GENDER IN MOTION

Asia/Pacific/Perspectives

Series Editor: Mark Selden

Woman, Man, Bangkok: Love, Sex, and Popular Culture in Thailand
by Scot Barmé

Making the Foreign Serve China: Managing Foreigners in the People's Republic
by Anne-Marie Brady

The Mongols at China's Edge: History and the Politics of National Unity
by Uradyn E. Bulag

Transforming Asian Socialism: China and Vietnam Compared
edited by Anita Chan, Benedict J. Tria Kerkvliet, and Jonathan Unger

China's Great Proletarian Cultural Revolution: Master Narratives and Post-Mao Counternarratives
edited by Woei Lien Chong

North China at War: The Social Ecology of Revolution, 1937–1945
edited by Feng Chongyi and David S. G. Goodman

Social and Political Change in Revolutionary China: The Taihang Base Area in the War of Resistance to Japan, 1937–1945
by David S. G. Goodman

Local Democracy and Development: The Kerala People's Campaign for Decentralized Planning
by T. M. Thomas Isaac with Richard W. Franke

Islands of Discontent: Okinawan Responses to Japanese and American Power
edited by Laura Hein and Mark Selden

Women in Early Imperial China
by Bret Hinsch

Postwar Vietnam: Dynamics of a Transforming Society
edited by Hy V. Luong

Wife or Worker? Asian Women and Migration
edited by Nicola Piper and Mina Roces

Biology and Revolution in Twentieth-Century China
by Laurence Schneider

Contentious Kwangju: The May 18th Uprising in Korea's Past and Present
edited by Gi-Wook Shin and Kyong Moon Hwang

GENDER IN MOTION

Divisions of Labor and Cultural Change in Late Imperial and Modern China

Edited by
Bryna Goodman and
Wendy Larson

ROWMAN & LITTLEFIELD PUBLISHERS, INC.
Lanham • Boulder • New York • Toronto • Oxford

ROWMAN & LITTLEFIELD PUBLISHERS, INC.

Published in the United States of America
by Rowman & Littlefield Publishers, Inc.
A wholly owned subsidiary of The Rowman & Littlefield Publishing Group, Inc.
4501 Forbes Boulevard, Suite 200, Lanham, MD 20706
www.rowmanlittlefield.com

P.O. Box 317, Oxford OX2 9RU, UK

British Library Cataloguing in Publication Information Available

Library of Congress Cataloging-in-Publication Data

Gender in motion : divisions of labor and cultural change in late imperial and modern China / edited by Bryna Goodman and Wendy Larson
p. cm. — (Asia/Pacific/Perspectives)
Includes bibliographic references and index.
ISBN 0-7425-3824-9 (cloth : alk. paper) — ISBN 0-7425-3825-7 (pbk. : alk. paper)
1. Sex role—China—History. 2. Women—China—Social conditions. 3. Women—China—History. I. Goodman, Bryna, 1955– II. Larson, Wendy. III. Series.
HQ1075.5.C6G46 2004
305.3'0951—dc22

2004022274

In memory of Christine Egan
(June 20, 1946–September 11, 2001)

Contents

Acknowledgments

THIS BOOK BEGAN AS A DISCUSSION among members of an interdisciplinary faculty reading group on gender in China at the University of Oregon (UO), which was organized under the auspices of the UO Center for the Study of Women in Society (CSWS). As our discussions deepened, CSWS provided funds for the planning of a conference, which took place at the University of Oregon in October 2001. We are grateful to Cynthia Brokaw, Deborah Davis, Susan Mann, and Ellen Judd for participating in the conference planning and helping us to refine our focus.

The UO Center for Asian and Pacific Studies (CAPS) provided support for conference planning, fund-raising, and administration. We received substantial grants from the Chiang Ching-kuo Foundation and the Association for Asian Studies China and Inner Asia Council. Additional support was provided by the Ford Foundation–funded Oregon Consortium for Asian Studies, the Admiral David E. and Mrs. Connie Jeremiah fund, the Oregon Humanities Center, and the College of Arts and Sciences. We would like to thank all of the sponsors for their contributions to the conference and book project.

Many people have worked to bring this volume to publication. We are particularly indebted to Lori O'Hollaren, the assistant director of the Center for Asian and Pacific Studies, who has overseen the project from the initial conference planning to the final submission of the volume. Matthew Wells, a graduate student in East Asian Languages and Literatures, helped in many ways with editing, translation, and computer work, and Hongwei Lu, a former UO graduate student in East Asian Languages and Literatures now teaching at University of Redlands, produced the first draft of a translation of the chapter by Luo Suwen. We thank both Matthew and Hongwei for their talented and timely work.

We thank Francesca Bray, Cynthia Brokaw, Carolyn Cartier, Susan Glosser, Theodore Huters, Elizabeth Perry, Lisa Rofel, and Wen-hsin Yeh, together with our University of Oregon colleagues Arif Dirlik, Stephen Durrant, Maram Epstein, Richard Kraus, Charles Lachman, and Deborah Sang, for their stimulating intellectual discussion and their cheerful contributions as participants, conference discussants, and colleagues in the field. We are especially grateful to Mark Selden and Susan McEachern at Rowman & Littlefield Publishers, for their early encouragement, conscientious reading, and principled, constructive criticism. Their efforts have improved our volume greatly.

Finally, we wish to thank all of the conference participants and contributors to the volume for their patience and meticulous efforts in revision and rewriting. This collective intellectual labor has deepened our insights into and helped us create pathways through the vast field of gender and labor in China, bringing alive the fascinating questions that stimulated our initial inquiries.

Introduction

Axes of Gender: Divisions of Labor and Spatial Separation

Bryna Goodman and Wendy Larson

LATE IMPERIAL CHINESE TEXTS—ranging in topic from statecraft to family management—are striking for their repetition of what Susan Mann has called the "rhetorical signs" of normative gender relations.[1] Taken from the language of classical texts and from later scholars' elaborations on these texts, these words, phrases, and sentences recur like a linguistic pulse throughout the Late Imperial era, across the space and time of China and at different levels of Chinese society. Though actual practices varied over era, region, and social class, this rhetoric of normative gender relations nonetheless emphasized that the social and political order depended on a strict gendered division of space and of labor.[2]

The essays in this volume examine the cultural meanings of these rhetorical signs of spatial and occupational division, and their relation to social practices and conceptions of gender. As governing notions of the social order (and interrelated constructions of gender) changed radically in the modern era—initially with the questioning of the imperial, dynastic order and the creation of a Chinese republic in the early twentieth century, later with the creation of a Communist government, and, most recently, with China's political and cultural transformations in the post-Mao era—the persistence of these older rhetorical signs in the interstices of new political visions has complicated the social projects and understandings of modernity, especially in terms of the creation of new public spaces, new conceptions of work and virtue, and new configurations of gender.

The call for gendered divisions of labor and of space is marked clearly in classical texts from early China, which later scholars intoned like mantras. The

Book of Rites emphasized strict separation of the sexes (*nan nü zhi bie*): "The Rites are founded on the correct relation of man and wife. In the dwelling house, outside and inside are clearly divided; the man lives in the outer, the women in the inner apartments . . . the men do not enter, neither do the women leave them." Early Chinese statesmen affirmed the political urgency of differentiating the "inner" (*nei*) from the "outer" (*wai*) and maintaining gender segregation. Any breach could bring danger. As the Later Han Confucian statesman Yang Chen (died 124 C.E.) memorialized: "If women are entrusted with tasks involving contact with the outside, they will cause disorder and confusion in the Empire, harm and bring shame on the Imperial Court, and sully sun and moon. The *Book of Documents* cautions against the hen announcing dawn instead of the cock, the *Book of Odes* denounces a clever woman overthrowing a state. . . . Women should not be allowed to take part in government affairs."[3]

The third-century philosopher Ge Hong elaborated on the segregation of information that accompanied the gendered segregation of space:

> The *Book of Odes* praises the union of husband and wife, but attaches supreme importance to the separation of the sexes. . . . Further, that news from outside shall not penetrate into the household, and that news from within the household shall not become known outside. . . . Such are the shining regulations on the separation of the sexes instituted by the Sages.[4]

These sentiments, habitually invoked in the centuries that followed, were forcefully restated by Song scholars, solidifying into orthodoxy in Song neo-Confucianism. The eleventh-century Song dynasty statesman and historian Sima Guang reenunciated classical notions of gender separation: "In housing there should be a strict demarcation between the inner and outer parts. . . . The men are in charge of all affairs on the outside; the women manage the inside affairs."[5] Twelfth-century neo-Confucian theorist Zhu Xi reiterated and emphasized key passages from the *Book of Rites*: "Men do not discuss inside affairs, nor women discuss outside affairs." Zhu Xi insisted that women should remain within the "inner quarters" in order to avoid "the disaster of the hen announcing the dawn."[6] Women who spoke or stepped beyond spatial boundaries created a cosmological impropriety that threatened social stability. In the high Qing embrace of neo-Confucianism, state interest in female seclusion became obsessive, with numerous proclamations designed to ensure women's containment within domestic space.[7]

As these quotations indicate, the separation of the sexes prescribed not only spatial division but also a gendered division of labor. Classical formulations of this separation identified proper and improper spheres of activity for each sex. Men managed affairs outside the house, while women's duties were domestic. According to one classic definition of a woman's place, which the second-century B.C.E. writer Liu Xiang approvingly attributed to the mother of Mencius, "The proper conduct of a woman is found in her skill in preparing the five foods, fermenting wine, caring for her husband's parents, and making clothes, and that is all. A woman's duty is to care for the household and she should have no desire to go [out]."[8] Women's role in making cloth was particularly emphasized: "Men till, women weave" (*nan geng nü zhi*), a phrase derived from concepts in the *Mencius*.[9] This ideal gendered division of labor became an orthodoxy in the Late Imperial era, "heralded high and low in the late Ming and Qing eras, in statecraft texts, illustrated manuals and family instructions."[10]

Although these labor categories did not explicitly distinguish among social classes, nonetheless, the boundaries of daily life clearly were marked not only by gender but equally by class. If the *Mencius* refers to a ritual display of plowing by a feudal lord, and if propriety in Late Imperial times required the emperor to ritually plow, in the daily life of many if not all areas of China, it was commoner males who engaged in agriculture. The most prestigious forms of masculine work in the Late Imperial era—scholarship and statecraft—were the province of elite men, almost exclusively.

Women were legally barred from public service and, ideally, from serious scholarship and outdoor occupations. For all women, work was to be manual and interior: food and cloth production and ornamentation. As recent scholarship has shown, peasant women in some areas of China departed from these ideals and engaged in agricultural production.[11] For cultivated elite women, however, special emphasis was placed on fastidious seclusion as well as skill at weaving, a female occupation understood to parallel male scholarly activity.[12]

Although spatial and occupational distinctions were influenced by class, the fundamental *nei/wai* feature was important, as a rule, for men and women across class. Some scholars have noted the comparative interest of China in considerations of gender because of the mutability of premodern gender roles as relational, rather than operating as a fixed, essential binary.[13] For example, in the position of family elder, the matriarch of an extended family was owed deference by younger generations of male relatives, even though she was a woman. Research on the conceptual foundations of gender distinctions and on the importance of the modern period in the development of a new, Western-influenced sexual binary has stimulated considerable reflection on the ways in which biologically sexed bodies could assume different gender positions within Chinese society in the course of the life cycle. Studies of gender in China have readily noted the way in which recognition of social roles "frequently overpowered thinking in terms of gender."[14] Nonetheless, in contrast with the mutually interpenetrated and relational concepts of *yin* and *yang*, which also informed Chinese notions of gender, ideas of spatial divisions and gendered differentiation of work were *theoretically* more rigid and less mutable. If male bodies contained female elements, and women's bodies similarly encompassed both *yin* and *yang*, the spatial principles indicated by *nei* and *wai* worked differently: "A woman may be relatively *yang* to her son, but she is not relatively outer."[15] If the widowed matriarch assumed a relative *yang* position in the family, no one imagined that she would leave the inner quarters, drop her embroideries, and take up public affairs.

The relative conceptual inflexibility of space as opposed to certain other aspects of gender in Chinese culture makes it important to understand the nature of the *nei/wai* division and its associated division of labor in processes of cultural change. It is therefore of great interest to look at the relations and connections between *nei* and *wai*. What types of mobility were possible in the context of these boundaries? What may be learned by looking at individuals who transgressed *nei/wai* boundaries? How were these boundaries reproduced and challenged in the context of economic and political change? When boundaries were moved through reconceptualization or simply social behavior, did the spaces available to male and female existence also change? Under the pressure of transformation, were spatial relations delineated in a rigid conceptual manner but practiced with more flexibility? How, precisely, were *nei* and *wai* mapped onto twentieth-century concepts of a public realm of modern citizenship and the modern workplace?

Although the notion that the seclusion of women and the separation of the sexes were essential to public morality commanded respect well into the twentieth century, new economic opportunities and self-consciously modern ideologies demanded the transformation of modern women into educated public citizens. In a seemingly contradictory way, women often stood for the backwardness of the past yet also indicated the potential of the future, a double-edged position that opened possibilities for new spaces and increased mobility while implying that there may be limits in how far these spaces and mobilities could go. How did public sentiment accommodate the shifting employment practices, mixed gender models of modern education, and transgression of canonical gender locations that the new conditions required? Throughout the modern period, women were asked to adjust and readjust the way in which they occupied space, existed in the public's eye, and associated with men. How, for example, are we to interpret the symbolic appearance of women into a very visible "outer" realm and women's engagement in politics during the 1911 Revolution, May Fourth, or Cultural Revolution eras? Finally, how have recent economic reforms and the ideological turn away from socialist revolution yet again deployed and reshaped gendered concepts of space and labor?

Hierarchy, Mobility, and Virtue

The flourishing field of gender studies in China now encompasses several generations of scholarship, with centers of research in North America, Europe, East Asia, and Australia. This scholarship most recently has begun to seriously examine connections between gendered divisions of labor and culture, making the relations of work, gender, and culture central to understandings of political, social, and economic change from the Late Imperial period through the Republican and People's Republic eras.[16]

This developing body of scholarship has introduced caution into our understanding of the Chinese rhetorical *nei/wai* dichotomy as a tool for understanding Chinese society. Though Chinese gendered spatial distinctions are often understood to be analogous to the Western private/public distinction, recent scholarship suggests that any notion of these spheres as exclusive is problematic for China, where the order of the home was understood to be deeply interconnected to the order of the state.[17] For example, in Confucian lore, it was filiality, moral education, and household management rather than worldly expertise that qualified men for public service.[18] The nineteenth-century Western experience of capitalism naturalized as opposites the categories *domestic* and *public*, and modern interpretations that privileged psychologies or subjective experience often translated that dichotomy into *private* versus *public*. Yet are these concepts illuminating or even adequate when evaluating gender relations in the Late Imperial period?

Similarly, can we accept a rhetorical distinction as descriptive of actual practices, or is it "more prescriptive of an ideal norm than descriptive of the realities of gender interactions?"[19] The question posed by Francesca Bray, "To what extent did the spatial boundaries marking female seclusion translate into real or perceived separation of worlds?" highlights the difficulty of interpreting a discourse of separate spheres—even one as lengthy and oft repeated as that indicated by *nei* and *wai*—as indicating material reality and social practice. Bray's work provides testimony to the argument that the spatial *nei/wai* boundaries "were not so much absolute as contextually defined, for they did not denote separate moral and conceptual worlds."[20]

However, even if the worlds of *nei* and *wai* were contextually defined and connected into a larger whole, their distinctions were experienced by many men and women as both clear and real well into the modern period.[21]

Explaining her initial reluctance to leave the confines of her family courtyard in the Republican era even when she and her children were starving to death, the elderly Mrs. Ning commented to the missionary Ida Pruitt that "it was no light thing" for a woman to step outside her home: "A woman could not go out of the court. If a woman went out to service, the neighbors all laughed. I did not know enough even to beg."[22]

As this example indicates, the language and ontology that contained and expressed normative spatial locations and occupational frameworks for men and women persisted beyond the imperial period into the twentieth century and later. As in other cultures, but following forms specific to China, gender segregation and classical notions of virtue continued to retain authority in the modern era, despite the efforts of both Republican-era reformers and communist revolutionaries to "liberate" Chinese women from their seclusion and oppression and to create new sexually integrated public spaces and notions of civic or revolutionary virtue. Ideals of the gendered division of labor remained so powerful in China that when John Buck surveyed North China in the 1920s, they still manifestly structured rural life. As Buck reported, men labored in the fields, and women worked inside in textile production.[23] Throughout the Maoist and Reform eras, rural marriage practices, as evident in Ellen Judd's chapter in this volume, have reflected an ongoing, if not entirely inflexible, gendered division of space.

When newly educated women entered professions in the twentieth century, those who taught in women's schools or ministered to female patients remained within acceptable gender boundaries.[24] Those who embarked on coeducation or worked in sexually integrated offices were far more controversial; in these cases, women's virtue appeared to be called into question by their "outer" location in society. Such traditional notions of space persisted and conflicted with efforts to create new and transformed social spaces that corresponded to what was imagined to be modern. Even in the most radical moment of women's emergence into the outer sphere—the Cultural Revolution—questions of female virtue haunted women's political integration into society. For women who were public figures, criticism of their public actions was accomplished by a highlighting of their sexual identity and their violation of what might be called *nei* morality. To mention two well-known examples, when Liu Shaoqi's wife, Wang Guangmei, was criticized by Red Guards, she was forced to dress as a prostitute; similarly, those who raised questions about Jiang Qing's conduct highlighted her past career as a Shanghai film star and her previous lovers.[25]

For the most part, foundational work on gendered divisions of labor has focused on specific politically defined periods (Late Imperial, Republican, People's Republic, or subsets of these categories). Scholarly examination of the cultural practices and social meanings of canonical gendered spatial and occupational divisions in China has concentrated primarily on imperial China.[26] Insofar as research tendencies separate contiguous time into "premodern" and "modern" (or revolutionary and postrevolutionary) blocks that are studied independently, studies of gender in twentieth-century China have often highlighted the theme of radical breaks with tradition or, minimally, changes in gender concepts and practices that result from new conditions and ideas. Different generations of scholars have variously identified the May Fourth/New Culture movements, the communist movement and revolution, or the post-Mao reform era as transformative moments of rupture with the traditions of the Chinese past. The expectation of such ruptures often persists, even in studies that aim to unmask the "failures" of particular political visions.[27]

Recent scholarship has questioned the claims of "the modern" and reexamined continuities linking later and earlier periods. This research on the Late Imperial period has done a great deal to call into question modern assumptions about Chinese tradition by shaking up the static, if pervasive, image of traditional gender relations disseminated in May Fourth journals and literature. In the iconoclastic May Fourth vision of the Chinese past, Chinese women—prior to the emergence of May Fourth feminism—were understood to be oppressed victims of patriarchal traditional Chinese culture. This early twentieth-century movement, which advocated the creation of a more democratic and individualistic culture, was less concerned with a nuanced representation of the past than with the creation of a politically useful model to serve as a foil. Within this vision of a monolithic unchanging tradition—which also bore similarities to Western images of a culture-bound and stagnant China—Chinese women were understood to be socially isolated, ignorant and uneducated, economically dependent, legally powerless, and oppressed by the patriarchal "three bonds" to father, husband, and son, which governed their lives.[28]

Gradually a more complex understanding of the diversity of men's and women's historical experiences has emerged, one that has revealed finer distinctions in power relations (if still a sobering history of gender hierarchy and inequality), as well as a great variety in male and female experiences. The study of gender in China, like the field of gender studies more broadly, now encompasses a diverse range of approaches. It is not simply the question of whether women's lives have improved or whether the May Fourth construction of an inhuman and patriarchal Chinese past distorted that past, or whether Chinese women were liberated by the Communist Revolution. Recent studies make it possible to assess varied practices within the so-called Chinese tradition, inquiring into the validity and meaning of the recurrent canonical rhetoric concerning the normative social order.[29] And in the modern period, more research on "traditional" concepts and practices has taken a position alongside studies that focus on the new.

Some scholars have proposed that the divisions of labor in classical texts and the spatial locations of men and women in society are somewhat ambiguous in terms of the social value of female labor as compared to that of males. Ideas of gender segregation in China commonly placed a wife in a position of hierarchical subservience to the family of her husband. Normative statements of female inferiority and submission, however, were tempered by suggestions of complementarity rather than simple subordination. The parallel construction of the canonical expression "Men till, women weave" suggests the equivalence of male and female work rather than a strict hierarchical structure. The notion of complementarity is explicit in Liu Xiang's account of the wise mother of Mencius, made familiar to Late Imperial readers through myriad editions of biographies of virtuous women that invariably repeated the same narrative. To reprimand the young Mencius for his sloth, his mother "took up a knife and cut the web of her loom," saying, "Your being remiss in your studies is like my cutting the web of my loom. . . . What difference is there [in your studying] and my weaving?"[30] In terms of economic value, women's labor in weaving and embroidery could be recognized by the family as highly lucrative.[31]

Recent studies have demonstrated that women's labor in the production of cloth was understood by moralists and officials throughout the imperial period as a high moral activity.[32] Until the late Ming, households were required to pay taxes in the form of cloth and yarn; the production of textiles was fundamentally important to the state and connected female labor and the political polity. What Francesca Bray terms "gynotechnics," or the technology of everyday role definition for women in Chinese society, functioned at economic, moral, and political levels. Through this structuring of daily life with multiple planes of significance, women were understood to contribute to the social order just as men did, though their contributions were not identical but, rather, complementary.[33]

Questions remain as to the connections between ideas, social value, power, and real-life conditions. The difficulty of interpreting moral texts and proclamations about women's place has become obvious with recent scholarship that contextualizes this discourse within economic, political, and social change. For example, it is possible that the strident moral rhetoric of female seclusion in Song neo-Confucianism reflected a backlash against women's prominence in the Song commercial boom.[34] If this is indeed the case, the heightened rhetoric indicates not merely the continuation of older ideals of female behavior but, perhaps more important, an attempt to mold these ideals to concerns of the times by putting women in their economic place. As a backlash would imply, the furor about women's space may imply not that women had been and still were severely sequestered but that they had made significant inroads into activities that were formerly handled by men. It may have been the case that changes in the textile industry between the Song and Qing removed women from the more profitable sectors of weaving, and these material changes translated into declining social status for women.[35] Judicial records have revealed startling, apparently antitraditional gender behavior by people living at the bottom of the social scale in the Late Imperial era, behavior that suggests that the state may have been more concerned with controlling the mobility and behavior of poor, unmarried (and therefore unorthodox) men than in maintaining or promoting rigidly separate spheres.[36]

This volume is part of the reenvisioning of the diverse meanings and complex practices of gender construction in the Late Imperial era. This said, our project extends beyond the rethinking of Late Imperial traditions and practices, into a reconceptualization of the modern through the recognition of dynamic cultural continuities and resonances that weave Late Imperial and modern eras together into an interconnected web. Recognizing normative gender inequality in both these periods, our volume also considers the meanings of nonnormative contexts in which the experiences of men and women diverged from any clear-cut assumptions of normative social relations associated with "tradition" or "modernity."

Gender in Motion

The title of this volume, *Gender in Motion*, conveys the flexibility of Chinese gender categories in practice and the historical fluidity of changing gender practices across space and time. Overall, the essays that comprise the volume address two central questions: (1) What were the meanings, limits, and possibilities of gendered spatial and occupational divisions in Late Imperial and modern Chinese culture? (2) What happens when gendered occupational or spatial boundaries are crossed? Both literal and figurative forms of *motion* are in play here; local circulation in the spaces of village or urban society and long-distance travel, as well as activity that crossed the symbolic terrain of gendered political and occupational identities all figure in our analyses.

The chapters in this volume traverse three periods that are usually separated in studies of Chinese history: the Late Imperial, Republican, and People's Republic (encompassing both the Mao and post-Mao years). The chronological reach of the volume permits comparisons across the *longue durée*, as well as of transformations in gender notions associated with commercialization, industrialization, ideological change, and other processes associated with modernity. It also incorporates in it a theoretical interest in time as it intersects with space, and in scale across both time and space. While paying some attention to historical change within the sections, we have chosen not to organize this volume exclusively in terms of chronology. Through this means, we hope to disrupt assumptions of a linear process of change or progress from a state of tradition to a state of modernity. The China field is hardly unique in its historical susceptibility to teleologies of enlightenment, revolution, or modernization. As a means of problematizing these simplistic but nonetheless pervasive interpretive tendencies, we deliberately juxtapose, in thematic sections, a focus on issues examined in different time periods. In terms of scale, the chapters range from close focus on the day-to-day lives of people living within defined spaces and relationships to larger concepts of the city and the countryside, the nation and the world, all important in material as well as conceptual realities.

The three parts of this collection, "Patterns of Mobility," "Spatial Transformations," and "Boundaries," group together inquiries into (1) the flexibility of normative spatial and occupational categories, (2) their transformations at moments of social, political, and economic change, and (3) the margins and boundaries of gendered spatial and occupational identities, and the resonance of older boundaries in the context of cultural and political transformations in society. Each thematic section is organized to include material from different periods in order to facilitate consideration of analogous issues at different points in time. Consideration of the Late Imperial and Republican eras as well as the Maoist and post-Mao periods permits, additionally, a sense of multiple pasts and multiple understandings of modernity.

Each part expresses a theme chosen to convey symbolic and metaphoric as well as literal and material meanings. This dual emphasis on concepts and material reality shown in the volume as a whole represents our attempts to think of these categories as they were expressed in texts and other conceptual theorizations as well as in daily life practices.

Part I, "Patterns of Mobility," rethinks normative divisions of space and labor, by considering the ability of women and men to move around within or despite normative prescriptions of virtue. The thematic focus encompasses literal movement across space as well as figurative movement, in terms of occupational redefinition or movement from female-identified to male-identified activity and role, and the conditions facilitating such movement. The chapters grouped together here all examine forms of mobility or boundary transgression that coexisted with normative boundaries and were not tied to new ideological motivations such as feminism or nationalism.

Part II, "Spatial Transformations," emphasizes the historical transformation of conceptual and lived space. Here the interpretive focus is less on the mobilities of individuals or groups that coexisted with normative gendered spatial and occupational divisions. Inquiry turns instead to changes in the conceptualization of space, the construction of new ideologies, and arenas of significance (e.g., new notions of "the public," or "the private," which don't correspond to canonical apprehensions of space). The chapters included within this section identify moments of spatial redefinition and associated reorientations of practice and social meaning.

In part III, "Boundaries," the interpretive emphasis is placed on the intangible and material lines that separated women and men in their work and spatial locations, and the conditions under which those lines became emphasized, muted, or revised. Of interest in this section is the relevance of canonical boundaries and their persistence despite ideological transformations that aimed to redefine work and space.

The three thematic categories expressed in parts I through III are intended more as overlapping explorations than as mutually exclusive units, facilitating consideration of the historical intertwining of gender, labor, and spatial distinctions. Boundaries did not exist without transgression, even when such transgression was not intended as a conscious challenge, and it is important to note the forms of mobility that coexisted with the normative categories. Similarly, conscious efforts to transform the gendered divisions of space and work, though striking in their bold redefinition of ideas and practice, were necessarily complicated and often limited by the persistence of older notions. The three-part division of this volume is intended as a means of ensuring reflection on both the complexities of "tradition" (encompassing traditions enacted in the past and in the present), and the dynamism as well as the limitations of changes that claim modernity.

While our interest in space, labor, and gender has benefited greatly from recent scholarship on China, we also have drawn on ideas that have emerged out of similar research on other cultures or in cultural, feminist, historical, and geographic theory. The most basic concept of cultural geography—that space is not neutral but like gender and labor, is culturally constructed—is built into the foundation of our work.[37] We understand both space and labor to be not only gendered but also saturated with multiple meanings that result from changing social relations. Social changes produce spatial changes, even as older meanings of space and labor are complexly woven into new practices. We examine theories of space, gender, and labor as they emerge through specific cultural practices including the creation and circulation of texts, although we do not imagine that texts provide a transparent window onto actual social life. Rather, we hope to illustrate the complex interplay between concepts developed by people and groups at various times and through various means, and their expression within concrete daily life.

Women and men inhabit, understand, and work within space differently, although at times boundaries shift, are muted, or become heightened. If *nei* and *wai* are significant, they are not the only important relational terms within this discussion. Locality, nativeness, and the nation; the home and the world; remunerative, important, and virtuous work—these are but a small sample of the multiple and shifting issues that interact with the organization of space, gender, and labor. In the twentieth century, revolutionary ideology and other cultural, political, and economic changes demanded configurations that often seemed to be directly opposed to older ideas of how women and men should live and work. Our goal in linking more recent concepts and social practices with those from the Late Imperial and Republican eras is not to show that tradition persists and never changes but rather to trace the continuous renegotiations of space, gender, and labor in relation to changing historical circumstances.

It is not accidental that the organizing categories of this volume use spatial metaphors. Space and spatial metaphors serve, literally and figuratively, to define gender and labor and their interrelation. The foundational concepts of *nei* and *wai* describe the spatial, mutually bounded, but interdependent relationships of gender and work that are anchored in rich textual development and changing practices. Although one could argue that the canonical influence of *nei* and *wai* diminished in the twentieth century, particularly as new identity-fixing spatial divisions emerged in the Maoist era,[38] we found that boundary distinctions and spatial differentiation not only persisted in various forms, but, even more importantly, always provided useful analytical perspective. As the chapters of this book amply illustrate, labor and gender emerge in practice through the organization of space, and spatial concepts inform the movement of women and men through time, locality, and social value.

Interpretations

In both Late Imperial and modern times, certain forms of mobility coexisted with normative gendered boundaries. That is to say that some individuals or groups regularly transgressed recognized boundaries without articulating a conscious challenge to normative behaviors. In some cases, this was because respecting such boundaries was impractical for reasons of economic survival. In other cases, individuals who in practice transgressed the normative spatial boundaries of gender nonetheless took great care to insist that, on the contrary, their behavior did conform to normative practices. Such individuals sought to conceptually reframe their divergent practices as perfectly in alignment with canonical behaviors.

Part I of this volume, "Patterns of Mobility," begins with two chapters on Late Imperial China that present new explorations of mobility across gendered boundaries at different ends of the social scale. At the lower end of the social scale, for example, conformity with normative boundaries was a luxury individuals could not always afford. This is immediately clear in "Making Sex Work: Polyandry as a Survival Strategy in Qing Dynasty China," Matthew H. Sommer's provocative exploration of sex work and family strategies among people at the bottom of the social scale. As Sommer demonstrates, it was not uncommon for behaviors to transgress the gender orthodoxies of the state—amounting to what Sommer describes as a stigmatized, illegal variation of nonfraternal polyandry—even as social actors intoned the rhetoric of the normative gender order. Poor women, motivated by economic necessity, flexibly interpreted their role as wives, taking on extra "husbands" to increase the well-being of their households. Such acts commonly incurred the criticisms of relations and neighbors, who described such households as transgressing *nei/wai* boundaries (*bu fen nei wai*). Nonetheless, such practices gave hard-pressed individuals a degree of relative mobility and power.

The novel family practices and occupational mobility examined by Sommer, involving the strategic manipulation by both husbands and wives of wives' sexual labor, clearly were not an attractive option to women of the elite class, who were better cloistered and could not have shared poorer women's desperate motivations for so radically transgressing gender norms. Elite women did, however, engage in other forms of mobility that potentially challenged normative gender roles. In her chapter "The Virtue of Travel for Women in the Late Empire," Susan Mann examines travel narratives by elite women. Normally considered the province of sojourning males, travel raised questions of virtue particular to women bound by the discourse of *nei* and posed narrative problems for those who recorded their journeys. Yet the stories of their journeys were not disinterested record keeping. Rather, as Mann demonstrates, women resolved the interpretive ambiguities through an ingenious narrative inattention to the scenery or delights of their trip. Instead of emphasizing pleasure, their travel narratives were consciously fashioned, above all, as testimonials to familial virtue and devotion.

If these two chapters on the Late Imperial era indicate the dimensions and limitations of mobility within or around the canonical rhetoric of gendered spatial division, the other two chapters in this part I, on the Republican and People's Republic eras, explore mobility in the twentieth century and locate similar concern with what mobility means for women. In "Gender on Stage: Actresses in an Actors' World (1895–1930)," Luo Suwen examines the entry of women and girls—motivated by financial necessity, not any articulated feminism—into the exclusive male preserve of Beijing opera performance.[39] Initially, well-known male performers would not allow their female relatives to learn opera, partially because of the improprieties of public exposure, and partially because they feared women's performances would invariably be viewed as licentious and the women as loose or available for abuse. Even though actresses were mocked as unskilled, criticized as immoral, and often banned, over a period of some thirty years women gradually were accepted into this prestigious form of opera. In this process, Luo highlights the crucial role of a certain unorthodox space, the foreign settlements of modern Shanghai, in facilitating a climate of operatic innovation that permitted the entry of actresses. If the new Beijing opera actresses of the early twentieth century might be retrospectively claimed as feminist heroines, the field of opera performance was broken into largely by poor girls who, similar to the women studied by Sommer who took on an extra man for economic gain, had a strong economic incentives to disregard the moral strictures against women entering the outer male sphere. While audiences may have interpreted female acting as lewd, thereby keeping actresses away from the status and recognition regularly bestowed on excellent actors, actresses also took advantage of the audiences' desire for the display of female bodies onstage to gain their livelihood, in the process acclimating audiences to female performers and ultimately transforming Beijing opera.

In "Women on the Move: Women's Kinship, Residence, and Networks in Rural Shandong," Ellen R. Judd examines the local circulation of women between rural localized communities of men in Shandong villages in the People's Republic period. Although it generally is true that women's mobility overall is more limited than that of men, Judd demonstrates that within the traditionally female-defined activities of matchmaking, women have developed extensive networks of acquaintances and contacts that not only expand their mobility but also significantly increase their ability to set up the kind of family relationships that are beneficial to them. Furthermore, women define these activities not as work but as part of their female home life, conceptually removing them from the outer sphere of male activity where women are not supposed to go. Susan Mann in chapter 2 traces how a potentially transgressive activity was made acceptable through the molding of narrative reconstruction. Similarly, in chapter 4, Judd's probing of women's understandings of their spatial circulation reveals efforts to locate such mobility in a familial context, placing women's activity back into the family, or the realm of *nei*. Judd's research illustrates that activities often deemed traditional may produce both physical and conceptual mobility, as long as these activities are properly defined, normatively speaking. Both chapters evoke the power of language and discourse in situating and interpreting women's movements.

These first four chapters work together to show the importance of classical ideas of gender segregation as well as the complex relationship between these ideas and the divergent realities of daily life. Differences in class are important in determining what kind of strategies women and families develop to improve their lives through extending female mobility across space. In the two examples provided by Sommer and Luo, the lower-class women who had least access to economic resources altered their restrictions by engaging in sexual or sexually defined labor. These women—and their family members, who at times placed them in these positions—were not self-consciously, as feminists, resisting the limitations put on them. Rather, they were simply trying to upgrade their living conditions. In the larger picture, however, this attempt effectively changes the expression of normative gender regulations and expands women's mobility. Rural women with some standing within their village can engage in "female" activities and slowly build up networks that provide them with more mobility and power than the conceptual limitations of women's place would normally permit. In contrast, when elite women ventured out of the household and into the male outer world, they used writing to defuse the conceptual dangers their travel posed and recontain their activities within traditional gender boundaries.

Part II, "Spatial Transformations," emphasizes moments of historical change, and the transformation of normative gendered divisions of space in the last years of the Qing dynasty, the early Republican era, and the Maoist and post-Mao periods. The four chapters in this section identify key moments and processes of social, cultural, and political redefinition across the long twentieth century to locate the reconfigurations of space, gender, and work. These essays investigate distinctive new notions of public and private, and their relation to older concepts of gendered space.

In "Between *Nei* and *Wai*: Chinese Women Students in Japan in the Early Twentieth Century," Joan Judge examines both the transnational travel of Chinese female students in Japan and these students' claims on the symbolic space of the Chinese nation. She suggests that the experience of female students in Japan should be assessed not simply from the perspective of the developing nationalism that characterizes male students' changing attitudes, but rather from a cultural/social focus that directs attention to the models of womanhood and female citizenship provided by modern Japanese women. Judge's research highlights the transformations that took place in women's worldviews and sense of the gendered social order during their sojourn in Japan, arguing that Chinese women were profoundly influenced by both Japanese models of womanhood as well as by the previously inaccessible spaces of social intermingling with Chinese men in which they found themselves abroad. These changes in the social circumstances of their lives blurred the *nei/wai* boundary and facilitated their developing sense of connection with the Chinese nation. Though their experiences in Japan were radically new, these women ultimately chose to embrace certain aspects of normative female behavior, urging women to work for the nation within the family.

In contrast to Judge's investigation of elite women abroad, Catherine Vance Yeh, like Luo Suwen, focuses on unorthodox and foreign spaces within China. In "Playing with the Public: Late Qing Courtesans and Their Opera Singer Lovers," Yeh studies courtesans who appeared in the new public spaces of Shanghai theaters and public parks. While fascinating Shanghai residents with the spectacle of their visibility, high-class courtesans also cultivated love affairs with male opera actors, relationships that asserted personal choice rather than following more traditional notions of business and the proprietary interests of male patrons. These interactions were marked private but were quite distinct from the domestic *nei*. Courtesans' so-called private life—really a space for the exercise of personal choice and autonomy—was of course very public. As it emerged, the new private space of courtesan love immediately aroused public fascination through the published journalistic essays of jilted literati lovers. As Yeh illustrates, late Qing newspapers created a public realm that contradictorily consisted of forays into the private lives of the courtesans. Yeh identifies a spatial realm that is less commonly explored by scholars than the construction of a new, politicized, citizen-identified public.

Madeleine Yue Dong, in "Unofficial History and Gender Boundary Crossing in the Early Chinese Republic: Shen Peizhen and Xiaofengxian," similarly interrogates the contentious terrain of political citizenship. Focusing on the early Chinese Republic, she traces the paths of women who set out deliberately to assert political citizenship, as well as stories of women who became progressive political symbols despite their political passivity. Women who broke into male political spaces such as the senate floor or physically attacked male politicians to protest for their rights were excoriated both in the press and in unofficial histories. Yet prostitutes who associated with political figures could receive political praise. Dong finds that these disparate receptions followed from their different modes of behavior. As the unofficial histories (*yeshi*) suggest, prostitutes could be imagined as working behind the scenes to influence powerful men. Their invisible but imagined activities did not directly challenge gender roles but rather reinforced fundamental spatial distinctions between men and women. In contrast to Judge's chapter, Dong's research suggests some of the ironies of gendered spatial arrangements. Judge shows that *nei* could be materially confronted through the appearance of new social spaces yet persists strongly as a state of mind. Dong's research not only illustrates the relevance of more popular sources such as unofficial histories in investigating gender practices but also shows how spatial segregation was an important symbolic structure that was difficult to dismantle. In her focus on public print media as vehicles for new displays of private behavior, Dong's research, like that of Catherine Yeh, provides additional evidence of the crucial role of the commercial press in the production and transformation of gendered notions of space.

In contrast to the groups and individuals who were able to initiate transformations in the spatial boundaries of their lives in the context of changed commercial, political, and ideological environments, as depicted variously in the studies of Yeh, Judge, and Dong, Wang Zheng's chapter in this section examines a prominent, but largely unexamined, reorganization of gendered space enacted by the new communist state. Wang's research on women's participation in urban neighborhood work, in "Gender and Maoist Urban Reorganization," delineates spatial change in gender divisions of labor in the early People's Republic. After the Communist Revolution, in a fashion resembling efforts in the early twentieth century to reshape women into citizens, unemployed urban women were regarded in a contradictory fashion: they were considered both backward and also potentially revolutionary in their ability to be formed into active agents of the state. In an extension of both female work space and occupational role, formerly unemployed wives were organized for neighborhood work. The usefulness of these women in local social management and surveillance, coupled with the cost-effectiveness of the venture, led to a gradual expansion in the range of duties assigned to women by local communist officials. Despite their volunteer status, these women gained organizational skills and found new public identities, functioning effectively as the lowest level of the civil service administration. They also gained local power through their linkages with the state security apparatus. Although women often felt empowered by their new positions, their work was denigrated by men in their neighborhoods, who found ways to delegitimate the new public roles of women by recourse to culturally available negative images of the dangers of meddling women.

The final chapter that engages the theme of spatial transformation is Wendy Larson's analysis of the symbolic and gendered meaning of work within urban life, and the connection between morally significant labor and contemporary intellectual discourse. "He Yi's *The Postman*: The Work Space of a New Age Maoist" examines a film that creates a male character with many of the attributes of the self-sacrificing, revolutionary Lei Feng, who provided the model for individual devotion in work for the communist state. Lei Feng was male, but the model was considered universally applicable across gender boundaries; indeed, the legendary "Iron Girl" heroines of the Maoist era, together with the female stars of Cultural Revolution films and opera, cleansed of their sexuality, all embodied the Lei Feng spirit. In this post-Mao film, Lei Feng is no longer a universal model. Female agency (as opposed to female sexuality) is out of the picture. The main character in the film labors in a highly regularized, monotonous job with perverse sexual undertones, and he lacks any of the articulate optimism associated with the universal revolutionary hero. Whereas the Maoist era delegitimated both the old realm of *nei* and the newer realm of the private, projecting an impossibly all-encompassing new public realm of universal service to the state, the collapse of Maoism punctured the model of the heroic workplace and along with it, the sense of open, positive space of which it was constructed. Larson sees in the film of He Yi (He Jianjun) a self-conscious, savvy attempt to salvage the notion of "serve the people" from within exaggeratedly bad contemporary conditions, especially the deadened and flattened space of work. The film's protagonist exhibits an oddly distorted male moral agency as he negotiates the confused historical remnants of space that surround him. Thus, *The Postman* sides with those who claim that China's revolutionary history and its vision of socially engaged work remains relevant and potentially liberatory, if barely so. At the same time, with the female characters representing little more than various positions for the protagonist to consider as he carves out his mission, this potential is not equally available to all. By investing that vision in a lone male character, the film presents a conventionally gendered division that mimics the *nei/wai* separation of the past.

The five chapters by Yeh, Judge, Dong, Wang, and Larson in part II emphasize processes of redefinition and creation of spaces of activity and signification at moments of historical change. This renegotiation of space reworks, extends, or marginalizes notions of *nei* and *wai*, as well as the more modern notions of public and private. In different ways, as well, these chapters closely examine the complex interplay between identity and spatial location. For Judge, the conceptual break from the idea of *nei* is fragile and cannot be sustained, at least within this early group of women students abroad. Dong demonstrates strong resistance to—yet also active success in—the integration of male and female activity in a new space of public political citizenship. For Wang, the broadening of female space to encompass the neighborhood becomes a novel source of management training, altering both the women who work there and the space itself. And Larson locates a distressing makeover of urban space that shrinks and limits the supposed gains of industrialization and liberation of sexual mores, while simultaneously putting moral agency back into its proper male body.

Part III, "Boundaries," moves the interpretive focus toward the conceptual and material boundaries of gendered practice. Here the emphasis is on the influence of normative boundaries in people's minds, even when such boundaries were disregarded in practice, or even after economic, ideological, or political changes brought transformations in the symbolic spaces of daily life.

In "Women's Work and the Economics of Respectability" Kenneth Pomeranz addresses, for the Late Imperial and Republican periods, the difficult problem of actually tracing the gendered division of labor expressed in the normative formula "Men till, women weave." Despite significant regional variation, gender divisions of labor were always culturally meaningful. In frontier areas, gendered spatial separation was often rigidly enforced, partially as a means of distinguishing Han cultural practice from that of other groups. Like Sommer, Pomeranz notes the greater likelihood that impoverished people historically transgress normative gender boundaries. His interpretation of this boundary crossing, however, differs significantly from that of Sommer. Whereas Sommer's analysis emphasizes mobility and agency, Pomeranz is less inclined to interpret the gender boundaries as so easily dispensable. Recognizing that the difficult circumstances of individuals' daily lives might require boundary flexibility, he argues that this flexibility did not render the boundaries irrelevant. Individuals who transgressed boundaries for purposes of economic survival could experience not freedom but loss of virtue and symbolic value. When lower-class women engage in male-identified labor, they do not gain power or respect but rather open themselves to exploitation. In Jiangnan, at least, Pomeranz notes, rather, a basic correlation between relative prosperity and a normative gender division of labor.

In his discussion of boundary issues, Pomeranz also articulates methodological questions that haunt studies of gender divisions of labor, arguing that while gender boundaries were highly significant for individual experience, it is impossible to abstract "women's" or "men's" calculations from family units and family strategies. Pomeranz questions the value of an abstract notion of "women's labor" and argues for understanding women through family strategies in which each individual's occupational deployment was understood and channeled in ways that cannot be calculated separately from family interests. In these respects, male and female, individual and family, cannot be sharply counterposed.

The remaining three chapters in this part all address the persistence of older normative gender boundaries despite radical shifts in ideology and politics in the modern era. Shifting to an urban setting, in "The Vocational Woman and the Elusiveness of 'Personhood' in Early Republican China," Bryna Goodman examines the contradictions of the New Culture discourse of gender equality, considering the ideal of female personhood (*ren'ge*) and the goal of female vocations (*funü zhiye*), both of which were understood by feminists to constitute prerequisites for female citizenship in the early Republican era. Although women's personhood was widely discussed and promoted, in practice the language of personhood was class based and occupation-specific. Poor and uneducated women were excluded, as well as women who were financially dependent on men. Only educated working women could qualify for personhood. In practice, not surprisingly, older gendered boundaries permeated new sexually integrated workplaces. Working women faced persistent evaluation with reference to earlier markers of female virtue and—in the office buildings or entertainment spaces of the city—could be vulnerable to their employers' desires. Their virtue, moreover, was tainted by the simple fact of their association with male coworkers, as well as by their material desire to work for money. Women activists who proclaimed their devotion to feminist goals often deployed a language of female chastity and purity as they created feminist martyrs. Though Goodman's urban working women were worlds away from the rural women studied by Pomeranz, their work in male-identified spaces could similarly expose them to insult and exploitation.

Tze-lan Deborah Sang, in "Women's Work and Boundary Transgression in Wang Dulu's Popular Novels," examines gender boundaries through Republican-era popular literature. Sang argues that beyond Wang's overt interest in creating female martial arts fighters with almost unlimited physical ability to cross boundaries lies a concern with female poverty and a claim that in real life, women were still disadvantaged by their lack of economic resources. Wang's most famous novel, *Crouching Tiger, Hidden Dragon*, appears to focus on the boundary transgressions and moral quandaries of an elite woman. Sang argues, however, that the novel is grounded in a larger interest that depicts the boundaries women must cross to sustain themselves as impossibly rigid obstructions. This novel is thus a fundamental revision of the Chinese chivalric tradition; it and other novels by Wang deploy the boundary-breaking female martial arts figure to investigate the stark social realities of lower-class female life. In a dozen social novels, Wang repeatedly analyzes the lives of poor young urban women who are compelled to seek work outside the home. His novels engaged in prevalent social contemplation of the question of whether work outside the home was a new social right or an unwanted burden. Sang's work suggests, finally, that boundary crossing—even in the most physical form of flying—can be used in literature to present the contrary message that women are often hopelessly constrained and limited by the boundaries that mark their existence.

In "Virtue at Work: Rural Shaanxi Women Remember the 1950s," Gail Hershatter returns our focus to the countryside to consider rural women's memories of the 1950s. Hershatter's narrative reveals identities that appear to inherit and continue an overarching structure of female virtue that has persisted despite political and ideological campaigns; the communist reorganization of rural family, economic, and legal structures; and increases in mobility that these women experienced after 1949. Describing themselves as pitiful, capable, and harmonious, these women see themselves less as revolutionary agents free to move through new social spaces than as family and community actors whose efforts could smooth and realign conflicts, even when these actions were disadvantageous to themselves. Although many of these women contrasted their ability to move through public space in the 1950s with childhoods that were more spatially and materially constrained, ideas of dramatic rupture are largely absent from their narratives. Instead, women crafted self-characterizations with recurring themes of prerevolutionary notions of female virtue, integrating into this notion of virtue more recent categories of self provided by the revolution, notably labor, though without its attachments to either the revolution or the state. In this regard, the construction of a remembered self in commonly understood terms of virtue creates a contrast with state narratives of transformative political change.

If these individuals marked their identities with clear lines of virtue, it is striking that the narratives Hershatter elicited contain few references to canonical notions of gendered boundaries of either labor or space. Both before and after the revolution, many of these poor peasant women apparently provided the primary means of financial support for their children, and even parents-in-law, as their husbands left for other areas or, in other cases, predeceased them. Their lives focused on family survival, and, if these women emphasized virtue, they had learned to define the category in ways that were practical and personally resonant. In this regard, Hershatter's findings echo themes in the work of Sommer and Pomeranz, regarding the weakness of *nei/wai* boundaries in the context of poverty. Hershatter's oral histories also resonate with Pomeranz's caution against imagining individuals outside family contexts. Despite their revolutionary experiences, Hershatter's rural women self-identified largely within traditional female capacities. If their notions of traditional female capacities do not strictly conform to canonical notions of *nei* and *wai*, the overwhelming impression created by their narratives is not one of freedom but, rather, of the family and community boundaries that mark their lives.

The four chapters in part III together present a nuanced, if sobering, view of both the crossing of gender boundaries and of modern or revolutionary claims for women's liberation. If these chapters allow us to see that boundary crossing in itself does not necessarily indicate either freedom from gender-based restrictions or even new ideas about women's work, they nonetheless reveal the shifting nature of boundaries, their transgression in particular circumstances and at particular historical moments, as well as the complexities of self-conscious boundary redefinition.

Notes

This introduction has been enriched by comments and suggestions from Cynthia Brokaw and Mark Selden, as well as the articles and discussion of the contributing authors.

1. Susan Mann, "Work and Household in Chinese Culture: Historical Perspectives," in *Re-Drawing Boundaries: Work, Households and Gender in China*, ed. Barbara Entwisle and Gail Henderson (Berkeley: University of California Press, 2000), 26.

2. The language of normative gender relations was promoted by imperial officials and, to some extent, cooperative local elites in border areas as part of a civilizing mission. See William T. Rowe, "Women and the Family in Mid-Qing Social Thought: The Case of Chen Hongmou," *Late Imperial China* 13, no. 2 (December 1992): 1–41. Notions central to Chinese philosophical texts were of course not evenly influential among various populations within China, nor was normative language unvaried over time. As recent work by Eric Mueggler, Ralph A. Litzinger, and Stevan Harrell has shown, even today, the influence of Han texts, ideas, and cultural practices is often more minimal in non-Han areas and border regions than many imagine. See Eric Mueggler, *The Age of Wild Ghosts: Memory, Violence, and Place in Southwest China* (Berkeley: University of California Press, 2001), especially chapters 4 and 5; also see Ralph A. Litzinger, *Other Chinas: The Yao and the Politics of National Belonging* (Durham, N.C.: Duke University Press, 2000); and Stevan Harrell, *Ways of Being Ethnic in Southwest China* (Seattle: University of Washington Press, 2001).

3. Cited in R. H. Van Gulik, *Sexual Life in Ancient China* (Leiden: Brill, 1974), 58, 87.

4. Cited in Van Gulik, *Sexual Life*, 103.

5. Cited in Patricia Buckley Ebrey, *The Inner Quarters: Marriage and the Lives of Chinese Women in the Sung Period* (Berkeley: University of California Press, 1993), 23–24.

6. Cited in Ebrey, *The Inner Quarters*, 24.

7. Susan Mann, *Precious Records: Women in China's Long Eighteenth Century* (Stanford, Calif.: Stanford University Press, 1997), 220.

8. Translated in Albert Richard O'Hara, *The Position of Woman in Early China* (Washington, D.C.: Catholic University Press, 1945; Hyperion reprint, 1981), 42. We have modified O'Hara's translation here to more clearly reflect the sense of the passage.

9. *Mencius* III:B and VII:A, trans. D. C. Lau (London: Penguin, 1970), 108, 186; see also discussion in Mann, "Work and Household in Chinese Culture," 19, 26. For a foundational discussion of this theme that emphasizes women's high production of value as weavers in the Song, see Francesca Bray, *Technology and Gender: Fabrics of Power in Late Imperial China* (Berkeley: University of California Press, 1997), 237–72.

10. Mann, "Work and Household in Chinese Culture," 26.

11. Mann, "Work and Household in Chinese Culture," 26. In particular regions and at particular times, women clearly participated in agricultural production, although overall, more men than women worked in agriculture. For a discussion of Han women working in the fields in North China, see Ellen R. Judd, *Gender and Power in Rural North China* (Stanford, Calif.: Stanford University Press, 1994), 41–50. In the Huaili records that Judd studied, men without other status were recorded as "grain peasants" and women as "cotton peasants," divisions that referred to different kinds of agricultural work by men and women. As Judd states, it is clear that "women are well-established elements of the agricultural labor force on this area" (41). For a reference to women's tea picking in South China, see Ono Kazuko, *Chinese Women in*

a Century of Revolution, 1850–1950, ed. Joshua A. Fogel (Stanford, Calif.: Stanford University Press, 1989), 1–2. Ken Pomeranz's article in this volume synthesizes recent work on temporal and regional variations in female employment.

12. Mann, *Precious Records*, 148–53.

13. For elaborations on this idea, see Rowe, "Women and the Family," and Tani E. Barlow, "Theorizing Women: *Funü, Guojia, Jiating* (Chinese Woman, Chinese State, Chinese Family)," both in *Body, Subject and Power in* China, ed. Angela Zito and Tani E. Barlow (Chicago: University of Chicago Press, 1994), 253–89. For analysis of *yin/yang* and gender, see Alison H. Black, "Gender and Cosmology in Chinese Correlative Thinking," in *Gender and Religion: On the Complexity of Symbols*, ed. Caroline Bynum, Steven Harrell, and P. Richman (Boston: Beacon, 1986), 166–95.

14. Ebrey, *The Inner Quarters*, 44.

15. The quotation is from Ebrey, *The Inner Quarters*, 44. For discussions of the dispersal of *yin* and *yang* elements in male and female bodies, see Charlotte Furth, *A Flourishing Yin: Gender in China's Medical History, 960–1665* (Berkeley: University of California Press, 1999), 19–58; and Judith Farquhar, *Knowing Practice: The Clinical Encounter of Chinese Medicine* (Boulder, Colo.: Westview, 1994).

16. Rather than exhaustively detailing this scholarship in an extended footnote, we refer readers to the notes within the individual chapters in this volume.

17. The seminal classical text that lays out the relationship among the home, the person, and the state is the *Daxue* (The Great Learning):

> The ancients who wished to illustrate illustrious virtue throughout the kingdom first ordered well their own states. Wishing to order well their states, they first regulated their families. Wishing to regulate their families, they first cultivated their persons. . . . Their persons being cultivated, their families were regulated. Their families being regulated, their states were rightly governed. Their states being rightly governed, the whole kingdom was made tranquil and happy.

Translated by James Legge, in *The Chinese Classics*, vol. 1 (Hong Kong: Hong Kong University Press, 1960).

18. The classical story of the selection of the Sage emperor Shun is narrated in the Shu Jing, Canon of Yao, 3:12. According to the story, Emperor Yao sought a worthy successor. His court advisers identified the commoner Shun. When the emperor asked about Shun's qualifications, they responded that Shun had a difficult family: "'He has been able, however, by his filial piety to live in harmony with them, and to lead them gradually to self-government, so that they will no longer proceed to great wickedness.' The emperor responded, 'I will try him!'" Translated in Legge, *The Chinese Classics*, 3:26–27.

19. Dorothy Ko, *Teachers of the Inner Chambers: Women and Culture in Seventeenth-Century China* (Stanford, Calif.: Stanford University Press, 1994), 12.

20. Bray, *Technology and Gender: Fabrics of Power in Late Imperial China*, 96.

21. Mann, "Work and Household in Chinese Culture," 27.

22. Ida Pruitt, *Daughter of Han: The Autobiography of a Chinese Working Woman* (Stanford, Calif.: Stanford University Press, 1967), 55, 62.

23. As noted in Mann, "Work and Household in Chinese Culture," 27. For recent, contrasting, scholarly discussions of the persistent association of seclusion with female virtue in rural China, and the limitations of women's occupational ventures in public, see Philip Huang, *The Peasant Family and Rural Development in the Yangzi Delta, 1350–1988* (Stanford, Calif.: Stanford University Press, 1990), 111; and Kenneth Pomeranz, *The Great Divergence: China, Europe, and the Making of the Modern World Economy* (Princeton, N.J.: Princeton University Press, 2000), 91, 106. See also the chapter by Ellen Judd in this volume, and Mark Selden, "Family Strategies and Structures in Rural North China," in *Chinese Families in the Post-Mao Era*, ed. Deborah Davis and Stevan Harrell (Berkeley: University of California Press, 1993), 139–64.

24. Constance Orliski, "The Bourgeois Housewife as Laborer in Late Qing and Early Republican Shanghai," *Nan Nü* 5, no. 1 (2003): 43–68.

25. Politically active women married to well-known men found their fate governed by their husband's situation. Jiang Qing could not be directly criticized in public until Mao was dead; on the other hand, when a husband fell from power, his wife almost always accompanied him in the fall.

26. One notable exception is Entwisle and Henderson, eds., *Re-Drawing Boundaries: Work, Households and Gender in China*, which presents social science research on the (mostly contemporary) People's Republic of China.

27. For example, Judith Stacey, *Patriarchy and Socialist Revolution in China* (Berkeley: University of California Press, 1983).

28. For an influential critique of the May Fourth construction of a problematic "tradition," in relation to gender, see Ko, *Teachers of the Inner Chambers*, 1–5.

29. For a broad sampling of contemporary trends in gender scholarship for China, though it does not focus on either spatial segregation or gender divisions of labor, see Susan Brownell and Jeffrey Wasserstrom, *Chinese Femininities, Chinese Masculinities: A Reader* (Berkeley: University of California Press, 2002).

30. O'Hara, *Position of Woman*, 40.

31. Bray, *Technology and Gender*, 200–203.

32. Bray, *Technology and Gender*, 237–52; Mann, *Precious Records*, 148–53.

33. For this approach, see Bray, *Technology and Gender*, 237, 260-61.

34. Mann, "Work and Household in Chinese Culture," 24.

35. Bray, *Technology and Gender*, 237.

36. Matthew Sommer, *Sex, Law, and Society in Late Imperial China* (Stanford, Calif.: Stanford University Press, 2000).

37. Some seminal texts that elaborate theories of space, gender, and labor are Doreen Massey's *Spatial Divisions of Labor: Social Structures and the Geography of Production* (New York: Methuen, 1984), and her *Space, Place, and Gender* (Minneapolis: University of Minnesota Press, 1994); Gillian Rose, *Feminism and Geography: The Limits of Geographic Knowledge* (Minneapolis: University of Minnesota Press, 1993); *Space and Place: Theories of Identity and Location*, ed. Erica Carter, James Donald, and Judith Squires (London: Lawrence & Wishart, 1993); and *Postmodern Geography: Theory and Praxis*, ed. Claudio Minca (Oxford: Blackwell, 2001).

38. Most notable in the Maoist era was the fixing of residence by a system of permanent urban or rural registration, or *hukou*.

39. Scholars have recently begun to examine gender and the modern transformations of the multiple forms of Chinese dramatic performance. See, in particular, Weikun Cheng, "The Challenge of the Actresses: Female Performers and Cultural Alternatives in Early Twentieth Century Beijing and Tianjin," *Modern China* 22, no. 2:197–33, for an overview of the varieties and transformation of female stage performance in these northern cities; and Jin Jiang, "Women and Public Culture: Poetics and Politics of Women's Yue Opera in Republican Shanghai, 1930s–1940s," (Ph.D. diss., Stanford University, 1998), for an inquiry into *yueju*, the popular, exclusively female opera form that emerged in twentieth-century Shanghai.

I

PATTERNS OF MOBILITY

1

Making Sex Work

Polyandry as a Survival Strategy in Qing Dynasty China

Matthew H. Sommer

"Getting a Husband to Support a Husband": A Case of Polyandry on the North China Plain

IN 1743, PEASANT WANG YULIANG REALIZED that he could no longer feed his family. Therefore, he decided to use his wife to recruit into the family a man who could.

Wang (age forty-nine[1]) lived in Fangshan County, Zhili (about fifty kilometers southwest of Beijing); his household consisted of himself, his wife Li Shi (forty-one), his widowed mother Fu Shi (seventy-nine), two young sons, and a daughter. The six of them shared a one-room house. Wang owned only four *mu* of poor-quality land, so much of the family's income depended on what he could earn by hiring out his labor to others (an example of the "semi-proletarianization" typical of the North China plain[2]). To make matters worse, for several years Wang had suffered from a chronic illness that made it difficult to keep down food, and he was bedridden much of the time.

These circumstances prompted Wang to approach He Shixin (thirty-seven), an immigrant from Neiqiu County, Zhili (about 350 kilometers to the southwest), who was working in the village as a casual laborer. He Shixin had neither land nor family, but he was strong and healthy. Wang proposed that He move in with Wang's family and sleep with his wife Li Shi in exchange for "farming and supporting the family" (*gengzhong yangjia*), and He readily agreed.

At first Wang's wife refused to cooperate, but eventually he persuaded her. As Li Shi later testified, he told her "I have this sickness and I can't take care of you anymore, so all we can do is get him to support (*yanghuo*) us and get along as best we can." Li Shi protested that they had only one room and sleeping platform in their house, so Wang explained, "Everyone will sleep together, but you don't need to be ashamed." She finally relented out of resignation and disgust, because if the family were to survive, they would need the help of some other man. Wang's mother was unhappy, too:

> [I] saw that my son had brought (*zhao*) He Shixin into our family. My son told me that he was going to let He Shixin live with us and sleep on the same sleeping platform with my daughter-in-law, so that he would farm our land and support our family. I said, "We may be poor, but how can we do something like that?"

But she, too, bowed to the inevitable.

So it happened that He Shixin moved in with Wang Yuliang's family, shared their sleeping platform, had sexual intercourse with Li Shi, and supported them as best he could by working their land and hiring out his labor. Neighbors later testified that everyone had had a pretty good idea what was going on, but no one interfered—after all, what better solution did they have for the family's problems?

But sometimes He could not get work, and the family continued to go short on food, provoking Wang Yuliang to complain and to abuse his wife; moreover, Wang was ill most of the time and by throwing up everything he ate, he was seen to be wasting quite a bit of all-too-scarce food. Wang had become a taxing burden to his family, something especially difficult to tolerate when all were going hungry. Finally, in the summer of 1744, Li Shi persuaded He Shixin to help kill her husband so that they could be a couple and have a better life together. After the murder, they were quickly found out, prosecuted, and sentenced to death—which is the only reason we know their story.[3]

How Widespread a Practice?

This story illustrates a practice known as "getting a husband to support a husband" (*zhaofu yangfu*), a form of nonfraternal polyandry that, with some variation, appears to have been remarkably widespread among the poor in China during the Qing dynasty (1644–1912). How widespread? It is impossible to quantify the practice in any exact way, and I would not suggest that most people—even most poor people—participated in such relationships. But it certainly was no isolated phenomenon.

Two major kinds of sources document this form of polyandry in China: Qing legal case records and early twentieth-century surveys of popular customs. The story of Wang Yuliang's family is found in a "routine memorial on criminal matters" held at the First Historical Archives in Beijing. These memorials from provincial governors report capital cases, which the archivists have sorted into categories according to the background situation that framed the central crime for which the death penalty was recommended (usually homicide).[4] In the archival category "marriage and sex offenses," a very common scenario found is the impoverished couple being supported by one or more outside males in exchange for sexual access to the wife. From a judicial point of view, such behavior constituted the crime of "abetting or tolerating one's wife or concubine to engage in illicit sexual intercourse with another man" (*zongrong qiqie yu ren tongjian*), for which the Qing code mandated ninety blows of the heavy bamboo (for the woman and both men) and compulsory divorce.[5] The "marriage and sex offenses" category contains countless memorials related to this crime, and I have collected several hundred from the Qianlong (1736–1796), Jiaqing (1796–1821), and Daoguang (1821–1851) reigns.

These are nearly all homicide cases, and homicide, of course, is an exceptional event. But I am convinced that the background situations that *framed* these homicides were not rare at all. This conviction is strengthened by the fact that such practices are well represented also in the routine caseloads of local courts in Ba County, Sichuan, and Baodi County, Zhili, most of which involved offenses far less serious than homicide.[6]

In addition to criminal records, two surveys of popular customs from the early twentieth century provide valuable documentation of polyandry (as well as related practices like wife selling). *Report on an Investigation of Popular Customs* contains data collected from local authorities in a number of provinces during the late Qing and early Republican eras as part of the preparation for drafting a modern civil code. This survey's reports from Fujian, Gansu, Hubei, Shaanxi, Shanxi, and Zhejiang all mention the "evil custom" of "getting a husband to support a husband."[7]

We need to bear in mind the limitations of this survey when weighing the significance of its evidence. Its reports vary widely in quality and detail, and it is far from complete: it leaves out most counties and many provinces altogether, including the far south and entire southwest of the country. It would be wrong to assume that the practice did *not* exist in places that are not specifically mentioned in the survey.[8]

A second survey, *The Common Law of Taiwan* published by Japanese colonial authorities, reproduces the text of a written contract for "getting a husband to support a husband" dated 1869.[9] This contract, which I translate here, documents a practice identical to that described in *Report on an Investigation of Popular Customs*. Based on these surveys, it seems safe to assume that for every instance of polyandry mentioned in a legal case, there must have been a great many others that left no specific written record.

A limitation of both surveys is that since their compilers sought to document "customs," they included only the most formally contracted version of polyandry, in which an outside male was openly incorporated into a couple's household. This practice—which should be understood as a form of marriage—represents only one end of a wide and varied spectrum of polyandrous practices that combined elements of both marriage and sex work in different ways and proportions. The common denominator among all these practices is that a wife, with her husband's permission, would have sexual relations with one or more other men in order to help support her family. In other words, the surveys reveal only the tip of the iceberg: there was an awful lot going on that the compilers either did not know about or (more likely) considered too deviant to mention in a report on local "customs." Since the entire spectrum of polyandrous practice was criminalized as "abetting or tolerating one's wife to engage in illicit sexual intercourse with another man," however, we can turn to the legal archives for a fuller picture of social reality.

The main challenge in interpreting the legal cases is to get beyond the judiciary's criminal categories to understand why people behaved as they did and how they themselves understood their own behavior. One should also keep in mind that since polyandry was illegal, participants had a strong interest in avoiding official attention. Legal cases record only those relationships that ended in serious trouble; harmonious relationships rarely left any trace in the public record. On the other hand, the main challenge in interpreting the surveys is to get beyond the compilers' definition of "custom" to understand their evidence in the broader context of practices they have left out. By combining these diverse sources, we can find evidence of some variation of polyandry in every province of China proper.

The Big Picture

Bearing this evidence in mind, let us consider the larger context for the story of Wang Yuliang. One precondition for the arrangement proposed by Wang was his ability to recruit He Shixin as a second husband for his wife. He Shixin was an able-bodied man with no wife or property of his own, who had migrated far from home in search of a livelihood, and Wang had no trouble at all persuading him to accept the proposal. There seems to have been no shortage of men like He, the ubiquitous "rootless rascals" or "bare sticks" (*guanggun*[10]) at the bottom of Qing society. The larger context, of course, is the skewed sex ratio and concomitant shortage of wives among the rural poor that were already very widespread and troubling phenomena by the mid–eighteenth century. One reason for men to share a wife was that there simply were not enough wives to go around, and in some rural communities, as many as a fifth of adult males would never marry, even though marriage was universal for women.[11]

A second precondition was a pervasive market for women, specifically their sexual and reproductive labor. It required no wild stretch of the imagination for Wang Yuliang to come up with this solution to his family's problems. When all else failed, his family had one more asset: his wife's body. Nor was it really very difficult for other people to understand and accept the arrangement, Li Shi's professions of distaste notwithstanding. This was a society in which it was both possible and easy—one can even say that it made sense—for a man to pimp or sell his wife in order to survive.

A third precondition, of course, was the desperate poverty of Wang Yuliang's family, exacerbated by his peculiar illness. The larger context is that there were many downwardly mobile families, living on farms too small to support themselves, who were turning to a range of desperate strategies in order to survive. The situation would only grow worse over time. Female infanticide was one such strategy and no doubt was the main reason for the shortage of wives and the surplus of single men among the rural poor; children also could be sold off (a transaction often euphemized as "adoption"), as could wives. In this particular case, we are reminded of Philip Huang's analysis of the involutionary pressure on peasant families to mobilize underutilized labor and engage in sidelines and risky cash cropping in order to survive.[12] One available form of "underutilized" labor was the sexual and reproductive labor of women, and one possible sideline was sex work.

This context helps us make sense of the myriad legal cases where we find a wife taking one or more patrons who chip in to supplement her family's income, with her husband either openly embracing her entrepreneurial initiative or simply pretending not to notice. In these situations, sex work is usually not the only kind of work going on; rather, it is part of a portfolio of strategies that enable a family to get by. In that sense, it is typical of most sex work that goes on in the world, which is part-time, temporary, or seasonal activity designed to supplement other sources of income in order to help support women's families. The women who do this work do not necessarily see themselves as "prostitutes"; that is, they do not necessarily see sex work as the most important or defining aspect of their lives.[13]

These three larger phenomena—the shortage of wives and consequent surplus of single men, the market for women's sexual and reproductive labor, and the problem of widespread downward mobility and involutionary pressure on poor families—were interrelated, and at their *intersection* we find people like

Wang Yuliang, Li Shi, and He Shixin engaged in survival strategies that combined elements of marriage and prostitution in a range of polyandrous forms. Some arrangements were formalized with matchmakers and written contracts or with some type of chosen (or "fictive") kinship; others were more casual, even ad hoc, and depended on verbal contracts or more indirect ways of reaching an understanding (such as the husband turning a blind eye to what he knows full well his wife is doing on the side). Each legal case tells a unique story full of specific details. But among the countless individual anecdotes we can discern common patterns and logic that make sense only when considered at the intersection of larger forces.

A Spectrum of Polyandrous Practice

Qing legal cases reveal a spectrum of different arrangements by which a wife, with her husband's approval, would have sex with one or more other men, in order to help support her family. Marriage and prostitution are the opposite poles of this polyandrous spectrum: some scenarios look more like marriage, and others more like sex work. Most, perhaps, lie somewhere in between.[14]

A number of variables can be used to plot a given scenario along this spectrum. For example, how many outside sexual partners did the wife take, and how long did their relationship(s) last? At the marriage end of the spectrum, we find a stable long-term relationship between the wife and one partner in addition to her husband. I have examples of such alliances lasting over ten years. At the prostitution end of the spectrum, we find multiple partners (typically, the wife cannot remember how many), each of whose relationship with her lasted only the duration of each "trick."

Second, to what degree, if any, did the couple incorporate an outside male into their family and household, and how did they represent that relationship to themselves and others? At the marriage end of the spectrum, we find the outside male fully incorporated as a second husband by means of contract, kinship vocabulary, coresidence, resource pooling, the sharing of meals from the same hearth, and sometimes even change of surname. For example, in Hubei "the second husband who was brought in" would adopt the surname of the first husband, in order to formalize his integration into the family.[15] In legal cases, we also find examples of the couple and their children adopting the outside male's surname. In their dealings with this man, the couple does not maintain boundaries; a phrase that repeatedly appears in testimony is "*bufen neiwai*"—literally, "they do not distinguish between inner and outer," a reference to the inner female space of the household from which outside males were normally to be excluded. In other words, they treat him as a member of their family.

At the prostitution end of the spectrum, however, the woman's multiple sexual partners may be completely anonymous strangers. They are simply customers, and the couple is fully self-conscious about being engaged in prostitution.

Third, what sorts of benefits were exchanged between the couple and the outside male(s), and were they exchanged in a "wholesale" or "retail" manner? At the marriage end of the spectrum, we find an ongoing exchange of a variety of different benefits over time; this is a "wholesale" exchange, in that we find no itemized calculation of compensation for each discrete sexual favor, and more is involved than just sex and money. The heart of this quid pro quo may well be an exchange of economic support for sexual relations, but once incorporated into the family, the outside male will also partake of the entire package of domestic caring work performed by the wife for her family, including preparing food, mending and making clothes, cleaning, caring for the sick, and so on. He also gains the less tangible benefits of membership in a family, including both chosen kinship (e.g., sworn brotherhood or adopting the couple's children as *ganqin*, something like a godfather) and the opportunity to have children of his own with the wife. For their part, the couple gains security through the pooling of labor, income, and whatever other resources the outside male can contribute on an ongoing basis.

The benefits a wife provided her second husband were simply an extension of her ordinary tasks within the family. Paola Tabet's description of the context of sex work in rural Niger applies equally to our Chinese cases of polyandry: "In the villages, giving sexual service is integrated with the other services women give in marriage: domestic labor, reproduction, and all the tasks allotted to women by the sexual division of labor."[16] Sex was just part of the package, and the second husband did not pay "by the trick" any more than did the first. Of course, at the opposite, prostitution end of the spectrum, we find straightforward, "retail" transactions: discrete acts of sex for discrete payments of money, which constitute the family's cash income.

For reasons of space, this chapter focuses on practices that most closely resembled marriage, in which the outside male was formally incorporated into the family. Readers should keep in mind that we are examining only one end of a wide spectrum of polyandrous alliances. It is my belief—which I shall elaborate and substantiate in a larger project—that this entire spectrum, along with related practices like wife selling, needs to be included in our analysis of the traditional Chinese marriage system.

The Polyandry Contract

The term "getting a husband to support a husband" (*zhaofu yangfu*) generally referred to a formally contracted relationship. It should be understood as a form of marriage, despite its official illegality and its unacceptability to elite standards; it was certainly understood as such by its participants, and even by the community at large. What stands out is the formality and openness of the arrangements, in conscious imitation of more widely accepted forms of marriage.

Report on an Investigation of Popular Customs notes that polyandry might be formalized through the use of matchmakers and written contracts. In Shaanxi, for example, "The couple will talk it over and agree to ask a matchmaker to bring a second husband into their household to support the first husband (*zhaofu rujia, yi yang qianfu*). They will draw up a 'bringing in a husband contract' (*zhaofu juzi*), which clearly states that 'the second husband may not mistreat the first husband.'"[17] The Japanese colonial survey of Taiwanese customary law reproduces the text of a written contract for *zhaofu yangfu* dated 1869:

> Wang Yunfa hereby establishes this contract for getting a husband to support a husband (*zhaofu yangfu zi*). Years ago I married Li San's daughter, Li Xiuliang, who is now twenty years old. We have lived together for four years. Xiuliang is filial in serving my parents and she takes care of the household without creating trouble or stirring up quarrels. It makes one very content to have such a good wife.
>
> Unfortunately, some time ago I contracted a disease and have become paralyzed. We are poor and have no source of income to meet our expenses. Although at the present time we are not starving, we have considered the fact that "there are three kinds of unfilial conduct [and the worst is not to have heirs]" (*buxiao yousan*).[18] When my wife's youth expires, it will be impossible to have a son. After long discussions, we have decided that there is no other alternative: if we insist that Xiuliang preserve her chastity (*bao qi zhenjie*), the whole family will be threatened with starvation. The only solution is to get a husband to support a husband.
>
> We have, therefore, consulted a matchmaker, and it has been arranged for Wu Jiusheng's first-born son, Wu Jinwen, to enter our family as an uxorilocal husband (*dengmen jinzhui*), and he [and Xiuliang] will become husband and wife (*chengwei fuqi*). We have, on this day, agreed that there will be no bride price, but that Wu Jinwen should provide the family with 20 yuan a month to cover expenses. Regardless of how many sons and grandsons Wu and Xiuliang may have, they will be heirs to the Wang family as well as to the Wu family.
>
> Both parties have reached this agreement voluntarily and without regret. Since spoken words alone are unreliable, I hereby establish this contract for getting a husband to support a husband, which can be presented as proof of our agreement.

Dated Tongzhi 8.3.?, and signed with marks of husband Wang Yunfa, the matchmaker, the scribe, and two witnesses.[19]

The agreement documented by this contract closely resembles those described by *Report on an Investigation of Popular Customs* as being customary in several mainland provinces. In both sources, we find the same basic vocabulary, including the ubiquitous "*zhaofu yangfu*," which appears to have been used everywhere from Taiwan to Gansu.

The Taiwan contract is written in the voice of the first husband, and it begins with a narration of hardship that justifies the unorthodox transaction as a last resort undertaken with regret; in both respects, it closely resembles contracts in which husbands sold or divorced wives, or parents sold ("adopted out") their children. Contracts for widow remarriage also justify themselves with a preamble of hardship and regret. Such narratives of woe have a formulaic quality, but all the evidence suggests that no one was proud of the kinds of transactions documented by these contracts.[20] Many of these transactions were illegal, even if local society accepted them—for example, wife selling, widow remarriage during the mourning period, and "getting a husband to support a husband."

The editors of the Taiwan survey and several contributors in *Report on an Investigation of Popular Customs* point out that "getting a husband to support a husband" was a form of uxorilocal marriage, in that the new husband would be incorporated into his wife's family. It specifically resembled uxorilocal remarriage of a widow, who (with permission of in-laws from her first marriage) might "bring in" (*zhao*) a second husband without changing her surname or surrendering her place in her first husband's household. The latter practice was called "*zhaofu yangzi*" (getting a husband to support one's sons), "*zhaofu yanglao*" (getting a husband for old-age support), and other similar terms.[21]

An important issue addressed by the Taiwan contract is the two men's (and, by extension, their respective lineages') claims to any sons born to the wife. Practice apparently varied quite a bit—and the matter was especially important where contracts set a time limit on the arrangement, meaning that eventually the second husband would leave the couple's family. *Report on an Investigation of Popular Customs* cites limits of anywhere from three to ten years in various counties. In Gutian County, Fujian, these relationships were generally limited to a decade:

> Any sons born within the ten years go to the second husband for him to raise. There are also some first husbands who lack sons, who stipulate that the first son born during the ten-year period will go to the second husband, but that any subsequent sons must become successors to the first husband himself.[22]

This focus on progeny indicates there was more at stake in these formally contracted relationships than just sex and money. Indeed, one of the most important benefits being exchanged was reproductive ability or labor, in the form of surrogate motherhood or fatherhood. All of the formally negotiated contracts described in *Report on an Investigation of Popular Customs* make clear that the second man was entitled to at least one of any sons produced by the polyandrous relationship. In effect, the wife would function as a surrogate mother, enabling the outside male to secure his own line of descent.

We are reminded of a related form of surrogate motherhood—namely, a husband's "conditional sale" (*dian*) of his wife to a creditor. The latter (typically a man whose own wife had failed to have children, but who could not afford to buy a concubine outright) would lend a sum of money to the husband; in exchange, the borrower's wife would share the creditor's bed for the duration of the loan, and any children she bore during that time would become the creditor's to keep. After the principal of the loan was repaid—her sexual and reproductive services having constituted the interest—she would return to her own husband, and the conditional relationship would be terminated.[23]

The Taiwan contract adds surrogate fatherhood to the picture. In the situation it describes, the husband's illness prevented him from impregnating his wife. By recruiting a second husband, therefore, he hoped to secure both his family's immediate survival and his own future line of descent. The contract states explicitly that any sons born out of polyandry should be successors to *both* husbands. The same provision is reported in Zhejiang: "If the first husband has no issue, then sons born to the second husband may serve as successors to the first husband as well."[24] In this way, the outside male served as a surrogate father to continue the first husband's line of descent, as well as his own.

In many places, the polyandry contract might be verbal, instead of written, but in other respects the arrangements appear to be identical. In Gansu, for example,

> If a man takes a wife, but later on he grows old and weak, suffers from severe illness, or becomes impoverished, so that he cannot make a living, then with his permission his wife can go through a matchmaker to bring a second man into their household as a husband (*zhao zhi qi jia wei fu*); this second husband will take responsibility for all the needs of the household. The two sides will strike a verbal contract (*koutou qiyue*) to settle questions such as which husband will get [as successors] any children who are born.[25]

In Qing legal cases, it is not always clear if the terms of an agreement were written down. Verbal contracts do seem to have been far more common than written ones, although the balance may have shifted by the twentieth century, when the surveys were conducted.

Two Examples of Formal Negotiation of Polyandry

We find an example of the open, formal negotiation of polyandry in a case from Shaanxi, in which a poor family contracted consecutive relationships with two different outside males; the record provides a detailed account of how the second relationship was negotiated. "Old Wang" (fifty-one) and his wife Wen Shi (thirty-one) were originally from Pucheng County, but in 1748 they fled famine with their young son and made their way to Yijun County (about seventy-five kilometers to the northwest). Wang found work as a casual laborer, but he soon came down with tuberculosis and could no longer make a living. The couple coped by allying with an immigrant laborer named Li Wen'ge: they moved in with Li and "ate from the same hearth" (*hecuan chifan*), in exchange for which Wen Shi slept with him. This relationship continued for about a year, and it ended only when Li decided to return home to Shanxi, leaving the couple with no means of support.

At this point, another immigrant laborer named Hei Jing noticed their difficulty. Hei was a widower from Yichuan County (about 150 kilometers to the northeast) who had no children and could not afford to remarry, and it occurred to him that "it would be less complicated and expensive just to contract a relationship (*bao*[26]) with Old Wang's wife." He sent a mutual acquaintance to propose that he replace Li Wen'ge as the couple's patron, and they agreed. Hei then asked the village head to act as "matchmaker" (*mei*) to negotiate the terms. With this man as witness, Hei promised husband Wang to "support him for the rest of his life" (*yanglao*) and to raise his son to maturity and secure him a wife; Hei then presented Old Wang with a cloth jacket to seal the deal. In exchange, Wang promised to "yield" (*rang*) his wife to Hei; as she later testified, Wang "agreed to use me to bring in Hei Jing as husband" (*jiang ming ba xiaofuren zhao Hei Jing wei fu*). The family moved in with Hei Jing, Wen Shi began sharing his bed, and they all "ate together as one family" (*tongjia chifan*). In her testimony, Wen Shi referred to this relationship as "getting a husband to support a husband" (*zhaofu yangfu*).

The parties to this transaction clearly understood it as a form of marriage, in which (to use their terms) an outside male was "brought into" the family as a "husband." An interesting detail is the second husband's promise to secure his predecessor's line of descent, by raising that man's son and eventually providing him with a wife. This provision resembles the surrogate fatherhood included in the Taiwan contract; it also resembles a common feature of widow remarriage, in which the deceased husband's son would accompany the widow into her new marriage, with guarantees of being raised to maturity and married, without being forced to take the second husband's surname.

The formality of this transaction reinforces its identity as a marriage that was seen as legitimate in the eyes of its participants and even the local community. The formal elements include the use of a go-between to make the initial proposal, the engagement of a respected person of authority as matchmaker to negotiate and witness the terms, and the ritualized presentation of a gift to the first husband, to signify the second husband's assumption of responsibility for his welfare. This case record does not specify whether the contract was written down, but either way, there is no questioning its formality or openness—indeed, the record suggests no sense of stigma on the part of either the couple or the outside male in this case.[27]

A case from Zhejiang reported in 1753 illustrates the use of a written contract for polyandry. Ma Shiyin (forty-five), Lin Shi (thirty-one), and their son Ma Ake (eight) were poor landless peasants from Yongjia County in southeastern Zhejiang; poverty had driven them from home, and they ended up begging and sleeping in empty temples. Ma had acquired some sort of chronic illness, and they were having serious difficulty getting by.

Just after the new year of 1753 they fell in with an itinerant fortune-teller, Mao Yuanfu (thirty-four), who had saved up several taels and was hoping to marry. Mao lent the family some money to buy rice, and they began migrating together and sharing meals. After two months, Ma proposed to formalize their relationship, yielding his wife to Mao in exchange for a promise of continuing support. Mao agreed, and while Lin Shi at first refused to cooperate, she soon conceded that they had no good alternative. Ma engaged a man they met on the road to write a "marriage contract for getting a husband to support a husband" (*zhaofu yangfu de hunyue*) and gave this document to Mao; that night, Lin Shi began sleeping with Mao, and the couple instructed their young son to address Mao as "uncle" (*shushu*). From this time on, Mao covered all their expenses. In testimony, witnesses referred to this arrangement as "*zhaofu yangfu*" (getting a husband to support a husband), "*zhaofu yangbing*" (getting a husband to support an invalid [husband]), "*zhaozhui yangbing*" (getting an uxorilocal husband to support an invalid [husband]), and other similar terms.

In another six months, however, Mao had used up his savings, and Ma's illness had greatly improved. Ma began to talk about taking his wife back home to Yongjia County and settling back into their old life, but Mao objected vehemently: "You already used Lin Shi to bring me into your family (*ni yi ba Lin Shi zhao le wo*)—how can you say you're going to take her back?" Lin Shi told her husband privately that it would be impossible for them to leave Mao unless they could retract the marriage contract. One day, when Mao was out telling fortunes, Lin Shi stole it from his pack and Ma burned it. The next day, Ma informed Mao that he and Lin Shi would depart the following morning for home. Mao angrily retorted, "You already '*zhao*'ed' your wife to me (*ni qizi zhao yu wo le*), and I have a marriage contract to prove it, so if you want to take her back you should come up with the money to redeem (*shu*) her!" (Note here the use of *zhao* as a transitive verb with the wife as its object, as shorthand for "contracted your wife to me in a getting a husband to support a husband relationship.") Mao then tried to produce the contract in order to cite its terms, discovered it was missing, and realized that the couple must have stolen it back. The quarrel quickly turned into a fight, and Mao ended up killing Ma.[28]

Stigma and Loss of Face

The openness and formality of such contractual arrangements imply a high degree of social acceptability and even accountability—why else have witnesses and a contract? Some of the commentary in *Report on an Investigation of Popular Customs* confirms this implication, despite the condescending and disapproving tone of the compilers. In Gansu, for example, we learn that "the first husband's relatives never interfere in these arrangements, and there is no social stigma attached to them whatsoever (*shehui shang yi jue bu yiwei kechi*)."[29]

But the evidence from legal cases is mixed, and we find many examples of significant stigma and shame (gossip and ridicule being the most common). In the middle range of practices between the poles of marriage and prostitution, especially, we find many instances of couples trying to maintain secrecy or at least ambiguity about the wife's extramarital relations. There are also examples in which the husband or other family members try to maintain a certain deniability by never openly acknowledging what is going on, although they know about it. Not infrequently, the crisis that produces a legal record occurs precisely because the husband can no longer face ridicule about his domestic arrangements and tries to break his family's connection with the second male.

The following case—from Gansu, it happens—illustrates the paradoxical quality of polyandry as a widespread, well-known, and formally contracted alliance that many people were ashamed of all the same. In some ways its story parallels the last case. In 1735, the harvest failed in Guyuan Subprefecture, Gansu, and by the New Year, peasant Ha Qijun (fifty-seven[30]) and his family had begun to starve. Ha and his wife, Zhang Shi (fifty), decided to head south to Fengxiang Prefecture in Shaanxi, about a hundred kilometers away, where they hoped to find work and food; the couple's son (thirteen) and adopted daughter-in-law (seven) went with them.

After a day's walk, the family stopped at a Guan Di Temple to shelter for the night and beg for food. There they encountered a teacher named Ye Ce (forty-eight), who worked at the temple; Ha knew him slightly from a previous visit during another famine many years before. Ye Ce was an immigrant from Wu-gong County in Shaanxi. He was not a typical "bare stick," in that he was literate enough to market himself as a teacher and had saved up a little money; even so, he had no wife or family and certainly could not be called prosperous by any ordinary standard. But prosperity is a relative concept, and Ha Qijun decided to approach him. According to Ye Ce's testimony, Ha told him, "Teacher, you have no family of your own; how would it be if I used my wife to bring you into my family, so we could all get by together? (*ba wo laopo zhaole ni, women yi tong guo rizi*)." Ha agreed, but it was not easy to persuade Ha's wife. Zhang Shi testified:

> My husband told me, "There's a teacher named Ye, I know him from before, and he has money. . . . I have it in mind to use you to bring him in and have him support our family so that we can survive (*ba ni zhaole ta yanghuo women yijia*)." When I heard this talk I rebuked him, saying "I'm already old, and our son is already grown up, how could I do such a thing?"

Zhang Shi and her husband argued for four days until she finally gave in:

> My husband said, "If we lose this man, and don't bring him into our family, then who else are we going to find who can help us? I've already acknowledged him as family (*ren ta zuo qinqi*), and there's no one who will know what's going on. If you don't obey me, then I'll die here, I refuse to go on!"

Once the problem of immediate survival was solved, Ha became concerned that word of their new arrangement might spread back home, which was only a day away. So he insisted that Ye join them in walking to Shaanxi. They ended up some two hundred kilometers from home in Jun County, where Ye found work as a teacher and supported the family; they told neighbors that Ye was Zhang Shi's brother, everyone in the Ha family called him "Uncle Ye" (Ye *shu*), and the sexual relationship between Ye and Zhang Shi was kept secret. This arrangement continued for about two years.

One day Ha Qijun and Zhang Shi heard that the famine in Gansu had ended, and they insisted on returning home. After some argument Ye agreed, but when they neared home, Ha told him they no longer wanted his company. Incensed, Ye Ce murdered him and then forced Zhang Shi to accompany him back to Shaanxi as his own wife.

Two points are crystal clear. As in our other cases, everyone who testified in the case was clearly familiar with polyandry and used a consistent vocabulary to characterize it ("bringing in"/*zhao* a second man to "support"/*yang* the family). Nevertheless, this couple found the relationship shameful—hence Zhang Shi's reluctance, Ha's anxiety about public exposure, their effort to use kinship of one kind ("Uncle Ye") to conceal another (polyandry), and the fatal attempt to sever relations.

The dispute that led to murder focuses our attention on the emotional as well as material investment that individuals could make in such alliances. In rejecting Ye, Ha had reneged on what had been stipulated as a permanent arrangement. According to Ye Ce, "That day he also said that since he was already old, after he died, his wife would be mine. Only then did I agree to hand over the money I had saved." Ye Ce obviously did not see himself as some sort of customer, to be rejected when his patronage was no longer wanted. On the contrary, Ye saw himself as part of a *family*: "I had joined his family by marrying his wife (*zhao zhei furen*) and had supported the entire family for two years—but now he was going back home and wanted to get rid of me! So I decided to kill him instead." He clearly did not share the couple's shame about their relationship.[31]

To reiterate, we must remember that legal cases record only relationships that ended in serious trouble, so they may give us an exaggerated impression of the impact of stigma and shame. Also, there are plenty of cases in which couples seem quite open about their arrangements and simply do not care what the community thinks. Attitudes may vary within families, too. Often the husband and his relatives seem more worried about losing face than the woman herself: her lack of chastity seems to bother them a lot more than it bothers her. When the couple was part of an extended lineage, then elders might try to suppress their behavior to protect the family reputation. The attitude of the community varies, too, but perhaps the most common attitude found in the case records is "don't ask, don't tell"—where fellow villagers have a pretty good idea what is going on, but it is never explicitly confirmed, and despite gossip, no one interferes.

Polyandry within Sworn Brotherhood

Chosen kinship was a prominent feature of this field of social practice, and sworn brotherhood between the husband and the outside male was one of the most common variations. In some cases, it is the pledge of brotherhood that frames the incorporation of the second man into the family, rather than an explicit contract for "getting a husband to support a husband." In other words, the second man's connection to the wife is a function of his relationship with her husband.

For example, in a 1750 case from Tangyi County, Shandong, a peasant named Ding Bi (thirty-two) pledged brotherhood (*bai xiongdi*) with Yuan Congren (forty-eight) out of gratitude, because Yuan had helped him financially during an illness. Yuan was a single migrant who worked as a casual laborer. Ding Bi had no money to repay Yuan and felt acutely his inability to reward the other man's charity. But Ding did have a wife, and, as Yuan later testified,

> I told him, like it was a joke, "I don't want any reward from you. But we brothers are very close friends: if we share your wife, it will show that we're *really* close to one another! (*ni de xifu dajia huozhe, zhe cai shi xianghao le*)." At first, Ding Bi wouldn't agree, but I often gave him a few hundred cash to spend, and when I got the chance, I would ask him again [to let me sleep with her], so finally he agreed.

Material interests definitely played a role here, but more important, it seems, was Ding's genuine gratitude toward the other man—Ding seems to have agreed with Yuan's suggestion that true friendship meant sharing *everything*, even a wife. Eventually, the couple ended up living with Yuan and farming together in another village, after Ding Bi's uncle (shamed by their unorthodox relationship with Yuan) forced them to leave home.[32]

Sometimes, a husband swore brotherhood with another man as a self-conscious strategy to gain access to his resources. For example, Zhu Gan (thirty-two) and his wife Liu Shi (twenty-nine) were peasants in He Subprefecture, Sichuan; they had no land, and Zhu worked as a casual laborer. They had two small children (a third had already died), and the family was too big for Zhu to feed on his own. In 1740, Zhu got to know Wang Hu (thirty-four), a single migrant from Guizhou who did odd jobs as an agricultural laborer, as a musician in funerals, and occasionally as a peddler. When Zhu saw that Wang had ready cash, he proposed that they swear brotherhood. Wang later recalled, "I was on my own, far from home, and it was a good idea to have a friend. So we pledged and became brothers (*rencheng xiongdi*)."

That winter, Zhu borrowed three taels from Wang Hu to buy food. Zhu knew that he could not repay the loan, so he invited Wang to spend the night and sent Liu Shi to his bed. At first Wang was alarmed, but after she explained that this was her husband's way to repay the debt, he relaxed and they had sex. Thereafter, Wang would work at various jobs and when finished would come stay with the couple, turning his pay over to them and sharing Liu Shi's bed. In this way, he became part of the family; as several witnesses testified, "They did not distinguish between inner and outer" (*bu fen nei wai*).

Zhu Gan's older brother Zhu Ming observed Wang Hu living with the couple, and he was not happy. Zhu Ming later testified,

> I asked my brother, "Who is this guy? Why do you let him sleep over at your house, and let him come and go as he pleases, without distinguishing inner from outer (*bufen ge nei wai*)?" My brother said, "His name is Wang Hu, he's from Zunyi, and he's my good brother who's pledged brotherhood with me (*tong wo jieyi de hao xiongdi*). So there's no need to treat him as an outsider (*meiyou fen shenme nei wai de*)."

After six months, Wang persuaded the couple to move about a hundred kilometers west to Anle County, where they lived together and worked on land belonging to a distant relative of his.[33]

The exchange between Zhu Gan and his brother is remarkable. Zhu Ming clearly knew what was going on, and Zhu Gan did not deny it. Instead, he *justified* it in terms of sworn brotherhood: as Yuan Congren asserted in the last case, sworn brothers need no boundaries, because they share *everything.*

The prominence of chosen kinship here points to the fundamental definition of the family-household unit (*jia*) in Chinese society as a group of people who live together, pool resources, and eat from the same hearth. (Thus, household division between brothers traditionally culminated in a final ritual meal together, followed by the establishment of a separate cooking hearth by each sister-in-law for her own newly separate household.[34]) Usually these factors coincided with the traditional kinship connections of blood and marriage, but they also seem to have helped *define* kinship.[35] From this point of view, the pledging of kinship in polyandrous relationships ratified the facts of coresidence, resource pooling, and wife sharing; it was a strategy to reinforce bonds of mutual trust and dependence. Pierre Bourdieu argues that kinship should be seen as a product of "strategic practice," rather than an automatic, natural result of bloodlines.[36] The function of chosen kinship in Chinese polyandry is a prime example of what he means.

Poverty as a Motive for Polyandry

The principal motive for couples to recruit an outside male was poverty. Even in cases where the wife's adultery preceded the economic support and was motivated by passion (the archives contain many examples of this scenario), these were invariably poor people, and it was the outside male's promise to provide food, cash, or other resources that would win the husband's acceptance of the relationship. Poverty was sometimes compounded by an illness or disability that prevented the husband from working, so that the family felt compelled to seek the help of another man. *Report on an Investigation of Popular Customs* confirms this pattern. In Hubei, for example, "a woman whose husband is handicapped, so that he cannot make a living, will be allowed to bring in a second husband to support the first (*lingzhao yi houfu, yi fuyang qianfu*)."[37] Polyandry's incidence and regional distribution probably correlated with those of poverty.

Poverty distinguishes the nonfraternal polyandry found in China from the socially acceptable, fraternal polyandry traditionally practiced in Himalayan societies. In the Himalayas, reasonably well-off families practiced polyandry in order to prevent household division and to concentrate and preserve their property across generations. It also tended to limit the birthrate in such families, since one woman can get pregnant only so often (polygyny would tend to have the opposite effect). This important social benefit was reinforced by the existence of large establishments of celibate clergy. The relatively low population density that resulted tended to protect the delicate ecology of that high-altitude region. The situation in China was completely different: in China, the illegal polyandry practiced among the very poor was an inverted reflection of the legal polygyny practiced by elite men.[38]

Here, it is useful to recall the argument of Russian economist Aleksandr Chayanov that the fortunes of a peasant family would change in a cyclical pattern, depending on the ages of family members and the ratio of laborers to mouths that had to be fed. According to Chayanov, a young couple with small children would be the most vulnerable to hardship, and in the majority of cases I have seen, it was precisely such couples who resorted to polyandry in order to survive. Sometimes there were elderly dependents as well as children.[39]

Of course, the rogue males who typically allied with these families were poor, too. But a single man had to feed only himself, so it was often possible for him to earn a little extra, as long as he could find work. Most of these men were simple peasants or laborers, but some had special skills by which they could earn a humble living: Qing case records include storytellers, fortunetellers, thieves, carpenters, musicians, many peddlers and clergy, and even teachers.

In some cases, the single man was simply the one with the wits and the initiative to keep the family fed. For example, in 1745 the governor general of Zhili reported a case of "one wife with two husbands" (*yifu liangfu*), in which a "propertyless single man" (*guangshen Han*) named Zhang Liang had employed a variety of means to support a peasant couple and their two children for over a decade. When husband Dong Si (from Xingtai County) first invited Zhang Liang to share his wife, Zhang Shi, in exchange for supporting the family, Zhang Liang was working as a casual laborer; after he moved in with the family, he managed to get together enough cash to start a little business peddling cooked food, which the three adults worked at together. Several years later, when they ran short on funds, Zhang fed them by means of theft—eventually being beaten and tattooed for that crime—and later on, he supported the family for another year or two by peddling tobacco. Finally, he arranged for the entire family to move to a busy market town in Yongnian County (at the southern end of the province), where they again peddled food and Zhang also did odd jobs on the side. (The whole family adopted the surname Zhang, and Dong pretended to be Zhang Liang's brother). Zhang Liang may have been a classic "bare stick," but he was also a tenacious entrepreneur.[40]

Whatever his resources, a single able-bodied man could help alleviate the distress of a poor family with whom he allied; in Chayanovian terms, his addition to the family would raise the ratio of labor to mouths. In exchange he would benefit from the sorts of family life and female caring labor he otherwise could not hope to enjoy.

How poor was "poor"? In some cases, families clearly faced starvation or at best the prospect of breaking up in order to survive (with the husband selling off his wife and children, one by one). Here, bringing in an outside male was a strategy not just to feed the family but also to preserve it *as* a family—a fact completely missed by the sanctimonious moralizing of dynastic officials and modern survey investigators alike. In other cases, the situation was not nearly so dire, but couples were still poor enough to welcome the support a second man could provide.

Polyandry and the Chinese Marriage System

When I first encountered in Qing legal cases the kinds of practices described in this chapter, I had no idea what to make of them. They certainly did not fit my image of "Chinese marriage." I knew that among the wealthy, polygyny was the rule: a main wife (*qi*), of the same social background as her husband, would be supplemented by concubines (*qie*) and maidservants (*bi*) purchased from less well-off families. Among the broad majority of peasants, however, monogamy prevailed (although there was considerable variation and flexibility within that overall pattern).[41] Dowry was a status symbol, and the daughters of more prosperous families incorporated the bridal gifts into the dowry they took with them to their husbands' households.[42] Among less prosperous families, daughters were more or less sold for bride-price, although this cash transaction would be masked as much as possible—"misrecognized," to use Bourdieu's term—by face-saving gestures. I also knew that there were many surplus males at the bottom of society with no wives at all, but I had no idea how they got along.

The evidence shows that in addition to polygyny and monogamy, the Chinese system for exchange of women included a third pattern, polyandry, that was practiced by a significant section of the poor. By *polyandry*, I refer to the spectrum of strategies that combined elements of both marriage and sex work in varying proportions and degrees of formality. The unifying theme of these diverse strategies is the naked instrumentality by which a wife slept with one or more men other than her husband, with his approval, in order to help support her family.

The reason that dowry was such a potent status symbol in Late Imperial China is that most families simply could not afford it. Dowry served to proclaim that "we are moral enough and wealthy enough not to sell our daughters"—unlike the great majority. The same logic applies to widow chastity and perhaps to foot binding. These were strategies to transform material capital into symbolic capital, and their utility as status symbols depended on remaining out of reach for the poor majority.

Among the poor, all marriage was instrumental to a high degree: basically, daughters were sold into marriage by their parents, and any endowment (direct or indirect) was trivial in material value, perhaps no more than a few small items to save face. This instrumentality is also obvious when one considers several variations of marriage that were common among the poor: *widow remarriage* (in which a widow sold herself or was sold by her in-laws, often using the bride-price to clear her first husband's debts or even to pay for his burial), *divorce* (in which the first husband typically would be compensated by the woman's natal family out of the new bride-price paid by a second husband), and *wife selling* (i.e., the direct sale of a wife by one husband to another), In fraudulent wife sale (a common variant, in which the wife usually posed as a remarrying widow), it was nigh impossible for the buyer to discover the fraud unless the woman told him the truth, for the simple reason that such a transaction appeared identical in every respect to a normal widow remarriage. In fact, some people did not understand that wife selling was a crime, since it was easy to confuse an illegal wife sale with all the legal kinds of marriage that also constituted sales. All of these variations of marriage were straightforward cash transactions.[43]

The spectrum of polyandrous practice depended on what Qing officials saw as the sexual promiscuity of a relatively small number of women with a much larger number of men: it was an ironic mirror image of the female chastity that underpinned the polygyny enjoyed as a status symbol by elite males. To the official mind, this was sexual anarchy, a dangerous trend with politically subversive implications.[44] It was this perspective that misrecognized custom as crime, polyandry as adultery, and survival strategies as sensual license.

But—some may protest—if this behavior was illegal and frowned upon, how can it be considered a part of traditional Chinese custom? This objection only begs another, more fundamental, question: What counts as "custom," and who gets to decide? "Custom" has a positive connotation, especially in the Chinese language; it implies a value judgment, behind which lies a power structure. Therefore, while delayed transfer marriage may have been the dominant norm in much of the Pearl River Delta, local gentry stigmatized the practice and Qing officials tried to suppress it outright.[45] Fraternal levirate (in which a widow is inherited through remarriage by her unwed brother-in-law) was far from unusual in China, but Qing law treated it as a capital offense.[46] More fundamentally, the celebration of female chastity combined with legal protection of polygyny was an ideological program that protected the interests and privileges of elite men. When a rich man who already had a wife bought another woman to be his concubine, the practice counted as "marriage"; but when a poor woman with her husband's approval contracted a uxorilocal marriage with a second man, *that* counted as "adultery."

Because "custom" has a positive connotation, people may resist applying this label to practices, however widespread, of which they are ashamed. In some Taiwan villages, "minor" marriage was the universal practice, yet villagers, when asked about "Chinese marriage" by a Western anthropologist, would invariably describe the "major" form, even though none of them practiced it themselves.[47] Of course, prostitution never counts as custom, even where ubiquitous and known to all.

Polyandry was a minority practice, but in weighing its significance, we should bear in mind, too, how few marriages were polygynous. Concubinage was most common among the gentry, who have been estimated to comprise less than 2 percent of the Qing population. In a study of twenty-three South China genealogies, Liu Ts'ui-jung has estimated that, on average, only 3.7 percent of married women were concubines/*qie* (i.e., the rest were main wives/*qi*).[48] Since a rich man might have more than one concubine, it is safe to assume that less than 3.7 percent of the men in these lineages had concubines. The percentage of Qing dynasty men who never married was certainly far higher than that—and it seems likely that many "bare sticks" were never recorded in any lineage genealogy.

But surely no one would argue that concubinage is trivial to our understanding of Chinese marriage; on the contrary, polygyny has usually been seen as paradigmatic and has consequently received a degree of scholarly attention far out of proportion to its actual incidence. If polygyny was paradigmatic of Chinese marriage, then so was polyandry—and I would guess that polyandry was by far the more common of the two practices. In fact, there is a logical connection between polygyny among the rich and polyandry among the poor, in that the transfer of young women to rich households (to become concubines and maidservants) exacerbated the shortage of wives in poor communities.

Polyandry was part of a larger field of practice in which people who could not buy into the normative pattern of marriage and family, because of poverty and other factors, would bond with others of similar condition in a variety of ways. These "unorthodox households" also included same-sex unions among marginalized males, alliances between independent widows and their hired laborers, and relationships in bands of itinerant beggars, in which one or more women allied with a group of men. In each scenario, sexual relations deemed illicit by the state combined with coresidence, resource pooling, emotional bonds, and chosen kinship. Unorthodox households may have been illegal and stigmatized, but they nevertheless constituted a basic and very widespread part of Qing social practice.[49]

Marriage and Prostitution

From the standpoint of Qing orthodoxy, marriage and prostitution constituted irreconcilable opposites. Marriage depended on the absolute chastity of a secluded wife—a clear separation of *nei* from *wai*—while prostitution implied the untrammeled promiscuity of a public woman. This basic distinction was vital to elite status and lifestyle as well as imperial ideology throughout the Ming-Qing period.

But if we survey the Chinese marriage system from the bottom of the socioeconomic scale, that distinction cannot be sustained. On the contrary, we learn that sex work in one form or another might even play a decisive role in the preservation of marriage and family. In poverty-driven polyandry, the distinction between marriage and sex work collapses, as a wife exchanges her sexual and other domestic labor with one or more outside males, with her husband's approval, in order to help maintain her family. This collapse of boundaries requires us to rethink marriage and kinship in Late Imperial China. If we look at the Chinese marriage system from the bottom up, then it suddenly makes sense, because polyandry falls into place as the necessary third piece of the puzzle, alongside the polygyny of the elite and the monogamy of the middling peasantry. If we define kinship as strategic practice, then we can account for the many chosen relationships of people who found it necessary to seek alliances outside the normative family system in order to survive. This reconsideration does not mean we should glamorize the often sordid and desperate lives of the Qing dynasty poor. But it does require us to get past elite norms and judicial categories, to understand why these people behaved as they did and how they understood their own behavior.

Polyandry in its various forms was a survival strategy, one means by which "the little people" coped with the very big social and economic problems that afflicted China over the last few centuries. To recapitulate, three larger forces that converged in these strategies were the skewed sex ratio and concomitant surplus of single men, the pervasive market for women's sexual and reproductive labor, and the subsistence crisis of a growing number of rural families. At the intersection of these larger forces, we find the case examples described in this chapter.

What changed over time? It may be impossible to answer with much certainty, but we can speculate. It seems likely that the three interrelated problems that framed polyandry were all getting worse over time—that is, they were affecting a growing number and probably a growing proportion of people, from the mid-Qing on. (For example, even if we assume that the percentage of "bare sticks" in the overall population held steady from 1700 to 1900, the absolute numbers of such men would have more than tripled during that time.) If that is correct, then it seems reasonable to guess that the incidence of polyandry and related practices would have increased as well.

In *Report on an Investigation of Popular Customs*, the section on Gansu contains a remarkable flash of insight:

> According to our investigation, this evil custom [of "getting a husband to support a husband"] exists almost everywhere in the province (*ji yu quansheng jieran*). It seems likely, therefore, that to enforce the law and prohibit this custom would pose an immediate threat to the survival of a very large population.[50]

This frank statement cuts through all the moralizing rhetoric, right to the heart of the matter. Polyandry was a response to survival exigencies that had rendered the normative standards and values of the late empire irrelevant. One might even read it as a harbinger of their collapse.

Notes

The research for this chapter was supported by funds from the CSCPRC, the American Philosophical Society, the American Council of Learned Societies and the Social Science Research Council, and the University of Pennsylvania. My sincere thanks to all who provided comments on early versions of this essay, especially Karasawa Yasuhiko and my students at Stanford.

1. I provide ages of protagonists in legal cases when possible (ages at time of first trial, unless noted), in *sui*. An age calculated in *sui* is on average one more than the number of years old according to a Western reckoning: someone aged twenty *sui* was probably nineteen years old.
2. Philip C. C. Huang, *The Peasant Economy and Social Change in North China* (Stanford, Calif.: Stanford University Press, 1985).

3. *Neige xingke tiben* (Grand secretariat memorials on criminal matters) (held at First Historical Archives, Beijing), Qianlong 10.7.23. Memorials collected before 2000 are identified by date; those collected since 2000 are identified by new serial number and date. All are from archival category "marriage and sex offenses."

4. For more on these sources, see Matthew H. Sommer, *Sex, Law, and Society in Late Imperial China* (Stanford, Calif.: Stanford University Press, 2000), 18–22.

5. For the history and application of this law, see Sommer, *Sex, Law, and Society*, chapters 6 and 7.

6. These documents are held at the Sichuan Provincial Archives in Chengdu and the First Historical Archives in Beijing, respectively.

7. *Minshi xiguan diaocha baogao lu* (Report on an investigation of popular customs) (two volumes), compiled by the Administrative Law Department of the former Nanjing National People's Government (Beijing: Zhongguo zhengfa daxue chubanshe, 2000), 2:840, 894, 904, 928–29, 938–40, 968, 977, 997, 1006, 1036, 1051. Kishimoto Mio also cites this survey in "Tsuma o uttewa ikenai ka? Min-Shin jidai no baisai/tensai kanko" (Is it forbidden to sell a wife? The custom of selling/pawning wives in the Ming-Qing period), *Chûgoku shigaku* 8 (December 1998): 179–84.

8. This survey leaves out Guangdong, Guangxi, Guizhou, Sichuan, Taiwan, and Yunnan, but legal cases document variations of polyandry in these provinces, too.

9. Rinji Taiwan Kyûkan Chosakai (Temporary committee on research of customs and practices on Taiwan) (1910–1911), *Taiwan shihô furoku sankôsho* (The common law of Taiwan, with reference materials appended) (thirteen volumes) (Taipei: Nantian shuju, 1995) (reprint), IIB:129–30.

10. For analysis of this term, see Sommer, *Sex, Law, and Society*, 96–101.

11. See Sommer, *Sex, Law, and Society*, introduction and sources cited therein.

12. See Huang, *The Peasant Economy*.

13. Kamala Kempadoo and Jo Doezema, eds., *Global Sex Workers: Rights, Resistance, and Redefinition* (New York: Routledge, 1998), especially 3–4; Alison J. Murray, *No Money, No Honey: A Study of Street Traders and Prostitutes in Jakarta* (Singapore: Oxford University Press, 1991); Paola Tabet, "I'm the Meat, I'm the Knife: Sexual Service, Migration, and Repression in Some African Societies," in *A Vindication of the Rights of Whores*, ed. Gail Pheterson (Seattle: Seal, 1989), 204–26; Luise White, *The Comforts of Home: Prostitution in Colonial Nairobi* (Chicago: University of Chicago Press, 1990).

14. In her study of African prostitution, Paola Tabet posits a "continuum" of "sexual-economic exchange" that in many ways resembles the spectrum of polyandrous practice I am describing here: "One aspect along the continuum of sexual service concerns time length; there is a whole range of sexual-economic relations between the two extremes of lifelong marriage and few minutes' intercourse in prostitution" ("I'm the Meat," 206–7). The lifelong marriage she refers to is monogamy or polygyny, however, not polyandry.

15. *Minshi xiguan diaocha baogao lu*, 2:977.

16. Tabet, "I'm the Meat," 206.

17. *Minshi xiguan diaocha baogao lu*, 2:1006.

18. This well-known proverb from Mencius is typical of the moralistic clichés used in contracts and legal plaints during the Qing.

19. Rinji Taiwan Kyûkan Chosakai IIB: 129–30; for an alternative translation, see Patricia B. Ebrey, ed., *Chinese Civilization and Society: A Sourcebook* (New York: Free Press, 1981), 235.

20. For a good example of a widow remarriage contract, see Sommer, *Sex, Law, and Society*, 184. Qing and Republican-era contracts for land sales contain formulaic language lamenting the need to sell family property, and household division documents typically apologize for violating the ideal of many generations living harmoniously together. See David Wakefield, *Fenjia: Household Division and Inheritance in Qing and Republican China* (Honolulu: University of Hawaii Press, 1998), 59. The popular imagination seems to have viewed all such transactions as transgressions against the family ideal that could be justified only imperfectly by reference to material need.

21. Kishimoto also makes this point ("Tsuma o uttewa ikenai ka," 183). In the Qing, a widow could get away with uxorilocal remarriage only if in-laws from her first marriage did not object, but the practice seems to have been fairly common; see Sommer, *Sex, Law, and Society*, 193–97, and Arthur Wolf and Chieh-shan Huang, *Marriage and Adoption in China, 1845–1945* (Stanford, Calif.: Stanford University Press, 1980).

22. *Minshi xiguan diaocha baogao lu*, 2:928–29.

23. See Kishimoto, "Tsuma o uttewa ikenai ka."

24. *Minshi xiguan diaocha baogao lu*, 2:894.

25. *Minshi xiguan diaocha baogao lu*, 2:1036.

26. *Bao* means to contract something for one's own exclusive use: for example, to purchase the exclusive services of a prostitute or to reserve an entire restaurant for a private party.

27. *Neige xingke tiben*, #554-3/Qianlong 19.5.27.

28. *Neige xingke tiben*, #527-4/Qianlong 18.9.24.

29. *Minshi xiguan diaocha baogao lu*, 2: 1036.

30. In this case, I provide ages in 1735.

31. *Neige xingke tiben*, Qianlong 3.9.7.

32. *Neige xingke tiben*, Qianlong 15.5.24.

33. *Neige xingke tiben*, Qianlong 10.5.17.

34. Wakefield, *Fenjia*, 60–62.

35. Qing law defined "a single household" (*yijia*) by coresidence and pooling of resources; blood kinship was not a necessary factor. See Derk Bodde and Clarence Morris, *Law in Imperial China, Exemplified by 190 Ch'ing Dynasty Cases* (Philadelphia: University of Pennsylvania Press, 1967), 193–94, 323–26.

36. Pierre Bourdieu, "Marriage Strategies as Strategies of Social Reproduction," in *Family and Society: Selections from the* Annales, économies, sociétés, civilizations, ed. Robert Forster and Orest Ranum, trans. Elborg Forster and Patricia M. Ranum (Baltimore: Johns Hopkins University Press, 1976).

37. *Minshi xiguan diaocha baogao lu*, 2:968.

38. The scholarship on Tibetan polyandry is summarized by William H. Durham, *Coevolution: Genes, Culture, and Human Diversity* (Stanford, Calif.: Stanford University Press, 1991), chapter 2, who explains Tibet's marriage system in terms of the logic of domestic economy. Also see Jack Goody, *The Oriental, the Ancient, and the Primitive: Systems of Marriage and the Family in the Pre-industrial Societies of Eurasia* (Cambridge:

Cambridge University Press, 1990), 137–53. Nonfraternal polyandry among the poor in Ceylon may resemble the Chinese case more closely than Tibetan practice does. See Nur Yalman, *Under the Bo Tree: Studies in Caste, Kinship, and Marriage in the Interior of Ceylon* (Berkeley: University of California Press, 1967), 108–12.

39. Aleksandr V. Chayanov, *The Theory of Peasant Economy* (Homewood, Ill.: Irwin, 1966).

40. *Neige xingke tiben*, Qianlong 10.6.19.

41. For variations of monogamy among the Chinese peasantry, see Wolf and Huang, *Marriage and Adoption in China*, and Janice E. Stockard, *Daughters of the Canton Delta: Marriage Patterns and Economic Strategies in South China, 1860–1930* (Stanford, Calif.: Stanford University Press, 1989); for elite polygyny in Late Imperial China, see Francesca Bray, *Technology and Gender: Fabrics of Power in Late Imperial China* (Berkeley: University of California Press, 1997), and Patricia B. Ebrey, *The Inner Quarters: Marriage and the Lives of Chinese Women in the Sung Period* (Berkeley: University of California Press, 1993).

42. Goody, *The Oriental*, sees this "diverging devolution" as a Eurasia-wide pattern in which women were not sold, as in sub-Saharan Africa, but instead took property with them into the conjugal funds of their new marriages. Here he has grasped the normative ideal of Chinese marriage far better than actual practice among the poor. The farther down the socioeconomic scale one looks, the more China resembles Goody's characterization of Africa.

43. Wife selling and compensated divorce will be explored in detail in my second book, now in preparation, tentatively entitled *Polyandry, Sex Work, and Wife Selling as Survival Strategies in Qing Dynasty China* (under contract to Stanford University Press).

44. See Sommer, *Sex, Law, and Society*, conclusion.

45. Stockard, *Daughters of the Canton Delta*, 105–10.

46. *Report on an Investigation of Popular Customs* contains many references to levirate.

47. Wolf and Huang, *Marriage and Adoption in China.*

48. Liu Ts'ui-jung, "Demographic Constraint and Family Structure in Traditional Chinese Lineages, ca. 1200–1900," in *Chinese Historical Microdemography*, ed. Stevan Harrell (Berkeley: University of California Press, 1995), 130.

49. Sommer, *Sex, Law, and Society*, 16, 155, 320.

50. *Minshi xiguan diaocha baogao lu*, 2:1036.

2

The Virtue of Travel for Women in the Late Empire

Susan Mann

In late imperial China, no successful elite man remained at home: he had to travel. Scholar-officials traveled to attend school, to sit for exams, to teach, to take up office, and—along the way—to see and celebrate the famous sights immortalized by writers before them.[1] Often, men sojourned in the company of wives, daughters, and daughters-in-law,[2] and often it was far from home that they died. If his widow survived him, it was she who brought her husband's body home for burial.[3] These journeys by families in motion continually bent the spatial boundaries marking off the domestic realm (*nei*) where women were supposed to preside. When in the spring of 1847 Zhang Wanying set off from the city of Wuchang on a small riverboat bound for the eastern coast of Jiangsu province, she was embarking on a journey whose moral contours were well defined. Her travel diary, later published by her younger brother and translated in full here, is in some ways unique. Wanying's husband, an uxorilocally married man, died far from his own native place though well ensconced in the household of his wife.[4] Her search for a resting place for his body reads like a pilgrim's progress: a record that encodes and inscribes her wifely virtue while reiterating her distinctive place as a woman whose charge is home and family. To place that record in its cultural context, we must first understand the concerns about women's travel that occupied scholarly men during Wanying's lifetime.

Late Imperial Debates about Women in Motion

Writings about women's travel in the late empire display conflicting worries. On the one hand, women were supposed to stay home. The ideal of the woman who is "still" (*jing*) or quiescent, who doesn't "move about," was a powerful trope in representations of the late imperial "cultivated woman" or *guixiu*. The *jing* ideal was traced to the Book of Odes (*Shijing*), where it was a read as a metaphor for sexual purity.[5] As Wang Duanshu (1621–c. 1706) put it in a preface to her anthology of poetry and criticism, *Mingyuan shiwei*: "The entire *Book of Odes* has its source in the poem about the 'pure and secluded girl'; the *Airs of the States* were chosen from among the songs of 'wandering girls.' By reading those poems, we learn to distinguish between pure and decadent mores, and vividly to bring to mind whatever is sagely and good."[6]

At the height of the eighteenth-century classical revival, quiescent or cloistered women were celebrated by conservative commentators, notably Zhang Xuecheng, who drew a derisive contrast between the *guixiu* ideal and the notorious ladies in Yuan Mei's circle of female poets. At the heart of the dispute between Zhang and Yuan over womanly ideals was the contradiction embodied in the woman writer, who by the very act of writing violated the classical injunction that "a woman's words should not pass beyond the inner apartments into the world outside" (*neiyan buchu menwai*).[7] Women's commitment to their honor as embodied and concealed within the home is a dramatic theme in all kinds of stories, from tales in Liu Xiang's Han classic *Biographies of Women* (*Lienü zhuan*) to stories of the fall of the Ming. Records of women's suicide during periods of invasion or social unrest—and operas like *Peach Blossom Spring* celebrating women's suicide—continually reminded women that when armies come and men flee, it is the women left behind who will stand firm and die at home. The *Biographies of Women* epitomized those virtues in the story of a king's wife who drowned in a flood rather than trust the man her husband sent to rescue her. Such tales of virtue were sometimes ridiculed by late imperial writers, who considered them examples of "propriety taken too far" (*guoli*).[8] They nonetheless served to dramatize the importance of women's honor and its association with cloistering in the home.

Ideas about womanly virtue may have been firmly anchored in the home, but they sparked broad disagreement about the effects of cloistering on women's talent. Some said (this was Zhang Xuecheng's own view) that women's writings were especially fine precisely because they were not exposed to the moral contamination of the worldly pleasures and pressures outside the home. For example, contemplating the relationship between women's place in the home and the writing of pure poetry, Zhong Xing (1574–1624) wrote:

> [T]o achieve all these [ideals of pure poetic expression], no man can do as well as a woman. Not burdened with the hustle and bustle of business and travel, with nothing but green moss and fragrant trees around her dwelling and no other work than tying curtains and burning incense, a woman is in touch with peace and elegance. Men must travel to all the corners of the earth in order to know the world. When Yu Shiji compiled his *Records of Ten Prefectures*, for example, he had to go and describe mountains and rivers, the various prefectures and counties, cities and their surrounding moats before he could draw maps representing them. But women never have to do that. They have country villages right on their pillows and mountain passes in their dreams, all because they are so pure.[9]

Here women's untrammeled imagination (freed, one may assume, from the mind-drying effects of studying for the examinations) combines with their freedom from worldly contamination to make them consummate writers.

On the other hand, women's inability to travel was sometimes cited to explain their limited ability in prose or poetry writing. For instance, wondering why there were so few women's poems in the standard collections, Wang Pengyun (1848–1904) opined:

> [I]s it more because . . . these women were born and bred in the confines of their boudoirs, and voices from the inner chambers could not reach the outside? Is it also because . . . they did not have the privilege of traveling to the great mountains, climbing to the top of the well-known pagodas, or having the occasions to expose their talent by engaging in verse exchanges with friends? These must be the reasons that there have been so few poems produced by women and that, among those produced, so few are known in the world far and wide.[10]

Male and female writers alike also worried about the psychological and emotional cost of cloistering. The early nineteenth-century anthologist Wanyan Yun Zhu noted that the poet Yan Wansi became depressed and eventually died because her jealous husband locked her in the house every time he went out.[11] The poet Hao Feng, whose *guining* poem is translated here, suffered from self-imposed psychological cloistering in her unhappy marriage, which she refused to discuss with her own parents to spare their feelings. Luo Qilan, a "disciple" of Yuan Mei and one of the most articulate critics of cloistering and its insidious effects, wrote, "Confined to their boudoir, Chinese women are extremely limited in experience. They have no friends for discussion whereby to open up their sensibilities, no mountains and rivers to visit and behold whereby to fructify their literary propensity." And so, she declared, "[After I was widowed] now and then I would leave the house and meet with celebrated men of letters north and south of the Yangzi River, with whom I would compete in poetry contests in order to disprove the unjust charge of plagiarism and to stop the mouths of ignorant people."[12]

To critics of cloistering, travel freed women's minds and talent, making it possible for them to circumvent or loosen the constraints imposed by the norms of their status and upbringing.[13] Would-be female travelers of the eighteenth century, when classical revival called new attention to Han dynasty works, looked to Ban Zhao as an exemplary female intellectual whose own work offered a model for travel writing. Ban Zhao's rhapsody "Traveling Eastward" (*Dongzheng fu*) chronicles a journey in which she follows her son from the capital at Luoyang to his post in Chenliu, about 180 miles to the east. In that work, written partly in response to a similar poem by her father titled "Traveling Northward," Ban Zhao alludes approvingly to the Confucian adage that "To cling to one's native place characterizes a small nature" (*xiaoren huai tu*).[14] Wanyan Yun Zhu was a famous example of an inveterate traveler who made her son take her places and who (according to him) planned the routes herself to ensure maximum coverage of "famous vistas."[15] Her peregrinations are a reminder that women traveled safely and even widely with their sons, whose filiality was thereby displayed for all to see—a point not lost on mid-Qing emperors Kangxi and Qianlong.[16]

Leaving home to travel was increasingly common for women after the Ming commercial economic revolution.[17] The visual culture of painting "famous scenes" made it possible for cloistered ladies to learn about and contrive to visit those places themselves, should the opportunity present itself.[18] And whether they were able to travel or not, female artists painted landscapes at home, relying on painting manuals and classical models for inspiration.[19] Women's writings often show the unmistakable impact of this kind of traveling in the imagination, or traveling through pictorial images.[20] As Wu Xiao put it, writing in the middle of the seventeenth century:

> Traveling around the five sacred mountains of China or floating on the three mountains of the boundless sea is not an activity fit for women, but when I look out upon clouds and mists or gaze at the sun and moon, these domains do not seem far away. Accordingly, I have devoted myself to a Daoist style of life, wear simple clothes, and eat vegetarian foods.[21]

Ideas about distant places were also brought home to women by a husband's or brother's or son's travels. Elite women's poems "seeing off" a departing loved one and their frequent correspondence—often through poetry—with a sojourning male relative display a keen awareness of distance and of the hazards of travel. To be sure, most such poems were situated in the boudoir or firmly lodged in domestic space. The infamous "balustrade" against which forlorn women leaned to search the horizon for an absent loved one is the most hackneyed of the many pieces of domestic architecture used to frame the female body in Chinese classical poetry. Poems to a distant man usually stressed not the cosmopolitan knowledge of the writer but her isolation. Poems about travel written by wives left behind were also suggestively sensual and sexualized, further emphasizing their femininity. An example is the poem "Far Journey" (*Yuanxing*) by the poet Chen Jing of Lou county, Jiangsu:[22]

A gusty wind suddenly blows, as if to uproot the trees.
In the middle of a sleepless night, I rise to light a candle.
Wind and rain (passion?) are always with us;
Small consolation for this lonely person whose heart turns over and over. The wild winds blow against me, and I worry about you;
Where is your slip of a boat moored this evening?

Men's fiction about female travelers invoked the opposite sexual images. A woman traveling by boat set the scene for rape, robbery, and suicide, dramatizing for readers the risks to body and virtue facing any woman who boarded a vessel for any reason, even in the company of her husband.[23]

Writing about Travel

In the midst of this debate and conflict over traveling women, we can identify several legitimate modes of womanly travel that also became occasions for elite women to display their talent as writers. The most constrained was the ladylike visit, which occupied a large part of the time of leisured *guixiu*.[24] Poetry clubs and casual tea brought women out of their homes and into the homes and gardens of other ladies, which they wrote about, as in the late eighteenth-century account of "an excursion with my lady friends to the Li Garden, east of the city"[25] or a poem recalling a surprise visit to a friend.[26] The intimate tone of such verses captures a mood akin to the graceful *guixiu* notes of thanks or regret studied by Yu-Yin Cheng[27] and anchors them unambiguously in the polite and genteel domestic realm.

A more ambiguous mode of travel for women was "wandering" for religious quest or spiritual development. Poems about wandering in the mountains bring women closer to the world of men's travels. Liu Shi (1618–1664) wrote this in her biography of Wang Wei's life after becoming a Buddhist adept:

> In cotton robe and with a bamboo staff, she traveled all over the Yangzi River region and the Chu area. She climbed the Dabie Mountain, looked out from the Yellow Crane Pavilion, and scanned the Parrot Isle and many such scenic sites. She visited Mount Xuan, scaled Tianzhu Peak, went upstream on the Yangzi River to Mount Kuang and Mount Lu, visited the thatched hut of Bo Juyi, and had an audience with the Buddhist Master Hanshan on Mount Wuru.[28]

Chen Jing, whose poem of longing for a traveling husband is quoted earlier, most certainly did not spend her whole life at home. In this poem, "Written for my Personal Maid As We Roam to a Mountain Temple,"[29] she presents herself as a cultivated devotee of nature:

Glittering, gilded and bejeweled, precious lotus altars,
Open in every beautiful spot amid stream and mountain. I myself delight in losing myself in this beautiful scenery;
I don't climb mountains to worship Buddha.

In Chen's poem, we see a would-be pilgrim spurning Buddhist devotions, posing instead as a Confucian or Daoist gentlewoman exploring the mountain landscape in pursuit of self-cultivation. As it turns out, poems by *guixiu* about pilgrimage (as opposed to poems about homebound devotions such as embroidering a sutra or the Bodhisattva Guanyin, or meditating or chanting sutras) seem to be relatively rare. Here is the only one included in Wanyan Yun Zhu's anthology, a decidedly secular piece by Luo Qun titled "Rustic Temple" (*Ye si*)[30]:

Ancient temple from Qi and Liang covers half the mountain,
Without a monk to open the door.
Year upon year the color of spring grass,
Green creeping onto the altar for chanting sutras.

Fictional accounts of pilgrimages show why respectable ladies found them problematic. In the seventeenth-century satirical novel *Xingshi yinyuan zhuan*, a shrewish and willful wife of a weak and ineffectual husband joins a pilgrimage to Mount Tai, only to find herself the only "proper lady" amid a crowd of tenant farmers' wives, hired staff from an official's compound, and "wet nurses from the Meng household or married-off maids from the Keng household."[31] It is the ultimate comment on the wife's lack of virtue that she feels right at home in this company.

Although some *guixiu* surely refrained from visits or wanderings, all upper-class women moved beyond the home—their words moving with them—when their proper roles as daughters, wives, and mothers demanded it. By far the most pervasive, respectable, and vaunted travel for women was travel for family duty. At marriage women moved out of their natal families, sometimes traveling a great distance to the place where a spouse or his father held office. A married woman then went on traveling, paying at least one required ritual visit to the natal family each year (*guining*) and sometimes many more, depending on the local custom of her place of residence.[32] If married to a traveling official, a wife had to accompany her spouse to each new post, an obligation that increased and also varied the distance she had to travel to make the *guining* visit. And if her husband died while sojourning, as his widow she escorted his body to its proper burial place in the ancestral home.

Like men's travel accounts, those of women writers are coded to display both their virtue and their learning—they became, to borrow Cynthia Brokaw's words, "vehicles for expressing appropriate emotions."[33] In the line of duty—following the obligations of a daughter, wife, or mother—upper-class women could move about free of scrutiny, though not, as we shall see, without risk and deep anxiety. Some of these moves were exhausting, especially when an entire household had to pack up and follow a sojourning man. Fang Weiyi (1585–1668), writing in a preface to her sister's collected poetry, observed sympathetically that the overburdened Mengshi, who married an official posted as a magistrate, "traveled [with him] far and wide, trekking through Beijing, Fujian, the land of Chu, Guangdong, Qingquan [Hunan province], and Xunyang [Jiangxi province]."[34] The endless literati search for a decent job kept countless families on the road, as Mengshi would sadly have attested, especially if they lacked land or sufficient funds to maintain a separate residence while the man of the house sojourned to teach, conduct business, or pursue some other genteel occupation. Such laments, however heartfelt, were artfully crafted to achieve the most refined expression of wifely sentiment, conveying both fidelity and strength: the obligation of a wife to "support her husband" (*fu fu*) under any circumstances.

Married women might travel alone, or with a child or two, to visit their natal families. The "visit home" (*guining*) was the occasion for writing much of the sentimental poetry that fills women's literary anthologies. Two examples show the range of expressive possibilities presented by this opportunity to travel. The first, titled simply "Guining," is by the Shandong poet Hao Feng:[35]

> A daughter travels far from her loving mother
> But once each year she may return.
> My brothers, delighted, all ask how I am,
> My sisters, happy, all greet me at the door.
> Together we enter the old house,
> Sit in a circle and talk of what has happened while we were apart.
> My mother takes my hand and asks
> Why have you grown so thin?
> I remember the last time I left her,
> She was ill, and her condition is still unstable.
> My thinness arouses her concern,
> I start to weep, then stop myself.
> If my mother is at peace, then I will be too.
> I must not wound her with my own loneliness.

My little problems with hunger and cold,
I dare not speak in my mother's hearing.

Here the shock of encountering a beloved daughter after a long separation can be expressed in a poem where other voices are silenced.

In a more sentimental and artful vein is a *guining* poem by Pan Zhengxin, the younger sister of Pan Suxin (Xubai), written to rhyme with a poem on the same theme by her elder sister. Notice how the poet takes care to annotate the reasons for travel alluded to in the poem:[36]

"Rhyme on 'Returning for a Visit Home,' Composed in Harmony with My Elder Sister, Xubai"
Since the time we were young nestlings together
We swallows have flown off to our separate houses.
From Wu down to Yue
Poet's note: this refers to the fact that Suxin married into a Hangzhou family
From the center of the earth to the margins of the heavens
Poet's note: i.e., from the capital, Beijing, to the far southwest, Yunnan
Though we were able to communicate through letters,
Letters cannot compare to traveling the distance in person.
So at last today when we finally meet,
Sorrow and joy mix and sharpen each other!
At our old home, with you in your brightly decorated carriage,
When they beat the gong to signal your departure,
Everyone hailed the high position of your husband
Poet's note: your husband had been appointed an inspector of education in Fujian and you were to accompany him to his post
But I could think only of your new poems,
Your sure hand with no trace of femininity.
All your life you've been faithful to your filial duties.
Approaching the trail back over the mountains, we grow more and more agitated.
At midnight I shall board the boat slowly.

Zhong Huiling's study of what she calls "thinking of home" (*sigui*) poems by Qing women writers[37] shows the many ways in which these poems worked to express women's consciousness as well as displaying their talent. So, for example, a *sigui* poem becomes the occasion for regretting that one is not a man, as in Xi Peilan's anguished verse lamenting that she cannot be with her mother to mourn her late father.[38] Writing *sigui*, the poet remarks on the difference between her own will and the will of the larger social order; composing a "poem about a thing," another compares her life to the fate of the floating willow catkin, utterly subject to currents beyond her control.[39] In other words, as noted, poems about travel can also take the form of imagined journeys that one never took. Imagined travel could be as powerful as travel in real time, nurturing the creative mind of a woman writer whose very thoughts of home constituted a field of knowledge and a way of knowing that she identified exclusively with women and women's experience. In the conclusion of this chapter, we shall return to the problem of imagination and travel.

Family Travel in the Nineteenth Century: The Case of Zhang Wanying

The most somber travel undertaken by a respectable cloistered woman was to escort her deceased spouse's corpse home to his native place for burial.[40] Although wives were not specifically charged with this duty, the record of Zhang Wanying's journey with her husband's body, translated here, shows that at least some women felt compelled to do it themselves, either because a son was too young or because of other kinds of attachments and concerns about the deceased that might require a widow's presence or intervention.

Zhang Wanying (b. 1800) was the youngest of the four daughters of Zhang Qi, one of the founders of a school of song lyric writing named after the family's native place of Changzhou, Jiangsu. Her younger brother (her father's only surviving son) Zhongyuan (Yuesun) was her lifelong confidant and, at the time of her husband's death, the head of the household in which she lived, since her marriage to Wang Xi was an uxorilocal one. She was the mother of four sons and four daughters; the eldest son and three of her daughters play a role in the story we are about to hear.

"Record of a homeward journey south" (Nangui jicheng)
by Zhang Wanying[41]

In the dingwei year of the Daoguang era, second month, 27th day [April 12, 1847], *I took my deceased husband's body from Wuchang back to his native place for burial. With me I took my eldest son Chenbi and my nephew Chenyang, leaving behind in our Wuchang quarters my other three sons, Chenliang, Chenjin, and Chenkai, four daughters, Caipin, Caifan, Caizao, and Cailü, and the concubine Zhou* [birth mother of the three sons left behind]. *At the time my eldest sister Mengti was about to return to the capital* [to rejoin her husband]. *Learning that there were bandits about in Shandong and Henan, she changed her plans to go by the Yangzi as far as Jingkou* [i.e., Zhenjiang, the point where the Grand Canal and the Yangzi River meet], *then travel northward from there to the point where the Yellow River and the Huai River enter the Zha River. So she came too.*

On the day of our departure we spent the night outside the North Gate of Wuchang. My brother Zhongyuan and my middle sister Wanxun came down to the boat to bid us farewell. They did not leave us 'til the sun set. We departed early next morning, on the 28th, passing from Qishui to Bahe and Lanqi and docking at Huangshigang, just on the border between Wuchang and Daye. The following day a headwind made it impossible to travel. On the first day of the third month we passed through Daoshifu and on to Qizhou. The following day we lodged in Xinzhakou. The third day of the month a great wind blew all day so we had to stop. The next day we passed through the customs station at Jiujiang and moored in Hukou county. The day after that the wind would not stop blowing, but the boathands hoisted the sails and went along for 300 li before stopping at Anqing. On the sixth day there was a huge storm, with thunder and rain and heavy winds all day and night. Our bedding and pillows were soaked through. On the seventh and eight days we remained halted by heavy winds. The next day we set out at dawn, spending the night in Qingqi. The following day we passed through Datong courier station, stopping as it began to rain. Next day we passed Tongling and again encountered rain. The following day we forged ahead but within several li the wind had once again brought us to a halt. On the fourteenth day we passed Digang and moored at Banziji. My sister was sick with chill. The next day it was still raining but we braved the storm and got as far as Luxijia [Rush Mat Narrows]. *In the middle of the night a furious wind rocked the boat and we could not sleep. I stayed up the whole night talking with my sister. And the following day the wind would not subside. A day later we were finally able to start out again, but we made only a little more than ten li before the gales returned, so we moored on the river's edge. That night the winds were so fierce that the boathands were afraid to sleep. But at dawn next day the weather was calm and we reached Wuhu. The day after, we were again halted by winds and had to remain in port for three days. On the 22nd my eldest sister began to feel better. We passed by the inspection station and traveled as far as Niutunhe. The next day we reached Caishiji, the following day we passed through the inspection station at Longjiang, then on the next day through Yanziji, Qingshan, and Fanshan* [Alum Hill], *finally reaching Jingkou. On the 26th I sent a servant to rent another boat, and on the 27th we removed my late husband's body [and placed it on the new boat] while my sister and I spent the night on the old boat talking about our coming separation. On the 28th we parted.*

When I planned this trip south, I was thinking about being in the same boat with my sister, and I did not fully appreciate how hard it is to travel. Now that I am on my own [lit., "my form comforts my shadow"], *I must endure my suffering alone. And my sister—she will be traveling where the Qing-Huai crosses the Yellow River and enters the Zha River, and the Zha is easily silted and blocked so she cannot possibly move quickly, and in the long summer's heat, her lonely boat will be like an oven, still more difficult to bear!*

On the 29th we reached Danyang. On the first of the fourth month, we finally arrived at Changzhou [Wanying's old home] *and docked outside the East Gate. Friends and relatives came in great numbers and held a memorial service. We spent three days moored there. I sent my son Chenbi to fetch Gong Shaobai* [Maocai] *to come with us to Taicang. Maocai is adept at grave siting and geomancy and he was a longtime good friend of my late husband.*

On the fourth day of the month our boat left Changzhou, reaching Wuxi the next day. The day after that we got to Suzhou and on the 7th we arrived in Taicang. We anchored at Caochi. I led my son and my nephew to pay our respects before the elders in my husband's family home. We saw my late husband's father's brother, Nianjiao, and his two sons Mianzhi and Zhuanxiang. Also my late husband's aunt Lady Shi and another aunt Huang, and various sisters-in-law. We then returned to our lodgings on the boat.

My husband's family has lived in Taicang since the Ming dynasty. My late father-in-law was always traveling and he died in Shaanxi when my husband was very young, so my husband grew up as a dependent of my own father. Later, when my father was holding office in Shandong, he arranged for my husband to enter our family as an uxorilocally married son-in-law. After my father's death, my husband sojourned for many years in Shandong, Anhui, and Zhejiang, unable to return to his native place. By the time we married, his parents were already deceased. For these reasons, I had never had an opportunity before to see the graves or ancestral halls of his ancestors, nor to become acquainted with the towering figures and great deeds of the men in his family. This was my first encounter with them. Yet the family's funeral ceremony was reverent and solemn, with hempen garments white like the snow. When members of the family saw us they grieved sorrowfully with truly pitiful tears.

On the eighth day we visited the graves of the Lord of Qin and the Lord of Yongzhou. The next day I asked Chenbi to take Gong Maocai to Liuhe and measure the grave site of my late husband's father. Upon their return the following day they reported that there was no land available for an additional grave. So we created a temporary grave shelter and took the body to Liuhe. We got to Liuhe on the 13th, and spent the next several days visiting the graves of my late father-in-law's relatives. On the 17th at the mao hour [the hour of the hare, 5–7 A.M.], *we placed my late husband's coffin in its temporary shelter to the right side of the grave of his father. The next day we made offerings beside the grave, and that same day we resumed our journey by boat. The following day we again moored at Caochi and the day after that I asked my son Chenbi to pay his respects at the ancestral shrine honoring his paternal ancestor the Lord Wensu* [the Ming grand secretary Wang Xijue, discussed later], *which is part of the main ancestral hall. Then the day after that we bade farewell to my husband's relatives and departed, stopping over at Suzhou. On the 28th we arrived at Hangzhou, where I took my son and my nephew to Tiequangang to my late husband's elder brother's residence during his term as an official there. We saw both my brother-in-law and his wife, Lady Zhang. She urged us to stay on, and so we spent three days with them. On the fourth day of the following month we moored at Tangxizhen, and on the day of the Dragon Boat Festival* [5th of the 5th] *we reached Shimenzhen, the next day passing through Jiaxing and on to Pingwang courier station; the following day through Pengqiao and Xuyeguan to Wuxi. On the 9th we arrived back in Changzhou, where on the 10th day we took up temporary residence at a remote house owned by my father's sister's son. On the 11th, the anniversary of my husband's death, I went to the Yanshou Convent and asked a nun there to chant a sutra for him.*

My husband's temporary burial arrangement had been judged most unsuitable by his elder brother, so while we were en route from Hangzhou back to Suzhou, I sent my nephew Chenyang back to Taicang in search of a burial plot. He could find nothing. In the sixth month I sent him again. Finally in the eighth month a letter came from him saying that he had found a possible plot, but when Gong Maocai went to see it, he decided it was not in a propitious location. In the eleventh month we finally found a piece of land in the 18th ward, some two mu in extent, costing more than 80,000. Maocai said that neither the year nor the month was propitious for the burial and that we ought to postpone it for several years. So we rented a boat to return to Wuchang.

On the 10th of the 12th month [January 15, 1848] *we boarded the boat and sailed from the East Harbor in Wuhu into the current of the Yangzi River. It was windy and snowy by turns, and bitterly cold. Chenbi became sick with chill and did not recover for several days. It took us 35 days before we reached Wuchang on the 15th day of the first month of the year wushen* [February 19].

My river journey there and back covered altogether a distance of more than 4,400 li [1,467 miles]. *We spent seven months in Changzhou and we were traveling for over 100 days. In 1824 when I accompanied my mother as she followed my father to his post in Shandong, I first knew the perils of travel. Ten years later, in 1834, I returned to the south; and a decade after that I came to Wuchang. But none of these journeys was much longer than 1000 li. I have never traveled so far as I did on this trip. This floating life is unpredictable and I do not know what the future may hold for me. Truly it makes me sigh with sorrow.*

Earlier when I was stopped in Taicang my brother Zhongyuan sent a courier to ask after me, and so I made a record of the journey and sent it in a letter to him. Zhongyuan wrote a poem at the end of it. Then when I got to Wuchang I revised it to make this record of the traces of my steps through time.

Dated: Daoguang wushen [1848], *second month.*

Tracking the timetable of Wanying's arduous journey, we see that the dates in her record speak for themselves. What is not apparent is that she was tracing a route that her husband had earlier traveled, one that evoked all kinds of memories. Her collected poems include sets of paired rhymes (exchanged between them) remembering his late mother, a native of Wuxi, during a trip he took through that city,[42] a poem about a climb her husband took up Tiger Hill, in Suzhou,[43] and poems exchanged with her husband while he was employed in Hangzhou in the 1830s.[44] (Among Wanying's poems written before her husband's death can also be found verses addressed to him in places far distant, such as Jiujiang, Jiangxi.[45]) Read in conjunction with Wanying's collected poems, her terse record reveals more than she intended about women's family travel and its meanings.

Zhang Wanying's late husband Wang Xi was a descendant in the fifth generation of the great painter Wang Yuanqi, who was in turn the great-grandson of the late Ming official and grand secretary Wang Xijue. The family claimed descent from the illustrious "Taiyuan Wangs," Taicang descendants of the original Taiyuan line from Shanxi. Between Wang Xijue's generation and Wang Xi's, the line produced two Grand Secretaries and nine *jinshi* degree holders. Thus when Wanying remarks on the "towering figures and great deeds" of her late husband's family, she is not merely being polite. At the same time, her record points to anxieties and tensions that go far beyond the bodily and psychological strains of travel in the monsoon and winter seasons.

The first thing to note about Zhang Wanying's travel diary is her selection of traveling companions. Her eldest son is also her only birth son. Wanying gave birth to four daughters, but the other three sons of her late husband were born to a concubine. The nephew who comes along seems to be the son of her late husband's elder brother, the one who is so kind to her in Hangzhou. This elder brother and his wife (who is also surnamed Zhang and may be a kinswoman of Wanying's as well) appear to be the only members of her late husband's family who are concerned about his final resting place. The fact that no space has been reserved for Wang Xi's body in his father's grave site, and that the temporary shelter Wanying finally settles on is clearly an uneasy compromise, points to the politics of burial in a large and ambitious family such as the Taiyuan Wangs of Taicang. Wanying's bravery—her fortitude in undertaking this arduous journey and her determination to find a secure resting place for her husband's body—becomes clearer as we observe the uncaring remoteness of the relatives who greet her and the difficulty she has in locating at last some acceptable if very expensive grave land. I have not yet been able to determine the names of most of the people whose graves Wanying visited, but many appear not to have been Wang relatives. One grave she mentions, for example, honors the Donglin leader Gu Xiancheng of Wuxi. Thus, she undertook some rather far-reaching travels about the countryside in search of the graves of great statesmen and also, perhaps, desirable land for her own husband's grave.

Wanying's record is most detailed in specifying places and dates. One can track her boat precisely day by day, as it makes its way from port to port, dock to dock, along the Yangzi River and the Grand Canal. Her cryptic notes about the weather, the terrified crew, the abrupt departure from Taicang, and the anguish of traveling on after her sister's departure leave us to imagine the enormous pain of that journey, with her husband's body, through her own birthplace with all its memories, and on to unknown relatives to whom she was an utter stranger and among whom her husband's own place was in some doubt. That the Taiyuan Wangs of Taicang received her haughtily and judged her own family beneath them seems all too plain from her story (why else would she lodge on her boat?). Perhaps, as people who prided themselves on their northern roots, the Taiyuan Wangs of Taicang disdained the widespread practice of uxorilocal marriage in the Lower Yangzi region. Even if this was not the case,

Wang Xi's father's early death made it possible for rival siblings to lobby against his interests. The warm reception accorded Wanying in Hangzhou by her late husband's elder brother and his wife also implies that the two brothers had found themselves allied against rival kinsmen.

Zhang Wanying's intimate relationship with her late husband, captured in countless poems and correspondence over the years, and her appreciation of his erudition and of his close ties to her own father and brother can only have heightened her resentment of her husband's relatives and their unseemly coldness. But she had little recourse if she wished to criticize them directly, other than to produce this masterly piece of understated narrative. In his afterword to her travel diary, her brother Zhongyuan focuses his attention on her stay in Changzhou, their old home, and avoids reference entirely to the Wang family:[46]

> This simple, tranquil essay is good.
> The sojourning guests are deeply tied to me.
> In my dreams I know this route,
> After reading, I felt I had returned to our old home.
> We white-haired people are all old,
> But we have not forgotten our "green mountain" [47] promises,
> In the old compound there are new swallows
> Who know to seek the Turmeric (*curcuma longa*) Hall.[48]

Spatial Stories: Travel as a Record of Virtue

In his discussion of what he calls "spatial stories," Michel de Certeau calls our attention to the relationship between "maps" and "routes"—between the places that mark out an itinerary and the spaces traversed to connect one place to another.[49] Wanying is composing just such a spatial story. Her focus is on the route, on getting there and back. But she marks her progress by the map: naming one river landing after another, and so accurately, in fact, that a contemporary reader can follow the entire journey on a modern Chinese map, where most of those landing names remain unchanged. Held together by these dots along the Yangzi and down the Grand Canal, Wanying's fragile narration moves us inexorably downriver, toward her husband's burial and, from there, on the circuitous route back up to the comfort of home. Why did she feel compelled to map her route this way? Why name the places? The reader who has passed the same spots will remember sights and sounds, noticing that Wanying herself is oblivious. Wanying rejects the adventures of travel and its delights. Instead, she focuses—stop by stop—on her misery and on the dangers of weather, illness, and a skittish crew. In this way, Wanying bends not only her own will but the will of her readers to the moral purpose of her journey: delivering Wang Xi's body to its final resting place, no matter what the cost. The terse map gives Wanying's travel narrative its ultimate power to display her virtue.[50]

So Zhang Wanying's travel journal, with its "simple" language and matter-of-fact observations, encloses unexpected worlds of meaning. Reading her poems with her travel journal in mind, in fact, enables us to see through Wanying's eyes a map of her world that follows her husband through space even as his poems and letters reach her by courier and she sends her responses, often encoded in "harmonizing" rhyme. There is yet another layer of meaning in Wanying's writings about her husband's travels and her own. At the end of each chapter of her collected poems appears the small notation: "proofread (*jiao*) by . . . ," followed by the names of three of her daughters and her eldest son. As Wanying's children, these four experienced yet another mode of travel in their filial roles as copy editors. Along with them, we can imagine their parents' lives in space and time, year by year, as they turn the pages of their mother's poetry collection. That Wanying's poems are printed side by side with the poems by her husband to which she was responding also suggests that the poet kept the paired poems together in her own literary archive, reinscribing the bonds between husband and wife in her bequeathed manuscripts.

All of this reminds us in turn that the intimate exchanges of a traveling man and his wife at home were on some level intended for a larger audience of would-be travelers, loved ones, admirers, and, of course, critics. A poem that might have caused Zhang Wanying's children some reflection, then, is one sent by their late father, Wang Xi, to their mother, following his departure on a trip to Hangzhou.[51] The poem describes the tearful scene at the door, as Wang Xi's youngest daughter clings tearfully to his leg, his wife and concubine look distraught, and his eldest daughter begs to go with him. So, the poet asks, if the family is neither cold nor hungry, must he leave? Answering his own rhetorical question, Wang Xi's concluding stanza replies:

> A man must set his sights on distant places;
> How can he let the mood of a moment break his ambition?
> Brushing off my clothes, I force my way out the door;
> My insides want to rip apart.
> *Qi qi* the raven cries into the night;
> By the flickering lamp, I sob right back.

Wang Xi's comment on the plight of "a man" (*zhangfu*), condemned by his gender to set his sights on distant places, is difficult to read. Is he complaining or explaining? Is he valorizing or apologizing? No matter how we read his poignant final stanza, he makes it clear that the man in the family must be the sojourner and that it falls to women and tearful offspring to endure his absence. Wanying's own "response" to this poem, which precedes it in her collected works, is wholly sentimental, intended to comfort and reassure the traveler. In fact, the language of these husband-and-wife poems about travel and separation privileges her as the centered person and pities his privations as a wanderer. To be sure, these are poems exchanged by a married-in son-in-law and a wife safely lodged in a home where she is surrounded by natal kin. Perhaps the dynamics of travel have a different gendered effect on couples in what Arthur Wolf and Huang Chieh-shan have called a "major" marriage.[52] Still, catching Zhang Wanying in this exchange with her husband permits us to revisit questions raised at the beginning of this chapter.

First, in the Confucian value system of late imperial China, travel was a man's world, at least for the leisured elite. Sojourning for scholarly success, official duty, or business profit was the business of men. Travel to famous sites or beautiful landmarks, part of the sojourning ritual but sometimes undertaken for its own sake, was also part of the process of self-cultivation that belonged to the male literati elite. Some *guixiu* sought travel for these same reasons, viewing travel opportunities as part of their own process of development as learned persons and fully realized human beings. But in the larger construction of things, which placed home (the "native place") and its grave sites at the center of every person's life cycle, the center of emotional and physical gravity remained the domestic space occupied by women, and women's travel diaries did not emerge as a venue for displaying the self. In other words, the construction of the meaning of travel itself has a particular valence in late imperial gentry culture, at least before the late nineteenth century. To appreciate this valence, we can contrast the *guixiu* with Victorian English "adventuresses," who sought out travel for "the freedom both to construct an identity and to embrace anonymity, to scrutinize and to retreat from self." In nineteenth-century England, women's travel writing became emblems of their taste, class, and race, part of their quest for independence and self-definition, and essential to their own growing awareness of cultural difference and civilizational hierarchies.[53] The *guixiu* of China's late empire in fact shared with Victorian women many of these same values (recall Ban Zhao's allusion to Confucius's admonitions about narrow minds and lack of travel). In both cultures, women's writing itself was a form of metaphorical travel, a mode of self-definition and self-cultivation. But we need to rethink the extent to which contemporary understandings of travel are colored by the Victorian legacy that viewed travel as a kind of "adventure" framed by encounters with the exotic Other. The self-discovery and self-cultivation sought by (mainly) male travelers in late imperial China derived not from encounters with the exotic Other but rather from viewing "famous vistas" from a long-familiar past. Writing about travel, and correspondence with travelers, flowed largely within family networks, as men wrote while they sojourned and the women at home responded. This only served to heighten the importance of the family ties that converged at home, the end point of every journey.

We cannot pretend that adventure played no part in the travels of upper-class men, and the occasional woman, in the Ming-Qing period. But their underlying assumptions about the purpose and the value of travel itself could not contrast more sharply with the Victorian example. Indeed, reflecting on Zhong Huiling's observations about *sigui* poetry, we see that travel away from home produced a heightened consciousness of self and identity among elite Chinese women precisely because of their longing *not* to travel. Ironically, it was not being away from home, but remembering home, that stimulated their awareness of their own will and desires, their suborned place in the social order, and their differences from men. Here, too, seeing how family duty framed ideas about *guixiu* travel takes us one big step away from the Victorian paradigm and closer to an understanding of how travel shaped gender identities in late imperial culture. The domestic realm defined as *nei* constituted a site for the continual reproduction and reinvention of ideas about gender difference and gender performance, as powerful in the female traveler's imagination as it was in the practice of homebound women who never went out the door.

Notes

The author acknowledges with appreciation the advice and assistance of Ye Baomin and the critical suggestions and scholarly inspiration of Grace Fong. I am indebted to Zang Jian, Wang Zheng, Weijing Lu, Yu-Yin Cheng, and Dorothy Ko, for help in obtaining copies of Zhang family writings, and to Cynthia Brokaw, Matthew Sommer, Maram Epstein, Lisa Rofel, Elizabeth Perry, and other participants in the Gender in Motion conference for illuminating criticism and comment.

1. See Richard E. Strassberg, *Inscribed Landscapes: Travel Writing from Imperial China* (Berkeley: University of California Press, 1994); and Pei-yi Wu, *The Confucian's Progress: Autobiographical Writings in Traditional China* (Princeton, N.J.: Princeton University Press, 1990).

2. Zeng Jifen recalls such a trip in Thomas L. Kennedy, trans. and annot., *Testimony of a Confucian Woman: The Autobiography of Mrs. Nie Zeng Jifen, 1852–1942*, ed. Thomas L. Kennedy and Micki Kennedy (Athens: University of Georgia Press, 1993), 26–27.

3. See the eloquent analysis in Grace Fong, "Authoring Journeys: Women on the Road," chapter 5 of *Herself an Author: Gender, Writing, and Agency in Late Imperial China* (forthcoming). See also the four-month journey described by Zeng Jifen in *Testimony of a Confucian Woman*, 37–38.

4. Uxorilocal marriage was not uncommon among elite families of the Lower Yangzi region during this period. See Weijing Lu, "Uxorilocal Marriage among Qing Literati," *Late Imperial China* 19, no. 2 (1998): 64–111.

5. The locus classicus for the phrase is Mao Ode 42, "Jing nü," which begins with the line "How lovely is the retiring girl!" and goes on to celebrate the virtues of the cloistered lady. See James Legge, ed. and trans., *The Chinese Classics: The She King,* vol. IV (Taipei: SMC, 1991), 68. Legge discusses the controversy alluded to by Wang Duanshu, noting that commentators had disparate readings of the import of these poems. Song dynasty commentators contrasted the "retiring maiden" with the "wandering girls" described in Ode 9 (*The Chinese Classics,* vol. IV:15) who "ramble about" as they gather plantain.

6. Kang-i Sun Chang and Haun Saussy, eds., *Women Writers of Traditional China: An Anthology of Poetry and Criticism* (Stanford, Calif.: Stanford University Press, 1999), 691.

7. Susan Mann, trans., "Zhang Xuecheng (1738–1801), *Fu xue*" (Women's learning), in *Women Writers of Traditional China,* 783–99.

8. Joanna F. Handlin, "Lü K'un's New Audience: The Influence of Women's Literacy on Sixteenth-Century Thought," in *Women in Chinese Society,* ed. Margery Wolf and Roxane Witke (Stanford, Calif.: Stanford University Press, 1975), 19–21.

9. From *Preface to Mingyuan shigui,* translated in Chang and Saussy, *Women Writers of Traditional China,* 740. See the slightly different translation in Ko, *Teachers of the Inner Chambers,* 62.

10. See preface to Xu Naichang, *Xiao tan luan shi huike baijia guixiu ci* (Song lyrics of one hundred famous women) in Chang and Saussy, *Women Writers of Traditional China,* 805.

11. Wanyan Yun Zhu, comp., *Guochao guixiu zhengshi ji* (Anthology of correct beginnings from our august dynasty) (1831):10:18a.

12. From Luo Qilan's (late eighteenth-century) preface to *Tingqiu guan guizhong tongren ji* (An anthology of fellow women writers, from the Listening-to-Autumn Studio). See Chang and Saussy, *Women Writers of Traditional China,* 704–5.

13. See Dorothy Ko, *Teachers of the Inner Chambers: Women's Culture in Seventeenth-Century China* (Stanford, Calif.: Stanford University Press, 1994), 219, 224, 251–93.

14. Translated in Nancy Lee Swann, *Pan Chao: Foremost Woman Scholar of China* (1932; repr. Ann Arbor: University of Michigan Press, 2001), 113–30, including a map on 118. On the importance of travel, see 114–15, and 124, n. 31; also *Analects* 4/11 (Legge, trans., *The Chinese Classics,* 1:168): "the small man thinks of comfort"—as opposed to the superior man, who thinks of virtue.

15. Susan Mann, *Precious Records: Women in China's Long Eighteenth Century* (Stanford, Calif.: Stanford University Press, 1997), 94–95.

16. Mann, *Precious Records,* 197–98.

17. Ko, *Teachers of the Inner Chambers.* See also Timothy Brook, *The Confusions of Pleasure: Commerce and Culture in Ming China* (Berkeley: University of California Press, 1998), 182–85. On travel in the lives of women writers of the Ming-Qing period, see accounts of Huang Yuanjie (one of whose sons drowned when their boat capsized

during one of her trips to a new teaching position), in Chang and Saussy, *Women Writers of Traditional China,* 358.

18. On travel through painting, see Craig Clunas, *Pictures and Visuality in Early Modern China* (Princeton, N.J.: Princeton University Press, 1997), 83*ff.*; quotation on 83.

19. See Marsha Weidner, "Women in the History of Chinese Painting," in *Views from Jade Terrace: Chinese Women Artists, 1300–1912,* ed. Marsha Weidner et al. (Indianapolis: Indianapolis Museum of Art, 1988), 23–24. Also Ellen Johnston Laing, "Women Painters in Traditional China" in Weidner, *Flowering in the Shadows,* 91–93.

20. On "armchair travelers," see Ko, *Teachers of the Inner Chambers,* 224–26.

21. From her *Preface to Xiaoxue an gao* (Manuscripts from Howling-Snow Studio), in Chang and Saussy, *Women Writers of Traditional China,* 690.

22. Wanyan Yun Zhu, *Guochao guixiu zhengshi ji,* 8:10b.

23. Mayumi Yoshida, "Mindai hakuwa shôsetsu ni okeru kawa to fune: Tenki, shi, saisei no ba ni tsuite" (Rivers and boats in Ming vernacular fiction: Crisis, death, and rebirth), *Sinica* 7 (July 2001): 96–103.

24. Chang and Saussy, *Teachers of the Inner Chambers,* 226–42.

25. Wanyan Yun Zhu, *Guochao guixiu zhengshi ji,* 13:20b.

26. Wanyan Yun Zhu, *Guochao guixiu zhengshi ji,* 16:22b–23a.

27. See Yu-Yin Cheng, "Letters by Women of the Ming-Qing Period," in *Under Confucian Eyes: Writings on Gender in Chinese History,* ed. Susan Mann and Yu-Yin Cheng (Berkeley: University of California Press, 2001), 169–78.

28. Chang and Saussy, *Women Writers of Traditional China,* 697–98.

29. Wanyan Yun Zhu, *Guochao guixiu zhengshi ji,* 8:10b–11a.

30. Wanyan Yun Zhu, *Guochao guixiu zhengshi ji,* 17:17a.

31. Translated in Glen Dudbridge, "Women Pilgrims to T'ai Shan: Some Pages from a Seventeenth-Century Novel," in *Pilgrims and Sacred Sites in China,* ed. Susan Naquin and Chün-fang Yü (Berkeley: University of California Press, 1992), 56.

32. See Ellen R. Judd, "Chinese Women and Their Natal Families," *Journal of Asian Studies* 48, no. 3 (1989): 525–44.

33. Discussant's remarks, Conference on Gender in Motion, University of Oregon, October 5, 2001.

34. Chang and Saussy, *Women Writers of Traditional China,* 687–88.

35. Wanyan Yun Zhu, *Guochao guixiu zhengshi ji,* 16:19a–b.

36. Wanyan Yun Zhu, *Guochao guixiu zhengshi ji,* 18:4a.

37. See Zhong Huiling, "Nüzi youxing, yuan fumu xiongdi—Qingdai nü zuojia sigui shi de tantao" (When a woman travels, she leaves her parents and brothers far behind—A study of "thinking of home" poems by women writers of the Qing dynasty), in *Zhongguo nüxing shuxie: Guoji xueshu yangaohui lunwen ji* (Writings by Chinese women: Collected papers from an international scholarly conference), ed. Danjiang daxue Zhongguo wenxuexi (Taipei: Xuesheng shuju, 1999), 127–69. Zhong argues that these genres of writings, exclusive to women, produced a kind of collective and individual consciousness about gender differences and constituted a mode of resistance against, or a critical commentary on, women's plight.

38. Zhong, "Nüzi youxing," 162.

39. Zhong, "Nüzi youxing," 163, 165–66.

40. See J.J.M. de Groot, *The Religious System of China, Its Ancient Forms, Evolution, History and Present Aspect, Manners, Customs and Social Institutions Connected Therewith* (repr. Taipei: Literature House, 1964), 3:834–44.

41. Zhang Wanying, *Canfeng guan wen ji chubian* (Collected prose from the Living-on-Breezes Studio, V.1) (1850) 1:29a–31a.

42. Zhang Wanying, *Linyun youyuezhiju shi chu gao* (Dwelling near the clouds and befriending the moon: Poems, early drafts) (1829), 2:1a.

43. Zhang, *Linyun youyuezhiju shi chu gao*, 2: 1a–b.

44. Zhang, *Linyun youyuezhiju shi chu gao*, 2:7b.

45. Zhang, *Linyun youyuezhiju shi chu gao*, 2:12a–b.

46. Reprinted in Zhang, *Linyun youyuezhiju shi chu gao*, 4:4a.

47. The term *qingshan* is another gloss on travel, probably a reference to a Tang poem by Xu Ning titled "Parting from Master Bai" (*Bie Baigong*), in which the "green mountain" is the old home to which the aged drunken traveler returns.

48. *Yujin tang* is a poetic allusion to the dwelling of a beautiful woman; here Zhongyuan must allude to the home where the four Zhang sisters grew up.

49. See Michel de Certeau, *The Practice of Everyday Life*, trans. Steven F. Rendall (Berkeley: University of California Press, 1984), 115–30.

50. Compare Wanying's terse account with the travel diary of Wang Fengxian, whose record of a trip back home from a remote posting in western Jiangxi lavished attention on "the minute pleasures and moments of revelation on the road" (including some comic relief about the cramped quarters on their upstream barge). See Ko, *Teachers of the Inner Chambers*, 221–22. Notice, in contrast, Wanying's focus on the journey's end and purpose; casual observations about the scenery find no place in her narrative.

51. Reprinted in Zhang, *Linyun youyuezhiju shi chu gao*, 2:7b.

52. Arthur Wolf and Huang Chieh-shan, *Marriage and Adoption in China, 1845–1945* (Stanford, Calif.: Stanford University Press, 1980).

53. See Maria H. Frawley, *A Wider Range: Travel Writing by Women in Victorian England* (London: Associated University Presses, 1994), 17.

3

Gender on the Stage

Actresses in an Actors' World (1895–1930)

Luo Suwen

BANNED FROM PUBLIC PERFORMANCE in the context of Qing neo-Confucian orthodoxy, actresses began to emerge in Beijing opera (*jingju*) in the late nineteenth century. The historical exclusion of women reinforced the male-centered culture of *jingju*, which was undergoing early professionalization just as women appeared on its stage. As the new actresses pursued careers and encouraged other women to work in opera, the male culture of *jingju* complicated actresses' professionalization, creating working conditions, restrictions, and opportunities quite different from those available for actors. This chapter examines gendered aspects of opera training and performance, and actresses' strategies of adaptability and manipulation of their medium as they worked to further their professional development.

Actresses' struggles for professional autonomy reflected not only concerns related to gender divisions of labor but also social class. It was commonly the case that poverty combined with gendered social stigmas to create particularly devastating conditions for girls and women. Opera troupes purchased poor girls from the countryside and coerced them into training. Performances by experienced actresses often were regarded as simply lewd entertainment. Public fear of female exposure and gender mixing led to an association between female actresses and sexual immorality that tainted even skilled performers. These associations were heightened by an actual and imagined overlap between female performers and prostitutes. Social prejudice discouraged famous opera families from initiating their daughters into the arduous training process, leaving few opportunities for actresses to attain advanced skills. It took some time, therefore, for actresses to rival the best actors. During most of the early period of female opera performances (1895–1930), actresses were regarded as inherently inferior to actors.

Yet the conditions that forced young, poor girls into opera in the first place, together with actresses' discursive association with lewdness, pushed the boundaries of gendered space. In time, the paradoxes of their position opened the field of opera to professional female performers. Not surprisingly, the foreign settlements of Shanghai, physically and conceptually marked as separate, offered some of the earliest venues for *jingju* actresses, despite attempts by Chinese authorities to regulate the performances. The development of opera troupes that used female performers within the settlements acclimated audiences to women's appearances in public and paved the way for wider public acceptance.

This study focuses on the late Qing and early Republican era, a period of intensified urbanization and professionalization in Beijing opera. The first section details late Qing changes in *jingju* that facilitated the entrance of women and girls. The second section outlines the various routes girls and women took to *jingju* performance and some of the difficulties they encountered. Throughout, my focus is on the seemingly contradictory social change that occurred as actresses struggled: On one hand, poverty drew most actresses to the stage, where they were vulnerable to economic abuse and social stigma. On the other hand, women's appearances expanded public notions of what was possible or desirable for women, gradually altering the occupational constraints of the traditional realms of *nei* and *wai*.

The negotiation and tension between *nei*, the inner realm that ideally enclosed women, and *wai*, the outer, male realm, took on special significance when a woman was physically on display, as in opera performance. Although the public found female performers scintillating, this impetuous entry of women into *wai* was both welcomed and scorned. The spectacular nature of opera lent itself to women's (actual and staged) forays into the outer realm; nonetheless, such forays were interpreted as unchaste. Whereas the critics of political women examined in Madeleine Yue Dong's chapter in this volume constructed caricatures to insist on their unnatural obscenity, critics of actresses could simply point to the extremity of public performance itself. Another level of complexity lay in the fact that opera contained both male and female roles—implying, in other words, a "rightful" place for women. If many critics insisted that men could perform femininity better than women, such a stance conflicted with new social ideologies of modernity that eventually helped open the stage to female performance.

Setting the Stage: Late Qing Changes in Beijing Opera

Beijing opera, unlike other regional operas, was fashioned over time through the gradual incorporation of melodies and performance skills from various local operas. This capacity to adapt elements from a variety of local operas may have facilitated Beijing opera's successful and rapid modern development. It also, I argue, is what set the stage for women's successful, if difficult, integration into operatic performance.

In the late Qing, *jingju* was centered on the imperial capital of Beijing, an environment that provided several advantages. First, Beijing's competitive cultural environment stimulated constant innovation. The capital of the Yuan, Ming, and Qing dynasties, Beijing enjoyed a galaxy of talent, commercial prosperity, and a lively entertainment market, all of which nourished a thriving environment for regional operas. Since the mid-Qing, the court favored *kunxi* (Kun opera), but other regional operas still performed and competed in Beijing, which gave rise to an exchange among styles that normally would not interact. In the mid–eighteenth century, *kunqu* and *jingqiang* were fashionable in Beijing, but sometimes these troupes also collaborated with performers from other regional operas. Early *huixi* (Hui opera) won over Beijing audiences with beautiful *erhuang* tunes, rich expression, and popular stories, and parts of these forms of expression were incorporated into the Beijing opera. Kun opera gradually lost favor in the late Qing, but learning to sing in *kun* style remained mandatory in the early training of Beijing opera actors. The Kun opera *chou* role (clown) was preserved on the Beijing opera stage. Elements of Hui and Han opera led to the formation of the *pihuang* tune.[1]

The mixing of formerly unrelated styles created an aesthetic shock that attracted audiences to Beijing opera. The constant competition and rise and fall of opera troupes provided a rich pool of talent for Beijing opera, talent that was both already trained and, by virtue of the mixing of local traditions, innovative. Compared to regional operas, Beijing opera enjoyed diversity in its performances, highly skilled performers, effective training for young performers, and, of course, imperial patronage. Under these conditions, Beijing opera changed rapidly and retained audience interest.

As is well known, the professional training of Beijing opera actors is characterized by long practice and high elimination rates, with a great deal of attention given to young talent. Many actors lost their voices early in their careers and were forced to teach or become musicians. This turnover increased opportunities for younger actors and also allowed for the rapid incorporation of new techniques.

The relatively high income of some performers in the late Qing, together with changes in the way performers were paid, marked the early modernization of *jingju*. Prior to this time, ensemble manager and opera actors signed yearly contracts for a fixed amount of money, independent of performance earnings. Such contracts did not permit actors to perform privately or with other troupes. Only a few famous actors received extra pay or payment for individual performances. In the 1880s, several famous actors successfully pressed for a commission system, a set percentage of performance earnings. Troupes adopted this system to retain famous actors. Actors welcomed this change, which offered not only the possibility of increased income but also greater mobility. On the other hand, the commission system increased wealth discrepancies among actors, helping produce the star system that became the norm in later years. Performers who did not become stars developed other means of producing income, such as offering training classes for students. There were six such classes in Beijing in the late Qing.[2] Palace performances also stimulated Beijing opera performance art and increased actors' income.[3]

By the late Qing, actors began forming their own ensembles and created new singing styles and roles. Actors gained fame in a variety of roles, departing from the conventional emphasis on old-man roles.[4] In 1909, Wang Yaoqing proclaimed himself a pillar of the stage and became the first actor *in a female role* to be the lead actor in a Beijing opera performance. To be competitive, famous actors needed—and could afford—the cooperation of musical specialists, drummers, or cosmeticians. This structure, which created production teams, increased actors' public prestige and enhanced the star system; it also resulted in innovative content, singing styles, accompaniment, costumes, and cosmetics.[5]

In the late Qing, a regional market began to take shape. In the two major cities of Beijing and Shanghai, a systematic reform took place, organizing opera through a commercialized management system and marketing network. Other cities also participated. Ensembles and famous actors were invited for periodic commercial performances at treaty ports, usually beginning in Tianjin, then moving to Shanghai, Jinan, and Yantai. Commercial *jingju* performances also blossomed in Harbin, Fengtien (Shenyang), Yingkou, and Andong (Dandong). In the late Qing and the early Republic, *jingju* spread from Shanghai to Hangzhou and Jiaxing, and it penetrated southern cities such as Changzhou, Wuxi, Suzhou, and Nanjing along the southern end of the Grand Canal.[6]

In the late Qing, boat and train transportation links developed first among treaty ports and other commercial centers. The pioneering commercial cities were also the earliest to be incorporated into the information network of the newly developing newspapers, publishing industry, and postal services. Performance tours in these cities—also sites of Western cultural exchange—expanded Beijing opera's influence and enlivened the opera itself. Beijing opera began to change rapidly. It was under these shifting cultural, commercial, and material conditions that actresses first began to appear.

The Emergence of Beijing Opera Actresses

Actresses first appeared in Shanghai, in "southern-style" Beijing opera. The first female ensemble was also established in Shanghai.[7] As one of the first treaty ports established by the 1842 Treaty of Nanjing, Shanghai became a special administrative zone in the 1860s. Foreign settlements, which were under the autonomous administration of foreign residents, allowed Chinese and foreigners to reside together and run businesses freely. This unique situation resulted in Shanghai's rise as the economic center of the Yangzei River Delta. In their first decades, the foreign settlements became a venue for female performers in both "obscene" mixed-sex performances, as well as in all-female performance. As a newly created Shanghai opera market blossomed inside the foreign settlements, female performers became integrated into southern-style *jingju* performance.

In the 1870s, *huagu xi* (Huagu opera), also known as "obscene opera," penetrated the amusement halls of the foreign settlements in the form of mixed male and female performance. Although Huagu opera was banned, its popularity continued and soon it was performed in teahouses:

> Huagu opera is performed in the Shanghai concessions. Actors and actresses perform together with vulgar singing and licentious attitudes. . . . After Chinese and Western officials banned it, Huagu opera disappeared from public view for two years. Yet the other day, outside the old north gate of the French Concession, a scoundrel gathered a Huagu troupe to sing. Although female and male performers just sang without performing, we already see public anxiety. Rumor has it that recently two actresses and three or four actors got up to perform together after singing opening tunes. The prohibition is mere formality.[8]

An 1875 article reported nine theaters in the city: "Most of them stage performances day and night. The audience assembles in crowds."[9] Most of the performers were from the north.

Until the 1880s, the so-called obscene operas encountered little resistance when promoters advertised and arranged public shows at settlement theaters. Chinese magistrates repeatedly promulgated prohibitions increasing the punishments for violators, but under the autonomous administration of the foreign settlements, Chinese decrees were ineffective. Moreover, the settlements provided attractive venues. In June 1877, the Municipal Council of the International Settlement issued fire regulations that required theater passageways, floor slabs, enclosing walls, railings, and running water.[10] These regulations ensured an architecturally secure and comfortable venue for actors and audiences inside the settlement, where tea garden theatrical performances became a leading entertainment business.

Female performers had been active in Shanghai since at least the mid-1850s, attracting audiences in a growing entertainment industry. Female performers were named "*nü changshu*" (female storytellers).[11] Little by little, female performers both assimilated *jingju* techniques and moved beyond teahouses to mount the formal stage. By 1890, as Beijing opera ensembles gained an advantageous position in settlement theaters, female performers were performing *jingju* onstage. During the Tongzhi reign (1862–1875), Xinghuayuan was a famous tea garden venue for female performance. Danfeng Teahouse (established 1876 or 1882) also invited female troupes. Among sixty-nine theaters opened between 1850 and 1889, fifty-three showed only Beijing opera.[12] The Shanghai newspaper *Shenbao* listed local and nonlocal opera performances, reviews, and audience responses as key elements of entertainment news. The fact that northern opera became mainstream entertainment among Shanghai residents is related to both the immigrant nature of the city and the colorful qualities of the opera itself.

As *jingju* became popular in Shanghai, the distinctive southern style of Beijing opera continued to develop. Commercialized management of opera in Shanghai appeared in response to market demand for entertainment, location requirements for commercial performances by troupes from different regions, and negotiations between local administration and theater management. The 1870s also saw the beginning of professional training in Shanghai for *jingju* actors, such as that offered by the Xia Family troupe, which was attached to Dangui Teahouse. In 1877, the Yongshengyu troupe (Clapper Opera troupe) from north China settled in Shanghai, and its performance aesthetics influenced the southern style.[13] Thereafter, between 1890 and the 1920s, Shanghai *jingju* began to experiment with reforms in play adaptation, staging, and performance innovations, some of which developed from interaction with regional operas, and some of which were inspired by Western performance models. The result was the Shanghai school of Beijing opera or *haipai*, and out of *haipai* came the female *jingju* ensemble.

The earliest female *jingju* ensemble was named *maoer xi* (Maoer opera). Although the origin of the term is not totally understood, one historical fact is clear: a performer named Li Maoer launched the first female Beijing opera ensemble.[14] Li Maoer followed examples set by Kun and Hui opera entrepreneurs, purchasing poor girls in Anching to bring to Shanghai. They were taught Hui tunes and performed only at private parties. The girls, from ages ten to seventeen, performed male characters, female characters, painted-face characters, or clown roles, and they were trained by only one instructor. The small troupe of around ten performers performed at familial celebrations organized by local gentry or merchants. For lack of a better name, people called it *maoer ban* (Maoer ensemble). In the beginning, the Maoer ensemble performed mostly episodic drama that did not require multiple roles. Three or five actresses performed episodes about teaching children, palace life, visiting brothels, romance, and selling rouge. The troupe was paid less than male ensembles, and the girl performers were not paid a monthly salary. Except for meals and meager pocket money, their performance income went to the head of the troupe.[15]

The Maoer ensemble was different from the *jingju* ensembles that performed at theaters, and it also was different from children's performance troupes that were attached to specific ensembles. Even though the first Li Maoer ensemble eventually disappeared, performances by this kind of female ensemble—with low investment cost and rudimentary training—soon became popular at private Shanghai parties. The economic incentives are evident. Compared to male troupes, these low-cost female troupes were more profitable for their organizers. After the Maoer ensemble disbanded, the Xie Family ensemble and the Lin Family ensemble appeared. Female ensembles soon became the rage, eventually performing at grand theatrical shows. In the late Qing, people began to name all female ensembles *maoer.* The most famous was the Qiu Ruyi Family Maoer ensemble at Qinghefang. This predominantly female ensemble (the twenty performers included some boys) performed at entertainment venues such as the Zhang and Xu Gardens.[16] The origin of *maoer xi* was recorded in *Tuhua ribao,* published in Shanghai in 1910: "*Maoer xi* was the beginning of female theater. As the first female ensemble is named after the organizer, people habitually use the name of Maoer for female ensembles."[17]

Maoer xi was marked by its liveliness, and there is no doubt that it influenced the development of women's *jingju* performance. The first female *jingju* ensemble theater, the Meixian, emerged in 1894. It was followed by the Nixian, Qunxian, Nüdangui, Dafugui, and other theaters. In 1900, after Qunxian and Nüdangui opened to the public, Maoer ensembles from other parts of the country were invited to Shanghai for performance tours. These included the Chen Family Warrior Ensemble and the Ning Family Ensemble from Tianjin, the Wang Family Ensemble from Suzhou, and the Yun Family Ensemble from Hangzhou.[18] The far-reaching influence of the Maoer ensemble perhaps lies in its early training of girls as professional actresses, as well as in opening up performance stages for female *jingju* ensembles, or *kunban.* However, female ensembles still faced multiple obstacles achieving recognition within the strictly organized professional environment of Beijing opera.

From *Maoer xi* to *Kunban*: Opportunity and Challenge

Beijing opera was dominated by male actors for reasons of repertoire, skills, and notions of gendered space. There were four major roles: *xusheng* or *laosheng* (old man), *zhengdan* (young woman), *wusheng* (military men and fighters), and *jing* (male painted-face roles). Not surprisingly, the repertoire emphasized male roles, especially the old-man role. Standards for selection of actors were strict, with priority given to a powerful voice.[19]

Beyond singing, there was a need for acrobatic talent, or *bazi*, which required training from childhood. Actors took pride in showing their abilities and considered performing bit roles to be shameful. Singing and stylized acting were highly competitive, and they required stamina, energy, and physical strength. In regard to these requirements, most male performers and fans found actresses technically deficient.

However, it was not just lack of skill that kept women out of Beijing opera but also a cultural disinclination to display women in public. Generally, Beijing opera actors followed the rule that their art was passed on only to men and accepted only male students. In the late Qing, actors' sons usually continued their fathers' careers, while daughters were often married to other actors. Famous performers who might have wished to train their daughters had reason to fear that such girls would be abused if they appeared in public. Many well-known actors did not allow their daughters to learn Beijing opera. The belief that women who performed in public were lewd was sufficiently strong that only the most impoverished would take the risk.

A few examples will illustrate the nature of this social bias against female performers. Yan Huizhu, who became an actress in the early twentieth century, recollected that her father, Yan Jupeng, opposed her training for fear that she would be bullied by officials and landlords. As a result, she did not start learning opera until she was seventeen.[20] Ye Chunshan drew up a family rule that no girls in the Ye family were allowed to learn opera. None of his four daughters were actresses, although three of them married *jingju* actors. Ye Chunshan's Xiliancheng ensemble (later Fuliancheng) in Beijing refused to accept female students to avoid "offending decency."[21] Even if they did not become performers, women born in Beijing opera families almost never stepped outside the circle, marrying actors, raising their sons as actors, and eventually marrying their daughters to other actors. They were thoroughly imbued with opera, yet it remained a forbidden zone, not only as a career but sometimes also as a physical space:

> There used to be a rule that women and mutes could not go backstage. Both were regarded as ominous. Once Yu Sansheng's wife went backstage because of family matters. She was punished by being forced to drink wine, and her infraction was publicly discussed, with the result that she was to be permanently barred.[22]

Despite articulated and implicit injunctions against women performers, in the late Qing there were still a few girls who learned Beijing opera from their fathers. For example, the Hebei native Ying Honglan learned the old-man role from her father and began performing onstage at Haisenwei. In the early Republic, she joined a female ensemble in Beijing.[23] Zhang Wenyan learned opera in her childhood from her father. Niu Guifang, the daughter of *jingju* actor Niu Songshan, learned the young-man role from her father. Xiao Yuexian, the daughter of *jingju* actor Wang Hongshou, learned the lively-maiden role of *bangzi* opera as a child. Occasionally *jingju* actors and fans accepted girl students.

In the early Republic, more actresses were trained, and *kunban* became increasingly common outside the foreign settlements. Nonetheless, associations with prostitution continued to demean the profession. In Shanghai, actress training focused on singing, and students were commonly from brothels, linking female performance and sexual services. Even when students were not prostitutes, there was often only a thin line of distinction:

> Elderly actors, actresses, and local landlords invested in village girls and forced them to learn opera with the threat of selling them to brothels. By purchasing twenty or thirty poor girls, they could form a troupe with male, female, painted-face, and clown roles. These girls were like beggars in the household of their troupe heads.[24]

As such material suggests, the professional development and conditions of *jingju* actresses differed from those of actors. Initially, girls could not perform in Beijing but were organized as *kunban* to perform in the vicinity of treaty ports. Most early *jingju* actresses learned to perform individually, working with a master. In the Qing, formal Beijing opera training schools, most of which were located in Beijing, did not admit female students. Schools in other areas also had restrictions against their admission.[25] The Shanghai Xiaojingtai School, associated with the Tianxian Tea Garden, was established in 1900 and admitted fifty to sixty exclusively male students. The Hangzhou Fang School, which later moved to Shanghai, also did not admit female students.[26] Still, some classes were open to girls. The Bangzi Opera Troupe admitted both boys and girls, training mostly in *bangzi*, with some *jingju* on the side. Around 1900, these students gave performances in Dalian and Yingkou. In Dalian, one of the earliest Beijing opera actresses, Liu Xikui, trained in classes open to both girls and boys.

In the context of the changing gender politics of the Republican era, a *bangzi* opera lively-maiden actor named Tian Jiyun organized the Chongya Female Ensemble Training Class in 1916, the first formal female Beijing opera training class in Beijing. Fifty-seven students studied both Beijing opera and *bangzi* opera at the school. The class staged its first public performance only two weeks after its establishment and was disbanded in its second year. Some students continued their artistic training and performance in the Chongya Female Ensemble. The short duration of this female training class suggests the difficulty of maintaining formal training for girls, and it forms a sharp contrast with the Xiliancheng Training Class of the same period (later called the Fuliancheng Training Class), which trained male students for another twenty years.[27] Under these cultural restrictions, artistic development was quite limited for actresses. There is little evidence to counter the belief that onstage, women were inferior to men. It would not be until fifteen years later, in 1930, that standard professional training for actresses was established through the founding of the Zhonghua Theatrical School, which admitted both male students and female students.

As I have noted, in the late Qing, Beijing opera actresses who were trained via private tutorship were often from poor families from which parents had sold them or given them up for adoption. Other young actresses were put into training by their biological parents, out of economic motives. One example is that of Wang Keqin, who was born into an old Manchu family. After her father died, her mother, a habitual gambler, "pawned clothes and accessories to invite a well-known instructor to train Wang in musical instruments, *erhuang* singing, and the *bangzi* opera lively-maiden role."[28] Such training was an investment strategy for parents or foster parents. Some *jingju* actresses were prostitutes who learned basic singing and instrumental skills and later performed onstage. They were usually prostitutes first and later became actresses, and some continued to work in both professions.[29]

In all of these situations, early Beijing opera actresses came from lower-class families, and their singing was not judged by strict professional standards. Their foundational skills were weak, and often what skills they did have reflected *bangzi* rather than *jingju* training. As a result, they were triply marginalized, as lines were drawn between professionals and amateurs, between Beijing and outsider performers, and between male and female performers.

In the late Qing, female *jingju* ensembles based themselves in cities like Shanghai, Tianjin, Hankou, and northeast treaty ports, where they sometimes could perform with male actors. In early Republican Beijing, actresses were banned from performing together with actors. The situation in Shanghai was somewhat more flexible. The well-known actress Liu Xikui was invited by

Wang Hongshou (a prominent figure in southern Beijing opera) to perform in the city. Zhou Xinfang also volunteered to perform with Liu.

Because the performance styles of urban and rural ensembles differed, actresses found that they needed additional training to enter the higher levels of urban performance. Beijing ensembles emphasized body language and facial expressions, while rural ensembles emphasized tunes and generally ignored facial expressions.[30] This created problems for ambitious actresses. For example, *bangzi* opera actress Yu Lanfang was among the first to learn and perform the Cheng style of Beijing opera. She was not able to study directly with Cheng Yanqiu (who declined to instruct her) but received indirect guidance from Wang Yaoqing and others who had performed with Cheng. Yu began learning opera at age nine, but by age fifteen, she was infatuated with the Cheng style. Along with her elder brother, she learned by positioning herself in theater corners to observe Cheng's performances. When giving her own performances, Yu imitated the Cheng style. After becoming a star, she changed her stage name to Xin Yanqiu in tribute to Cheng Yanqiu's style.[31] Lacking formal professional training and faced with rejection from famous teachers, early *jingju* actresses found it difficult to hone their skills or compete with male actors.

Another major obstacle faced by actresses was that their performing space was crowded and confined. In the early Republic, Tianjin boasted the largest number of stages for female *jingju* performances.[32] Yet even in Tianjin, actresses were confined to smaller stages and excluded from the more spacious world of male ensembles. In Shanghai around 1900, five theaters staged commercial performances, of which three were exclusively at the service of male ensembles: Tianxian Theater, Dangui Theater, and Chunxian Theater. As Kun opera and Yue opera declined over the next ten years, only one of the five theaters (Qunxian Theater) staged female ensemble performances.[33]

In the early stages, *kunban* met powerful opposition by male ensembles. In Shanghai, "when the Qunxian Theater opened with female ensemble shows, crowds were drawn to the theater and enormous profits were made, making it the target of jealousy from other theaters. [Male performers] agreed that if any actor gave instruction at Qunxian, he would be banned from performing at the other theaters."[34] *Kunban*'s rise at Qunxian Theater did not last, partially as a result of such hostile tactics. Another competitive challenge came from elderly palace actors from Beijing who stimulated the excitement of Shanghai audiences: "For the first time, southerners were able to view the orthodox school of Beijing opera."[35] The orthodox school did not include actresses, and Qunxian's business suffered in the face of this competition.

Fortunately, female ensembles from all over China joined in strengthening Qunxian's business. To compete with male ensembles, they adjusted their repertoire and developed additional roles. Famous actresses such as En Xiaofeng, Jin

Yuemei, Bai Lanhua, and Guo Fengxian were invited to perform, and they tried their hands at acrobatic plays. The Wang Family Ensemble and Ning Family Ensemble, which specialized in acrobatic operas, performed for several years at Qunxian Theater. Such creativity, combined with the collective participation of ensembles from around the country, enabled Shanghai female ensembles to withstand the challenge from famous northern *jingju* actors.

Other locations sustained only scattered performances by female ensembles. In Tianjin, there were initially two female troupes: Chen Family *kunban*, known for acrobatic operas starring Chen Changgen, and Baolai *kunban*, starring Ying Honglan. Though banned in late Qing Beijing, there were two *kunban* in Koudai Lane (in the west of the city) that performed at private parties (gatherings of men from the same hometown, same-year graduates of imperial exams, or businessmen in the same trade). Opportunities were limited. Birthday or other celebrations by rich households were rare, and extravagant displays of wealth were not fashionable. Female ensembles that depended on private parties could hardly survive. After 1900, they were disbanded, with famous actresses such as En Xiaofeng moving to Tianjin.[36] The female ensembles that entered Beijing during the early Republic came from Tianjin in 1912, when organizers successfully petitioned the Beijing police to lift the ban on female ensembles in the city.[37]

Mixed ensembles emerged in the north only in the early Republic. When a mixed ensemble appeared in Tianjin in 1906, it was banned as an "offense against decency."[38] Gradually, however, ideas and practices were changing. In Beijing, at a private party held in the president's residence in 1912, the actress Xiao Lanying performed along with Sun Juxian, Tan Xingpei, Chen Delin, Yang Xiaolou, Mei Lanfang, Liu Yongchun, and Huang Runfu.[39] Actresses participated with actors in ensembles; for example, the actresses Du Yunfeng and Yu Zhixian were in the Shuangqing She ensemble, Sun Yueqiu and Yu Zhiyun were in the Xiliancheng ensemble, and Yang Cuixi and Xiao Cuixi were in the Qing Chunhe ensemble. But generally, although these ensembles contained both female and male actors, they did not perform onstage together, as local officials and landlords continued to regard coperformance as indecent. When actors felt threatened by actresses' appeal to the audience, they also resisted coperformance. Their motive was self-preservation and elimination of dangerous competition, securing the stage for actors alone.[40]

The situation was different in Shanghai, where only the French Concession banned coperformance in the late Qing. Feng Theater, along with Tiansheng Theater, staged male and female coperformances. The Qiankun Opera House at the Great World Amusement Hall got its name (*qiankun*, implying male/female) when actress Jing Shaomei started performing with actors there. Although *kunban* roles were less rich than those of male ensembles, after several years *kunban* was able to manage on its own. At times it even supplanted male ensembles in popularity. In 1915 and 1916 when *kunban* was all the rage, only one male ensemble—that of Mei Lanfang—could compete.[41] In the development from *maoer* performance to *kunban*, from vignettes to grand opera and acrobatic opera, *jingju* actresses slowly achieved independence. Strenuous efforts on the part of actresses who wished to develop their skills, along with the acquisition of new techniques through exposure to different styles as the troupes traveled, allowed *kunban* actresses to progress.

One distinctive feature of late Qing Shanghai *jingju* was that new operas were constantly performed to pique audience interest. Moreover, troupes constantly innovated and experimented in repertory, props, singing style, acting skills, music, makeup, and costumes. Some innovators influenced opera in a fashion that opened the door for female performers. For example, Feng Zihe (1888–1941) altered the female role. Perhaps influenced by theories of Western drama, he developed the idea that an actor should act out a human being rather than a role type.[42] He also created fashionable costume operas, Western costume operas, and Qing-style costume operas, emphasizing eye expressions, female-role singing style, makeup, costumes, and instrumental accompaniment. Shanghai *jingju* increasingly appealed to audiences with melodramatic plots, ever-changing settings, fabulous costumes, vivid acting, and scenes of bustle and excitement.[43]

Yet, even in Shanghai's more open and innovative climate, *kunban* was not powerful enough to share the stage with male ensembles, a situation caused by complex social and cultural circumstances. Because actresses lacked formal training, they did not use their real names when they acted. They were mostly called "Chu," following the name of Jing Chu, the first actress who performed as an amateur in Shanghai.[44] Early *maoer* performances were considered "guest performances by prostitutes," because of overlap between actresses and prostitutes.[45] Actresses' performances were considered inferior to the standard of even mediocre professional actors.

Nonetheless, "guest performances by prostitutes" appealed to audiences, revealing that *kunban* had its selling point. The Shanghai saying, "Watch opera at male ensemble performances, but find excitement at female ensemble performances," shows that audiences were interested in actresses, if not entirely for their operatic art. Liu Xikui arrived in Shanghai during the early Republic, and whenever she took a rickshaw in public, young men followed her, even going so far as to throw gold bracelets into the rickshaw.[46] When En Xiaofeng first performed in Tianjin, her fame was instant. According to one anecdote, several rich and powerful men in the city were frustrated in their desire to get acquainted with her. Some conspired to boycott her performances, and others hired thugs to make a distracting commotion when she was onstage. Such distractions only added to her fame, compounding the delights of Xiaofeng's clear and outstanding voice.[47]

Although actresses often tried to improve their skills, early *kunban* at times exploited audience prurience. At one titillating performance, the famous Shanghai lively-maiden actress Feng Yue's skirt was loosened onstage by the actress playing her boyfriend. The next day, Feng was fined fifty yuan and the opera was permanently banned. Zhou Chu, a famous late-Qing bearded-man actress, reportedly removed her clothes onstage at a customer's request, in return for an extra hundred in gold coins.[48] To some extent, actresses and audience alike regarded these performances as bawdy entertainment. Nonetheless, it was precisely this environment that allowed actresses the opportunity to be onstage and develop their skills.

Kunban acrobatic operas performed in the early Republic also had a distinctive appeal. In the Shanghai French Concession, Feng Theater mainly staged acrobatic operas starring the bearded-man actress En Xiaofeng and lively-maiden actress Wang Keqin. The actresses' acrobatic skills appealed so much to the audience that Feng Theater's business surpassed that of Qunxian Theater and the male ensemble theaters.[49] Dan Guiyuan Theater also enjoyed good business along these lines from 1912 to 1917, even without particularly famous actresses.

In the early Republic, audiences and performers divided among theaters and amusement halls. Theaters were larger and housed more seats. In order to maintain business, they had to invite stars who could fill the house. Small ensembles had no choice but to perform at amusement halls with lower artistic standards.[50] As they positioned themselves in amusement halls, small *kunban* troupes created and defined for themselves a certain kind of audience. At the time, most *kunban* played for low-income audiences who purchased inexpensive seats. In 1916, Qunxian Theater closed its doors and the higher-level *kunban* that had performed there disbanded. Several famous actresses joined in performing with actors at different theaters while others moved to perform at amusement halls.[51]

In the mid-1920s, the *Shenbao* called female ensembles that performed in Shanghai theaters *kunban*. Advertisements for female ensembles at the Great World Amusement Hall referred to them as *maoer xi*. The two ways of naming the female ensembles indicate two different levels of audience and their respectively refined and popular tastes. During the Spring Festival holiday season of 1925, the lowest ticket prices for traditional operas in Shanghai were thirty cents at Gong Theater, twenty cents at Tianyan Theater, Yi Theater, and Gengxing Theater, and fifteen cents at Yue Theater and Xing Theater. At the Great World Amusement Hall, ticket prices were much lower: ten cents for male ensembles and eight cents for *maoer* performances.[52]

In the early Republic, *kunban* performances in Beijing were limited in role types and unappealing in repertoire. The Chengnan Amusement Hall, which showed films, magic performances, and new plays, sometimes featured *kunban jingju* actresses. For a ticket price of twenty cents, audiences could watch all the performances they pleased. *Kunban* performances emphasized mostly female roles, complemented with bearded-man, warrior, and painted-face performances. In the early 1920s, Beijing *kunban* troupes were constantly reorganized. Some performed in public only once or twice before reorganization or mergers. By 1927–1928, *kunban* stars were constantly in flux. Zhang Eyun, Jing Youqin, Xin Yanqiu, and Yang Jufen were once the stars of their troupes, but none of them could last long and their troupes were time and again disbanded.[53]

In the summer of 1928, the capital moved to Nanjing, and Beijing theaters declined. Troupes could not maintain full houses and had to cut performances. Major actors and actresses went to other parts of the country to make money, while those remaining made a living by performing for several troupes.[54] Thus, the financial decline of opera in Beijing caused early Republican Beijing *kunban* to experience its rise and decline in less than ten years.[55]

The historical development of female performance was constrained by types of audience, lack of comprehensive roles, and poor training. This may be illustrated with a few details. First, although some actresses performed male roles, few were highly skilled. Male roles, which were usually given to the star of the ensemble, required talent and solid acting skills. Early bearded-man actresses were inclined to imitate male actors. Although they worked very hard and succeeded in their costume and makeup, they were still considered incompetent. Early Republican opera critics used famous bearded-man actors as the standard to judge bearded-man actresses. Some actresses lost their voices as they tried to adapt, while others achieved a male-sounding voice but still lacked fundamental training. For example, Liang Xinhua achieved a masculine look, but her singing and acting were not competent, according to critics. Qilin Tong was gifted with a good voice, but she overused it, and her stage gait was terrible.[56] Zhao Zhiyun was perfect in the roles of civil servant and warrior, yet her singing was drab.[57]

Second, *kunban* was always inferior in acrobatic skills. Warrior roles, learned by many actresses in the 1920s, required the harshest practice. Critics often found something to criticize in the actresses' performances (although now and then exceptional talent was recognized): "Warrior characters on the whole lacked actual strength. Famous warrior-role actresses were mostly just adopting a stance." Young warrior actress Xie Xiange, who played the part of Zhao Yun in *Huanghe lou*, was considered the best in the role; her makeup and costume produced the impression of handsomeness, and her stylized acting and sonorous tones impressed the audience.[58]

Third, according to critics, lively-maiden role performances were also of poor quality, although critical judgment was divided on lively-maiden actress Jing Yuemei and female-clown actress Xiao Lanying, the earliest female Beijing opera stars in Shanghai. The lively-maiden role made the greatest breakthrough in the late Qing and the early Republic. But the late Qing actresses' singing was not good enough. For example, Cai Ziyun was gifted with a fine voice but "didn't know how to make good use of it." Jing Yufeng's voice was "high and sonorous but not soft enough."[59] Critics evaluated actresses' performances against the performances of actors who impersonated women. For example, Liu Shaorong, who played young-maiden and lively-maiden roles, was praised as "resembling the appearance of Xiao Cuihua." They also complimented actress Miao Xingru, who played the old-woman role, as the "Number One Old-Female-Role Actress" but still found that her style was derived from that of the old-female role actor Gong Yunfu.[60]

As a result of this habitual contextualization within the circles of male talent, early Republican actresses worked hard at imitating famous actors, and some made use of male actors' fame to create their own. For example, Zhang Jieyun (1911–) learned opera at age seven and performed at eleven as an amateur onstage in Beijing. After watching her performance, Wang Yaoqin praised her as "a female Mei Lanfang" and volunteered to take her as his student. Xin Yanqiu's rise to stardom was related to her "resemblance in voice and makeup to Cheng Yanqiu—'as if Yanqiu had actually appeared.'"[61] Such critical judgments discouraged originality. Framed and confined by existing performance styles, female actresses could not develop to their potential or innovate artistic perspectives.

Although mainstream traditional critics believed actresses were not as good as actors, one school of thought departed from this perspective, claiming that "women playing female opera roles were by nature competent. Actors could not surpass them. In all the years since the beginning of Qunxian Theater, male actors have not been able to compete with Jing Yuemei's lively-maiden role."[62]

Early Republican criticism of female role actresses tended to emphasize looks more than artistic skills, but actresses who showed off their looks courted rebukes. For actresses, the message was contradictory: they were, on one hand, criticized for their poor appearance and, on the other, blamed for using their attractiveness to woo the audience.

The final difficulty facing actresses was an insufficiency of role specialization. In the late Qing, because male roles enjoyed a higher social status, more actresses focused on male roles. Yet the small size of late Qing *kunban* ensembles required that actresses be trained to play multiple roles rather than develop specialized skills. Although critics noted the high cost of this practice as well as its poor results—women ended up with some skill in many roles but no commanding presence—it continued for another twenty years into the early Republic. This practice limited the full development of actresses' individual potential.

Rightful Performers

Moving along in fits and starts, female performance in Beijing opera eventually became an accepted part of stage life. After 1930, actresses entered a period of greater professionalization. During the early period explored in this essay, however, it is apparent that the field developed largely through gains made by performers who worked under very bad conditions. Young girls at the margins of survival were forced into the profession by desperate parents, who had little choice but to ignore the cultural taboos that restricted those from more elite ranks. Although accomplished female performers realized they could only achieve the higher reputation afforded the male troupes by improving their art, they often did not have adequate conditions or training. Pressured by physical needs of survival, they sometimes willingly catered to the demands of the popular audience.

The strange symbiosis between audiences' revulsion at seeing women onstage and their lust for the spectacle of female entertainers created a unique opportunity for change. Rural poverty and the higher cultural value of males provided opera with an exploitable resource in the form of young girls whose parents could not afford to keep them. Innovations in opera occurring in the context of treaty ports, commercialization, urbanization, and new communication links, combined with forces of poverty and public curiosity about women on display. The conjuncture of forces broke the male monopoly of public *jingju* performance. It is important for us to understand how, over a thirty- or forty-year period, these changes could alter the meaning of what it meant to be female, primarily through the assault on the traditional idea of *nei* that the actresses provided.

These conditions propelled the field forward. Although the inability to ascend center stage in Beijing limited female performers, they found a marginal point of entry in which innovation and experimentation were not just possible but also encouraged. It is not coincidental that it was in the foreign settlements of the brash commercial city of Shanghai, where new styles of Beijing opera were rapidly developing, that the door was first opened to actresses and the first all-female ensembles were created. These were precisely the locations, as Catherine Yeh describes in her essay in this volume, for the public emergence of actresses' twin sisters, courtesans. In such unorthodox spaces, actresses slipped in at society's edges, eventually establishing themselves as skillful performers whose right to the stage eventually became unquestioned.

Notes

1. *Pihuang* singing combines Han *xipi* and Hui *erhuang* tunes, with local Beijing accent, and Kun melodies and style. Zhao Huirong, *Yandu liyuan* (Pear garden of Yandu), (Beijing: Beijing chubanshe, 2001), 12.

2. Beijing yishu yanjiusuo, Shanghai yishu yanjiusuo, eds., *Zhongguo jingjushi* (History of Beijing opera; hereafter referred to as *History*), vols. 1, 2, and 3 (Beijing: Zhongguo xiju chubanshe, 1990), 1:203, 205–6, 497, 446.

3. Actors who were selected for palace performances had to be ready at any time for an imperial summons. In the late nineteenth century, palace performers received one hectoliter of grain and three taels of silver monthly. Actors selected for palace performances included Yang Longshou (1883), Mu Fengshan (1885), Sun Juxian (1886), Wang Guifen (1902), and others. Actors selected by the royal palace to be opera instructors included Shen Jinchen (1879), Shi Xiaofu (1886), Bo Ruyi (1892), and Xie Shuangshou (around 1896). Zhao, *Yandu*, 37, 39; also *History*, 1:469, 205.

4. Yang Yuelou, Yu Jusheng, Huang Yueshan, and Li Chunlai established the formal warrior role. The old-woman role started with Gong Yunfu. The *jing* (painted-face) developed into the subtypes of *tongchui* (emphasizing singing) and *jiazi* (emphasizing body carriage), as represented by Jing Xiushan and Huang Runfu. Female role performance required skills in young-maiden, lively-maiden, and armored-maiden roles. Representatives were Yu Ziyun, Chen Delin, and Wang Yaoqing. See *History*, 1:139.

5. The star system began with Cheng Changgen, who toured with his own musicians and drummers, ensuring a coordinated performance. Other troupes soon followed this practice. *History*, 2:36–38.

6. Kaifeng, Hankou, and Changsha also were sites for *jingju*, although to a lesser extent. *History*, 1:373–78.

7. "Southern style" refers to *jingju* styles outside Beijing, also called *waijiang pai* (outsider's style). *History*, 1:274.

8. "Huaguxi yijin" (Banning Huagu opera), *Shenbao*, October 1, 1877, 317.

9. "Xiyuan zhujubing" (Theater regulations), *Shenbao*, November 3, 1875, 122.

10. *Shenbao*, June 16, 1877, 553.

11. Ge Yuanxu, *Huyou zaji* (Miscellaneous travels in Shanghai), 1871 (Shanghai: Shanghai guji chubanshe, 1989), 157.

12. Lin Mingmin, "Shanghai xiqu yanchu changsuo bianqian yilanbiao" (A table of Shanghai traditional opera performance), in *Shanghai xiqu shiliao huicui* (Collected historical material of traditional Shanghai opera), ed. Zhongguo xiquzhi Shanghai juan bianjibu, vol. 3 (1987), 126–30.

13. Yongshengyu troupe admitted students and gave itinerant performances in Jiangsu and Zhejiang provinces for about twenty years, emphasizing both Beijing and *bangzi* opera and greatly influencing southern-style *jingju. History,* 1:292–94.

14. Li Maoer, a native of Tianjin, was one of three famous clowns (the other two are Tu Bianer and Zhu Xiaoer) who arrived in Shanghai in the late nineteenth century.

15. Haishang shushisheng (One holding stones in the mouth in Shanghai), "Haishang jiushi linzhua lu" (Shanghai pear garden records), in *Xiju congbao* (Opera collectanea), vol. 1, no. 3.

16. Zhongguo xiqu zhi Shanghai juan, bianji bu, ed., *Zhongguo xiqu zhi—Shanghai juan* (Chinese opera gazetteer, Shanghai volume; hereafter referred to as *Gazetteer*) (1992), 249. The similarly pronounced "cat opera" (also *Maoer xi*) was an earlier and unrelated development, dating to the early nineteenth century, involving child performers six or seven years old, attached to brothels, who performed at private parties.

17. Huanqiushe Editorial Group, ed., *Tuhua ribao* (Pictoral daily), 1909–1910 (Shanghai: Shanghai guji chubanshe reprint, 1999), 5:572.

18. *History,* 1:281–82.

19. Su Kuangguan, "Wangmen dizi shuping" (Stories of kings and their disciples) in *Xiju yuekan* (Opera monthly), vol. 1, no. 3.

20. Yan Huizhu, "Huainian wode fuqing Yan Jupeng" (Remembering my father Yan Jupeng), *Jingju tanwanglu xubian* (Further memoirs of Chinese opera), ed. Beijing wenshi ziliao yanjiu weiyuanhui (Beijing: Beijing chubanshe, 1988), 210.

21. Oral history of Ye Shengchang, recorded by Chen Saowu. See *Liyuan yiye* (One page from the pear garden) (Beijing: Zhongguo xiju chubanshe, 1990), 240, 244.

22. Zhang Xiaochang, *Jubu congtan* (Collected discussions of the chrysanthemum group), (Dadong shuju, 1926), 21.

23. See *Gazetteer,* 285.

24. Zhi Qing, "Shinianlai kunling zazhi" (Miscellaneous notes from ten years as an actress), *Shenbao,* August 19, 1921 [vol. 172], 386.

25. Zhang, *Jubu,* 18.

26. *Gazetteer,* 250.

27. *Zhongguo dabaike quanshu* (China encyclopedia), Xiqu (Opera) volume (Zhongguo dabaike quanshu chubanshe, 1983), 40. Zhang, *Jubu,*18.

28. Boduoye Qianyi, *Jingju erbainian zhi lishi* (Two hundred years of Chinese opera; hereafter referred to as *Two Hundred Years*), trans. Luyuan Xueren (Shanghai: Shanghai qizhi yingshua gongsi, 1926), 132, 295–96, 290.

29. *Two Hundred Years,* 294; *History,* 1:285.

30. Qi Rushan, *Jingju zhi bianqian* (Transformation of Chinese opera) (Beijing: Beijing guoju xuehui, 1935), 52.

31. Zhongguo xiqujia xiehui Beijing fenhui Chengpai yanjiu xiaozu (The Cheng group of the Beijing branch of the Chinese opera association), *Qiusheng ji* (Autumn sound collection) (Beijing: Beijing chubanshe, 1983), 165–68. Though she did not study with Cheng, Yu learned several operas from Mei Lanfang.

32. *Shenbao,* Sept. 12, 1912 [vol. 118], 739.

33. The other theater was Mantingfang (across the street from Chunxian), which sometimes staged Kun opera or Yue opera. Ju Ping, "Nian wunianqian Shanghai xiju

gaikuang" (Thinking of Shanghai opera five years ago), *Shenbao*, February 5, 1925 [vol. 209], 533; *Gazetteer*, 249–50.

34. "Xinju xianping" (Casual discussion of the new opera), 5, in *Haishang liyuan zhi*, ed. Ge Youshen (Shanghai: 1911), vol. 2.

35. Ju Ping, "Nian wunianqian Shanghai xiju gaikuang," 533.

36. Zhao, *Yandu*, 82; Qi, *Jingju*, 96–97.

37. *History*, 1:289.

38. "Qing jin nannü heyan xiban" (Ban male-female performance troupes), *Shenbao*, April 19, 1906 [vol. 83] 182.

39. Zhang, *Jubu*, 35.

40. Xiao Yin, "Pinju yuhua" (Chrysanthemum talks), 95, in Zhou Jianyun, *Jubu congcan* (Collected chrysanthemum talks) (Jiaotong tushuguan, 1918); Liu Jingyuan, *Jingju yishu fazhan jianbian* (Brief history of the artistic development in Beijing opera) (Anhui wenyi chubanshe, 1984), 110; Zhu Qianfu, *Haishang guangfu zhuzhici* (Bamboo branch poem, Shanghai guangfu) (Shanghai: Minguo diyi shuju, 1913), 14; *History*, 2:44.

41. Qi, *Jingju*, 96–97; Liu, *Jingju yishu*, 71.

42. Shanghaishi zhengxie wenshi ziliao weiyuanhui (Historical and literary research materials editorial group of the municipal government of Shanghai), ed., *Xiqu jingying* (The best of opera), vol. 1: *Shanghai wenshi ziliao* (Shanghai historical and literary research material), vol. 61, (Shanghai: Shanghai renmin chubanshe, 1989), 222, 166, 223.

43. Qi, *Jingju*, 14. Audience taste in the two cities differed partly because of different performance environments. In the early Republic, Beijing opera venues were not comfortable, nor were the shows spectacular. Emphasis was placed on singing and acting, so the Beijing audience went to the theater to "listen to opera" rather than "watch opera." Shanghai performance style was different from Beijing style, and purists sneered at it, calling the performances "slippery shows" (*huatouxi*). "Lun Shanghai ren zhi guanju" (How Shanghainese see opera), Ge, *Haishang*, 1:7.

44. *Tuhua ribao* (Pictorial daily), 5:66; "Ershinianqian hushang zhi kunban gaikuang" (Female opera troupes in Shanghai twenty years ago), *Shenbao*, March 4, March 5, 1925 [vol. 210], 65, 83.

45. Ying Xian, "Nüling zhi fada" (The development of actresses) in *Shenbao*, 1912 [vol. 118], 739.

46. *Zhou Xinfang wenji* (The collected works of Zhou Xinfang) (Zhongguo xiju chubanshe, 1982), 389; Hu Sha, "Liu Xikui," in *Zhongguo mingling chuanqi congshu* (Collections of stories about famous Chinese actresses) (Beijing: Renmin yinyu chubanshe, 2000), 22.

47. *Two Hundred Years*, 132.

48. Haishang shushisheng, "Haishang jiushi linzhua lu" (Shanghai pear garden records), in *Xiju congbao* (Opera collectanea), vol. 1, no.10.

49. Yang Guo, "Shinianqian hushang maoerxi gaikuang" (Maoerxi in Shanghai ten years ago), *Shenbao*, March 10, 1925 [vol. 210], 181.

50. Liu, *Jingju yishu*, 125.

51. Xuan Lang, "Hushang zhi kunban" (Female opera troupes in Shanghai) in *Shenbao*, February 20, 1913 [vol. 120], 506; See also Zhi, "Shinianlai."

52. *Shenbao*, February 5, 1925 [vol. 209], 532.

53. Beijing yanshan chubanshe, ed., *Gudu yihai xieying* (The best of ancient art) (Beijing: Beijing yanshan chubarshe, 1996), 224; Liu, *Jingju yishu*, 134, 136.

54. Liu, *Jingju yishu*,137.

55. *Kunban*'s rise in Beijing started around 1915–1916. After 1923–1924, it gradually declined. Qi, *Jingju*, 97.

56. Guangleishizhu (Master of the glistening stone studio), "Tan Chuyan xinsheng zhu nujue" (The new voice of female-role actor Tang Chunyan), *Shenbao*, August 19, 1924 [vol. 215], 672.

57. *Liyuan jiahua* (Lofty talk of the pear garden), Liuyi congke jiaji (Edition name), (Shanghai: Shangwu yinshuguan, n.d.), 145.

58. "Nüling xiaoping III" (Brief critique of actresses, part 3), *Shenbao*, November 12, 1924 [vol. 207], 204; Ju Ping, March 4, March 5, 1925 [vol. 210] 65, 83; *History*, 1:284.

59. Xiao Yin, "Pinju," 19; See also Zhang, *Jubu*.

60. *History*, 1:284.

61. Su Zhongwei, "Pinju yutan" in *Xiju yuekan* (Opera monthly)1, no. 3. When Qi Rushan first watched Xin Yanqiu, she still bore the name Yu Lanfang. He remarked that she looked like Cheng Yanqiu—why was she named Yu Lanfang? Qi invited her to his home and suggested the name change. See *History*, 2:715.

62. Ju Ping, "Nian wunianqian Shanghai xiju gaikuang," 65, 83.

4

Women on the Move

Women's Kinship, Residence, and Networks in Rural Shandong

Ellen R. Judd

A DEFINING FEATURE OF RURAL COMMUNITIES in China has long been the prevalence of patrilocality. Men have preferentially and predominantly remained in their community of birth upon marriage, while women have preferentially and predominantly married out into another rural community where they can normally expect to remain for the rest of their lives. This pattern of movement has widely resulted in rural communities of very great continuity in the male line based on a fundamental discontinuity in the lives of women.

The focus of most attempts at understanding rural social life has been on the resulting localized communities of men. Much less is known about the mobility of women between these communities. Where there has been some significant effort at examining the movements of women and the ties formed through women, these have commonly been conceptualized as affinal relations (from the men's point of view) and as being relations formed by men with other men through the generalized exchange of women in marriage.[1]

But during household visits and interviews with women in three Shandong villages in the 1980s and 1990s, it became evident that the patterns of mobility of women among local communities were highly significant and that women were more active agents in managing this mobility—primarily through marriage—than might be apparent from previous discourse on the subject. Women were active as those who, by virtue of moving between communities, had knowledge about people and households that transcended community boundaries. Typically this knowledge would also extend within the walls of related and neighboring households and constitute a valuable source of intimate knowledge about potential matches and their close kin. Women married out into other communities were a trusted source of information on households and communities to which a daughter might confidently be sent in marriage, and they often served as "introducers" (*jieshao ren*) on their own or in conjunction with their husbands. Mothers also appear in these accounts as major decision makers in the matches of their children, both sons and daughters.[2] Mothers were obviously concerned with who would be joining their own households as daughters-in-law, and they were also commonly concerned with the matches their daughters would make. At least in these areas of rural Shandong, it was common for mothers and daughters to maintain close ties beyond the daughter's marriage out and, in many cases, for married daughters to continue to visit and help their parents as long as either parent was alive.[3] Young married women occasionally sought matches for younger sisters, while it was more common for sisters to marry into different communities. Young women themselves are increasingly agents in their own marriage arrangements, although this had rarely been the case in earlier generations.

In this chapter, I will venture to explore how women (and men) make the movement of women among rural communities operate. I will show how this mobility shapes the structure of rural communities, how it is conceptualized by those involved, and why women's mobility and the resulting forms of network and kinship make a practical difference as women assume a critical role in the outer as well as the inner domain in contemporary rural society.

This exploration will be based on fieldwork in three geographically dispersed Shandong villages described in more detail elsewhere.[4] Two are single-surname villages; one is a multisurname village in which one surname predominates; all are characterized by local patrilines of about twenty generations in depth. None is located in a suburban or particularly affluent area, and each has had periods of relative poverty as well as of relative affluence, with the effects of these changing conditions upon marriages into each community evident in interviews. At least one of the villages had recently become exceptionally attractive as a marital village for women at the time of fieldwork. For present purposes, I will not attempt to trace local differences or historical change and will examine the data set as a whole, while recognizing that it incorporates a substantial range of differing circumstances.

In total, I have recorded information on 255 ever-married women (of all living generations) in these villages, of whom all but eighteen had married out of their natal villages in the major or patrilocal manner. The proportion of women marrying patrilocally is slightly understated in this sample, since I sought to include all atypical marriages in my field study. The eighteen exceptions, distributed among all three villages, consist of two cases of small daughter-in-law (*tongyangxi*) marriage, five uxorilocal marriages, and eleven intravillage marriages.

With many of the women interviewed, I particularly explored issues regarding the arrangement of their marriages and the nature of their ties with their natal families after marriage as well as their networks of social ties more generally. Women in older generations, including many married as late as the early 1960s, commonly had marriages arranged by senior kin, and might well not have met their spouses prior to their wedding day. However, this was not uniform, and there were "free love" matches at least as early as the 1940s, especially in the village (in Changyi) that had been located in a border region prior to Liberation. There were also occasional divorces and remarriages initiated by women in the early 1950s.[5] The more recent norm is for marriages to be semiarranged. Essentially this means that the couple to be married will meet at least once before engagement (and often just once and formally) but may meet several times while engaged (especially for shopping trips on their own). In this form, as still practiced in the late twentieth century, senior kin retain the main responsibility for locating a suitable partner and making the match, although the young people to be married have an opportunity for veto. As young people become more economically independent and are able to meet potential partners through school or work outside their own communities, matches are initiated by the young people themselves, although they then arrange to be formally introduced. However, very large numbers of young people—perhaps still the majority—continue to enter into semiarranged marriages.

Not Marrying Out

The standard practice whereby women marry out of their own communities has been repeatedly identified as a major disadvantage for women, placing them across significant rural divides (of lineage, collective unit, or administrative village) from their closest natal kin. This removes women from familiar networks of cooperation and help in everyday life, even if they retain close ties with their natal families. It also breaks patterns of nurturing careers and preempts education or training, since the young women are seen by their natal communities as well as their natal families as destined to depart early and permanently.[6] And the mobility and dispersion of women among different communities impede possibilities for the creation of strong women's networks within their communities of residence.

Could the situation be better for women who, despite the prevailing patrilocal tendency, remain in the communities of their birth or childhood after marriage? It is difficult to assess the exact prevalence of alternative forms of postmarital residence, and the literature on alternatives consistently views these as deviations from the norm that require explanation, but they may have provided a wider repertoire of possibility and potential than the discursive dominance of patrilocality might suggest.

Norma Diamond[7] has summed up some earlier evidence, including instances in the work of Isabel and David Crook,[8] pointing in this direction in the revolutionary period. Some particularly interesting cases involved women who had been "small daughters-in-law" (*tongyangxi*), that is, women who were "adopted" at a young age and raised in their marital families to become future daughters-in-law within the same family. More recently, Gregory Ruf has reconstructed the local history of a Sichuan community that had rates of "small daughter-in-law" marriage as high as one-third in the early twentieth century, although he does not observe an advantage for these women.[9] Indeed, most women in these circumstances were very poor, since this marriage form was associated with households unable to afford the expenses of a conventional, major marriage, and such girls were not always treated as well as a family's own daughters. These disadvantaged women were priority targets of mobilization for the Communist Party during the revolutionary period when it sought both to organize women and to have women replace men (who were departing for the military and higher levels of leadership) in local politics. There may well have been a temporary window when political conditions opened opportunities for women in such marriages, which had not been possible before.

I was able to interview at some length two elderly women in one village who had been married as "small daughters-in-law" into other poor families following the death of one or both parents. One of these had served as a village head in 1949, after joining the party in 1946. While she had an important leadership role around the time of Liberation, she did not enjoy a political future[10] or a particularly happy marriage. "Small daughters-in-law" were not common in this area,[11] and this form of marriage appears to have been effectively stopped after Liberation. Women already married in this form did not necessarily seek divorce, even though women were initiating some divorces in the early 1950s and this woman village head was herself involved in supporting cases of divorce and remarriage.[12]

If remaining within the community of her youth is important for a woman's future in the countryside, a more promising alternative may be uxorilocal marriage. This form of marriage is a widespread part of the cultural repertoire and does not have the disadvantages of childhood arranged marriage. The potential of uxorilocal marriage for promoting change in gender relations meant that it was viewed positively by the state after Liberation and was actually advocated in the late Cultural Revolution period. But it also encountered renewed indirect opposition from the force of collectivization, which effectively reinforced the boundaries between collectives that resembled corporate agnatic communities.[13] Uxorilocal marriage is a traditional alternative designed to provide descendants for those without sons—a daughter would bring in a son-in-law and one of their sons would take the mother's father's surname. As recently encountered in these Shandong villages, there is less emphasis on ritual descent than in the pre-Liberation era, and surnames may wholly pass in the patriline, but uxorilocal marriage has continued as a recognized means to provide for the care of parents without sons. Nevertheless, closed androcentric communities have remained resistant to the entry of outside men and few men here are willing to enter uxorilocal marriages. Many cases of uxorilocal marriage encountered in these villages involve men with urban household registration who are present in their marital households only on a part-time basis. Despite the apparent or potential benefit of remaining in her natal village, the predominant reality in uxorilocal marriage seemed to be that of a daughter making the sacrifice of accepting a less desirable match in order to provide for the care of her father and mother. In occasional cases, as in the marriage of a woman to a sent-down youth, she may be able to remain in her natal village in more desirable circumstances, but this remains exceptional.

A particularly interesting change in postmarital residence has been an increase in the acceptability and frequency of intravillage marriage. While the overwhelming majority of marriages represent village (lineage, collective, or administrative village) exogamy, there has been an increasing but still uneven and limited acceptance of intravillage marriage. This change may be related to political changes that favor new marriage patterns, as observed by Chan, Madsen, and Unger, as well as by Liu Xin,[14] although there has also been local resistance to the added complexity of intracommunity social relations created by village endogamy. It is possible that the move toward intravillage marriage has been more pronounced in south China[15] or that it could be related to specific local or historical factors. Chan et al. note the importance of Chen Village's relative poverty, as well as the salience of political and personal advantage. In northeast China, Yan Yunxiang notes banner endogamy in the early settlement period followed by later village endogamy in multilineage villages.[16] Liu Xin found a breakthrough toward intravillage marriage in the 1980s in Shaanxi in poorer communities having trouble attracting wives.[17] In contrast, Mark Selden found a major move toward intravillage marriage in Hebei in a large, multisurname village (which still retained three exogamous neighborhoods) that was much more prosperous than nearby villages, which allowed this village to retain its daughters as well as its sons.[18] Where options to leave the countryside were reduced for decades by the household registration system and boundaries between rural communities deepened by the corporate aspect of collectivization, there may have been a period when retaining daughters through intravillage marriage became a more attractive alternative than it had been earlier.

Intravillage marriage was not widely practiced in any of the villages studied here.[19] In one of the two single-surname villages, marriage within the surname is still considered unacceptable, no matter how remote the relationship, while the other single-surname village has moved toward accepting such matches provided the couple are only remotely related (beyond *wufu*, the customary mourning categories of close kin). In the multilineage village, intravillage marriage was possible but rare, and I am not aware of any such cases involving members of the same surname. Intravillage marriages appear to be of two types within these villages. In several cases they are explicitly an alternative to uxorilocal marriage as a solution for the problem of caring for parents without sons. While women in these situations do not face the particular difficulties of uxorilocal marriages, they have a restricted range of potential matches and are making a sacrifice for their parents. In other cases, the marriages appear to have arisen from the free choice of the couple and may have resulted in marital happiness, although I have found no indication that the women in these marriages have benefited in any other manner (leadership positions, educational opportunity, or employment) from remaining in their natal village. In either type of intravillage marriage, it is often a village leader (such as the party branch secretary) who acts as introducer, either to make the necessary match in order to care for community members without sons or to provide respectability for those making their own match. Such marriages are not yet unmarked or routine. An additional reason the increase in intravillage marriage has been modest here may have been the comparatively good situation of each of these villages during most recent years. To the extent that this has been the case, women have been attracted from other villages, but men have had no incentive to restrict their choice of spouse to their own village. This has been remarked as an obstacle by some young women approaching marriage age and is consistent with Lavely's[20] findings about spatial hierarchy in marriage choice.

In short, most women have little alternative except to marry out of their own community—not only to achieve upward mobility but also to avoid a restricted and undesirable match. While substantial numbers of young women succeed in leaving the countryside, those who remain in (or return to) the countryside and form the core of the rural labor force continue to move in the countryside through marriage, and their matches are still largely arranged.

Marrying into Other Villages

One of the paradoxes of the interweaving construction of place and gender in rural China is that women, who decisively move through marriage, are more firmly tied to rural places than are men. This is in part a result of the official barriers to mobility created by the household registration system, which effectively tied people to the countryside from the late 1950s until late in the twentieth century. The household registration system continues to link people to specific locations in the countryside, although actual location and movement have become increasingly flexible. For many women, and especially those married prior to this flexibility, the link to place—or, more accurately, to a succession of places—has been a central component in the construction of rural women's adult identities. For young women, leaving their natal village may now be a welcome step toward work experience and perhaps even a future life in a larger, urban world, but many of these women still marry according to the preexisting rural pattern. It remains the case that the majority of women can anticipate that marriage will take them to the rural home of the rest of their lives. At least some women look forward to this move as a transition to adulthood and prefer to move to another village even if a good intravillage match is available, since this provides independent adult standing.

Arranging where a woman will spend her adult life is a process that demonstrates not just a mobility but also a flexibility, in sharp contrast to the prescribed, fixed locations of her (nonmigrating) husband and brothers. While men are tied to localized communities, women can move to any of numerous communities. In the absence of fixed marriage exchange relations, women (and those arranging their marriages) have opportunities as wide as the connections of family, neighbors, and other contacts can provide. Most women have multiple suggestions made to their parents and may themselves experience more than one "introduction," but I will limit myself here to a description of some of those that were successful (or that were not successful in interesting ways) before proceeding to a discussion of the implications of this mode of movement.

A woman born in the opening years of the twentieth century, with bound feet, introduced my middle-aged landlady into the same marital village. She was actual father's sister (*gu*) to this woman and described herself as having been the person who initiated the introduction process. Her own husband was not closely related to the husband of her niece, although this was a single-surname village, and this was a matter of her natal family trusting her to find a good match (rather than a related match) for the niece. The niece attributed her marriage at some distance from her natal family to this introduction.

A woman born in the 1920s who had been introduced into the same village by her father's sister acted in her youth to introduce a schoolfriend of her younger sister to her own husband's younger brother when he returned to the village for his father's funeral. These two couples subsequently lived in a joint household for a lengthy period of time but eventually divided.

Another woman of that generation, who had been politically active as a party member and women's head in her natal village around the time of Liberation, was introduced by her own older sister who had already married into this village. The match was appropriately with a demobilized soldier and long-time party member, and it was a free-choice marriage in 1954.

A woman born in the 1930s, who had been introduced by her father's sister, had in turn introduced her sister's daughter and later her brother's daughter into her own marital village while still a young married woman in the 1960s. In neither case were the matches made with close kin of her husband but rather with neighbors, since marital possibilities are not prescribed and the goal is to find a good match with people one knows well. As she described her own work as an introducer, she first approached the prospective husband's mother (*popo*) to tell her about the young woman and her situation, and she also spoke with the prospective husband's father. This was done on her own initiative, as is commonly the case when people see youths approaching marriageable age, although either set of parents can start inquiries, as well. Once the prospective husband's side expressed interest, the introducer suggested the match to the prospective bride's side, that is, her mother. Once both sets of parents had agreed on the possibility, the young woman was approached. Then the young woman visited the home of the introducer, on her own, where she was introduced to the young man. The two young people were left alone to talk for a while, and later each reported their agreement to the match to the introducer. Not all introductions result in mutual agreement, and, even if there is an engagement at this point, the introducer may have the task of handling a break, but in this case the match was made and the introducer proceeded to mediate the details of the wedding date and property exchanges.[21] After the wedding, the work of the introducer was complete, or "Once the bride is on the bed, the introducer leans on the south wall" (*xifu zuole chuang, meiren kao nanqiang*). The introducer keeps in touch with the couples as a matter of course, in this case, since she is related to both women and lives in the same village.

A woman born in the 1940s who had recently had her son married to her brother's daughter was quite pleased with the arrangement, for which she took credit herself. She said she had known the young woman from visits to her brother and thought that she would make a good daughter-in-law. This is an interesting twist on the conventional explanation that the young woman's father would be the prime actor in a matrilateral cross-cousin marriage, in seeking a good home for his daughter, an explanation that makes no reference to the agency of the (senior) women involved.[22]

A woman born in the 1950s had been found a match by male relatives in Beijing that might well have taken her out of the countryside. This was a match arranged without her participation, but she professed little interest in being involved at the time and instead relief that she would no longer be troubled by people repeatedly attempting to arrange matches for her. However, her army husband with a political future was sent back to his natal village to turn around its desperate economic plight (with official support), which made her the wife of a village party branch secretary. He was also the head of a thriving village-run factory, and she had a management role there herself, which resulted in her being repeatedly approached by a merchant she often dealt with in another village to act as introducer for his daughter. The daughter worked in the factory, and he wanted her to be introduced to someone in that village, since it was now wealthy and she would be then able to continue her attractive job after marriage. The village weaving factory employed large numbers of young women in neighboring villages, many of whom had similar aspirations, so this determined young woman sought the aid of the party secretary's wife. After being pressed to help, she gave some attention to the young woman (whom she had not previously noticed) and introduced her to a young man in the village, who was still available in part because his father was deceased and his household therefore not affluent. The fiancée arranged through the introducer to offer all her salary for a year for the building of a new house and was evidently an active agent in arranging her own marriage.[23]

Another woman born in the 1950s (in a different county) married into a nearby village with a thriving factory that drew in workers from surrounding villages, including many young women. She got her younger sister a job in the factory, and, when the younger sister met a coworker she liked in the same village, the older sister's marital family provided an introducer.

A woman born in the 1960s was offered the opportunity by her married older sister in Shenyang to follow her there, a desirable urban alternative to life in the countryside, but their mother decided that she wanted a daughter to remain close (even though she also had a son). Consequently, the younger daughter was married into an adjacent, affluent village. The introducer was her father's younger sister, who was the actual sister of her husband's paternal grandmother.

There are numerous similar instances, from which these few have been selected to indicate range in generation and in detail. According to the accounts of older women in these villages, the common practice in their youth had been for poorer households to rely upon women kin for introductions. This may well have become a more common practice in the collective era as village men's contacts became more localized and as opportunity for affinal partnerships in the private sector disappeared. Managing relatives can be and is presented as part of women's "housework" (*jiawu*), and this practice extends to introductions.

Men have also been involved as introducers throughout the twentieth century. This has been a useful part of the prevalent strategy of using a wide range of contacts to gain knowledge and create possibilities for favorable marriages. Men, however, have rarely had kin contacts to households in other communities—except through women—and while they may serve as introducers on behalf of their wives, their contacts are typically different, where they exist at all. These tend to come from working elsewhere, from contacts made in former military service, or through political office or connections. The number of men lacking or having few such contacts has surely been one of the reasons for the strong role of women in providing and managing the knowledge requisite for a successful marriage introduction.

Where men have had promising contacts, this was associated in the past with elite building of alliances. Few men in the countryside in recent decades have been so privileged, although it is possible to find some instances of marriages between the immediate families of political leaders in neighboring villages, although even these may happen through the agency of a kinswoman as introducer. There has been less scope for commercial alliance, and I have found negligible indication of affinal ties in business in these villages even in the reform era. What was more clearly evident was a trend toward using connections to give a daughter a chance at exit from the countryside, through steps to obtain urban residence status, education (at this time to technical secondary level), or (usually temporary) employment. As more advantaged villagers used their superior connections to help their daughters as well as their sons to leave the countryside, there was less possibility or even point in attempting to make strategic alliances through marriage with other villagers. This is then a factor that reduces pressure on women to enter into particular matches, at least in villages such as these which are at least moderately attractive as marital villages.

Women's Kinship

Women benefit (in a certain sense) by their structural interchangeability. From the perspective of men's kinship and localized patrilineal communities, wives are absolutely necessary, but which women arrive as wives is structurally inconsequential. In contrast, from the perspective of women's kinship, where a woman goes in marriage is absolutely life determining. These two models of how marriages are constructed are able to coexist in each other's interstices. From a practice theory perspective,[24] men's kinship provides the structure, while women's kinship provides the people. This is no doubt a simplification, but I would suggest that it is a useful one in highlighting how a rigidly structured system can be open to countervailing practices. This was demonstrated in a somewhat different manner decades ago through the concept of the "uterine family,"[25] and the present chapter is part of a larger attempt to explore similar practices at the present time.

As with the concept of the uterine family, there is no implication that these arrangements are free of overt or covert conflict or that they unambiguously benefit women—still less that they benefit all women. Where each individual woman goes upon marriage is the result of a complex play of factors and the operation of power relations within and beyond households. Few young women enjoy the opportunity to meet enough men to make a choice from a great many possibilities or to know at all well the ones they may choose prior to the engagement or even the wedding. In the still more common cases where the weight of decision making rests with the parents, the parents are themselves constrained by limited circumstances and by a range of different considerations (including their own well-being), which may not always lead to decisions in the best interests of the young women. In the most troubling cases, this results in catastrophic matches from which there is no easy exit.[26]

To the extent that women have been major actors, it is older women who have had a significant say. One recent study elsewhere in Shandong may be indicative. Based on 170 responses in the Yimeng region, the following were said to decide upon the marriage of a couple's children: husband, 1.2 percent; wife, 10.6 percent; husband and wife together, 75.3 percent; members of a more senior generation, 4.1 percent; no reply, 7.1 percent; and other, 1.2 percent.[27] The young people themselves, if they had any choice, were either in the 1.2 percent or were making their wishes effective indirectly. This was a report of a survey of representations of decision making and may well have underreported women's roles. Determining how complex decisions are made by a conjugal couple should not be expected to be easy or clear cut. In addition to the numerous factors affecting the desirability of the potential partners and their households,[28] there is the question of the weighting of the interests of the parental generation, in more privileged cases for alliances, more generally to bring in a daughter-in-law who will get along well with her mother-in-law and often to marry a daughter nearby. At least in these areas of Shandong, a woman typically maintains close ties with her natal family as long as either parent is alive and mothers (at least in recent decades) often visit their married daughters. Unquestionably, there is much room in decisions as critical as the marriage of children for there to be major conflicts among the numerous interested parties who can legitimately claim a part in the decision making.

Any decision can be made only on the basis of available knowledge, of a type difficult to acquire and verify outside one's own community: What is the real nature of familial relations behind the household walls? Is the prospective mother-in-law kind or only adept at maintaining her public image? Will the new daughter-in-law insist on immediate division of the household and on what terms?[29] It may be very largely the challenge of acquiring good information on these critical issues that places so much of the actual arrangements of introductions in the hands of women, especially senior women. It is readily apparent that, given the gender divide in rural society, the introducers would be on closer terms with the mother than the father. And it is the mother who has more at stake in selection of a daughter-in-law.

Introductions are expressions of a form of knowledge/power about women and their households that enables the movement of women through the countryside on which rural society depends. Successful introductions can also create satisfied relatives and neighbors, and perhaps extend an introducer's social network. However, there appears to be little direct benefit now gained on a individual basis by the introducer (although gifts have been given in the past). In many cases, the result will be the movement of a younger woman to the marital village of an older introducer, but not necessarily to her own or a closely linked household. Given the depth of household boundaries, the link is not necessarily close and is more likely to benefit the younger woman than the older one.

It is possible that there is a more generalized advantage for women in having other women from their own natal village in their marital village. Introducers with whom I spoke were consistent in denying that this would be taken into consideration in making a match—factors of household and the likelihood of a successful match were much more important, and the presence of women from one's own village was not seen as affecting those critical concerns. Many married women did find themselves relatively close to their natal villages or had other women from their natal village in their marital village. In some cases, of course, this was obviously the channel through which they had been introduced, but in a few cases there were a larger number of women who shared both natal and marital communities.

In each of the three villages, I was given to understand that there were some local villages with which there were relatively dense ties of marriage. From the records in my samples, however, this appears either not to be very strongly the case or only the case if each household can consider itself connected through a quite large number of marital ties. It is possible, indeed, for there to be a large network of ties, without there being substantial concentrations of women from any particular natal village in any particular marital village. In the village for which I have the largest recorded number of married women with birthplaces other than the same village, seventy-four of the eighty-eight women were from the same township, but these seventy-four were from thirty-five different villages. One village did have a recognized predominance (twelve in my sample), including the village women's head, who had on at least one occasion been involved in facilitating a match with her natal village.[30] Other women had at least some chance of finding fellow villagers in their marital villages. In a second village, I had been told of a similar concentration, but it was less apparent in my sample of forty-four, as the thirty-four women from the same township came from nineteen villages and were more evenly dispersed. In the third village, dispersion seemed even more accentuated, since only twenty-five of forty-one came from other villages in the township, while fourteen others were from individual villages elsewhere in the county and two from still further away.

From a long-term perspective, women in this area, and perhaps more generally, may often have been able to enter their marital village knowing or having a potential tie with at least one senior woman. While women would not be able to intervene across household boundaries, such a contact may well have been useful to a woman in making her adjustment to her marital community, and perhaps in moderating the relationship with her mother-in-law. Certainly, some women have mentioned women from their natal village among their frequent contacts, although there has been no discernible formal recognition of these ties as there has been, for example, for the wives of a set of brothers (*zhouli*).

The highly dispersed nature of these connections limits their potential as a basis for communities of women and continues to divide most women from other women. But at the same time, the lack of formal recognition leaves women—and those arranging their marriages—more open choice than would be the case in a tightly structured circulation. In effect, women are selectively able to carve out small, informal networks nestled nonconfrontationally within the interstices of the dominant androcentric structure of rural communities. While women as introducers reproduce this androcentric structure, they also provide a basis for informal women's networks.

Connections between Women

The concern that motivated this examination was to find a basis for women to connect with other women within rural communities. While exit from the countryside is highly desired and now attainable by increasing numbers of young women, the majority of adult rural women remain in (or return to) the countryside and are indispensable for all aspects of rural social and economic life. By 1995, 210,000,000 women constituted roughly two-thirds of the agricultural workforce[31] and continue to provide, directly and indirectly, a labor force for the cities and surplus accumulation to fuel development.

In the past, women's work groups in the collectives were briefly viewed as a step toward women organizing on an effective economic base in the countryside. I found in talking with middle-aged and older rural women shortly after decollectivization that they did not look back on these work groups as having been advantageous.[32] Nor did they look on village factories or even cooperatives as being particularly promising. They were viewed as offering unattractive work that was not particularly well paid and over which they would not have much control.[33] While factory work offered employment and, especially when in an urban setting, wider opportunities for young women, many married women preferred to run household-based enterprises where they would either be independent or in a conjugal partnership.[34] Household situations vary, but rural women find individual men within small households generally less of a problem than large groups of men organized as corporate entities. Managing a prosperous, harmonious household is a mark of a mature, successful woman and fully consistent with both traditional and contemporary social values. As women work to accomplish this goal, household barriers are reinforced—both in relation to their husbands' agnates and in relation to other women. Ties that are structurally favored between households tend to be those between agnatically related households. How can women be brought together across household boundaries and in spite of their dispersed mobility among rural communities?

Some attempts in this direction have relied on state structures and the external interventions of the official women's movement, through women's committees, women's heads, and efforts to move women into local governing bodies, as in the initiative in the 1990s to break into the "two committees," that is to place the village women's head either in the party branch (if a party member) or in the less powerful village committee. These specific targets were largely accomplished in Shandong by the mid-1990s, which at least began the task of opening local power structures to women. Concurrently, in the late 1980s and 1990s, the women's movement made an effort to move beyond purely administrative means to draw women into local development measures through a Chinese variant of gender-and-development work, the "two studies, two competitions" activities (*shuangxue shuangbi huodong*) for educating rural women and promoting the women's role in the mainstream of rural economic development.[35]

These steps were accompanied by concerted, formal efforts to create new spaces where women could come together. The most visible of these were

"Women's Homes" (*funü zhi jia*), actual rooms in villages that could serve as a spatial base for women's activities. I saw such a dedicated room in one of the villages in this study in 1989, well appointed with materials and records, under the impetus of the county Women's Federation. It rapidly fell into total disuse, even though the women's movement in the village continued to enjoy official support in the following years. It appeared that this innovation ran against the grain of local organizing, which depended typically on operating from the homes of village political leaders. Later in the 1990s, as the "two studies, two competitions" moved to a more technical level, "research associations" were promoted at village and township levels. These were intended to bring together women learning or expert in applied agricultural or other rural technologies to share knowledge and to work together in local development. I have not been able to observe these in effective operation, although that may have occurred in other locations, and surmise that it has been difficult to introduce new formal structures to bring women together in more than an administrative manner.

Despite the efforts of the official women's movement to devise innovations that can organize women effectively, there is a sense in which its policies implicitly recognize the deep social divisions that isolate women from each other and leave women dependent on themselves and on what they can create in their individual households. Current women's movement initiatives focus strongly on individual women's internal capacities and aim to provide institutional supports to nurture these. This is partly a continuation of earlier approaches such as the "four selfs" (*sizi*) of self-respect, self-confidence, self-reliance, and self-strengthening. It is also rooted in contemporary recognition of central elements of rural social structure that require most women to make change on their own with little help from a weak and fragile official women's movement. Social relations in the countryside continue to be pervasively structured by kinship relations, especially those of local community and of household. Local communities that may (especially in the south) or may not (especially in the north)[36] have been corporate entities in the past acquired fixed boundaries and a corporate character in the collective era that has carried over at the administrative village level into the present. Within this context, households, especially nuclear households in which even very young married women can experience autonomy from a mother-in-law, are attractive as a social base for women. However, as each woman strengthens her own household, she is pursuing a path that separates her from other women.

Within the kin-structured world of a village, a woman is expected in the first instance to associate with the kinswomen of her husband—her mother-in-law and the wives of her husband's brothers as well as women more remotely connected through her husband— and, indeed, not to associate with others at risk of being described as "running around." These strictures limit the extent to which women can form ties with other women in their marital communities. Indeed, women may even choose to distance themselves from their affinal kinswomen, since creating such a space may provide a woman with a degree of independence and opportunity. This raises the difficult question of whether there might be any available channels through which women can informally connect with other village women. Without such an informally grounded social base, formal efforts such as Women's Homes may be very hard to establish or sustain.

From this perspective, women's own kinship ties clearly loom as important. Women in these villages commonly maintain fairly close ties with their natal families as long as either parent is alive, and daughters may visit their "mother's families" (*niangjia*) very frequently and also receive visits from their mothers and other kin. These are long-standing practices in this area, but ones that have been facilitated by the end of foot binding and the arrival of bicycles. Nevertheless, the depth of divisions between rural communities means that it has seemed highly important for women to be able to form significant ties with other women within their marital communities.

Ties with women from the same natal community—ties important enough that they may have been responsible for the marriage introduction—constitute one such resource. It is illustrative that in one village where I have been able to follow changes over time, the period when activity in the women's movement peaked was also the period when there was an active women's head who drew explicitly and effectively on ties with a handful of young and middle-aged married women from her own natal village. Ordinarily—and in the same village at other times—it has been possible to have the formal structure of a women's movement but little involvement on the part of village women beyond minimal compliance (at most) with official calls to attend meetings. There was a conspicuous peak in involvement during the brief term of this women's head (before she unofficially migrated to a city), based on her active work in drawing women into activities—in this case, the "two studies, two competitions"—including many women who had not previously been involved in this village. During the terms of the preceding two women's heads, no women from that village were active in the women's movement. With her selection as women's head, she was able to draw three others into active involvement. Two participated actively in the "two studies, two competitions," including one who had formerly been women's head in their shared natal village and a third who was then under consideration for a responsible position in the marital village.

Women from the same natal village share informal (and often kin) ties that can constitute a resource for building networks for individual and group benefit, direct and indirect. While the number of such contacts may not be great in quantitative terms, their absolute presence is a qualitative difference that adds another dimension of connectedness on which otherwise isolated women can draw. This is especially the case if it is not realistic to think of changes in residence ("small daughter-in-law," uxorilocal, or intravillage marriage) that will break down patrilocality and the consequent androcentry of rural communities.

Networks Crossing Community Boundaries

Women's kin connections remain spatially distinct from those of men—they are dispersed, contingent, and transitory. Conceivably, any effort to locate women's kinship in the spaces defined by patrilocality (including those in apparent opposition to it) may be misguided, and a different approach to the question of women's place in the countryside may be required—one that moves from an emphasis on community to an emphasis on networks crossing community lines. A further case is suggestive.

A pathbreaking instance of independent success in the early reform era was that of a woman who married out of her village in a variant of patrilocality in 1983, after having met her husband while both were working in a township-run factory in her own township. He has nonagricultural registration but was unable to give it to her, so she followed the usual practice of acquiring his mother's rural registration in a village in another township.[37] She remains registered there but has lived informally, with her husband, in her own natal village where both run small businesses from a premise neighboring the local highway. She has a sister and a brother and has not in any sense entered into a uxorilocal marriage, with its attendant disadvantages, although she has enjoyed having her mother care for her children (as her mother-in-law might otherwise have done). She and her husband have informally been able to take advantage of the superior commercial location available in her natal village. She had been an unusually successful seamstress, training other local women (including her younger sister) as apprentices and providing training classes for women in the village through the women's organization, before retiring to shopkeeping when sewing became less attractive. She has long been one of the local models of economic success and of sharing expertise with other women that is advocated in the countryside. Essential elements in her ability to do this have been her own technical and entrepreneurial ability, as well as her ability to move unconventionally across community divides and to reside where her networks and opportunities are strong.

A few more women could be cited as now managing to cross the divides between rural communities that were formally so deep and limiting for women and that still remain significant barriers, although the others of which I am aware have been less conspicuous. One woman managed to remain in her natal home years after marriage and the birth of a child, in order to retain her good job in a factory in her natal village. While staying with one's natal family prior to birth of a child or for short visits thereafter is unexceptional in this area, a move to the marital home is expected prior to the birth of a child. This woman was aware of pushing the limits further, with a supportive and powerful natal family, although she did not expect to be able to extend this arrangement beyond the marriage of her younger brother. The fact that she was able to retain her attractive factory position was also exceptional, since she would normally have been expected to give this up upon marriage, even if marrying into a nearby community.

Another young woman newly married into a village that has never employed a woman as a teacher, despite having several married women in the community who had been teachers in their natal villages, arranged to continue teaching in her nearby natal village, again crossing a border of employment usually not crossed. These and a few other cases indicate that some married women are now finding it possible to move more flexibly through the countryside than they have been able to do in preceding decades. As restrictions effected by the household registration system continue to be dramatically reduced, women will be creating more complex and mobile relations to place through marriage and work than hitherto possible.

Given the importance of kin ties, this flexibility may still advantageously involve networks in which a woman's natal kin and natal village are critical resources, but these are constructed and accessed in fundamentally different ways from those in which men build and use localized communities. Women's kinship consists instead of a distinctive combination of mobility and networks. As the barriers defining rural communities become more permeable, there may be viable border-crossing alternatives to change in postmarital residence that can open opportunities for work and for organizing to rural women. Three villages can do no more than raise questions: How do women move through the barriers between communities? How could reducing obstacles to women's mobility enable women to build stronger and more effective networks?

Notes

The field research and subsequent study reported here were made possible by a series of grants from the Social Sciences and Humanities Research Council of Canada.

Within China, the research was facilitated by the Chinese Academy of Social Sciences, the Shandong Academy of Social Sciences, the China Shandong International Culture Exchange Centre, the Shandong Women's Federation, and various levels of government in Shandong province. I am especially grateful to the residents of Zhangjiachedao, Qianrulin, and Huaili. Bryna Goodman, Wendy Larson, and Mark Selden have made valuable comments on the original draft of this chapter; remaining deficiencies are my sole responsibility.

1. For the most part, these issues are treated in passing in works concentrated on other aspects of rural life, but see especially Elisabeth Croll, *The Politics of Marriage in Contemporary China* (Cambridge: Cambridge University Press, 1981), and Bernard Gallin and Rita S. Gallin, "Matrilateral and Affinal Relations in Changing Chinese Society," in *The Chinese Family and Its Ritual Behavior*, ed. Hsieh Jih-chang and Chuang Ying-chang (Taibei: Academia Sinica Institute of Ethnology, 1985), 101–16. Also see Martin C. Yang, *A Chinese Village: Taitou, Shandong Province* (New York: Columbia University Press); Myron Cohen, "North China Rural Families: Changes during the Communist Era," *Études chinoises* 1–2 (1998): 59–154; Margery Wolf, *Women and the Family in Rural Taiwan* (Stanford, Calif.: Stanford University Press, 1972); and Margery Wolf, *Revolution Postponed: Women in Contemporary China* (Stanford, Calif.: Stanford University Press, 1985).

2. See Yang, *A Chinese Village*, 106; Janet W. Salaff, "The Emerging Conjugal Relationship in the People's Republic of China," *Journal of Marriage and the Family* 35, no. 4 (1973): 705–17; and Liu Xin, *In One's Own Shadow: An Ethnographic Account of the Condition of Post-reform China* (Berkeley: University of California Press, 2000).

3. Ellen R. Judd, "*Niangjia*: Chinese Women and Their Natal Families," *Journal of Asian Studies* 48, no. 3 (1989): 525–44.

4. Ellen R. Judd, *Gender and Power in Rural North China* (Stanford, Calif.: Stanford University Press, 1994). The villages are in three different counties, Changyi, Anqiu, and Lingxian, and may therefore be indicative of a reasonably large portion of Shandong.

5. Ellen R. Judd, "Reconsidering China's Marriage Law Campaign: Toward a De-orientalized Feminist Perspective," *Asian Journal of Women's Studies* 4 no. 2 (1998): 8–26.

6. Ellen R. Judd, *The Chinese Women's Movement between State and Market* (Stanford, Calif.: Stanford University Press, 2002).

7. Norma Diamond, "Collectivization, Kinship and the Status of Women in Rural China," in *Toward an Anthropology of Women*, ed. Rayna R. Rapp (New York: Monthly Review, 1975), 372–95.

8. Isabel and David Crook, *Revolution in a Chinese Village: Ten-Mile Inn* (Atlantic Highlands, N.J.: Humanities, 1959); and Isabel and David Crook, *The First Years of Yangyi Commune* (Atlantic Highlands, N.J.: Humanities, 1966).

9. Gregory Ruf, *Cadres and Kin: Making a Socialist Village in West China, 1921–1991* (Stanford, Calif.: Stanford University Press, 1998), 44.

10. This appears to have been part of a larger pattern resulting from the return from war of men who then displaced the women who had held local leadership positions in their absence.

11. The situation in Taiwan was quite different in this respect. See Wolf, *Women and the Family*; and Arthur Wolf and Chieh-shan Huang, *Marriage and Adoption in China, 1845–1945* (Stanford, Calif.: Stanford University Press, 1980).

12. See Judd, "Reconsidering China's Marriage Law."

13. See Croll, *The Politics of Marriage*; and Wolf, *Revolution Postponed.*

14. Anita Chan, Richard Madsen, and Jonathan Unger, *Chen Village: The Recent History of a Peasant Community in Mao's China* (Berkeley: University of California Press, 1984); and Liu Xin, *In One's Own Shadow.*

15. See Chan et al., *Chen Village*; William L. Parish and Martin King Whyte, *Village and Family in Contemporary China* (Chicago: University of Chicago Press, 1978); and Sulamith H. Potter and Jack Potter, *China's Peasants: The Anthropology of a Revolution* (Cambridge: Cambridge University Press, 1990).

16. Yan Yunxiang, *The Flow of Gifts: Reciprocity and Social Networks in a Chinese Village* (Stanford, Calif.: Stanford University Press, 1996).

17. Liu Xin, *In One's Own Shadow.*

18. Mark Selden, "Family Strategies and Structures in Rural North China," in *Chinese Families in the Post-Mao Era*, ed. Deborah Davis and Stevan Harrell (Berkeley: University of California Press, 1993), 139–64.

19. Also see Cohen, "North China Rural Families."

20. William Lavely, "Marriage and Mobility under Rural Collectivism," in *Marriage and Inequality in Chinese Society*, ed. Rubie S. Watson and Patricia Ebrey (Berkeley: University of California Press, 1991), 286–312.

21. The details of the ritual sequences culminating in weddings and of the property transactions involved followed explicit but varying local norms in each village. These are not significantly different from those recently reported for elsewhere in north China in Cohen, "North China Rural Families."

22. Although the wedding had taken place after the 1981 Marriage Law was proclaimed, which prohibited marriage between first cousins, there was no local concern about this issue, provided the match was not between patrilateral parallel cousins. National People's Congress, *The Marriage Law of the People's Republic of China (1 January 1981)* (Beijing: Foreign Languages Press, 1982).

23. Working conditions and income in this village's weaving factory were quite attractive, as were living conditions in the village. Many young women from neighboring villages were employed here before marriage, but normally the only married women employed were those married into the village. Young men in the village were consequently very attractive matches for whom numerous women were competing.

24. Pierre Bourdieu, *Outline of a Theory of Practice* (Cambridge: Cambridge University Press, 1977), and its application in Judd, "*Niangjia*" and in Judd, *Gender and Power.*

25. See Wolf, *Women and the Family.*

26. In principle, women can choose divorce, and I met a number of divorced women who had remarried, as well as remarried widows. In practice this is usually an extreme step, since it is difficult without the support of a woman's natal family (which may or may not be willing to allow her to return home and help her remarry). The government and the official women's movement are formally expected to help, but the

former may not be willing and the latter has a limited capacity to help. Remaining divorced in the countryside is not a viable option, so a divorced woman faces remarriage but will only be able to make a much less desirable match.

27. "Nongcun funü fazhan de zuji" (Traces of rural women's development), *Funü yanjiu luncong* (Collection of research on women) 1 (1996): 21–25.

28. There are sets of explicitly understood criteria for a good match, from each respective side. Among the considerations on the woman's side are whether the individual man, his family, and his community are well off; how many other siblings the prospective husband has and where he is in the birth order (a younger son may be preferred as the marriages of older brothers and the associated household divisions will already have happened; younger unmarried sisters may be viewed as an income-earning asset); there should be a mother (future *pomu*) present, even if the newly married couple plan to divide at an early point; the family should be relatively harmonious; whether the prospective husband works elsewhere or in the village is a factor, but there are differing views on which is preferable; a marital village near the natal village is preferred; and political status may be a factor, especially in the case of cadres and party members.

29. In contrast with the daughters-in-law of earlier generations, the current generation is—at least in these villages—in a much stronger position due to the young women's substantial earning power and the common local practice in which a new wife can spend protracted periods of time living with her natal family. This practice is sometimes used and understood as a mechanism to speed the construction of a new house or division of the family.

30. She was not the introducer in this case but was called on to try to overcome resistance to the match on the part of one of the mothers.

31. Han Baozhen, "Nongcun funü fazhan yu keji peixun" (Rural women's development and scientific and technical training), in *'95 di sici shijie funü dahui zhongguo nongcun funü fazhan luntan wenji* (Collected papers of the forum on Chinese rural women's development of the 1995 Fourth World Conference on Women), ed. Li Qiufan et al. (Beijing: Zhonghua quanguo funü lianhehui chengxiang gongzuo bu, 1995), 51. Also see Barbara Entwistle and Gail E. Henderson, eds., *Re-drawing Boundaries: Work, Households, and Gender in China* (Berkeley: University of California Press, 2000); Meng Xianfan, "Nongcun laodongli zhuanyi zhong de zhongguo nongcun funü" (China's rural women in the transformation away from agricultural labor), *Funü zuzhi yu huodong* 5 (1993): 52–59; and Meng Xianfan, "'Nangong nügeng' yu zhongguo nüxing de fazhan" ("Men work and women plow" in the development of Chinese women), *Funü yanjiu* 4 (1995): 48–51.

32. Where they did express regret for the loss of the collectives, it was for the social safety net that they had partly provided. See Wolf, *Revolution Postponed*, on women's relative marginality to collective work.

33. Interestingly, this was also strongly the view of the Women's Federation, notably in Lingxian, at this time, which was emphasizing household-based strategies for economic development in the interests of women. See Judd, *The Chinese Women's Movement.*

34. Typically these were very small enterprises that provided household self-employment and rarely employed anyone else or generated large incomes. As the

countryside opened to market activity, this option was available to many rural households on varying scales, ranging from petty commerce to incipient capitalist enterprises. On the Women's Federation's efforts to expand women's access to this option, see Judd, *The Chinese Women's Movement.*

35. See Judd, *The Chinese Women's Movement*, for an extended treatment of these issues in the same communities. Literally, the "two studies, two competitions" consisted of adult basic education, practical technical training, competition in economic success and recognition, and competition in social contribution. In effect, the "two studies, two competitions" activities comprised an organizational strategy for preparing disadvantaged rural women for income-generating economic activity through basic education and short-term practical training. The program was market oriented and linked with local development plans.

36. Myron Cohen, "Lineage Organization in North China," *Journal of Asian Studies* 49, no. 3 (1990): 500–534.

37. This was the standard practice here at this time, although sometimes with a delay. Recent relaxation of household registration practices means that many women in similar situations may not move their registrations. Note that in the earlier period access to land was tied to registration, but the thirty-year fixed term of land allocation means that this is no longer the case.

II

SPATIAL TRANSFORMATIONS

5

Between *Nei* and *Wai*

Chinese Women Students in Japan in the Early Twentieth Century

Joan Judge

IN THE 1908 NOVEL *XIN SHITOU JI* (New story of the stone) by Nanwu Yeman, the cultural icon Lin Daiyu is reinvented as an empowered overseas student and teacher. Rather than die when Baoyu marries Baochai, she leaves the Grand View Garden, studies abroad, and becomes a professor in Tokyo. Baoyu rushes to Tokyo when he learns she is there only to find that Daiyu has shed her former persona along with her Chinese dress. No longer pathetic and romantic, the new Lin Daiyu is more interested in scholarship than romance. When Baoyu enrolls in the Datong school, she informs him that the ethos of the new citizen (*guomin*) requires abandoning all sentimental talk of love and feelings.[1]

Nanwu Yeman's novel embodies the late Qing belief in the transformative power of overseas study, the source not only of modern shipyards and a Westernized army but of a new category of Chinese woman. Female students in Japan at the time the novel was published were themselves convinced that study abroad was the key to elevating Chinese women from their present state as "slaves and disparate particles of sand" to individuals capable of partaking in civilization (*wenming*). The most famous among them, Qiu Jin (1875–1907), liberated the female characters in her autobiographical *tanci* from patriarchal oppression by having them flee to Japan where they studied together and joined a revolutionary party.[2] Two female characters featured in a theater script published in the *Shuntian shibao* (Shuntian daily) in 1907 repeated the recurrent litany of tropes describing the degraded state of Chinese womanhood before voicing the solution to this host of evils: study abroad.[3] Current Chinese and Japanese secondary literature upholds the conviction voiced in these various sources that the late Qing overseas study movement represented a crucial moment in the unfolding of Chinese women's history.[4]

This chapter focuses on the significance of the Chinese female overseas experience in Japan in terms of changing understandings of gender distinctions. I analyze how the *nei/wai* (inner/outer) dichotomy functioned as a shifting continuum rather than as a rigid binary in the writings and activities of the overseas students by examining three dimensions of their experience abroad. First, their integration into the nonnormative social community in Tokyo contributed to the transformation of their gendered habitus and their sense of the gendered social order.[5] Second, their confrontation with Japan as a cultural mirror both reflected a repugnant image of sequestered Chinese women and offered literate, public Japanese women as models for the future. And, finally, their attendance in Japanese women's schools meant they were trained both in the arts of *nei* and in the skills necessary to become independent teachers in the quasi-*wai* zone of the women's school.

Shared Spaces: Tokyo as a Social Community

Students who traveled to Japan to study transgressed two layers of *nei–wai* boundaries, the boundaries between family and the broader society, and between nations.[6] Depending on the circumstances of their travel and their living arrangements in Tokyo, the students transgressed the first of these boundaries to different degrees. Many were companions to male family members who transported the constraints of the inner chambers with them to Tokyo. Others were envoys of their provincial governments with a limited degree of autonomy. The most independent group consisted of self-supporting students.

The Chinese female overseas study movement in Japan can be divided into three phases that roughly corresponded to these three trajectories. The first extended from 1901 to 1905, the period when programs aimed specifically at Chinese female students were first established at Japanese schools. The women who traveled abroad during this period were generally accompanying their husbands, brothers, or fathers. He Xiangning (1878–1972) first provided the funding for her husband Liao Zhongkai's studies at Waseda University in Tokyo and then followed him there in the winter of 1902. Fang Junying (1884–1923) went to Japan in 1902 shortly before her younger brother Fang Shengtong but lived with him once he arrived. Chen Xiefen (1883–1923) fled to Tokyo from Shanghai with her father, *Subao* editor Chen Fan, after the Subao Incident of 1903. One important exception in this period is Qiu Jin, who arrived in Kobe on July 12, 1904, not with a male family member but with a female Japanese mentor Hattori Shigeko.

The second phase of female overseas study was from 1905 to 1907, a period marked by the beginning of official overseas study as provincial governments, with Hunan at their lead, began sending groups of students to Tokyo. Tang Qunying, Wang Changguo, and Zhang Hanying, who were all active in China's suffrage movement in the early Republican period, were part of this first group of Hunanese students. Chinese women became more involved in social and political movements within the overseas student community during this period.

The final stage in late Qing female overseas study in Japan extended from 1907 to 1911. This was the period with the most students in both the independent and government-supported categories. Whereas the peak years for male overseas students were 1905 and 1906, for females they were the years between 1907 and 1910. This period saw the participation of Chinese students in activities related to the 1911 Revolution and in China's nascent suffrage movement.[7]

The women who traveled to Japan to study during these three phases were among the first Chinese females of elite background to travel abroad. Women of high social standing generally refused to leave the Chinese *nei*, and the first female overseas students in the late 1800s were generally poor women who had been educated in China and then sent overseas by foreign missionaries.[8] There are a number of indications of the elite status of the students who traveled to Tokyo in the early twentieth century. These included the generally high social status of male students who many women accompanied, government guidelines for students that encouraged them to dress simply and leave their maids behind, and the relatively high cost of enrollment in a Japanese school.[9]

Crossing national borders made it possible for the young women who lived in the Chinese overseas student community in Japan to also cross the gender and inner/outer divides in a way that would not have been possible in the mainland. The degree of gender integration in Tokyo was even greater than in the Chinese overseas community in the United States where students were more dispersed and coed socialization was often orchestrated.[10]

Wang Lian, who arrived in Tokyo in 1902 from Hubei province, described her journey from China to Japan in terms of a gradual naturalization of her relations with men. At her first stop in Hankou, she was uncomfortable with the idea of traveling with male companions. By the time she got to Shanghai she was a little more accustomed to her male fellow travelers. On the boat from Shanghai to Kobe as she shared meals with male passengers and allowed them to help her embark and disembark along the way, she felt even more at ease. Once settled in Tokyo, Wang was even less conscious of gender differences. She viewed the ten or so friends of both sexes who visited her every day like brothers and sisters who treated each other with mutual "respect and love." Wang contrasted this feeling of naturalness with "the barbarian Chinese custom of not letting males and females see one another."[11] When male students from her native Hubei graduated from the Kôbun College and the Military Academy in Tokyo and were about to return to China in 1903, Wang gave a speech at their farewell gathering, demonstrating how integrated she had become into the community of male overseas students.[12]

As Wang Lian's speech honoring her male colleagues suggests, men and women shared certain physical spaces in Tokyo, a reality that contributed to the transformation of gender relations among this privileged group of Chinese women and men in the early twentieth century. Female overseas students freely encountered male students in public spaces that were meeting grounds for the increasingly radicalized overseas community. One of the most common of these physical sites was the *Zhongguo liuxuesheng huiguan* (Chinese overseas student hall), a two-story building founded in 1902 in the Kanda section of Tokyo that had a bank, bookstore, auditorium, and reception hall on the first floor and classrooms where Japanese language was taught on the second floor.[13] Qiu Jin attended Japanese classes and weekend discussion sessions, and she gave lectures at the *huiguan*. In the monthly journal she founded, the *Baihua bao* (Vernacular journal), she also reported on debating sessions regularly held at the building on Sundays.[14] Political meetings attended by both male and female members of the overseas community, such as one organized in April 1903 to coordinate resistance to the Russian advance in Manchuria, were also held at the *Zhongguo liuxuesheng huiguan*.[15] Meetings of female organizations were frequently held in this space as well. The *Zhongguo liu Ri nüxuesheng hui*, for example, first met at the *huiguan* on September 23, 1906.[16] Similarly, the seventy to one hundred females who attended the first meeting of the *Zhongguo liu Ri nüxue hui* (Study society of Chinese women studying in Japan) on March 5, 1911, gathered at the *huiguan*.[17]

Other shared public spaces include the *Kinki kan* where Sun Yat-sen had given lectures and where the initial meeting of over five hundred overseas students protesting the Russian encroachment in Manchuria was held on April 29, 1903.[18] Qiu Jin and probably other female students also attended discussions at Kôbun College where Huang Xing had organized a *Doyôkai* (Saturday club) for college students from Hunan. One of the lectures Qiu Jin delivered at the club was the famous "Jinggao Zhongguo erwanwan nü tongbao" (Advice for the two hundred million women of China), published in the second issue of *Baihua bao* in October 1904.[19] Qiu also gave an important speech at the Fujimi building on December 5, 1905, in response to the Japanese government's "Control Regulations" (*Torishimaru kisoku*) that imposed increased restrictions on the Chinese students in Tokyo. In her speech, Qiu encouraged female students to go on strike and leave their dormitories.[20] Given the positive response she received (seventeen students left the Jissen dormitory alone), we can surmise that a number of women were in the audience.

In addition to meeting places, living spaces in Tokyo also became sites of new gender arrangements. Whether the female students resided in dormitories or with family members, they were freer in their social interactions in Tokyo than they would have been living with parents or in-laws in China.[21] While the school dormitories where the majority of the female overseas students lived were, in theory, closely regulated, there is evidence, particularly in the period before 1908, both of women freely leaving the school premises unaccompanied and of men secretly visiting the dormitories.[22]

Many of the young women who lived in the community with husbands, brothers, or other family members lived under the same constraints they would have been subject to in China, their fate remaining largely determined by their families.[23] For others, however, living outside the dormitories brought unprecedented freedom. He Xiangning, for example, moved out of a school dormitory setting in 1903 and, with her husband Liao, rented rooms first in the Ushigome and then the Koishikawa sections of Tokyo.[24] Finally, at the request of Sun Yat-sen, who hoped to use the Liao-He household as a front for his revolutionary activities, the couple moved again to the Kanda area where many of the overseas students lived. In their home in Kanda, He hosted and became acquainted with the radical students associated with Sun Yat-sen. She formally joined the *Tongmeng hui* (Revolutionary alliance), the first woman to do so, in her own household in 1905.[25]

Other female *Tongmeng hui* members lived under similar circumstances. Fang Junying, for example, lived with her brothers the revolutionary martyr Fang Shengtong and Fang Shengtao (1885–1934), her widowed sister-in-law Zeng Xing, Zeng's son Fang Xianchu, Shengtao's wife Zheng Meng, and, from 1908, Shengtong's wife Wang Ying (1889–?). This was another "revolutionary" household where all but Xianchu were members of the *Tongmeng hui* and where Shengtong, Zeng Xing, and Junying would formulate their plans for uprisings aimed at overthrowing the Qing dynasty.[26]

As the example of the Fangs suggests, in addition to sharing spaces with male students in Tokyo, female students also shared organizational practices, demonstrating a sense of collective social, political, and educational concerns. On April 29, 1903, for example, when male students announced the founding of the *Ju-E yiyong dui* (Volunteer corps to resist [the Russian advance in Manchuria]) members of the female organization, the *Gongai hui* (Humanitarian association) responded with a call to organize a parallel women's organization. Hu Binxia, the association's founder, first took the podium, followed by eight other students—Chen Yan'an, Wang Lian, Qian Fengbao, Lin Zongsu, Cao Rujin, Fang Junji (cousin of Fang Junying), Hua Gui, and Gong

Yuanchang—all of whom pleaded for their female compatriots to join the struggle against Russia. Together with four other women, these nine joined a wing of the Japanese Red Cross, the *Tokushi kangofu kai* (Association of determined nurses).[27] Similarly, in 1911, the *Zhongguo liu Ri nüxuesheng hui* was organized in response to the formation of the *Liu Ri Zhongguo guomin hui* (The association of Chinese citizens studying in Japan) by patriotic male students on February 26, 1911.[28] The educational concerns of female overseas students were also occasionally addressed in tandem with those of male students. In 1907, for example, the *Zhongguo liu Ri xuesheng jiaoyu xiehui*, a consortium of Tokyo schools with programs for Chinese students, was formed in response to Chinese student protests following the Japanese government's publication of the Control Regulations. The consortium's mandate was to encourage only serious Chinese students to enroll in programs in Japan by extending the length of short-term courses to three years. Nineteen schools, including the Jissen women's school, constituted the consortium.[29]

These shared spaces and parallel organizations reflected a new configuration of gender relations which was both product and source of a shared commitment to national and reform issues in the early-twentieth-century overseas student community. Previous identities and notions of gender separation were not completely unsettled by the new spatial and social arrangements in Tokyo, however. The women and men students remained rooted in different social and cultural positions that ultimately gave rise to gendered understandings of their respective roles within the nationalist project.

As had been the case in the preceding centuries, women intent on projecting their voices and concerns beyond the inner sphere depended on the mediation of sympathetic men. It was the female students who consistently crossed borders in Tokyo by entering the physical, political, and discursive spaces first established by their male colleagues. While women did publish their own journals in Japan, one of the most important forums for their ideas, particularly in the first phase of the overseas study experience, was the main overseas student organs. One of these journals in particular, *Jiangsu*, became the most important platform for the female overseas students, in part because the *Gongai hui* used it as its forum.[30] With the exception of Chen Xiefen's *Nüxue bao* (Journal of women's studies), which was published in Japan from October of 1903,[31] it was not until 1904 that women began publishing their own journals in Tokyo. The most influential among them were Qiu Jin's *Baihua bao* and the *Zhongguo xin nüjie zazhi* (Magazine of the new Chinese women), a monthly published between February 1907 and July 1907 for six issues and run almost single-handedly by Yan Bin.[32]

Whether they were writing in male-run or female-run journals, Chinese women in Japan did not call for the abandonment of the sphere of *nei* in favor of a new commitment to *wai*. They used their own unprecedented position as women living abroad and writing publicly to call for a new conceptualization of the *nei–wai* continuum set within a broader social and national context but still grounded in essentialized domestic female roles. With rare exceptions, these women did not criticize male oppression; rather, they appealed to men as allies in the struggle to recover the rights women had lost over the preceding centuries.[33] They defined their new roles in terms of an expansion rather than a denial of familiar familial roles, a merging of long-standing domestic and new national responsibilities.

Wang Lian, who had described how natural interactions between male and female students were in the overseas community, maintained that a woman's influence in the outer sphere would be via her relations with her husband and sons. If women understood patriotism, so would the male members of their families. Whether a man became a corrupt official or a great hero was largely dependent on the influence of his wife or mother.[34] Cao Rujin, who had arrived in Japan from Jiangsu province at the age of twenty-four with her elder brother, Cao Rulin, invoked what would become a familiar trope in the nationalist discourse up through the 1930s. She claimed the family was a microcosm of the nation and that in loving their families women had already displayed their love for the people and the nation. To become true patriots, they merely had to learn to treat the nation like the family and each member of the nation like a member of their family.[35] Even Qiu Jin, who had abandoned her own husband and children, called on women to encourage their husbands to work for the good of the community, their sons to study abroad, and their daughters to get an education in order to strengthen the nation.[36]

Divergent Agendas: Japan as a National Model/Cultural Mirror

In Tokyo, the Chinese female students attempted to integrate themselves into the overseas male political community by physically entering new public spaces and discursively investing essentialized female roles with new national meanings. Gendered *cultural* differences proved harder to overcome, however. In the national mirror that Japan became for all reform-minded Chinese in the late nineteenth and early twentieth centuries, China's political backwardness was coded male, with the braided queue as the marker of submission, while its cultural backwardness was coded female and symbolized by the bound foot.[37] These different images marked the divergent primary agendas which the male and female students set for themselves: whereas the male overseas community was most consumed with the need to overturn some 260 years of Manchu rule, the females confronted the more burdensome task of ending thousands of years of cultural oppression cruelly inscribed in the bodies of women.

The gendered representation of China's cultural decrepitude which had the most profound impact on the overseas student community was a Chinese display booth planned for the 1903 Osaka Exhibition. On March 8, 1903, two Japanese newspapers announced that the "Races of Man Pavilion" (*Renlei guan*) would have displays of peoples of China together with the Ainu, aborigines of Taiwan, and peoples of the Ryuku Islands, Korea, India, and Java. One of the objectives of the exhibit was to highlight premodern customs. In the case of China, these customs were exemplified by twenty-one Chinese women with bound feet (*xiaozu nüzi*), one smoking opium. The Chinese display was ultimately cancelled due to Chinese opposition. However, the Taiwan Pavilion continued to feature "elaborately ornamented women with bound feet" in one of its exhibits and had two "small-footed women" serving in the pavilion's tea shop.[38]

While I have not yet found any direct references to the exhibition in the writings of the female students, they were certainly aware of the controversy that was discussed in the same overseas student organs in which their own essays were published. These essays consistently referred to bound feet as the prime marker of Chinese women's isolation and degradation. In what was possibly an oblique reference to the exhibition controversy, an author writing in *Zhejiang chao* under the name Tai Gong criticized Chinese women for "dolling themselves up in the inner chambers and wriggling about all their days like playthings on exhibit in a zoo."[39]

These negative images of Chinese women refracted through various lenses in Japan were sharply contrasted with positive representations of Japanese women in the Chinese reformist discourse of the period. The most commonly compared value was literacy. While the arts of reading were often practiced in private, Japanese women were celebrated for the access to new public roles which literacy provided. As early as 1891, journals published in China commented on the high levels of enrollment in Japanese girls' schools[40] and contrasted China's low rates of female literacy with those in Japan, the Japanese being, according to the early reformer Song Shu, "the most literate of the yellow races."[41] Kang Tongwei bemoaned the fact that despite its "sagely teachings, physical beauty, and expansive territory" China did not measure up to Japan when it came to the education of its women.[42]

Early views of educated Japanese women from afar were reinforced by the impressions of Chinese who traveled to Japan in the late nineteenth and early twentieth centuries. All commented that Japanese women were both literate and publicly visible. Those who investigated the state of education in Japan, for example, commented that they were surprised to see women of lower classes in shops with newspapers in their arms.[43] Early male students such as Cao Rulin commented that the rate of literacy in Japan was so high and newspapers so available that "ordinary people, even women, were informed about world affairs."[44] A poem written by a certain Chen Daohua about his impressions of daily life in Tokyo in 1908 (*zhuzhici*) described neat and pure female students of the famous Japanese educator and founder of the Jissen school, Shimoda Utako (1854–1936) in their "white shirts and violet skirts," circulating in public and releasing the scent of a new literate culture.[45]

One of the notable characteristics of the young, educated women in Japan that Chen emphasized in his poem was their single status—a sharp contrast to Chinese women who tended to marry young.[46] Chinese female writers repeatedly remarked on the tendency among Japanese women to get an education before marrying or to not marry at all. The author of a 1904 essay in the *Nüjie zhong* (A tocsin for women) described how a friend of hers, a teacher in a Tokyo upper-level elementary school, studied for hours every evening to prepare for a Ministry of Education examination after having taught for six hours during the day. The author pointed out that this dedication and independent spirit provided an important contrast to Chinese women. While young Chinese women married at approximately age twenty (a relatively high estimate), Japanese women in elementary school were generally not married, and those who had graduated from a female high school, normal school, higher normal school, or university were predominantly unmarried. The author commended not only the diligent women who followed the life of the mind but the system that endorsed it by treating teachers as respected officials. Because of this system, she wrote, "Japanese women want to become teachers; they do not want to become wives."[47] This impression was supported by statistics published in education journals of the period that showed, for example, only approximately 44 percent of Japanese female school graduates were married.[48]

In an article written to encourage more Chinese women to study abroad, Chen Yan'an, one of the first Chinese women to graduate from the Jissen school, also focused on Japanese women's educational accomplishments. "It has only been thirty years since the Restoration," she wrote, "and already the sound of females reciting can be heard throughout the nation." According to Chen, these literate Meiji women had not only received a general education, but many had "brilliantly succeeded in specialized higher-level courses." She complained that Chinese women differed from these educated Japanese in a number of important ways: they had no curiosity about external matters, were not motivated to study, were dependent on others, and were ignorant of their own relationship to China's national survival.[49] Wang Lian also recorded how impressed she was with the level of Japanese education for females. "At home,"

Wang explained at the send-off meeting for her male colleagues in Tokyo, "I didn't study much, and it was not until I got to Japan that I realized all Japanese females could read, all could write letters and peruse the newspaper."[50]

Tai Gong, writing in the *Zhejiang chao* article mentioned here, also compared Chinese and Japanese women, admiring the latter for their public roles and integration into society. "Female education in Japan is almost exactly the same as for males," Tai Gong noted.

> Morning and evening they wander the city streets in the midst of busy traffic. Out of ten people, four are male students, three female, and the rest are merchants and members of the lower level of society. The female students all wear purple skirts, hold book bags, and walk in groups of three or five. How can they be compared to females in our country?[51]

In addition to being models of literacy, Japanese women were also models of social organization. The overseas student journals reported on the activities of a number of Japanese women's organizations which served as a sharp contrast to the more disparate female community in China. One of the organizations the Chinese students most admired was the Japanese Red Cross. In a petition to Prince Zaizhen, a member of the Qing imperial family, female students in 1903 bemoaned the fact that China was one of the only nations in the world that did not have its own Red Cross organization. They urged the prince to imitate the Japanese empress, who both attended Red Cross meetings and helped fund the organization.[52] An article that linked the expansion of women's rights to the establishment of women's organizations announced the establishment of a women's clubhouse (*fujin kaikan*) by Japanese female educators. The clubhouse provided facilities for the *Fujin kyôiku kai* (Women's educational society), the *Fujin eisei kai* (Women's hygiene society), and the *Joshi kyôritsu jizen kai* (Women's philanthropic society). These organizations held lectures and meetings, and entertained foreign guests. Their existence illustrated the progress of women's rights in Japan and supported the claim of a Mrs. Somerset from England that "the twentieth century would be the century of female autonomy" with women becoming educators, politicians, and diplomats.[53]

Chinese overseas students also admired Japanese women for their establishment of patriotic women's organizations. Members of the *Liu Ri nüxuehui*, founded by female students in Tokyo in 1911, declared that their role models included Red Cross workers in Europe and members of the Japanese *Aikoku fujin kai* (Patriotic women's association), an organization established by Shimoda Utako in 1901. Just as the *Aikoku fujin kai* had it own journal, the *Aikoku fujin* founded in 1903, the *Liu Ri nüxuehui* also published its own organ, the *Liu Ri nüxuehui zazhi.* According to an article in this journal, members of the *Aikoku fujin kai* were anonymous heroines intent on eliminating the foreign threat.[54]

The Chinese female overseas students were concerned with nationalist issues as their interest in the *Aikoku fujin kai* indicates. Their agenda, however, went beyond contemporary political matters. Chinese nationalism was, in their eyes, less a topical anti-Manchu issue and more a structural cultural problem. As a result, they did not view Japan primarily as a national model of wealth and power but, rather, as a cultural mirror that brought into relief thousands of years of female degradation in China. As the author of the "Inaugural Statement" to the *Liu Ri nüxue hui zazhi* wrote, "for several thousand years, women in our country were simple and honest. Their livelihood depended on others. Their duty was to serve. They did not know what the nation was. Moreover, they did not know what the relationship between women and the nation was."[55] Before women could begin to address the current political issues that consumed the male overseas student community, they had first to redress centuries of cultural oppression that had rendered them dependent, voiceless, and ignorant.

Some female writers tied this oppression to foot binding, a practice that they variously claimed had endured for nine, fourteen, or fifteen centuries.[56] They described their mandate not in terms of establishing women's rights but of recovering rights that had existed in ancient times. They claimed, for example, that Confucius himself had acknowledged women's rights by using the phrase *pifu pifu* (a man and a woman) and that it was the Han dynasty literati who first denied women these rights.[57] Overwhelmingly, however, these women focused on the issue of education as the force that would release women from their imprisonment in the sphere of *nei* and empower them as actors in the sphere of *wai.* Just as they emphasized female literacy in their admiring descriptions of Japanese women, they considered the lack of education to be the source of Chinese women's backwardness. Chen Yan'an claimed the primary objective of the overseas students was to put an end to "four thousand years of no education for girls and women," Huang Lingfang decried the two-thousand-year lack of female education in China, and Yan Bin described how Chinese women had been forced to keep to the old teachings for several millennia.[58] To overcome the neglect of women's learning in the Chinese cultural tradition, these authors claimed it was necessary to imitate foreign nations.[59] For this particular group of overseas students, Japan would serve as their site of transformation, the place where Chinese women would be educated, uplifted, and rendered capable of fulfilling both their personal and national destinies.

A New Women's Culture: The Japanese Women's School as a Site of Transformation

While the overseas students pointed to education as the crucial aspect of Chinese women's transformation, there was an inevitable blurring of national, cultural, and educational agendas in their writings and activities. They believed women had to challenge certain aspects of the Chinese cultural tradition in order to serve the nation and that the way to do so was through education. The providers of this education in Japan—many of whom were driven by pan-Asian concerns—also combined these various agendas but with a very different understanding of nationalism, culture, and the private or public ends to which female education should be put.[60] This resulted in a series of tensions concerning the kind of site of transformation Japan should be.

These tensions were clearly uppermost in the mind of Jissen school founder, Shimoda Utako, the woman responsible for the education of the greatest number of Chinese female students. At the first graduation ceremony for Chinese students in 1904, Shimoda made it clear that learning, not politics, should be the primary objective of overseas study in Japan. She stated in her address that she did not want her students to become "radical proponents of popular power" (*gekietsu na minken ronsha*) or "rebels" (*ranshin zokushi*) but contributors to the field of women's education in China.

There were a number of ways Shimoda and other teachers in Japan attempted to control the experience of the young Chinese women in Tokyo within newly defined boundaries of *nei*. The first was to encourage them to live in school dormitories like the Jissen dormitory, which was located on the second floor of the school building above the classrooms, reception room, dean's office, and kitchen.[61] The intensive classroom schedule at a more serious school like Jissen also made it easier to regulate the students' lives. Before 1908, the general course consisted of twelve classes with thirty-six hours of classroom time a week.[62] After April 1908 when the school revised its program and introduced the *Gaikoku ryûgakusei kitei* (Foreign student regulations) largely in response to the Torishimaru incident, it not only established three-year rather than one-year programs but also extended the hours of study. The new regulations also imposed stricter requirements on the Chinese students. To qualify for admission to the school, they had to have a guarantor and an introduction from the embassy. They could only leave the school if accompanied by a dormitory dean or teacher, and their activities in the dormitory were closely monitored.[63]

Despite the strictness of these regulations, as the discussion earlier on social community has shown, the female students did become involved in political and social activities outside of the school. As I've written elsewhere, the overwhelming majority of Chinese women who would become publicly and politically engaged in this period had studied in Japan, most in the classrooms of Shimoda's Jissen school.[64] Qiu Jin, perhaps Shimoda's most famous student, is the best-known example, but there were many others, including He Xiangning, a close collaborator of Sun Yat-sen's from 1903 until his death; the women who would be at the forefront of the suffrage movement in the early Republican period, Lin Zongsu, Tang Qunying, Zhang Hanying, and Wang Changguo; and Fang Junying. Fang, one of the earliest graduates of the *Tokyo joshi kôtô shihan gakkô* (Tokyo upper-level normal school), was among the most radical students before the 1911 Revolution. Together with Qiu Jin, Chen Xiefen, and others, she received instruction from a Russian nihilist at a weapon-making factory in Yokohama, and she also joined an assassination squad (*mousha tuan*) organized by Wang Jingwei (1883–1944) in 1908. In 1909, she went to Hong Kong, where she served over the next two years as part of the rearguard for a series of attempted uprisings and assassinations in China.[65]

These women clearly ignored their teacher's injunctions against involvement in "rebel" movements, and their activities demonstrate the inextricable interconnectedness of the educational, cultural, and political experience in Japan. The most fascinating example of the ways the Chinese students were able to adapt the cultural agenda of pan-Asian inspired teachers like Shimoda to their own political ends was the uses to which they put the Japanese language. In order to conceal their plans for the uprising that led to Fang Shentong's death as a revolutionary martyr, Fang Junying and her coconspirators communicated in Japanese.[66] He Xiangning put forward a scathing critique of the political cowardice of Chinese women at the time of the intrusion of the Joint Expeditionary Forces into Beijing in 1900 (an interpretation that sharply contrasted with Shimoda's) by making reference to a Japanese journalistic account of the incident, the *Hoku Shin kansen ki* (Observation of the war in northern China).[67] And the money Qiu Jin and others made from translating works from Japanese into Chinese was quite likely to have been funneled into revolutionary activities.[68]

The historical record has tended to focus on women like Qiu Jin and He Xiangning because of their role in the unfolding narrative of China's revolutionary history. The significance of the overseas female study experience cannot be reduced to these women's political contributions, however. While not denying their importance, I would like to shift our attention to the broader cultural meaning of female overseas study in Japan. To do so, it is necessary to highlight the educational component of the nationalism-culture-education nexus that defines this experience. I would argue that, ultimately, the greatest impact of the overseas study movement was not in the decidedly *wai* sphere of nationalist politics—women were refused the vote in the early Republic, for example—but in the quasi-*wai* sphere of female education. Their entrée into this newly developing sphere had implications for Chinese culture in general and women's culture in particular in the twentieth century.

Even the most radical female overseas students focused on education as the means of transforming China's women from sequestered dependents to autonomous citizens. In their often essentialized view of female nature, the overseas students believed that women's roles had to be extended not only from the family to the nation but from the domestic to the professional spheres. The student Gong Yuanchang wrote that women were equal to men and deserved to be granted equal rights. Because of their distinct nature, however, they would have different duties. "Duties result from natural endowments," Gong wrote, and each sex had its special strengths. While "males were superior to females in politics and military matters, females were superior to males in education and the fine arts."[69] For the overseas students who did pursue careers after returning to China, these careers were in fields that served as extensions of women's long-standing roles as nurturers and instructors of the next generation: medicine and, most commonly, education.[70]

The conviction that teaching was the destiny of the female gender is evident in the high enrollment figures for normal school courses. This was in part because students sent to Japan by their provincial governments were sent with the express purpose of becoming educators. When Hunan province sent its first group of government-sponsored students to the Jissen school in late July 1905, for example, the majority of them (thirteen) enrolled in the regular short-term normal course whereas seven chose the short-term handicraft normal course.[71] During the peak years for female students in Japan, 1909–1910, of the sixty-seven students who graduated from the Jissen school, the majority were from the teacher-training or the new nursery-training course.[72]

Interviews with overseas students also reveal their personal ambition to become teachers upon their return to China. Zhu Jingyi had come to Tokyo from Hunan province to study after her brother convinced her that Japan was academically the most advanced nation in East Asia. Zhu explained in an interview in the *Shuntian shibao* that whereas in China she had only had the opportunity to study calligraphy and embroidery, in Japan she was most enjoying her classes in physical education, singing, and composition. Her ambition was to share her new knowledge with uneducated women on her return to China.[73] Huang Guohou, who was also from Hunan province and the top student in her class at the Jissen school, explained in an interview that she had been able to develop her own thinking in Japan, particularly on the subject of education in China. She said she would surely contribute to the field of women's education when she returned to China.[74]

As these interviews suggest and the school enrollment figures indicate, the overwhelming number of returned students who pursued careers became teachers.[75] As either founders of girls' schools in their hometowns or teachers in one of the many girls' schools founded in the last years of the Qing dynasty and the early Republic, they became the first career women in China.[76] Out of the twenty Hunanese students who entered the Jissen school in 1905, for example, twelve out of the twenty graduated and three of those twelve started their own schools.[77] One of them, Li Qiaosong from Pingjiang county, became the principal of a private school, the *Qiming nüxuetang* (Enlightenment girls' school) in 1908.[78] While this issue awaits more systematic analysis, there is an abundance of anecdotal evidence of this kind. Six young women who had studied in Japan became teachers at one of the three *Chuanxi suo* (Institutes of teaching and learning) established by Jiang Hanghu in Beijing from 1905. The *Beijing waicheng nüxue chuanxi suo* hired a graduate of the Japanese *Bijutsu gakkô*, a Miss Wang, to teach drawing. The *Beijing neicheng nüxue chuanxi suo* also employed graduates from Japan.[79]

Even the students who defied Shimoda's injunction against becoming involved in politics served as teachers on their return to China. Qiu Jin, for example, taught Japanese language, science, and hygiene at the Xunqi Girls' School in Nanxun, northern Zhejiang, shortly after her return to China in 1906. She also managed the *Mingdao nüxue* (Girls' school of the enlightened way) and founded a physical education school for women later known as the *Datong tiyu xue tang* (Datong physical education school), both in Shaoxing. Qiu further assisted in establishing in Shanghai a school for students who had ended their studies in Japan, the *Zhongguo gongxue* (Chinese public school).[80] After the establishment of the Republic, Fang Junying returned to Fuzhou where she became the director of the *Fujian nüzi shifan xuexiao* (Fujian female normal school). Even when Fang was not in a formal teaching position, she devoted herself to instructing the children of her friends and family.[81] Chen Yan'an, who was involved in radical nationalist activities while a student in Japan, directed a kindergarten and an elementary school in Beijing after her return to China.[82]

Returned students were also involved in the writing and production of textbooks for the new schools for girls and women. Sun Qingru, a graduate of the *Shina jo gakusei bu* (Chinese female student department) of the *Seijo gakkô* (Women's school), wrote a textbook entitled *Nüzi shifan jiangyi* after she returned to China. The textbook was approved by the Ministry of Education in 1909.[83]

In becoming independent career women, the returned students helped create a new feminine culture based on women's increased self-sufficiency. This new culture was both intentionally and unintentionally nurtured by Japanese teachers in Tokyo. One of Shimoda's objectives in establishing a program of education for Chinese women was to help eliminate the "custom of weakness among Chinese women."[84] She insisted that students who lived in the Jissen dormitories learn to take care of themselves. Chinese girls who were accustomed to being served were required to get up at 5 A.M. and to sweep their own rooms, halls, and bathrooms.[85] Many of the students not living in the dormitories also learned lessons in domestic self-sufficiency. When He Xiangning agreed to let Sun Yat-sen use her home as one of his political bases, she was forced to engage in an unusual revolutionary activity—cooking. This made it possible for her to run the household without the help of a Japanese maid who might have compromised the *Tongmeng hui*'s activities.[86] These lessons in self-sufficiency made the overseas students both autonomous and independent minded. A Miss Liao who taught at a Zhili women's school after returning from Japan, for example, insisted on bringing her female students to a graduation ceremony at the local army school because she believed this experience would increase her students' respect for the army and invigorate a martial spirit. The school principal, who believed the sexes should not mix, opposed the idea. When Miss Liao brought her students to the ceremony nonetheless, she lost her job.[87]

The historical significance of this new feminine culture can be established by tracing the impact the returned student-teachers had on women in the early Republic. Wang Zheng's study of the May Fourth era provides a number of examples of young women who were strongly influenced by their Japan-educated teachers. All of career revolutionary Huang Dinghui's (1907–) elementary school teachers in Liuyang, Hunan, had studied in Japan as had the principal of the Zhounan Girls' School where she later studied, Zhu Jianfan, and his wife.[88] At the famous Shanghai *Aiguo nüxuexiao* (Patriotic girls' school), the future educator Chen Yongsheng (1900–1997) received training in a Japanese-style education from her teachers, who had all studied in Japan. Later, as a teacher herself, Chen worked at a school in Guangdong where the principal, the elder sister of He Xiangning's husband, Liao Zhongkai, had also studied in Japan.[89]

In addition to the instruction these teachers imparted, they also provided their students with new models of womanhood. Many of the returned students remained single, thus sanctioning an independent life for women for the first time in Chinese history. They also raised their students' awareness of gender issues and the need to struggle for sexual equality.[90] The more dramatic figures in the history of female overseas study, Qiu Jin and He Xiangning in particular, joined the ranks of icons like the legendary warrior Hua Mulan (c. 500). They served as inspirational *lienü* for later generations of young Chinese women.[91]

Language and Autonomy

The female overseas study movement in Japan in the early twentieth century provides an important example of gender in motion: motion across national borders as travel abroad by elite young women was sanctioned in the late Qing for the first time in Chinese history, and motion across social barriers as Chinese women lived within a more fluid social community in Tokyo and received a formal education—one of the markers of *wai* from ancient times. Educated separately, the overseas female students nonetheless shared certain physical spaces with men in Tokyo. In these diverse meeting places and living spaces, they began to question long-standing notions of the gendered order and joined their male compatriots in addressing the political and educational concerns of the overseas student community. The female students' understanding of normative femininity was further altered through their observations of Japanese women who served as a cultural mirror that both reflected an image of a degraded and isolated Chinese womanhood and projected a new Japanese model of femininity based on a publicly empowering literacy. While few of the overseas female students reached the level of the idealized professional Japanese woman, many learned important lessons in self-sufficiency while abroad. It was this newly acquired autonomy that allowed a number of them to use the language (both literal and metaphorical) that their experience in Japan had taught them, whether as radical activists or self-supporting educators.

The students used this new language to decry the more extreme manifestations of women's isolation in the sphere of *nei*—foot binding and ignorance. Rather than advocate completely erasing gender distinctions, however, they tried to recalibrate those distinctions in accord with both timeworn social assumptions and new political realities. These women who had transgressed the boundaries from *nei* to *wai* with such apparent ease in traveling to Japan staked out a new position for themselves from within physical and discursive spaces that had been established by men and formed segregated organizations with gendered mandates. Most significantly, they continued to view new female roles in essentialized terms. They encouraged women to serve the nation through their families, extending their love of kin to love of country and joining the work force by cultivating their innate feminine skills as nurturers and educators. The sphere of *nei* which the students continued to inhabit was less a well-defined physical location than it was a state of mind, an essential component of their gendered habitus. The historical significance of the overseas female experience in Japan lies in the ways that experience altered this habitus through the incorporation of new nationalist aspirations, cultural insights, and educational ambitions. What made these women "new Lin Daiyus" in the spirit of Nanwu Yeman's heroine was not their entrance into spheres of action explicitly coded as *wai* but their capacity to shift the parameters, without completely undermining the social and cultural meaning, of the realm of *nei*.

Notes

1. David Der-wei Wang, *Fin-de-Siècle Splendor: Repressed Modernities of Late Qing Fiction, 1849–1911* (Stanford, Calif.: Stanford University Press, 1997), 5, 29; "Jia Baoyu ye shi liuxuesheng—wan Qing de liuxuesheng xiaoshuo" (Jiao Baoyu is also an overseas student—Late Qing overseas student novels), in *Xiaoshuo Zhonguo: Wan Qing dao dangdai de Zhongwen xiaoshuo* (Narrating China: Chinese fiction from the Late Qing to the contemporary era), by Wang Dewei (David Der-wei Wang) (Taipei: Maitian chuban gongsi, 1993), 229–36; Yan Ansheng, *Nihon ryûgaku seishinshi: Kindai Chûgoku chishiki jin no kiseki* (The spirit of overseas study in Japan: Traces of modern Chinese intellectuals) (Tokyo: Iwanami shoten, 1994), 70–71.

2. Qiu Jin, "Jingwei shi" (Stones of the Jingwei bird), in *Qiu Jin ji* (Hong Kong: Changfen tushu gongsi, 1974), 119–60.

3. "Nüzi chuyang: Xin banen" (Females go overseas: A new theater script). *Shuntian shibao* (Shuntian daily), GX 33 [1907] 1:14; reprinted in *Jindai Zhongguo nüquan yundong shiliao: 1842–1911* (Historical materials on the early modern Chinese women's rights movement: 1842–1911, hereafter *NQYDSL*), ed. Li Yu-ning and Chang Yü-fa (Taipei: Longwen chubanshe, 1995), 2:1271–72.

4. On this secondary literature, see for example, Zhou Yichuan, *Chûgoku jin no jôsei Nihon ryûgaku shi kenkyû* (Research on Chinese female overseas students in Japan) (Tokyo: Kokusho kankôkai, 2001), 95; Ishii Yôko, "Shingai kakumei ki no ryû-Nichi joshi gakusei" (Female overseas students in Japan at the time of the 1911 Revolution), *Shiron* 36 (1983): 48; Wang Qisheng, "Cong shengui zouxiang shijie de nüliuxuesheng" (Female overseas students: From the inner chambers to the world), *Mingbao yuekan* (September 1993): 31.

5. For a discussion of Pierre Bourdieu's concept of habitus in relation to gender, see Beate Krais, "Gender and Symbolic Violence: Female Oppression in the Light of Pierre Bourdieu's Theory of Social Practice," in *Bourdieu: Critical Perspectives*, ed. Craig Calhoun, Edward LiPuma, and Moishe Postone (Chicago: University of Chicago Press, 1993), 156–77.

6. The quintessential literary example of respectable resistance to such transgressive travel was Madame Jin in the novel *Niehai hua* (Flower in a sea of retribution). See Sun Shiyue, *Zhongguo jindai nü zi liuxue shi* (The history of overseas study by Chinese women) (Beijing: Zhongguo heping chuban she, 1995), 27–28; Hu Ying, *Of Translation: Composing the New Woman in China, 1898–1918* (Stanford, Calif.: Stanford University Press, 2000), 36.

7. According to Japanese Foreign Office (Gaimushô) records, there were 139 Chinese female students in Japan in 1907, 126 in 1908, 149 in 1909, and 125 in 1910. Zhou, *Chûgoku jin no jôsei*, 55–94. Zhou dates the first period from 1870, but since we

cannot speak of a real overseas "movement" until there are significant numbers of students and formal Japanese programs for them, I date the first period from 1901. For the Gaimushô numbers, see 84.

8. See Ye Weili, *Seeking Modernity in China's Name: Chinese Students in the United States, 1900–27* (Stanford, Calif.: Stanford University Press, 2001), 116–29; Hu Ying, "Lishi shuxie yu xin nüxing xingxiang de chuli: Cong Liang Qichao 'Ji Jiangxi Kang Nüshi' yi wen tan qi" (The new woman and the writing of history: The case of Kang Aide). In *Jindai Zhongguo funüshi yanjiu* (Research on women in modern Chinese history) 9 (September 2001): 1–29; and Sun, *Zhongguo jindai nü zi liuxue shi*, 43–48.

9. On the social status of the male students, see Paula Harrell, *Sowing the Seeds of Change: Chinese Students, Japanese Teachers, 1895–1905* (Stanford, Calif.: Stanford University Press, 1992), 62–65. On government regulations, see "Nüzi youxue xuzhi" (What female students should know concerning overseas study), *Dongfang zazhi* (The eastern miscellany), quoted in Sun, *Zhongguo jindai nü zi liuxue shi*, 71–72; and Zhou Yichuan, "Qingmo liu-Ri xuesheng zhong de nüxing" (Females among late Qing overseas students to Japan), *Lishi yanjiu* 6, no. 102 (1989): 54. Expenses for the entire year would translate into approximately three hundred Japanese yen not including the cost of travel to Japan and personal purchases such as books. Cited in Sun, *Zhongguo jindai nü zi liuxue shi*, 72.

10. Ye Weili (*Seeking Modernity*, 164) has described how the Chinese Student Alliance in the United States held an annual summer conference with the mandate of encouraging socialization between men and women students from China.

11. Wang Lian, "Tongxiang hui jishi: Hubei zhi bu" (Record of same-place association meeting, section on Hubei), *Hubei xuesheng jie* 2 (February 27, 1903), 114–15. According to some sources, Wang Lian was married to Wang Xiaosong when she arrived in Tokyo, although there is nothing in her own writings that would indicate this. See, for example, Zhou, *Chûgoku jin no jôsei*, 57.

12. Wang Lian, "Tongxiang hui jishi," 115.

13. On the *huiguan*, see Sanetô Keishû, *Chûgoku jin Nihon ryûgaku shi zôho* (A history of Chinese students in Japan) (Tokyo: Kuroshio shuppan, 1970), 195–203; Harrell, *Sowing the Seeds*, 98–100.

14. Liu Mei Ching, "Forerunners of Chinese Feminism in Japan: Students Fighting for Freedom in Japan" (Ph.D. diss., University of Leiden, 1988), 291, 295.

15. Zhou, *Chûgoku jin no jôsei*, 67.

16. Ishii, "Shingai kakumei," 44.

17. Zhou, *Chûgoku jin no jôsei*, 88.

18. Sanetô, *Chûgoku jin Nihon*, 164, 166; Zhou, *Chûgoku jin no jôsei*, 66.

19. Liu Mei Ching, "Forerunners," 291, 295. Qiu Jin, "Jinggao Zhongguo erwanwan nü tongbao" (Advice for the two hundred million women of China), in *Qiu Jin xianlie wenji* (The writings of the national martyr Qiu Jin) (Taipei: Dangshi weiyuan hui, 1982), 133–35.

20. Sanetô, *Chûgoku jin Nihon*, 473.

21. In 1909, one of the peak years for female overseas study in Japan, out of over fifty-five students at the Jissen school, thirty or so lived in the dormitory, while twenty-five lived with family members. Ko Shimoda kôchô sensei denki hensanjo,

ed., *Shimoda Utako sensei den* (Biography of Professor Shimoda Utako) (Tokyo: Ko Shimoda kôchô sensei denki hensanjo, 1943), 406.

22. In the fall of 1904, for example, it seems that Qiu Jin lived in the Jissen school dormitory and took Japanese classes in the evening at the *Riyu jiangxi suo* at the student union building. Guo Zhanghai and Li Yabin, eds., *Qiu Jin Shiji yanjiu* (Research on Qiu Jin's achievements) (Changchun: Dongbei shifan daxue chubanshe, 1987), 128. One of the Jissen school deans, Sakaki Mitoko, mentioned that, despite harsh regulations, secret visits were made to the dormitory by male visitors. Sakaki Mitoko, "Sakaki Mitoko shi dan" (A conversation with Ms. Sakaki Mitoko), Jissen joshi daigaku toshokan, Shimoda Utako kankei shiryô (Jissen Women's University Library materials related to Shimoda Utako, filed by number), file # 3001-1, August 26, 1968, 6.

23. Zhou, *Chûgoku jin no jôsei*, 62.

24. He Xiangning, "Wo de huiyi" (My reminiscences), in *Xinhai geming huiyi* (Memoirs of the 1911 Revolution), Zhongguo renmin zhengzhi xieshang huiyi quanguo weiyuan hui, ed. Wenshi ziliao yanjiu weiyuan hui (Beijing: Wenshi ziliao chubanshe, 1981), 1:14.

25. He, "Wo," 15–20; He Xiangning, "When I Learned How to Cook." In *Chinese Women through Chinese Eyes*, ed. Li Yu-ning (Armonk, N.Y.: Sharpe, 1992), 135–43.

26. Li Yuning, "Xinhai geming xianjin Fang Junying nüshi" (Fang Junying, a progressive woman in the 1911 Revolution), *Zhuanji wenxue* 38, 5 (May 1981), 16-17.

27. "Liuxue jilu" (Record of overseas students activities), *Hubei xuesheng jie* 4 (April 27, 1903): 125 [0575].

28. Ishii, "Shingai kakumei," 44–45. This organization also published a journal, the *Liu Ri nüxuesheng hui zazhi* (Journal of female students studying in Japan), founded on April 27, 1911.

29. Sun, *Zhongguo jindai nü zi liuxue shi,* 100; Zhou, "Qingmo," 59; Ishii, "Shingai kakumei," 37.

30. On the involvement of Gongai hui members in *Jiangsu,* see Ishii, "Shingai kakumei," 43.

31. Sun, *Zhongguo jindai nü zi liuxue shi,* 110; Charlotte L. Beahan, "Feminism and Nationalism in the Chinese Women's Press, 1902–1911," *Modern China* 1, no. 4 (October 1975): 389–90.

32. On these and other journals of the period, see Ishii, "Shingai kakumei," 45–49; Sun, *Zhongguo jindai nü zi liuxue shi,* 11–12; Jacqueline Nivard, "Bibliographie de la presse féminine chinoise, 1898–1949," *Études chinoises* 5, nos. 1–2 (Spring–Autumn 1986): 185–236.

33. See, for example, Yi Qin, "Lun Zhongguo nüzi zhi qiantu" (The future of Chinese females), *Jiangsu* 4 (July 25, 1903): 143 (reprint, Taibei: Zhongguo Guoming dang, Zhongyang weiyuan hui, Dangshi shiliao bianzuan weiyuan hui, 1968, 761).

34. Wang Lian, "Tongxiang hui jishi," 115.

35. Cao Rujin, "Aiguo ji ziai" (Patriotism and self-love), *Jiangsu* 3 (June 25, 1903): 158 (reprint, 0588).

36. Qiu Jin, "Jinggao," 133–35.

37. This point deserves more elaboration than I am able to give it in the context of this essay. It is, of course, impossible to completely separate political and cultural back-

wardness—one constitutes the other—but foot binding, a practice that preceded the Manchus, and wearing the queue were used as ubiquitous markers of China's backwardness and singularity.

38. On the overseas students' reactions to the exhibition, see "Riben Daban Bolan hui Zhongguo Fujian chupin yichu Taiwan Guan shimo ji" (A complete record of the integration of Fujianese products in the Taiwan Pavilion at the Osaka Exhibition), *Jiangsu* 1 (April 27, 1903): 146–47 (reprint, 164–65); "Bolan huibao" (Report on [the Osaka] Exhibition), *Zhejiang chao* 2 (March 18, 1903): 1–3 (reprint, Taibei: Zhongguo Guoming dang, Zhongyang weiyuan hui, Dangshi shiliao bianzuan weiyuan hui, 1968, 133–35).

39. Tai Gong, "Dongjing zashi shi" (Poems on various topics concerning Tokyo), *Zhejiang chao* 2 (March 1903): 162.

40. According to one article, for example, in 1884, 3,190,000 males and 2,960,000 females were enrolled in schools of all levels in Japan—numbers close to those found in Western nations. "Yindu ji Riben nüxue zhi xingqi" (The rise of female education in India and Japan), *Wanguo gongbao* (June 1891): 5–6 (reprint, *NQYDSL* I:267).

41. It has been estimated that in China in the 1800s, 30 to 40 percent of males and 2 to 10 percent of females were literate. Evelyn Rawski, *Education and Popular Literacy in Ch'ing China* (Ann Arbor: University of Michigan Press, 1989), 140.

42. Sun, *Zhongguo jindai nü zi liuxue shi*, 53; According to Kang Tongwei, "in the last ten years there have been over two million female students, one thousand teachers, three hundred schools in [Japan] whereas China has not had a single women's school." See "Nüxue libi shuo" (The advantages and disadvantages of education for girls and women), *Zhixin bao* 52 (May 11, 1898). Reprinted in *Zhongguo jindai xuezhi shiliao* (Historical materials on the modern Chinese educational system, hereafter *XZSL*), ed. Zhu Youhuan (Shanghai: Huadong shifan daxue chuban she, 1986), 1: 2, 877.

43. Yan, *Nihon ryûgaku seishinshi*, 72.

44. Cited in Harrell, *Sowing the Seeds*, 80.

45. Chen Daohua, "Rijing zhuzhici" (Verse about Tokyo) (1908: n.p.), cited in Yan, *Nihon ryûgaku seishinshi*, 72.

46. Young women generally married between the ages of sixteen and seventeen in the eighteenth century. Susan Mann, *Precious Records: Women in China's Long Eighteenth Century* (Stanford, Calif.: Stanford University Press, 1997), 46.

47. "Rifu ren jiaoxi" (Japanese women become teachers), *Jingzhong ribao* (May 22, 1904), reprinted in *NQYDSL*, 1: 293–94.

48. This particular statistic was from the *Nihon joshi kôtô shihan gakkô* and based on a sample of 927 women, out of whom 405 were not married. "Nü jiaoshi yu jiehun" (Women teachers and marriage), *Jiaoyu congshu* 3 (July 1901): 3–4.

49. Chen Yan'an, "Quan nüzi liuxue shuo" (Exhortation for female overseas study), *Jiangsu* 3 (June 1903): 1–2 [155–56].

50. Wang Lian, "Tongxiang hui jishi," 115.

51 Tai Gong, "Dongjing,"162.

52. "Nüxuesheng shangzhen beizi shu" (Female students offer a petition to the Manchu noble [Zai] Zhen), *Hubei xuesheng jie* 5 (May 27, 1903): 137–38 (reprint,

Taibei: Zhongguo Guoming dang, Zhongyang weiyuan hui, Dangshi shiliao bianzuan weiyuan hui, 1968, 727–30).

53. "Dongyang nüquan kuozhang" (The expansion of women's rights in Japan), *Hubei xuesheng jie* 2 (February 27, 1903): 99 (reprint, 273).

54. Tan Sheying, *Zhongguo funü yundong tongshi* (A general history of the Chinese women's movement), 1936. Reprinted in *Minguo congshu* (Compendium of sources from the Republican period), 2:18 (Shanghai: Shanghai shudian, 1990), 19.

55. Xian Bin, "Fakanci" (Inaugural statement), *Liu Ri nüxuehui zazhi* (Female overseas students in Japan study society magazine) (May 1911), reprinted in Tan Sheying, 18.

56. Jiang Dong, "Ji Hangzhou fanzu hui" (Record of the Hangzhou foot liberation society), *Zhejiang chao* 2 (March 18, 1903), 1–6 (reprint, 173–78). Qiu Jin claimed the practice of foot binding had been introduced by Chen Houzhu (Chen Shubao, 533–604, last emperor of the Chen dynasty). Qiu Jin, "Jinggao," 134.

57. Chubei yingzi, "Zhina nüquan fenyan" (Indignation at the denial of Chinese women's rights), *Hubei xuesheng jie* 2 (February 27, 1903): 95–96 (reprint, 268–69).

58. Chen, "Quan nüzi," 156; "Huang Lingfang Nüshi Nüjiezhong xu" (Huang Lingfang's preface to *Wake-up call for women*), *Jiangsu* 5 (August 23, 1903): 133 (reprint, 943); Yan Bin, "Fakanci"(Inaugural statement), *Zhongguo xin nüjie zazhi* (Magazine of the New Chinese Women), reprinted in Tan Sheying, 15.

59. See, for example, Chen, "Quan nüzi," 156. For more on the pan-Asianism of Shimoda Utako in particular, see Joan Judge, "Talent, Virtue, and the Nation: Chinese Nationalisms and Female Subjectivities in the Early Twentieth Century," *American Historical Review* 106, no. 3 (June 2001): 765–803.

60. See Judge, "Talent, Virtue, and the Nation."

61. Ko Shimoda, *Shimoda Utako*, 80, 102.

62. Zhou, *Chûgoku jin no jôsei*, 71.

63. Zhou, *Chûgoku jin no jôsei*, 82–83.

64. See Judge, "Talent, Virtue, and the Nation."

65. Li, "Xinhai"; "Wen Fang Junying zijin zhigan (7.25, 1923)" (My feelings upon hearing about Fang Junying's suicide, July 25, 1923), in *Cai Yuanpei quanji*, ed. Gao Pingshu 4 (1921–1924) (Beijing: Zhonghua shuju, 1984), 336–37.

66. Li, "Xinhai," 17.

67. He Xiangning, "Jinggao wo tongbao jiemei" (A warning for my sister compatriots), *Jiangsu* 4 (June 25, 1903): 144–45 [762–63], 144.

68. Guo Changying and Su Xiaohuan, "Jindai Zhonguo nüzi liuxue tanxi" (An analysis of modern Chinese overseas study), *Shixue yuekan* 3 (1991): 62.

69. Gong Yuanchang, "Nannü pingquan shuo" (Equal rights for males and females), *Jiangsu* 4 (June 25, 1903): 145; reprinted in Zhongguo Guomindang zhongyang weiyuanhui, Dangshi shiliao bianzuan weiyuanhui (Taipei, 1968), 763.

70. Wang, "Cong shengui," 33.

71. Sun, *Zhongguo jindai nü zi liuxue shi*, 67.

72. Ishii, "Shingai kakumei," 36.

73. "Zai-Ri Zhongguo liuxue sheng, qi yi" (Overseas Chinese students in Japan, 1). *Shuntian shibao* GX 31 [1905] 6.19, 20, 21; reprinted in *NQYDSL*, 2:1256.

74. "Ji liuxue nüshi zhi tanhua" (Record of a conversation with overseas female students), *Shuntian shibao* GX 32 [1906] 8:19; reprinted in *NQYDSL*, 2:1269.

75. According to Sun Shiyue (*Zhongguo jindai nü zi liuxue shi*, 326), between 1909 and 1922, most returned female students went into careers in education.

76. Some female returned students did enter the publishing field or business enterprises, but most devoted themselves to careers in education. Wang Zheng, *Women in the Chinese Enlightenment: Oral and Textual Histories* (Berkeley: University of California Press, 1999), 130.

77. Ko Shimoda, *Shimoda Utako*, 405.

78. Li Qiaosong presented Shimoda Utako with a picture of herself and her students in late 1908. Ko Shimoda, *Shimoda Utako*, 431.

79. *NQYDSL*, 1127, 1151, cited in Guo Changying, 63.

80. Bao Jialin, "Qiu Jin yu Qingmo funü yundong" (Qiu Jin and the late Qing women's movement), in *Zhongguo funüshi lunji* (Materials on the history of Chinese women), ed. Bao Jialin (Taipei: Daoxiang chuban she, 1997), 371–73; Mary Backus Rankin, "The Emergence of Women at the End of the Ch'ing: The Case of Ch'iu Chin," in *Women in Chinese Society*, ed. Margery Wolf and Roxane Witke (Stanford, Calif.: Stanford University Press, 1975), 55, 59; Wendy Larson, *Women and Writing in Modern China* (Stanford, Calif.: Stanford University Press, 1998), 112. On the *Zhongguo gongxue*, see Liu Mei Ching, "Forerunners," 298.

81. Li, "Xinhai"; Cai.

82. Zhou, *Chûgoku jin no jôsei*, 62.

83. *Jiaoyu zazhi*, 1:10, 1909, 72, cited in Zhou, *Chûgoku jin no jôsei*, 75.

84. "Zhongguo liudong nüxuesheng" (Chinese overseas students in the East), *Shuntian shibao* GX 31 [1905] 7.4. Reprinted in *NQYDSL*, 2:1268.

85. Sun, *Zhongguo jindai nü zi liuxue shi*, 72.

86. He, "Wo," 15–20; "When," 135–43.

87. *NQYDSL*, 1187. Cited in Guo Changying, "Jindai Zhonguo nüzi," 63; Luo Suwen, *Nüxing yu jindai Zhongguo shehui* (Women and modern Chinese society) (Shanghai: Renmin chuban she, 1996), 149.

88. Wang Zheng, *Women in the Chinese Enlightenment*, 291, 292.

89. Wang Zheng, *Women in the Chinese Enlightenment*, 265, 267. I have only found reference to a younger sister of Liao's who studied in Japan, Liao Yongyun.

90. Wang Zheng, *Women in the Chinese Enlightenment*, 291, 292.

91. Huang Dinghui, for example, was encouraged to read the biography of Qiu Jin, and she also had great admiration for He Xiangning. Wang Zheng, *Women in the Chinese Enlightenment*, 295, 297.

6

Playing with the Public

Late Qing Courtesans and Their Opera Singer Lovers

Catherine Vance Yeh

IN THE LATE NINETEENTH CENTURY, the top-ranking Shanghai courtesans rose to become a new type of public personality. With their brazen public behavior, business practices, and lifestyle, they were able to garner attention and create amused controversy. In treaty-port Shanghai, the low social status that courtesans had in Chinese society ceased to prod them to self-censorship and restraint and even seemed to free them from existing constraints binding other groups of women. Here, the leading courtesans became stars in the new media and were instrumental in setting new fashions and forms of behavior in the public realm.

A core feature of this new lifestyle was the creation of an ever more clearly marked "private" or "personal" realm beyond their professional sphere. This became visible in their efforts to separate their public role as entertainers and "lovers," and the love affairs that they carried on outside their business, increasingly thought of as belonging to the private sphere. The former included relations with clients and patrons, which were part of their business of entertainment, unfolded in the spaces assigned for it, and might but did not necessarily have a sexual component. The latter would be "unofficial" love affairs away from their business; they took place in a space and time marked as private and did not involve the kind of business considerations dominating courtesan entertainment.

While the traditional concepts of *nei* (domestic) as the space reserved for females and *wai* (public) as the space reserved for males had an impact on the secluded way in which courtesan establishments were set up, they are not useful for the study of the Shanghai foreign settlements. The conquest of the public realm by the Shanghai courtesans, with their high public visibility in the city, and the coverage they received from the Shanghai press were new developments. These hinged on the premise that the authorities would not intervene. It is against the backdrop of their new professional and public role that, in an equally innovative move, they carved out an urban private realm they claimed as separate from their entertainment business and ruled by their own private interests.

The division between the two is most sharply visible in a new interpretation of time and space by the courtesans. For their own private love affairs, they set apart from their professional activities a marked time and space. The new space for love was created on the one hand by reinterpreting public space such as theaters, parks, and restaurants, not only as new business premises but also as space for private endeavors. On the other hand, they also explored new types of spaces such as *siyu* (private dwellings) as the site of their private love affairs. In creating the time for love, the intersection between professional and private was even stronger. It appears that they marked the late night for their own pursuits. This new reassignment of time and space challenged the cultural basis of courtesan entertainment where the role a courtesan plays in the game of courtship was deemed as her all-encompassing persona.

With the construction of this new private sphere, the courtesan in effect redefined her life as having both a private as well as a professional realm. This separation highlights its modern character when compared with the *nei* (domestic) versus *wai* (public) traditional construct. While her professional life already cuts across that demarcation line, in her pursuit of the private, there is no sense of a domesticity that contributes to a collective identity. The fact that the public perception of her role is precisely that of a lover makes the creation of the private, with its space and time dimension, all the more provocative and shocking.

This private realm was not private for long, however. Much of the information we get on this transformation comes from Shanghai's men of letters. Working as literati turned salaried journalists and editors in Shanghai's rapidly developing media industry, they readily publicized their opinion on this new trend. Their reaction was mixed. While they admitted a great deal of admiration for the courtesans, their unease and moral outrage at this new development was directly forthcoming. They were not neutral observers. The Shanghai *yangchang caizi* (Shanghai settlement intellectuals) saw their traditional privileged social position erode in this city, with its commercial spirit and financial might. Nowhere was this more striking than in the attitude of the Shanghai courtesans toward them. Instead of being, as tradition had it, the objects of the courtesans' devotion and the natural candidates for being their lovers and potential husbands, the Shanghai *wenren* found themselves in hopeless competition with rich merchants and compradors as far as courtesan entertainment was concerned. To their great consternation, top courtesans eventually even went further, picking their private lovers from the likes of lowly opera singers or even their chauffeurs.

Reflecting the rapid shifts in the evolving urban sensibility even on the part of the courtesans themselves, this private realm was eventually publicly claimed and stripped of its clandestine nature. The courtesans paraded the lovers who were not clients in their carriages, their private affairs were as extensively reported in the media as their professional entertainment, and some courtesans made active use of the new star status of their opera singer lovers to enhance their own professional stature and attractiveness.

The unfolding of this lifestyle with its new concepts of time and space and its extraordinary exposure in the public realm reflects the conditions in the Shanghai foreign settlements. With the development of the public sphere through institutions such as the newspaper or public places such as the teahouse, the park, the theater, the wide and clean avenues, and different types of private dwellings organized to suit new life arrangements, the Shanghai foreign settlements were unquestionably leading modern urban development in the Qing empire; in terms of city infrastructure, the settlements even prided themselves on competing with the likes of Paris or London. The development of these public and commercial features together with the city's self-administration offered options for the development of new and urban lifestyles. They helped attract sojourners to the city for a life that was not possible elsewhere in the empire. Shanghai was the most accommodating venue for the high-class courtesan to stage her new lifestyle and explore new emotional relationships.

The implied sexual aura of the courtesan's profession makes their existence and influence in the public arena an extremely sensitive issue. Of all the issues raised with regard to courtesans' increasing visibility and influence in the public realm, the social relations of their sexuality is one area not often discussed by either contemporaries or later scholars. Yet it was in this realm that they initiated one of the most profound social transformations at the time, namely a shift in the conception of love. Their blunt insistence on a space for their private feelings opened the doors for the emergence of a new urban sexual culture, or culture of love, that was defined as "private." Historically no such separation existed for courtesans, and the development of this private space hinged on their establishing, by contrast, a professional and public time/space for their entertainment. This new development separated work and love, public and private. It became part of an urban trend that had private love as the basis of the nuclear family, and it foreshadows some of the time/space arrangements for this new lifestyle.

I use here on occasion the term *courtesan* as a collective to denote a relatively small group of top courtesans; in reality, of course, even their situation was highly diversified. As a group, however, made up of oft-competing individuals they had a historical impact, and in this spirit I use the term *collective.*

The Ambiguous Position of the Courtesans as Public Personalities

The move of the courtesans from the walled city of Shanghai as well as from courtesan centers such as Suzhou to the Shanghai foreign settlements in the 1850s and 1860s marked a sharp change in their social position and public role.[1] Formerly, the courtesans as a social and professional group were defined by a set of well-smoothed-over paradoxes. While it was a courtesan's profession to entertain men of high social and economic standing in a playful simulation of social equality with even the most powerful and influential men of the empire, she herself belonged to the very low social rank of *yueji* or *yuehu* (entertainer in bondage) and was considered *jian* (low caste). Before the Qing period, the courtesan was either a slave belonging to the court (or a private family) or an inmate of a courtesan house controlled and taxed by the court office *jiaofang si.* Early in the Qing, this office was abolished and with it officially organized courtesan entertainment. The courtesan profession became entirely private, and courtesans became the inmates of privately run courtesan houses and brothels that continued to serve an elite clientele.[2] As there was no clear legal protection for them, both the courtesan establishments and their inmates depended largely on the unstable protection of local power holders. As their profession dictated, their services were accessible only to an elite group in a secluded environment. In this way, they were simultaneously both in the center and at the margins of society.

There is a traditional trope of the "beauty overturning a kingdom," and stories abound where ministers remonstrate with their ruler to take care of government rather than spending his time and energies in the inner quarters. This criticism, however, did not extend to the courtesan profession. It was well established socially and culturally, and considered sufficiently contained and even beneficial to social order, that the state set up official and exclusive courtesan houses for its bureaucrats. The Qing abolishment of this institution did not seriously undermine the social acceptance of courtesan entertainment. The courtesan was part of the cultural ambiance of the literati, and there was a well-established symbiotic and sympathetic relationship between the two. The courtesans' own projections of their persona and their close and often very emotional contacts with men from the lettered elite helped create a rich body of legends and literary depictions. This body of literature sets out to accord to the courtesans a high cultural as well as moral status that effaces their low social position.

However, neither the new public persona the courtesans sported in the foreign settlements in Shanghai nor their new private sphere was part of the traditional image. The shift came first with the availability and accessibility for the courtesans of public places in the foreign settlements, an opportunity they did not let go by as it offered new avenues both for their business and for their private amusement. Once the courtesans moved into the public space of the settlements' avenues, squares, parks, and theaters, the days of privileged male elite access were gone, and so were the old rituals and routines. As those who lost most in this shift, the pen-wielding men of letters began to ask what "public" the courtesans were wooing, how public they would become, and who was entitled to enjoy the entertainment they provided.

The courtesans' move to the Shanghai foreign settlements changed, among other things, the power relationship between them and the lettered elite. Wounded and dismayed by this behavior, the Shanghai *wenren* censured the prevailing vulgarity by bemoaning the loss of the great tradition personified by the Jiangnan courtesans of the late Ming.[3] Beneath the general irritation on the part of the late Qing writers, the issue was very much what kind of lover these two groups of courtesan had taken. The reputations of the late Ming Jiangnan courtesan and of the late Qing Shanghai courtesan rest on two diametrically opposite scenarios. The former, who is central to a real literary industry of late Qing nostalgia, represents ultimate cultural refinement and moral integrity. The latter, who also figures prominently in late Qing writing, has become the glowing emblem of the collapse of moral order and the corrupting powers of the Shanghai treaty port's commercial spirit.

The two scenarios do share one common feature, however: the strong individuality and self-determination shown by the famous courtesans of both periods in their own lives, and in their literary representations, in recklessly and passionately pursuing their ideal lovers. The difference is in the type of lover they pursued, and this difference accounts for the divergence in their reputation among literati. The late Ming courtesan sought out outstanding members of the literati class as ideal lovers and potential husbands.[4] The Shanghai courtesan defied this tradition and, in some cases, the institution of marriage altogether; instead she chose the beautiful man of popular fame but low social status, the Beijing opera star, as her romantic counterpart.

As the men of letters imposed their reconstructed cultural memory on the scene of Shanghai courtesan entertainment, the response of Shanghai courtesans seems to have been very negative. Also flamboyant and self-conscious in staging their public persona, the Shanghai courtesans largely turned their backs on the Ming tradition and thwarted the expectations of the literati.

They became legends in their own right and on their own terms; upholding the spirit of commercial culture of Shanghai port city, they did not follow the high ideal of the literati as the late Ming courtesans had done, but an ideal of personal pleasure they saw as separate from their professional success. They discarded the literati ideal of the courtesan in favor of one much more in tune with the attitudes of Shanghai's businessmen, their main clients. The professionalization, commercialization, and economic success of their entertainment gave them the confidence to claim the privilege of a private space and time in which they insisted that they were entitled to follow their own whims and passions.

The influence the courtesans had with the public was very much based on their visibility and exposure.[5] They performed in the new female storytelling halls, sang in the new all-female opera performances known as *maoer xi*, rode in their carriages with clients to view the scenic spots of the foreign settlements, and accompanied clients to the theater, to the parks, or to dinner parties in restaurants. This degree of public exposure for a female figure in general and a courtesan entertainer in particular was unheard of in the rest of the Qing empire and made them a unique sight of the Shanghai foreign settlements.

This exploration of public places by the courtesans initially had been driven by business considerations but quickly took on another dimension—namely, the courtesans' self-staging. The settlement culture with its glorification of money and its conspicuous spending was very much a culture of public display. Parading their newest fashions and knickknacks before the curious eyes of the public became a way of life for the top courtesans. Their names were published in the newspapers; entertainment papers sprung up to make money off their fame by giving them and their activities exclusive coverage. As a result, some of these courtesans became well-known public personalities who could expect to be recognized on the street or in the theater.

Courtesan entertainment was a thriving business in the Shanghai settlements. Relationships between the madams and the courtesans here lost much of their former legal and social constraints and were reduced largely to financial obligations and joint efforts to make their business thrive. In this environment, many of the courtesans, instead of pursuing marriage as the traditional way out of the bondage into which their parents had sold them, bought themselves free with the money they themselves were able to amass. This kind of transaction, which was called "buying oneself out" (*zishu*), was unheard of prior to 1870.[6] They would then set up their own business or join a courtesan house under a free contract that guaranteed them a share of the overall profits. Their new public personae gave them considerable stature, as the plethora of remarks and criticisms about their public behavior attests. The linkage of this public stature (or notoriety) with their new financial standing shaped their self-assessment.

The New Candidate for Lover

Courtesan houses were strongly focused on the entertainment business, and courtesans repeated that focus in their public performances. Their success and their new status in the settlements also offered them a new option, namely the development of a private and personal realm. For courtesans to realize this opportunity, social acceptance had to be secured and new spaces had to be created. The first sign of this claim of a separation between business concerns and private desires was having a nonpaying lover, which was called keeping a "graciously supported guest" (*enke*). In the early days, these relationships were kept secret. For top courtesans there was a potential conflict between entertaining clients and having a lover on the side; the efforts to keep the latter a secret signals the courtesan's attempt to keep her business intact while also following her private desires. Had her clients and especially the man who committed himself as patron found out about the existence of such a lover, she would have found herself in the awkward situation of being in effect the sponsor of this other man, who himself was unable or unwilling to finance the costly life of a courtesan.

The men chosen by the leading courtesans as their lovers, however, were not impoverished brilliant men of letters but most often opera singers. This choice exacerbated the problem dramatically. Becoming involved with an actor had been a taboo of long standing in the courtesan community, as actors were at the lowest of all social ranks, even beneath the courtesans. There seems to have been a custom that an actor would bow when meeting a courtesan;[7] this was based on the assumption that one day a courtesan might marry and become a concubine of a man of good family (*liangjia*), while actors remained in the slave cast (*nuji*) and were forbidden to marry a girl from such a *liangjia*. An actors' descendants, furthermore, were for three generations after abandoning this profession banned from participating in the Imperial Examinations.[8] During the Ming and Qing periods, young actors were trained to also serve powerful patrons as male prostitutes (*xianggong*).[9] Against this background, the courtesans' choice enraged connoisseurs and clients; it was unthinkable for them to share their privileges with a courtesan and then stand by idly as the courtesan shared those privileges with an actor. As long as the lover was kept secret, the face of the patron was, at least to a point, saved. But given the attention focused on these new stars, the newspapers, including as we shall see the *Shenbao*, could not forfeit such sensational news, and given the growing self-confidence of these courtesans, they made less and less effort to keep their lovers in the closet but began actually parading them around. In short, the secret was quickly in the open. Finally, this choice was seen as a debasement of the courtesan high cultural tradition. As many courtesans eventually were married to men of wealth or from good families and as it was assumed that this was all these women aspired to, this brazen behavior of the top courtesans put in doubt their suitability for this traditional role, not to mention their willingness to strive for it.

In Shanghai, the actual social status of actors was undergoing a momentous transformation, a transformation that eventually would propel some of them into national superstar roles in the coming decades. In the Shanghai foreign settlements, theater began to flourish after the Taiping War. As part of the emerging star system, the Shanghai theaters were organized from the beginning according to a different principle than the tradition long established in Beijing. Shanghai theaters owned their own basic troupe but invited lead singers from Beijing and Tianjin, who were singled out from the troupe to which they belonged. Coming as guest performers to Shanghai to lead the theater's program for a certain period, these singers were rewarded with extremely high payment.[10] Their work was then backed up by ample publicity and additional financial rewards. In this process, Shanghai set the stage for yet another new public personality, the actor as an individual star, and for the emergence of the star system.

The rise of the lead actor into stardom coincided with the Shanghai courtesan's interest in actors as lovers. Increasingly, the lead actor shared the limelight in the entertainment world with the courtesan. While he was thus entering the fray with a newly gained sense of his own importance, the power dynamics between the courtesan and the actor still gave the courtesan the initiative, since it is she who would see him perform in public and be the one to choose and pick. Actors, on the other hand, still were barred from entering courtesan establishments because of their inferior social status.

The new system of inviting actors to Shanghai thus ensured a regular supply of new talented singers. By the 1890s, it had become such a fashion among the top Shanghai courtesans to have an opera singer as lover that the entertainment newspapers could report on a fierce competition among the courtesans to catch the lead actors. The winner could claim that she had what it takes to be a leader in the world of courtesan entertainment.[11]

It is said that the fashion of going after actors was set by two of the most famous courtesans of the 1870s, Li Qiaoling and Hu Baoyu.[12] When Li Qiaoling took the unusual step of marrying Huang Yueshan, one of the most famous actors at the time, Wang Tao, the main authority on the early years of Shanghai-foreign-settlement courtesan entertainment, lamented, "Alas, such a downfall for a leading courtesan! All her sisters in the same profession have nothing but scorn for her [for marrying an actor]."[13]

Not all courtesans shared this attitude towards actors, and certainly not Hu Baoyu. Her love affair with the female impersonator Shisan dan became legendary. When she was pursuing him, she reportedly was already having an affair with another actor, Kang Heier. But it was her affair with Shisan dan that made her famous (or infamous). According to one of the earlier biographies on Shanghai courtesans published by the *Shenbao guan* in 1884—a story quoted and elaborated upon in many later collections of courtesan biographies—Hu Baoyu fell so deeply in love with Shisan dan that she abandoned her courtesan business in Shanghai to pursue him when he left for Beijing. Taking one maid with her, she took the steamship to Tianjin, where he came to meet her. At the time, this was an extraordinary way for a woman to proceed. It created quite a stir and was promptly reported in the *Shenbao*. When he fell out of love with her (or the other way around) and she had to return to Shanghai and reopen her business, the news of her return again made it into the news.[14] Reportedly, her business soon became even more prosperous than before.[15] According to a later biography, the reason for the affair's demise was that it caused Shisan dan to be jeered at by his companions and male patrons, and so he quickly abandoned Hu Baoyu.[16]

Shanghai New Space for Amorous Pursuits

The Theater

With the opening up of different types of public places such as parks, theaters, and Western-style restaurants, together with easily available transportation and more importantly, a Western-style city management that did not exclude women from these public places, Shanghai had by the end of the nineteenth century became a space for what might be called "private love" (as opposed to family-arranged marriages). The pursuit of this type of love affair involved a variety of persons and a variety of reasons. A pair of runaway lovers could come to the foreign settlements of Shanghai, and they would be able to find private living quarters for rent with very little community interference; in the city, courtesans who married rich men and did not want to join their extended families and live under the power of the main wives could rent apartments in the foreign settlements and set up their own households; to carry out their love affairs, courtesans and opera singers often rented a third dwelling for their meetings. Thus, together with its public places, it was the cultural and civic structure of the city that formed the foundation to create this new type of space for "private love."

By far the most controversial public place in Shanghai was the theater, because it was open to women. By contrast, Beijing's theaters admitted women only after 1900, in the aftermath of the Boxer Rebellion and the invasion by the Allied forces.[17] From the very beginning, women attended the theater in the foreign settlements. This was reported in the *Shenbao* from the time the newspaper was founded in 1872. The trend might have been started by courtesans, since courtesan guides from that time noted that it had become part of their business to accompany clients to the theater.

The courtesan's forming private love relationships with opera actors they had first admired onstage highlights the Shanghai theater as a public place. With their audiences of both sexes, Qing officials saw these theaters as a threat to public morals. The issue was brought to a head in 1874 with the case against the *wusheng* (martial) actor Yang Yuelou, who had married the daughter from a good family with the consent of the mother but against the later objections of her extended family. He was sent to the district town prison, tortured, tried, and sentenced to exile and hard labor in Xinjiang, while his bride was married off to some old man as a concubine.[18] Needless to say, the young woman had fallen in love with him while attending his performances at the Dangui chayuan theater.

Shortly thereafter, Shen Youdan, the *Daotai* of Shanghai at the time, tried to issue a public order prohibiting women from attending the theater. It was never officially put up because all the theaters were located in foreign settlements and prior consent of the foreign authorities was required. This he had not succeeded in securing and without that consent, the order was not enforceable. Thus only the draft of the order was published in the *Shenbao*.[19] The article quotes the Chinese judge sitting at the Mixed Court, who stated that this order was also not enforceable because theater was one of the important business locales for the courtesans; to ban them from attending (and deprive the clients at the same time of the chance to enjoy themselves in their company) was not a solution to the problem.

At the same time, the *Shenbao* carried a public and controversial discussion on the pros and cons of women attending the theater. An article entitled "On Prohibiting Women from Going to the Theater" argued that at least half the women in the Shanghai foreign settlements were courtesan entertainers or prostitutes. Even if the order was intended to affect women in general, the courtesans still would go to the theater as part of their business; they would use their influence to prompt the foreign authorities to be lenient with them. If it was directed only at women of good family, and the aim was to shame them from going out of fear of being taken for courtesans, by what means could these women be identified? And who was to decide which woman was from a good family and thus was breaking the law? How was the court supposed to handle such a caseload every day? Furthermore, the author argues that theater can be a very educational place where women can be taught Confucian values. The problem of women falling for the beautiful actors occured only because the lives of these women were so sheltered that they were inexperienced. Once they had become regular theatergoers, this problem would be solved.[20]

In a Bamboo twig ballad published early in 1874 in the *Shenbao*, two weeks after the other articles about women attending opera performances, the amorous dimension this theater experience was supposed to have for women was detailed. Entitled "A Bamboo Twig Ballad on Women Attending the Theater" (*Funü kanxi zhuzhici*), it relates the story of a famous opera troupe invited to town (Shanghai is not explicitly mentioned) and all the women getting extremely excited and sending their maids to secure the best places. The most attractive clothes are laid out the night before, but the excitement robs the women of their sleep. They rise early to see what kind of a day it will be, then follow a meticulous makeup and dressing routine. Once at the stage (or theater), all these women do is to look at each other and compare their outfits and ornaments as they enjoy the attentions of men. They then compare these dashing unknown young men with their husbands, who are neither fashionable nor handsome, and bemoan their bad luck. As the show goes on, the heart and mind of each of the women gets more and more confused and dazzled. When she reaches home, her longing and regret strain her looks, and her fantasy of an amorous affair makes her despair and become sad. The poem ends with the warning that it would have been best never to have entered the theater, for it is nothing but the realm of emptiness.[21]

In Shanghai the theater was a daily affair, and the interaction between male and female, audience and actor was part of an evolving urban lifestyle. The Shanghai theater with its audience and even actors from both sexes thus was a unique public place of private contention, especially among women, with the visiting actors from Beijing being the main target.

It is a signal of the public attention these affairs received that they were at times even reported in *Shenbao*, which in turn magnified their importance. One of the first cases so reported involved Li Qiaoling and Hu Baoyu, and, as I have mentioned, they were later blamed for starting the trend of courtesans' pursuing actors. The paths of these two courtesans now and then crossed unpleasantly over an actor pursued by both. According a biography of Hu Baoyu, the first time was over the *wusheng* (martial) actor Huang Yueshan. In this case Li Qiaoling was victorious as she became his wife a few years later. In the second case, the fight was over the *dan* (female impersonator) actor Shisan dan.

Under the title "A Virago Robber," the newspaper reported an incident of the previous evening when Shisan dan was performing at the Dangui shuyuan. Li Qiaoling had taken for herself the theater box reserved by Hu

Baoyu, and when Hu confronted the theater manager with this transgression, the manager was insolent to Baoyu. In anger, Baoyu smashed a teacup that had been prepared for Qiaoling. A few days later, when Baoyu went to the Daguanyuan theater also to see Shisan dan, she met Qiaolin, whose husband Huang Yueshan was a co-owner of the theater. Qiaoling began to curse Baoyu and the two got into a fist fight, ending with Baoyu the loser.[22]

By the 1890s, private love affairs (outside normal business transactions) between courtesans and actors were accepted as perhaps undesirable but inevitable. When these affairs spilled over into love affairs between actors and concubines of men of good standing however, public reactions were quite different. As we have seen, the question of public morals and the theater as a locale where people of both sexes gathered was a big issue with Qing officials. In most cases, the actor and the concubine involved were taken to court by the woman's husband, and both lovers were severely punished. Here the basic social order was under threat. In fact these concubines might once have been courtesans, but because of their new situation, a different set of rules was in force.[23] By being on the margin of social order, the courtesans had more leeway in designing their private and professional life.

Parks and Carriages as New Spaces for Love

The notion that a park could be public came from the West. By the turn of the century, Shanghai could boast many such public institutions.[24] As the rules governing behavior in these places had not yet been established and accepted within the community, they were a source for conflict. Perhaps surprisingly, the Western-style horse-drawn carriage belonged to the same category. As private property, it was clear who was entitled to ride in it. But because the carriage was a transportation vehicle that ran on public streets, the questions of how to drive it and how to behave while in it continuously generated conflicts and controversies, as in the case of public parks. The boundaries governing these new types of spaces were open for definition. The Shanghai courtesans exploited these new domains, making them into a public space for private love. In the process, they unwittingly were instrumental in defining the rules for them.

When a top-ranking courtesan like Lin Daiyu was caught by a Sikh policeman in the dark of the night while making love to opera singer Zhao Xiaolian in her carriage on a secluded road, the news made it into the *Dianshizhai Illustrated Magazine.* Under the title "The Startling Separation of the Mandarin Ducks," the paper reported (with illustration):

> In Shanghai there is a *jiaoshu* (courtesan honorific) Lin Daiyu who is extremely skilled in the battle for selecting [lovers] and has the reputation of a woman who travels between rivers [has many lovers at the same time]. Although she has encountered many men, there [appear] to be none to match the sexual skills of the martial actor Zhao Xiaolian from the theater Tianxian chayuan. Totally devoted [to each other], they are as close as if stuck with paint and glue. [In contrast] she treats the men of position and consequence as though they are dirt. Recently after just recovering from illness and with her health still fragile, she was nonetheless as always full of licentious desires. When all was quiet at night, she would, in a reverse role, get herself over to his house to continue there where they had left off last.
>
> Two nights ago the two of them left Zhao's place hand in hand and rode off in a carriage driven by the chauffeur Fuyuan to visit the Yu and Zhang gardens. At once their sexual desires overtook them, and they gave orders to Fuyuan to drive to the shady and quiet lane of Wangjia ku, which is all enclosed by vegetation, and there proceeded to make love [in the carriage]. Unexpectedly, a Sikh policemen patrolling on horseback saw them and came close to the carriage, yelling out that they were under arrest. The two of them got into quite a fright; they were obliged to end their lovemaking and were led away by the policeman to the police station.[25]

The story ends with the two lovers on their knees begging for mercy, and the police chief taking pity on them and releasing them with a warning that if they were caught again they would be brought before the court. The illustration focuses on the aftermath, showing the two on their knees in front of a standing foreign police officer and the carriage with the chauffeur waiting outside the police station.

Although evidently having fun at the expense of Lin Daiyu, this report reveals to what degree Shanghai's public space and the Western-style carriage were used by top-ranking courtesans like Lin Daiyu as a space within which they could conduct their private affairs. After falling in love with actors, they publicly paraded their lovers by driving in an open carriage to the gardens, a classical route on which courtesans normally took their clients.

The definition of the public park as a space for private love was even more controversial, as we can see from a case involving the courtesan Lu Lanfen and her actor lover Zhao Xiaolian. The same Zhao Xiaolian who had once been Lin Daiyu's lover but had been dropped by Lin became Lu Lanfen's lover. Late one evening, Lu Lanfen and Zhao Xiaolian were seen by Zhu Weifu, one of Lu Lanfen's clients, as they were hobnobbing in Arcadia, the Zhang Garden teahouse built in Western-style architecture. As this client was very passionate about Lu Lanfen, he was extremely jealous. He sent his chauffeur to bring some friends, whom he promised to pay handsomely afterward, and they

Figure 6.1.

planned to ambush Zhao Xiaolian and beat him up. Meanwhile, Zhao realized the danger he was in and sent his servant to summon other actors to come to his rescue, among them a martial actor who brought his knives. The park became a battleground with both sides charging at each other. The fight was broken up by the owner of the park and the owner of Tianxian Theater, to which the actor belonged. The event, however, was noted by the police as a major public disturbance, and they pressed charges against Zhu Weifu and Zhao Xiaolian. In the end, the client had to pay a huge fine, Zhao Xiaolian was reprimanded, and the actor who had carried a weapon was sentenced to carry the wooden cangue and to be evicted from the foreign settlements upon his release. To dissociate herself from this event, Lu Lanfen (who at that time was still called Hu Yue'e) changed her name to Lu Lanfen, the name under which she now is known.[26]

In this story, the park, a public space normally used by courtesans in the course of their entertainment business, was used for Lu's private affair. One might argue that Lu Lanfen was making a point in publicly staging her claim for a private life and love realm not shielded from the public eye. Another possibility is that there was genuine confusion in defining the demarcation between the public and the private, since these were such new concepts. Her client's reaction upon seeing the pair in the Arcadia meant that he considered this a time and space in which she was to be with him. Her taking her lover for an excursion was seen by him as a provocation and a loss of face. The fight between the two men was thus one over time, space, and face and was caused by the installment of a "private" realm by the courtesans.

Sidi: A New Kind of Love Nest

A private love affair, finally, needed a new intimate space outside work. Courtesans, especially those who were famous, initially tried hard to conceal their private love affairs from the public. Most often these affairs took place at neither the courtesan house nor the lodgings of the actor but at a secretly rented place that at the time was referred to as *sidi* or *sifang*—private dwelling.[27] The term is meant to contrast with the family house *fu* or *zhai*, where an extended family resides. Again, it is the Shanghai foreign settlements where such a private space that very much prefigures the later features of the bourgeois urban "love space" could be had. As these houses were not cheap, only well-paid lead actors and top-ranking courtesans could afford them. Often, much of the information about these new spaces comes from sensational events that made it into the press for quite other reasons. In the story of a triangle love affair Lu Lanfen was having with a businessman who owned a cloth-dying business and the martial actor Li Jihong, she resided first with the one and later with the other in such a house. The story became known because it ended tragically; according to one source, Li Jihong was so jealous of the businessman that he brought his friends from the theater to beat him up, and the businessman died shortly afterward.[28]

Inventing the Private Realm

Top-ranking courtesans such as Hu Baoyu and later Lin Daiyu, Lu Lanfen, or Zhang Shuyu might have affairs with actors, but they did not marry them. The relationship with an actor as conducted by these courtesans was strictly for private passion and pleasure. Although Lin Daiyu, for example, was married more than once, it was never to an actor. Marriage remained a decision based on social and financial considerations rather than matters of the heart. In this respect, Li Qiaoling's case was a rather rare exception.

The establishment of such a private realm of love involved a dissociation of the candidates for love from traditional business associations, a recarving of space and time to make place for this realm, and an exclusion of the monetary concerns which otherwise were very much at the center of courtesan entertainment. The two different kinds of "love affairs" were clearly separated: the client pays and the actor as lover does not. In their roles as entertainers the courtesans would often refer to themselves as businesswomen (*shengyi lang* [*shang*]*ren*) "doing business" (*zuo shengyi*) This "professionalization" of entertainment activities that before had engulfed their entire existence opened the space for a "private" realm. Between doing business and getting married as a concubine (in their terms, *ren jia ren*), there now was a third option.[29] Taking an actor as lover was neither part of the entertainment business nor the search for a suitable partner for marriage but was an event solely of her private concern.

There was, however, a public understanding of the role and expected behavior of courtesans, and the active recrafting of their life arrangement by the courtesans in the Shanghai settlements challenged this understanding. A courtesan was supposed to be skilled in entertaining a client and in arousing passion and desire in him without focusing on her own entertainment, passion, or desire. Private love affairs had no place in this concept, least of all with men of lower social standing, and the fact that no money was involved puzzled the critics and irritated the clients.

As the story goes, when Lin Daiyu was attacked for taking actors as lovers, she excused herself by claiming that they were (private) medicine for her very personal well-being.[30] In reality these relationships were often more complex. When Lin Daiyu married an official with a position in Nanhui county, she moved there with him, but she also took her lover at the time, the martial actor Li Chunlai, along with her. When her husband found out, he ended the marriage.[31] Later in the early years of the Republican period, she fell in love with Long Xiaoyun, an actor with the Dangui Theater, and openly set up house with him as husband and wife. Long became Lin Daiyu's kept man and was completely supported by her. She not only financed their livelihood but also hired teachers to educate Long both in Chinese and in a Western language so that he could make something out of his life. Using her connections, she later found him a post in the military office of the government, but he was forced to leave it due to protests from colleagues who had found out about his actor's background. When he returned to Shanghai and found that Lin Daiyu's resources were exhausted, he began an affair with another courtesan. According to her biographer, Lin Daiyu regarded his manipulative use of her as one of the most painful episodes of her life.[32]

A love affair needs time. To create opportunities for these private feelings to be lived out, the courtesans created a time "outside work." As we have seen, Lin Daiyu and Lu Lanfen found a time late at night to meet their lovers. This time also fit the actors' schedule, since it occurred after the evening's performance. Thus, many stories regarding the courtesan and the actor take place late at night. Like the public spaces, time was also a difficult category to define in the new public versus private context. As the stories demonstrated, the borders between the two time zones were still fluid and contested. The late evening could very well also be the time a courtesan and her patron spent together. When Lu Lanfen and her actor lover went out together, Lu's client Zhu was abroad, and her transgressions were amplified by her failure to accompany him on his trip.

The time/space question was played out in a scene described in the novel *Biographies of Shanghai Flowers* (*Haishang hua liezhuan*), first published in 1892. A long-term client unexpectedly arrives at the house of a courtesan and discovers his beloved in bed with an actor. This took place within the courtesan house, but in a room in the back of the main living quarters called *tingzi jian*, a small room created out of an enclosed balcony. This architectural feature was unique to the Shanghai settlements, and the space was accordingly based on a Western architectural tradition. The time was late at night when the courtesan thought the client would not be coming. Even after the client had appeared in the house, the courtesan continued with the actor, assuming the client had gone straight to sleep.

Two points in this story are of interest to our discussion. The courtesan seems to have treated her bedroom as a business premise reserved for clients, while the small room in the back of the house—a room with only a spare bed without curtains—was considered by the courtesan as her private space where she could act as she pleased.[33] Furthermore, the time being late at night, the courtesan assumed her duties for the day were over, and this was her private and leisure time. Through a reinterpretation of the space within her business premises and of her duties in terms of time, the courtesan in the story was silently pushing for a redefinition of the borders defining her professional life.

In the novel, a remark by the courtesan indirectly reveals the public perception of high-ranking courtesans taking actors as lovers. In her attempted self-defense, the courtesan claims that it was completely implausible for her to have an affair with an actor, for that was the common pasttime only of the most successful and famous courtesans. They could be "looking for some fun" (*zhao le zi*) because they were powerful enough not to care what clients thought of their virtues as professional entertainers. Having an actor lover had in fact become a sign of success for the courtesan.[34] This new personal freedom was based on the increasing independence of the top-ranking courtesans both in financial terms and in terms of their own growing social status, while their use of this new freedom also enhanced their standing.

The creation of this private time/space was instrumental in the development of a private sphere of life away from work for courtesan and actor alike. As we have seen, this arrangement was soon picked up and developed by courtesans, who moved out of their courtesan houses to share a flat with a patron who had become their exclusive lover for the time being. The courtesans' private love forays into spaces considered "public" such as the parks opened these spaces for their eventual use by others. By the Republican period, they had become the preferred and romantic place of private encounters between young urban lovers who had no private apartment to withdraw to and therefore chose public anonymity in the shade of trees and the darkness of night. At the same time, meeting in public meant that they were keeping things largely within the limits of propriety.

One might think that the notion of private space was connected to a desire for secrecy that for the dwellings is actually indicated by the term *si.* As an entertainer, a top-ranking courtesan would seem to want her reputation preserved and to appear fully devoted to those who paid for her services. It was standard practice of that period for a *changsan* courtesan to have one patron at a given time, and the financial obligations of this patron were substantial. A patron who discovered that the courtesan had a secret love on the side may feel obliged to leave her if for no reason other than to save face. The rapidly changing urban society of the foreign settlements and the new position of the actor, however, changed this logic. For the courtesan to show herself in public with her actor lover—now a rising star, adored by theatergoers and in general the object of passion for female and male alike—ended up in enhancing her own standing and attractiveness. As she must have been fully aware of the risks involved, the fact that she made no efforts to keep things a secret attests to the rising public acclaim of the actor.

The newspapers, and in particular the entertainment papers, generally continued to view such relationships as scandalous, but they did have news value. Their reporting might have ruined some chances for the courtesans, quite apart from giving the journalists a chance to vent their anger at being marginalized in the favors of the courtesans, but obviously the courtesans' self-confidence and income as entertainers were solid enough for them to take this risk. By then they had learned that sensational press reporting would not necessarily hurt them even if it was critical. The benefits of being seen as having caught a lead actor would increase one's status in the world of courtesans and possibly even among clients. As one contemporary observer exclaimed in dismay, "Courtesans are numerous; if one does not take an actor as lover, she can never distinguish herself from the crowd."[35]

The Shanghai Way of Life

The love affairs between courtesans and actors signaled the degree of independence these two groups of entertainers had achieved by the late Qing. As their protection depended more and more on the Shanghai treaty-port business environment and their own rising professional position, their traditional reliance on powerful patrons was reduced and, with it, their willingness to abide by the value judgments of the patron. There was, to be sure, a legal and material basis for the development of this private relationship and lifestyle. This basis was provided only by the Shanghai foreign settlements. While the differences in the legal environment for courtesan and actor between the foreign settlements and the rest of the Qing empire are evident, a look at the material conditions under which courtesan and actor publicly paraded each other in Shanghai shows how peculiar the new development was to this locale. The walled district town of Shanghai just across the Yangjingbang Creek makes this distinction amply clear. There, the streets were too narrow for horse-drawn carriages, for decades courtesans were forbidden from entering the parks, and there was no opera theater until early in the twentieth century when the New Stage (*Xin wutai*) was built, although even it was outside of the prefecture proper.[36] The outraged newspaper reporting in Shanghai catered to the comforting domestic morals of its readers while at the same time providing them with exciting news from the novel environment to which, after all, they had moved on their own initiative.

In 1899, the *Youxi bao* claimed that courtesans courting actors had become such a pervasive trend that it was no longer expected to be otherwise.[37] When Li Boyuan, the late Qing political novelist and the founder of the *Youxi bao*, held one of the paper's first "flower competitions" among the Shanghai courtesans, he claimed that if one of the criteria for participation would be not having actors as lovers, there would be no candidates left for the top ranks.[38] In 1918, a Beijing entertainment newspaper went so far as to publish "The Chart of Alliances between Prostitutes and Actors" (*Chang you lianhe biao*) listing the relationships between Shanghai courtesans and actors.[39]

Gradually irritation about these willful choices of the top courtesans gave way to a reluctant acceptance of this new urban way of life. An article in 1899 in the *Youxi bao* signals such a change. A client of a courtesan was holding a dinner party at her house, but she did not show up the whole evening. In his anger, the host tried to find out what had happened, only to discover that while his party was on, she did not have obligations to other clients but was making love with an actor.[40] There was no outcry. A few months later the paper even defended a courtesan star's antics.[41]

Why did the opera actors rather than other groups of men qualify as the preferred lovers of the top courtesans in Shanghai between the 1880s and the early 1910s? Opera actors were men of great public attraction, and their status within the new urban theater scene in Shanghai was growing. To catch such a prize was a challenge and a triumph, apart from greatly contributing to the fantasy image of the courtesan. For the courtesan, the criterion for choosing a lover obviously was different from that pertaining to a patron. Actors were often considered very handsome and well built, yet their social standing hardly qualified them to make trouble when dropped.

Underlining this choice of the courtesan was a new understanding of the question of class and status. For some of the late Qing intellectuals, it was shocking that the courtesans failed to take into consideration that their choice of actors for lovers was, in the eyes of society, self-degrading. In their eyes, the class and status of a woman was defined and redefined according to her association with a man. By choosing the actor in the full knowledge of this assumption, the courtesan in fact sported and personified the new modern notion of free love, which in its ideal form is based not on family approval or income and status consideration but on one's feelings. By choosing the actor, the courtesan signaled not only a new time/space construction but the coming of a new lifestyle in which the traditional rules governing the relationship between a man and a woman were challenged.

While we have a great deal of evidence indicating that top courtesans of this time found it fashionable to pursue actors as their private lovers, rare are the sources explaining to us in straight words what made these men preferable. One document, noted down only in 1928, allows us to have a glimpse at the emotional choices open to courtesans, and their ensuing strategies.

The position of love and marriage in the life of a courtesan was structured very much like that of the rest of society. It was difficult for courtesans to refuse a proposal of marriage from a man of good family with sound financial backing. Although their feelings toward the man are important, many courtesan biographies show us that emotions were not the decisive factor. The decision involves money, social position, and, if they are in bondage to a madam, the madam's opinion as well. On the part of a man who wanted to marry a courtesan, the consideration was exactly opposite. The marriage to his main wife had been arranged by the parents, and many social and financial matters had gone into this choice, but little of his personal feelings. As the courtesan was to become his concubine, this marriage depended entirely on his feelings toward her. The courtesan's passion and sexual fantasies were marginal to the decision, and in fact they could get in the way of a reasonable settlement for her future. Chen Wuwo quotes one client who, during the late Qing, had asked a courtesan, "Why an actor?" Her answer:

> In our profession as courtesans, we have seen a lot of people and we are not keen on getting close to anyone. The most important thing for us is whether we are "birds of the same kind" [with a lover, having mutual understanding]. Only then do we offer our body and heart. But among the wealthy clients today, even though they hold high positions within the state, are wealthy, and come from prominent families, on average, when seen from outside, we are unimpressed by their parochial manners; and when seen from within, we are again unimpressed by their meager airs. Thus it often happens that they are inferior to the actors. Therefore, with them, we only go for their wealth, but cannot give them our hearts![42]

The love for an actor is thus defined as a matter of the heart. The dilemma between social and financial considerations, on the one hand, and love, on the other, is nothing new; what is new is the way the Shanghai courtesans went about resolving it. By straightforwardly creating separate time and space for their business and matters of the heart, they insisted on continuing as professional and highly paid entertainers while enjoying the leeway and freedom of a private life of private passions.

Notes

1. For the move from the Shanghai prefecture to the foreign settlements see Wang Liaoweng, *Shanghai liushi nian huajie shi* (Sixty years of the Shanghai flower world) (Shanghai: Shixin shuju, 1922), section *yi*, "Jiyuan didian guize paibie yan ge" (On the transformation of courtesan house's location, rituals, and types), 1–2; Xue Liyong, "Ming Qing shiqi de Shanghai changji" (Shanghai prostitution during the Ming and Qing periods), 150–58; Christian Henriot, *Prostitution and Sexuality in Shanghai: A Social History, 1849–1949* (Cambridge: Cambridge University Press, 2001), 22–25.

2. On the legal status of courtesans under Qing law see Matthew H. Sommer, *Sex, Law, and Society in Late Imperial China* (Stanford, Calif.: Stanford University Press, 2000), 210–59; Wang Shunu, *Zhongguo changjie shi* (The history of prostitution in China) (Shanghai: Sanlian shudian), 261–63.

3. For a study on the late Ming nostalgia of Shanghai men of letters, see Catherine Yeh (Ye Kaidi), "Wenhua jiyi de fudan—Wan Qing Shanghai wenren dui wan Ming lixiang de jiangou" (The burden of cultural memory: The construction of the late Ming ideal by late Qing Shanghai *wenren*), in *Wan Ming yu wan Qing: Lishi chuanchen yu wenhua chuangxi*, ed. Chen Pingyuan, Wang Dewei (David Wang), and Shang Wei (The late Ming and the late Qing: Historical dynamics and cultural innovations) (Wuhan: Hubei xiaoyu chubanshe, 2002), 53–63.

4. The most important narrative on these relationships between the courtesans and literati was Yu Huai (1616–1696), *Banqiao zaji* (Random notes on [the pleasure quarters by] the wooden bridge), first published 1654, reprint in Zhang Tinghua, ed., *Xiangyan congshu* (A collection of books on fragrant beauty), orig. 1908, 5 vols. (reprint, Beijing: Renmin wenxue chubanshe, 1992), series 13, chap. 3, 4:3637–72.

5. See Catherine Vance Yeh, *City, Courtesan and Intellectual: The Rise of Shanghai Entertainment Culture 1850–1910*, (Seattle: University of Washington Press, 2005). It contains chapters on courtesan public behavior and its social impact. I here give just a very short summary of my findings.

6. See Henriot, *Prostitution and Sexuality*, 233–34.

7. Langyou zi, *Haishang yanhua suoji* (Miscellaneous notes on Shanghai flowers) (Block print, Shanghai, 1877), 3:8.

8. During the eighteenth century, a part of the laws restricting entertainers was lifted, but in reality the social status of the actor changed very little; for details, see Anders Hansson, *Chinese Outcasts: Discrimination and Emancipation in Late Imperial China* (Leiden: Brill, 1996), 42, 163–64; Sommer, *Sex, Law, and Society*, 270–72.

9. See Colin Mackerras, *The Rise of the Peking Opera* (Oxford: Clarendon, 1972), 151–53.

10. In the Beijing system, a troupe was independent from the theater; they only rented the space and divided the proceeds. For a preliminary study, see Catherine Yeh, "Where is the Center of Cultural Production? The Rise of the Actor to National Stardom and the Beijing/Shanghai Challenge (1860s–1910s)," *Late Imperial China* 25 no. 2 (December 2004): 74–118.

11. Chen Boxi, *Shanghai yishi daguan* (A collection of anecdotes on Shanghai's past) (first edition entitled *Lao Shanghai*, 1919; reprint, Shanghai: Shanghai shudian chubanshe, 2000), 433.

12. Lao Shanghai (Wu Jianren), *Hu Baoyu* (Hu Baoyu), first published 1907 (reprint in *Shinmatsu shôsetsu kenkyû* no. 14, 1991), 128.

13. Wang Tao, *Haizou yeyou fulu* (A supplement to *Record of visits to the courtesan houses in a distant corner of the sea*), Preface 1873, first published in Hong Kong, 1883; reprint in Zhang Tinghua, ed., *Xiangyan congshu*, series 20, chap. 2, 5:5685–786, 5720.

14. Xiaolantian chanqing shizhe (Tian Chunhang), *Haishang qunfang pu* (A register of Shanghai flowers) (Lithograph, Shanghai: Shenbao guan, 1884), 4:11.

15. Xiaolantian chanqing shizhe (Tian Chunhang), *Haishang qunfang pu*, 10–11. According to Wang Tao, the name of the actor was Heier, see his *Haizou yeyou fulu*, 5750; Zou Tao, *Chunjiang huashi* (Flowers from the Spring River) (block print, Shanghai, 1884), 1:13.

16. Lao Shanghai, *Hu Baoyu*, 128–29.

17. Beijingshi yishu yanjiusuo and Shanghai yishu yanjiusuo, eds., *Zhongguo jingju shi* (The history of Chinese opera) (Beijing: Zhongguo xiju chubanshe, 1990), 1:185.

18. For studies on the case, see Ye Xiaoqing, "Unacceptable Marriage and the Qing Legal Code: The Case of Yang Yuelou," *Journal of the Oriental Society of Australia* 27–28 (1995–1996): 195–212; Bryna Goodman, *Native Place, City, and Nation: Regional Networks and Identities in Shanghai, 1853–1937* (Berkeley: University of California Press, 1995), 111–17; Natascha Vittinghoff, "Readers, Publishers and Officials in the Contest

for a Public Voice and the Rise of a Modern Press in Late Qing China (1860–1880)," *T'oung Pao* 87 (2001): 393–455.

19. "Yizun ju pin yanjin funü ru guan kanxi gaoshi" (Public notice according to the draft form by his honorable magistrate on strictly forbidding women to enter theaters), *Shenbao*, Tongzhi 10 (January 7, 1873), 2.

20. "Jinzhi funü kanxi lun" (On "Strictly forbidding women to enter theaters"), *Shenbao*, January 6, 1874.

21. Lianxi tingxiangguan sumei xiaoshi, "Funü kanxi zhuzhici" (A bamboo twig ballad on women attending the theater), *Shenbao*, January 26, 1874, 2.

22. "Pofu qiangwu" (A Virago robber), *Shenbao*, November 11, 1878, 2.

23. For the case of Gao Caiyun see Catherine Yeh, "A Public Love Affair or a Nasty Game? The Chinese Tabloid Newspaper and the Rise of the Opera Singer as Star," *European Journal of Asian Studies* 3 (2003).

24. For one of the most famous controversies over the usage of the International Park, see Robert A. Bickers and Jeffrey Wasserstrom, "Shanghai's 'Dogs and Chinese Not Admitted' Sign: Legend, History and Contemporary Symbol," *China Quarterly* 142 (June 1995): 444–66.

25. "Jingsan yuanyang" (Startling the lovebirds), *Dianshizhai huabao, Yuan* (1897) 11:87; regarding the case, see also Chen Wuwo, *Lao Shanghai sanshi nian jianwen lu* (A record of things seen and heard by an old Shanghai hand in the last thirty years) (first published 1928; reprint, Shanghai: Shanghai shudian, 1997), 147–48.

26. Chen, *Lao Shanghai*, 56.

27. Chen, *Lao Shanghai*, 55.

28. Wang Liaoweng, "Huajian zhanggu" (Stories of courtesans), *Shanghai liushi nian huajie shi, Yibian*, 149–50.

29. Xue, "Ming Qing shiqi de Shanghai," 155.

30. Chen Wuwo, "Lin Daiyu yishi" (Anecdotes on Lin Daiyu), *Lao Shanghai*, 149.

31. Lao Shanghai, *Hu Baoyu*, 103.

32. Wang, *Shanghai liushi nian huajie shi*, 52.

33. Han Bangqing, *Haishang hua liezhuan* (Biographies of Shanghai flowers) (first published Shanghai, 1892–94; reprint of this illustrated lithography edition, Taibei: Huangguan zazhishe, 1987), 264.

34. Han, *Haishang*, 273.

35. The full quotation, "There are hundreds and thousands of courtesan establishments; if [a courtesan]did not take an actor as lover [she] would not be able to come out ahead from the crowd" (*Chu guan qin lou qianban bei, bu bing xizi tu chaoqun*); see Chen Wuwo, "Pin xizi you dao" (There is a reason for taking an actor as lover), *Lao Shanghai*, 30.

36. On the location of Shanghai theaters, see "Bai nian lai Shanghai liyuan de yange" (Changes in the Shanghai theater during the last hundred years) (Shanghai: Datong shuju, 1937), 2:44–60.

37. "Shimao guanren" (The fashionable courtesan), *Youxi bao*, May 6, 1899, 2.

38. Li Boyuan, "Youxi zhu da ke lun kai huabang zhi buyi" (The master of entertainment answers a visitor's comments on the difficulty of holding the flower competition), in Chen Wuwo, *Lao Shanghai*, 195.

39. See Chen, *Shanghai yishi,* 433–37; Wang, *Shanghai liushi nian,* section "Youxiwen," 137–40.

40. "Shimao guanren," 2.

41. "Lun Lu Lanfen pin dahualian shi" (On Lu Lanfen's taking a *dahualian* as lover), *Youxi bao,* July 18, 1899, 1–2.

42. Chen, "Pin xizi you dao," 30.

7

Unofficial History and Gender Boundary Crossing in the Early Republic

Shen Peizhen and Xiaofengxian

Madeleine Yue Dong

AMONG THE VERY FEW WOMEN whose names are remembered from the early Chinese Republic are Shen Peizhen and Xiaofengxian. They belonged to the two most visible groups of women in Beijing in the early years of the Republic, suffragists and prostitutes. In both cases, their notoriety resulted from their interactions with male politicians in Beijing. Shen went to the nominal capital city with her comrades to demand political rights for women; Xiaofengxian moved to Beijing from the south to take advantage of the flourishing entertainment business, where the most generous customers were officials of the new republican government.

On the surface, suffragists and prostitutes appear quite different. Suffragists—daughters and wives of elite families—were educated "new women" (*weixin nüzi*), some of whom had studied overseas. Most prostitutes came from poor families and entered their profession to make a living. However, while their class backgrounds were quite different, Shen and Xiaofengxian both became public figures because of their direct or indirect involvement in politics. Shen was a political activist whose work put her in constant contact with well-known politicians. Xiaofengxian's political activities, on the other hand, came through her relationship with Cai E, the famous general who led a rebellion against Yuan Shikai's monarchical restoration.

Despite their similar involvement with political men, Xiaofengxian eventually was adulated as virtuous and admirable, while Shen Peizhen was satirized as an unseemly woman. The different historical representations of these two women certainly had to do with their personal qualities but also reflected their contrasting positions in the gendered spatial order. They presented themselves in arguably two of the only urban spaces outside of the domestic where women and men mingled: the newly created political spaces and the brothels. But while Shen's actions altered gendered spatial relationships, those of Xiaofengxian confirmed them.

At issue in these differences is what constituted the public in the new Republic, and what the public meant in terms of gender relations and for women who had historically been consigned to domesticity. The appearance of women in spaces where they mingled with men challenged gender definitions as well as concepts of what constituted public space and stimulated extensive coverage in the newly emerging mass media. Media reports were obsessed with the mere sight of women in public spaces and their personal styles and behavior. In both the more formal newspapers that claimed to carry political discussions and in the popular readings that focused on private lives of eminent figures, representations of Shen and Xiaofengxian emphasized their relations to a gendered spatial order. It appears that the women's challenge to spatial propriety was more threatening than the potential consequences of their political agendas.

In addition to newspaper articles, sociological surveys, government documents, and other materials that historians conventionally study, this chapter analyzes representations of Shen Peizhen and Xiaofengxian in the popular genre *yeshi* (unofficial history),[1] in particular, Cai Dongfan's *Minguo yanyi* (Unofficial history of the Republic) and Tao Hancui's *Minguo yanshi yanyi* (Unofficial erotic history of the Republic).[2] *Yeshi* makes direct connections between the new Republican regime and gender relations by creating a narrative in which male politicians' relationships with women form the core, providing a rare opportunity for examining popular understandings of the connection between political and gender boundaries. Serving as the basis for storytelling, stage plays, and, in later times, movies and TV dramas, *yeshi* has a profound impact on society. *Yeshi* adopts historical chronology as an organizing frame but elaborates using anecdotes, gossip, and contemporary common sense. The genre thus enables the historian to move beyond state policies and elite discourses to access more popular perspectives on political events and social changes.[3]

From Shen Peizhen to Sun Beizhen

Once the Chinese Republic was established in 1912, women activists who had fought for the birth of the new regime pressed for citizenship with full political rights. After repeated petitions to leaders of the Republic, including Sun Yat-sen, the women were frustrated by indifference to their demand and turned to more radical measures, especially when the 1912 Provisional Constitution contained no clause on equal political rights between the two sexes. In March, the Hunan activist Tang Qunying led more than twenty women to a meeting of the senate, demanding that delegates discuss the issue of women's political rights. They ignored orders to sit in the auditors' section, took seats instead among the delegates, and argued loudly. Failing to locate the senators on the following day, they broke windows, fought with and injured guards, and took documents. Several days later, more than sixty women went to the senate again, this time carrying weapons. The gate was closed to prevent them from entering the building, and soldiers were dispatched to protect senate offices. On April 1, the provisional senate announced its election law, stipulating that only men who were twenty-five years or older were eligible for election into the senate.

In early April, Sun Yat-sen resigned from his position as the provisional president of the Republic. When Yuan Shikai assumed the presidency and moved the government to Beijing, the women followed. On August 13, Tang Qunying, Wang Changguo, and Shen Peizhen attended a meeting of the Revolutionary Alliance to discuss consolidating five political parties into the Nationalist Party. The program of the new party did not include equal rights between men and women, which enraged the three women members. Wang Changguo mounted the stage and hit Song Jiaoren, claiming that she was "venting anger on behalf of 200 million fellow women." At the Nationalist Party's inaugural meeting on August 25, 1912, at the *Huguang huiguan*, in front of several hundred representatives and three to four thousand spectators, including forty to fifty women,[4] female activists physically attacked Song Jiaoren again for eliminating the equal rights clause from the program. A vote, taken amid chaos, ended with little support for the women. This result was repeated on November 6, 1912, when the senate again discussed the women's petition. The suffragists' cause was vastly outvoted, effectively ending the early Republican women's suffrage movement.[5]

Media responses to the women's activities ranged from serious discussions of the issues to satires that ridiculed their efforts. Starting with Kong Hai's editorial, "Doubts on Women's Rights to Political Participation," *Minli bao* published a series of articles debating the issue. Justifying his points with the theory of evolution, Kong Hai argued that the natural order required men to work outside the home and manage the country's affairs and women to stay home, bearing children and taking care of the family. Breaking this system would harm society because family life was the foundation of social order. In short, politics was not in women's nature, which explained women's limited knowledge of politics.[6] When the woman activist Yang Jiwei wrote to the newspaper to argue that women's limitations resulted only from lack of opportunities and practice, Kong Hai replied that women were inherently weaker than men, both physically and intellectually. The repeated failure of regimes under the rule of women, such as Wu Zetian and Cixi, proved their violation of natural laws of evolution.[7]

The responses to Kong Hai included a letter from Zhang Renlan, a woman who had visited the United States. Zhang criticized the activists for being "neither men nor women, neither Chinese nor Western, neither monks nor nuns." Zhang argued that the family would be harmed if the activists, some of whom opposed marriage, got their way. This would result in the extinction of the Chinese nation. In her view, women's domestic duties were more onerous than men's, and a good woman should have no energy left for politics after caring for children, entertaining guests, cooking, and sewing. Men's working outside and women working inside was not inequality but a division of labor that belonged to the natural order of the world. This order also ensured harmony between the sexes. If the kind of freedom and equality the women activists were demanding prevailed, men and women would interfere with and fight against one another, preventing peace and tranquility. Zhang believed that this was contrary to freedom and equality.[8] It is noteworthy that both Zhang and Kong Hai glorified domestic duties: the domestic was pure, and politics was corrupt and "dirty."

The theme of breaking the gendered spatial order was continued in "Phenomena in the New Women's World" published in *Aiguo baihua bao* (Patriot vernacular). The article divides women activists into three categories according to their levels of education. The first class is criticized for blindly following Western women's examples in demanding political rights and ignoring Chinese reality. The motivation of these women is interpreted as desire for power. The second-class activists—the majority of them—are hardly educated and have no real ability. They run around every day without clear goals and never achieve anything. The opportunity to elevate their status as women reformers motivates them. The third class abandons all the rules that govern women's behavior. Groups of these women frequently present themselves at teahouses and markets, demonstrating and wandering around freely. The author sees the second- and third-class women as more dangerous than the first class for they are too loose (*fangzong*) and will harm social customs (*fengsu*) if their behavior is tolerated.[9]

In addition to direct attacks on the activists and their agenda, *Rizhi bao* (Daily learning) and *Aiguo baihua bao* published a series of satires that in many ways are more revealing of contemporary interpretations of the meanings of the women's suffrage movement. "Laws of the Provisionary Wife" stipulates that the wife organizes the family, controls all powers in it, and sets up rules for the husband to follow. She can freely leave the house, keep her own property, have extramarital affairs, control the couple's sex life, and divorce.

She can forbid her husband to go out at night or purchase a concubine. In contrast, the husband has the following rights: to petition the wife in bed, to take her to stores, theaters, and wine shops, to perform hard labor at night, to provide for the wife, and to entertain her.[10] "Explanations for the Regulations of the Women's Autonomous Association" suggests that the essence of women's liberation and freedom is to ensure the decline of women's moral quality. Members' activities such as appearing in theaters and temples are not to be restrained. The association studies strategies to resist the husband and to abuse in-laws. The association is located in the Village of New Beauties (*xinyan cun*) and will expand to the River of Love (*aihe*) and the Ocean of Desire (*yuhai*) once progress is made. The publication department of the association is headquartered at Street of Stealing Men (*touhan jie*), and officers are those members who can flirt and are good in bed.[11] "A Constitution for Equality between Men and Women" demands the president to allow brothels for male prostitutes to be set up across the country so that women can visit these places, hold tea parties and banquets, or stay overnight. Women have the freedom to purchase male concubines, but not to exceed one hundred. Men and women must get pregnant at the same time if they have sexual intercourse. Women give birth to girls; men give birth to boys. Men must wear flowers, face powder, and women's clothes, but out of respect for civilization, they are not required to bind their feet or pierce their ears. To correct a four-thousand-year problem and to demonstrate equality between men and women, in all written materials, the order of *nan nü qian kun fu qi* (man, woman, *qian, kun*, husband, wife) should be reversed to *nü nan qi fu kun qian.*[12]

Yeshi gives a face and name to all these offenses, which is Sun Beizhen, a figure modeled on Tang Qunying, Wang Changguo, and Shen Peizhen.[13] Tao Hancui's *Minguo yanshi yanyi* devotes three chapters to her. Sun is extraordinarily fat but wears a tight Western dress and a pair of glasses with a thin golden rim: "Although her appearance was repulsive, she was a 'new woman,' which was clear from her clothing." "According to herself, she has made major contributions to the success of the national revolution, but it is hard to tell from historical records what those contributions might be," the text comments. Articulate and lively, she jumps up to shout about freedom and equality during meetings. She is good at practicing her idea of equality between men and women—she does not feel any embarrassment inserting herself in a crowd of men.

Having established this image of Sun, the story describes her meeting with two male senators in her hotel room to discuss women's political participation. One of the senators originally has a date with a prostitute, but he shows up in her room "out of his fear of Sun." When the two men enter, Sun is lying in bed with her arms and legs outstretched, her big natural feet on the edge of the bed. The men are embarrassed, but she is not. She shakes hands with the men and calls the servant loudly to bring tea. After gulping down a whole cup of tea, she asks about opinions among the senators regarding the women's petition. Frightened by her appearance, the two men sheepishly answer, "The Republic emphasizes equality between men and women. Men have the right of political participation, why not women? Women should have the same right." Before the men can finish, Sun jumps in: "Yes, indeed. Men are human beings; women are human beings as well. They all have the same organs on their faces and four limbs; there is no difference between men and women. Why is it that men can be presidents, ministers, senators, and governors, but women can only manage the household for you men?"

In the middle of her eloquent delivery, Sun suddenly takes off her Western-style skirt and exposes a pair of pink flowery Chinese pants. She then sits on the chamber pot that is located in the same room and asks one of the men to hand her a cigarette and match. Smoking as she uses the pot, Sun continues to discuss women's rights, stating that the purpose of having a republican revolution is to give society freedom and equality. Quoting Madame Roland, Sun elaborates her new slogan that she would rather die than give up equality and freedom. While making a lot of noise on the chamber pot, she tells the men that she wants to be the Madame Roland of China, to fight for freedom and equality for Chinese women:

> Chinese men always treat women as playthings. We women live a pathetic life. Once we achieve equality between men and women, we will vent the anger and frustration of our 200 million fellow women by making the 200 million Chinese men wear powder and rouge on their faces, and bind their feet. . . . We will eliminate concubinage, or women will advocate male concubinage and male prostitution. If there are only female concubines and prostitutes and no males in those roles, what kind of equality between men and women is this?

After she has relieved herself, Sun calls the servant for a pair of scissors and starts cutting her toenails and scratching her disease-infected feet, all the time talking about freedom and equality. Sun finally dismisses the men after they have expressed their support for women's political participation. She then eats several cookies, drinks four cups of tea, sings some women's revolutionary songs, removes her leather shoes, and, carelessly wrapping herself in blankets, falls asleep on the bed, snoring loudly. The next day, Sun meets with a group of comrades in her hotel room, an event that ends with the overturning of the chamber pot filled by Sun the night before. One woman leaves the room covered in filth.

Sun and her comrades then go to a session of the senate to hear the discussion of their petition. Zhong Xiaorun (Song Jiaoren) claims that although women should have the right to political participation, Chinese women are too naïve to be involved in politics right away: "Many of the members of the association probably do not even understand what political participation means. . . . Allowing women into politics is both bad for them and for the country." Hearing these words, Sun jumps on the stage, grabs Zhong's tie, and slaps his face, with the women in the auditing seats chanting, "Hit him! Hit him!" Before she can strike again, the guards swarm in and drag her off the stage. Sun continues to stamp her feet and curse, and the meeting ends in chaos.[14]

In this story, Sun's main violation is apparently her transgression of gendered spatial order. Her inappropriate behavior, the story implies, results from her total lack of respect for basic gender boundaries. She stays in a hotel by herself and meets with men there, mixes with men, and has no sense of modesty. She is violent, publicly slapping a man's face. She is unfeminine: she carries a gigantic business card and has a loud voice, big feet, and a large, inelegant body. She talks too much and uses the new political vocabulary to excess. In short, she transgresses boundaries that spatially and behaviorally situate men and women in terms of political norms, cultural tradition, and historical practice. As David Strand argues:

> The violence of the protests was both real and symbolic, reflecting the militant and military background of many of the women and the deep sense of betrayal they felt when the full citizenship they had been promised was denied. If they were refused the legal status of voting citizens they could still act like citizens, and not in the more sedate and pliable form favored by many conservatively-minded politicians. Women who cut their hair short, walked unaccompanied in public, smoked cigarettes, and engaged in political acts like making speeches were liable to be stared at or worse. Brandishing weapons, shouting slogans, and laying hands on male delegates broke every Confucian taboo imaginable.[15]

The women's breaking of established gender codes, however, was often represented as threatening ideals central to the new republican order. One article in *Da ziyou bao* (Great liberty news, one of the many newly established and short-lived Beijing newspapers) saw the physical attack on Song Jiaoren as a demonstration of the suffragists' disrespect for law, public order, legal rights, civility, and progress.[16] Despite the fact that women were not allowed the same rights as men in the new system, they were nevertheless expected to respect the very law that denied them these rights. The new republican political ideals operate as a self-perpetuating system that excludes unwanted participation and maintains exclusion in the name of public order and law. The system, in theory, represents the interest of the public, which includes the whole population. In other words, the society produced by an equal republic should have no inside and outside—everyone is included—and any problem should be resolved by legal means within the system. But in this case, the women are treated as both subject to the new system and exterior to it, a troubling predicament that is not unfamiliar in the history of many modern nations.

The containment of unruly women, consequently, was to be achieved through republican ideals and institutions. Another article in the *Great Liberty News* suggests that instead of fighting for political participation, women should first reform their individual bodies:

> I have heard that among the enthusiasts for equal rights one woman has very small feet. When shouting at a man somewhere, she suddenly fell because her feet were small and weak. The man laughed and said: "You have to have equal feet first before you demand equal rights." . . . I will risk suggesting that instead of demanding political participation in the senate, our women compatriots should advocate a "natural feet society" in each county and prefecture. Instead of asking the Nationalist Party for equal rights in the constitution, you should set up more schools.[17]

These comments, if at first glance seem conservative, were in fact in accordance with the new ideal of feminine physical practices in the late Qing.[18]

Shen Peizhen was eventually contained, not by the old norms that she fought against, but by new republican institutions. In July 1915, Shen became the protagonist of a legal drama that entertained the capital city. After the Shanghai *Shenzhou ribao* published an article about her making a scene at a restaurant, Shen and a few friends of hers went to the paper's Beijing office to protest. The office was located in a courtyard shared with a family. As the result of an argument and fight between Shen and a man of that family, Guo Tong, a few household items were broken. Guo Tong sued Shen for breaking into his house and damaging his belongings. The media coverage was a colorful cocktail of rumors and speculations. Shen was described as thirty years old, wearing Western-style black suits and leather shoes. Her face was "yellowish, but her eyes are still shining." Although the case itself had nothing to do with sex, sex was nonetheless what was used to discredit Shen. In the middle of a report on the court scene, the reporter inserts that a man in his thirties fled Shen's hotel room when the police went to arrest her. The paper comments that Shen "shamelessly" accused Guo Tong of demanding that she and one of her friends spend a night with him to settle the case.[19] The paper further established Shen's "shamelessness" by recounting that when a man denied that Shen was his concubine, she "stated that he had a mole on his penis" to prove their relationship. One newspaper speculated that Shen was engaged to her lawyer.[20] The prosecutor argued that Shen had conducted many improper activities and needed to be punished severely to maintain social order. For improperly entering the house, for one broken chair and a shattered vase, a case that in local customs could have been settled outside of the court with a banquet hosted by Shen for Guo, Shen was given a ten-moth sentence with fifty days of imprisonment.[21]

Xiaofengxian

At the same time that Shen Peizhen was removed from the public for her spatial transgressions, another woman, the prostitute Xiaofengxian, was gaining fame through her relationship with her patron, Cai E. Cai was a participant of the 1911 Revolution and then served as the military governor of Yunnan and Sichuan. Distrusting Cai because of his early association with Sun Yat-sen's faction, Yuan invited Cai to Beijing in 1913, allegedly so that he "could play a more prominent role in promoting military education" but in fact to put him under surveillance. Cai eventually escaped and returned to Yunnan via Tianjin and Japan and organized an uprising against Yuan. Other provinces followed with their own uprisings and claims of independence. In November 1916, Cai died at the age of thirty-four from what a German doctor controversially diagnosed as syphilis.[22]

Cai frequented brothels when he was under Yuan's surveillance in Beijing. Most accounts suggest that his motivation was to mislead Yuan into believing that he had lost interest in state affairs. At this point Xiaofengxian entered Cai's life.[23] Born to a concubine in a family in Hangzhou, Xiaofengxian was forced by the first wife to leave the family. She was raised by her wet nurse when her mother died and was then sold to a man in Shanghai who trained her in opera. After a short career in singing in Nanjing, she moved to Beijing's Eight Lanes district to become a popular prostitute when she was still in her teens.[24] Cai spent much time in Xiaofengxian's residence and used it as a meeting place for his anti-Yuan associates. He also left from there when he escaped from Beijing.[25] Although it is unclear what role Xiaofengxian played in this process, there is no shortage of imagination about it. In fact, a significant portion of contemporary popular stories about Cai E focus on Xiaofengxian. In the stories, she recognizes Cai as an extraordinary man although he disguises himself as a merchant. They soon become soul mates and he shares with her all his thoughts and anti-Yuan plans. She understands the frustrated man and takes care of him.[26] Although a prostitute, she has the taste and talent of a scholar. Her elegant residence contains nothing vulgar, by her design. She always asks for poems when she has scholar visitors, so her room is filled with rolls of calligraphy. She most values a couplet from Cai.[27] She herself is a good poet, and her farewell poem for Cai and her elegiac couplet for Cai's funeral are cited widely.[28] She also reads and admires Liang Qichao's books, likes to wear men's clothes, and claims that loving the country is not only men's, but also women's responsibility.[29] If all these outstanding qualities are not enough to distinguish her from a common prostitute, she also controls her life. By making monthly payments to the brothel madam, she is able to choose her own visitors.[30]

Xiaofengxian makes sacrifices for Cai. She accompanies Cai to Japan and only returns to China after Cai reaches Yunnan. Afraid of Yuan's revenge, she hides in Shanghai. One story has it that one of Yuan's sons has long wanted to have Xiaofengxian as his concubine, but she loves the heroic Cai. Yuan's son thus takes revenge on Cai through his father's power. Aware that she is the cause of trouble for Cai, Xiaofengxian "gives her body to repay him."[31] She is also ready to sacrifice her life. After Cai returns to Yunnan, Xiaofengxian refuses to see any visitor and spends all her time reading newspapers, looking for news from Yunnan. One day when she reads that Cai has died in a battle, she cries until blood comes out of her mouth and cannot get out of bed for days.[32] Finally, she commits suicide with a sword.[33]

In reality, Xiaofengxian did not die, nor did she go to Japan or move to Shanghai. In 1951, Xu Jichuan, the assistant to the eminent Beijing opera performer Mei Lanfang, interviewed Xiaofengxian, who had by then changed her name to Zhang Xifei (washing away wrongs), in Shenyang. According to Zhang Xifei, she knew that Cai was a revolutionary but did not understand what it meant. In her mind, Cai E, who told her *Three Kingdom* and *Water Margin* stories and taught her to read, was simply a decent man. She asked Cai to explain the difference between an emperor and a president when she heard rumors that Cai was against Yuan. She did help Cai although she was aware of the potential trouble their intimacy might cause her. After Cai E died, Zhang first married a military officer of the Northeast Army and later a worker. She lived in Shenyang after 1949. To judge from the note Zhang sent Mei Lanfang in 1951, which contained some wrong characters and improper usage of phrases, she had limited education.[34]

Xiaofengxian in Cai Dongfan and Tao Hancui's *yeshi* closely resembles the figure in the popular stories. She is educated, wise, dignified, and a quiet and proud loner among the popular prostitutes in the capital city. Informed about current affairs and opposing Yuan's enthronement, she helps Cai fool Yuan and risks her life to assist his escape out of her admiration for Cai's commitment to the Republic. *Yeshi* elevates Xiaofengxian into a conscious political actor while transforming the dangerous Shen Peizhen into a laughable Sun Beizhen.

One important element that explains such positive representations of Xiaofengxian in the popular stories and *yeshi* is her relationship to gendered spatial order. The physical space in which Xiaofengxian interacted with Cai, the brothel, was highly controlled by the modern state through its regulations on sexuality and gender relations, and the symbolic space in which she acted did not present threat to established gender codes.

The kind of commercial space in which Xiaofengxian operated was in fact created in the Republican period in Beijing. Both male and female prostitution existed in Beijing prior to 1912, but for most of the Qing, "high-class female prostitution was effectively suppressed, yet male prostitution was allowed to flourish in such districts as the lanes off Qianmen Street in the capital's Outer City."[35] In his encyclopedic *Qing bai lei chao*, Xu Ke recorded that it was a fashion among scholars and officials in the capital city to be entertained by boy actors called *xianggu*, or *xianggong*, but visiting a female prostitute was considered a lowly practice.[36] The situation began to change at the beginning of the twentieth century. Tian Jiyun, an actor who participated in the 1898 reform, petitioned the Qing and Republican governments repeatedly to ban the practice of *xianggu*. In April 1912, Tian's petition was approved,[37] and the government announced the ban:

> The practice . . . has damaged the image of our nation and made us look ridiculous to other countries. . . . Drama can contribute to social reform, and being an actor should not hurt one's status as a citizen. . . . We cannot allow this decadent custom to remain in our nation's capital city. . . . [Men who are in the *xianggu* business] should develop a wholesome character and be respectable citizens.[38]

The citizen here is clearly defined as male. Actors, by virtue of being men, were included in the political realm. The practice of male prostitution generally disappeared from public view after this time.[39] Only rarely could one discern that male prostitution continued in the city.[40]

While male prostitution was disappearing from public view, female prostitution was legalized in the first year of the Republic.[41] The heyday of female prostitution in Beijing was the years between 1911 and 1928 when the capital city was crowded with national politicians of the Republic.[42] The American sociologist John Burgess, who conducted research in Beijing, observed that the rise in the number of prostitutes "far exceeded the increase of population in the city, which indicates that this institution is growing."[43] The connection between politics and prostitution is also corroborated by the almost 50 percent decrease of first- and second-class prostitutes after 1928.[44] An article in *Great Liberty News* commented, "All the businesses [in Beijing] declined after the Revolution, except brothels and theaters whose business blossomed. This is no doubt 'a revolution for the brothels and theaters.'"[45] Another piece claimed, "People who make huge amounts of money in the capital city are senators, prostitutes, and actors. . . . Now the senators are getting an increase in their pay; this means an indirect pay increase for the prostitutes. . . . Good fortune has arrived for prostitutes"[46]

Many of the national politicians were regulars at the entertainment quarters. Hosting parties and making business deals in brothels became a fashion in the capital city in the Republican period.[47] Sidney Gamble observed, "It is extremely difficult for a man to hold a high official rank without spending a very large part of his time in the licensed quarter attending dinners and wasting his energy in late hours."[48] Analyzing the reason why visiting the courtesan houses was so important for the male politicians, Yanjing University sociologist Mai Qianzeng noted:

> When Beijing was still the capital, from the cabinet ministers down to the clerks all took visiting brothels as a glorious deed . . . and many military and national decisions were made there. Society has become used to it, taking it as an unavoidable social activity. Even the representative of public opinion, the newspaper, promotes prostitutes: so and so is pretty, so and so is good at entertaining.[49]

Gamble's observation of newspaper advertisement for brothels and courtesan houses confirmed Mai's argument:

> Practically all the newspapers give extensive publicity to the houses of prostitution and derive from them large financial benefit. Beauty contests are conducted among the prostitutes for the sake of the publicity the press can give to the winners, and special "write-ups" of such events are published, together with pictures of the women. In some of the Peking newspapers attractive pictures of the women are pasted beside advertisements for houses, while in others an entire page will be given up to prostitutes' cards. These will give the girl's picture or her name in large type, her address and telephone number and then a bit of descriptions: "Her face is like a flower, and her body like a pearl." . . . Newspaper men are either paid in money or in trade, and in special cases may even be allowed the privilege of giving a feast in the house to which they may invite their friends.[50]

The *Great Liberty News* referred to drinking parties as "one of the worst fashions of Beijing." Men ranging from officials to senators, from political party members to newspaper editors "all threw away big money just to win a smile from the prostitutes. They take this as being masculine, wasting time at it and neglecting their duties."[51]

The Republican state took active measures to regulate prostitution, subjecting female prostitutes to strict administrative and medical control as well as moral scrutiny. The control of prostitution was characterized by police supervision, regular medical examination, and restrictions on business locations and architectural style.[52] These measures designated these women as a dirty, infectious, and morally dangerous inferior class while maintaining a pristine reputation for those who made use of their services, ensuring that even though these women were interacting with politicians or even acting in directly political ways, they would not gain political power for themselves or women in general. In a seemingly contradictory way, these women became necessary commodities as well as dangers to public health and threats to marriage and family life.

This was the world where Cai E met Xiaofengxian. Cai E would be one of the men hosting parties there, Xiaofengxian one of the women who sold themselves into that world and were controlled by contract, kept under police surveillance. Though subjected to regular medical examination and regulated financially, in the critics' view, prostitutes facilitated the decadence of male politicians. To solve the contradiction of a Republican hero's involvement in a world of decadence with a woman of dubious moral standing, both Cai E and Xiaofengxian are made to appear different from other men and women in the brothel. Cai E's visits to brothels are justified as revolutionary subterfuge. Xiaofengxian does not have the character usually imputed to a prostitute. In fact, her political commitment appears to be not too different from that of the women suffragists. Cai Dongfan even meant to use her as an example to "shame men."[53] But both *yeshi* ensure that her image is just positive enough not to degrade or overshadow the appeal of the hero; Xiaofengxian was only significant in her connection to Cai E. In Cai Dongfan's words,

> The center of this chapter is Cai E. Even where Xiaofengxian is brought in, the purpose is to use her as background for Cai E. Xiaofengxian was only a weak prostitute, could she really have such vision and wit? Cai E had a secret plan which he would not even tell his wife of twenty years until he was ready to leave Beijing, how could he have confided all his thoughts and feelings to Xiaofengxian, with whom he had only met two or three times? The author writes such a story totally for the purpose of casting more light on Cai E's character, and is only using Xiaofengxian to edify the readers.[54]

Cai Dongfan's way of positioning Xiaofengxian was echoed decades later in Xu Jichuan's account of his interview with Xiaofengxian, in which he emphasizes that his purpose was to "learn about Cai E's escape from the brothel," not to "write a laudatory biography for Xiaofengxian (*bushi wei Xiaofengxian lizhuan*)."[55]

The manipulation of the images of Cai E and Xiaofengxian reveals a failure in the old trope of hero and beauty in the Republican context, which is best expressed in Xu Zhuodai's preface to Tao's novel. On one hand, in Xu's view, women only add entertainment value to politics and history: "For history, beautiful women are accessories, ornaments, seasonings, and glue. Histories without beautiful women are like clothes without style, dishes without taste, and glue without adhesive material. . . . A stage cannot be without *huadan*; a banquet cannot be without a waiter. They are all for the purpose of making things interesting." On the other hand, women's involvement in politics was becoming dangerous: "After the 1911 Revolution, women's rights have been expanding and there are more women behind the political scenes. . . . Those who don formal clothes and uniforms, command tens of thousands of soldiers, and hang countless medals on their chests are in fact under the control of delicate thin fingers."[56] What the author failed to recognize was that women like Shen Peizhen challenged male dominance directly rather than manipulating politics behind the scene with "thin fingers." Does this failure of recognition result from misfit between women activists and the old trope of hero and beauty? Or is Xu trivializing women to discursively contain their threat?

In either case, *yeshi* does not imagine the Republic as giving women more public power, but proposes that Republican men should be stronger in resisting corruption and lust than men under the decadent, backward, and thus failed imperial system. Both *yeshi* explain Yuan's action as stemming from moral degradation. The stories criticize Yuan and his followers' political ambition to restore the throne by attacking their desire to copy the emperors' sex life. In other words, regression and corruption in the political system are interpreted as the result of decadent sexual morality. Tao explicitly compares the sexual behavior of officials of the Republic to that of the emperors, arguing that the emperors in the past lived a degenerate life, embodied in their sexual indulgence. But the emperor was the only person who could live such a life during the imperial period. Although the court officials wanted to imitate the emperor, out of fear, they had no choice but to respect limits. In the Republic, however, officials no longer had anything to fear. Every warlord had a large number of concubines, the majority of whom had been prostitutes. Visiting brothels became daily entertainment for Republican officials. Xu Chihen, an editor of *Xinwen bao*, believed that China's political stage was controlled by "degenerate, corrupt, and evil men." "Laws that are inconvenient can be abolished; inconvenient regulations can be changed. Neither public opinion nor people's views are enough to regulate these men."[57] The only way to correct the problem, then, lies with men themselves: self-cultivation for higher moral standards, a familiar Confucian prescription. Women fade into the background. When Shen Peizhen was contained by the Republican legal system in a prison, Xiaofengxian was contained too, by her brothel environment and by gendered narrative tropes. Acting not out of her own political will and staying within established gender boundaries, Xiaofengxian differs radically from Shen Peizhen. Her dedication to Cai E reasserts traditional gender boundaries. Such containment serves as the security mechanism that allows *yeshi* to show

Xiaofengxian as taking political actions without appearing threatening to normative gender relationships.

The disparate reception of the two political women, Shen Peizhen and Xiaofengxian, in popular media reflected their differences in personality, but, more importantly, followed the ways in which their presence in the new political and commercial public spaces confirmed or altered gendered spatial relationships. Shen and her comrades created new political spaces for both men and women through transgressions of male space, while the invisible but imagined political activities of Xiaofengxian did not directly challenge gender roles but rather confirmed governmentally sanctioned spaces and reinforced fundamental spatial distinctions between men and women.

The representations of both women reveal contradictions in the changing gender relations of the early Chinese Republic. Shen's experience exposed the distance between the ideals that legitimized the Republic—equality among all citizens—and the reality women lived. Such exposure led to questioning of men's behavior, challenging the categories "male" and "masculine" and their self-perpetuating connection to the legitimacy of the political system. When femininity was redefined, masculinity entered a crisis as well. If Shen's activism fell outside the old trope of hero and beauty, the *yeshi* writers' effort to fit Xiaofengxian into the familiar trope was not persuasive either; they were unable to resolve the moral contradictions of the hero and beauty in a space that was officially and socially recognized as decadent, neither could they decide on whether to make the prostitute politically conscious.

The commercial press played crucial roles in the production and transformation of gendered notions of space. *Yeshi* highlights the private lives of male politicians, leading readers into a sensational space of unstable moral boundaries that was not often represented in print. The gender boundaries *yeshi* polices are not necessarily exactly the same as those of the state. *Yeshi* suggests that the official reasoning for the rejection of the suffragists—that they were not ready for political participation—was not the primary reason the senate refused to grant the women the right to vote. Rather, in their strong challenge to gender relations, women went too far. While the newspapers ridicule women for their bound feet, *yeshi* mocks Sun's big feet and her unfeminine behavior. Although the Republican state designated prostitutes immoral through laws designed to control and define them, *yeshi* depicts Xiaofengxian as an admirable figure. Women were disqualified from citizenship in state legislation, but *yeshi* allows Xiaofengxian to act with a citizen's sense of responsibility. Her actions, *yeshi* seems to say, indicate the right way for women to act politically. If the Republican state legitimized the construction of new gender boundaries in the vocabulary of "progress" and "civilization," *yeshi* exposes the many common characteristics that such new boundaries shared with older notions. *Yeshi* does not directly challenge the boundaries set by the state, but neither does it follow them. Instead, it reveals the hidden truths of state regulations indirectly, and often unintentionally. If such popular representations turn the women's suffrage movement into a farce, they also discursively open up possibilities for women as indispensable actors in an important moment of Chinese history. Although thematically, *yeshi* disparages women's direct political acts, the popular genre also brings out the truth behind idealized government regulations and proclamations, showing them to be based on biased cultural notions rather than modern political ideas. In this sense, *yeshi* is productive as well as repressive. Its depictions highlight women activists' appearance in the discursive public space. Although the goal of the popular text may have been to depoliticize women's actions and relocate them in a more proper and manageable cultural sphere, its focus on women's behavior shows that the issue is at heart political.

Notes

1. First appearing in the Tang dynasty, the genre of *yeshi* matured in the Ming dynasty, and its popularity increased in the later half of the Qing. In 1897, *Yanyi baihua bao* (Vernacular popular history) was established. One of its most important stories was *Tongshang shimo yanyi* (The origin of the treaties) on the history of the Opium War, later published as a single volume, *Yingsu hua* (Poppy flowers). This was followed by Huang Shizhong's *Hong Xiuquan yanyi* on the Taiping Rebellion in 1905. In 1912, Ziyou sheng's *Xin Han yanyi* (A new history of the Han nationality, Shanghai shuju) on history from the Wuchang Uprising to the establishment of the Republic and Xue Xiang's *Shenzhou guangfu zhi* (The recovery of China) on events from the end of the Ming to the establishment of the Republic were printed. Late Qing reformers and revolutionaries saw new values in unofficial histories. Explaining the publication of fiction in the newspaper *Guowen bao*, Yan Fu and Xia Zengyou argued that popular histories could reach a larger population than classics and official history: "People's mentality and customs are controlled by popular (fictionalized) histories." Similarly, Liang Qichao advocated the adoption of popular histories for educational purposes. The appeal "to save the nation with fiction" and "to save the nation with *yanyi* (popular history)" regularly appeared in magazines in the late Qing, and the popularity of unofficial history grew even stronger in the early twentieth century with the new developments in urban popular print culture.

2. Cai Dongfan (1877–1945) was born in Xiaoshan in Zhejiang province. He won an imperial degree and briefly held an official post. After 1911, he worked for a publisher in Shanghai, editing and writing textbooks. The first part of *Zhongguo li dai tongsu yanyi* (Unofficial Chinese dynastic history) on the Qing was finished in 1916. The whole project, covering 2,166 years from the time of Qin to 1920, was completed in September 1926 and published by Huiwentang in Shanghai. In 1935, Huiwentang

added to Cai's original a fourth volume on the Republican period written by Xu Jinfu and published the whole series as *Lidai tongsu yanyi* (Popular unofficial dynastic history). Responding to the popularity of the series, a large number of copies were printed and sold nationally. Cai Dongfan, *Minguo yanyi* (Unofficial history of the Republic), 4 vols. (Shanghai: Shanghai wenhua chubanshe, 1980). Biographical information on Tao Hancui is hard to locate. Judging by the names of people who wrote prefaces to Tao's book, he had connections with some of the most famous writers of popular readings of the time, such as Xu Zhuodai. One of Yuan Shikai's sons, Yuan Kewen, wrote the calligraphy for the cover title. Tao's eight volume series was first published in 1928 and was reprinted three times in eight years.

3. In *Dangerous Pleasures: Prostitution and Modernity in Twentieth-Century Shanghai* (Berkeley: University of California Press, 1997), Gail Hershatter thoughtfully interprets popular literature as a source for studying the history of women and gender.

4. Ono Kazuko, *Chinese Women in a Century of Revolution, 1850–1950*, ed. Joshua A. Fogel, trans. Kathryn Bernhardt et al. (Stanford, Calif.: Stanford University Press, 1989), 87.

5. The summary of these events is based on accounts in Chen Sanjin, ed., *Jindai Zhongguo funü yundong shi* (A history of the women's movement in modern China) (Taibei: Jindai zhongguo chubanshe, 2000); and David Strand, "Citizens in the Audience and at the Podium," in *Changing Meanings of Citizenship in Modern China*, ed. Merle Goldman and Elizabeth Perry (Cambridge, Mass.: Harvard University Press, 2002), 44–69.

6. Kong Hai, "Duiyu nüzi canzhengquan zhi huaiyi" (Doubts about women's participation in politics), *Minli bao*, February 28, 1912, 2.

7. Yang Jiwei, "Yang Jiwei nüshi lai han" (Letter from Ms. Yang Jiwei), and Kong Hai, "Fu Yang Jiwei nüshi han" (Reply to Ms. Yang Jiwei's letter), in *Minli bao*, March 5, 1912, 2.

8. Zhang Renlan, "Zhang Renlan nüshi lai han" (Letter from Ms. Zhang Renlan), *Minli bao*, March 9, 1912, 2.

9. "Xin nüjie de xianxiang" (Some phenomena among the new women), *Aiguo baihua bao*, August 9, 1913, 1, and August 10, 1913, 1.

10. "Linshi furen yuefa" (Provisional constitution of women), in *Rizhi bao*, December 1913, 7.

11. "Xi ni nüjie zizhihui jianzhang yuanqi" (Bantering on the origin of the "Brief program for the Women's Autonomous Association"), *Rizhi bao*, November 28, 1913.

12. "Nannü pingquan jianzhang" (A brief program on equal rights between men and women), *Aiguo baihua bao*, September 17, 1913, 7.

13. The characters in Tao Hancui's book have names that can be easily matched to historical figures; for example, Yuan Shikai is Fang Shiwei, and Song Jiaoren is Zhong Xiaorun.

14. Tao Hancui. *Minguo yanshi yanyi* (An erotic history of the Republic), 8 vols. (Shanghai: Shihua shuju, 1936), 1:95–121.

15. Strand, "Citizens in the Audience," 57.

16. *Da ziyou bao*, August 28, 1912, 11.

17. *Da ziyou bao*, August 30, 1912, 11.

18. As Joan Judge writes: "Women were no longer valued for their delicacy, weakness, and refined adornment, but for their robust healthiness, rosy cheeks, and dignified bearing." Joan Judge, "Citizens or Mothers of Citizens? Gender and the Meaning of Modern Chinese Citizenship," in *Changing Meanings of Citizenship in Modern China*, ed. Goldman and Perry, 32.

19. *Qunqiang bao*, July 9, 1915, 2–3; July 10, 1915, 2–3.

20. *Qunqiang bao*, July 8, 1915, 2–3.

21. *Qunqiang bao*, July 7, 1915, 3.

22. Xie Benshu, *Cai E zhuan* (A biography of Cai E), (Tianjin: Tianjin renmin chubanshe, 1983), 140–41.

23. John D. Young, "Ts'ai Ao" in *Historical Dictionary of Revolutionary China, 1838–1976*, ed. Edwin Pak-wah Leung (New York: Greenwood, 1992). The love story of Cai E and Xiaofengxian was made into a movie, *Zhiyin* (Soul mates), in the early 1980s. When the Taiwanese popular history writer Gao Yang wrote the history of Yuan Shikai's monarchic restoration, he used *Xiaofengxian* as the title even though she appears only late in the book and is hardly a main character. Gao Yang, *Xiaofengxian* (Beijing: Zhongguo youyi chuban gongsi, 2001).

24. Xu Jichuan. *Xu Jichuan yitan manlu* (Xu Jichuan's memoir of the art world), (Beijing: Zhonghua shuju, 1994), 40–48.

25. Xie, *Cai E zhuan*, 94.

26. Shen Tianchan and Dong Shan, *Cai Songpo yishi* (Stories of Cai Songpo) (Taibei: Wenhai chubanshe, 1970), 94–95.

27. Shen Tianchan and Dong Shan, *Cai Songpo yishi*, 140.

28. Shen Tianchan and Dong Shan, *Cai Songpo yishi*, 101–2.

29. Shen Tianchan and Dong Shan, *Cai Songpo yishi*, 142.

30. Shen Tianchan and Dong Shan, *Cai Songpo yishi*, 141–44.

31. Shen Tianchan and Dong Shan, *Cai Songpo yishi*, 121.

32. Shen Tianchan and Dong Shan, *Cai Songpo yishi*, 143.

33. Shen Tianchan and Dong Shan, *Cai Songpo yishi*, 121. Also see "Cai E yu Xiaofengxian" (Cai E and Xiaofengxian) in *Cai Songpo ji* (Works of Cai Songpo), ed. Zeng Yeying (Shanghai: Shanghai renmin chuban she, 1984), 1465.

34. Xu Jichuan, *Xu Jichuan*, 40–48.

35. Gary P. Leupp, *Male Colors: The Construction of Homosexuality in Tokugawa Japan* (Berkeley: University of California Press, 1995), 15. A Japanese visitor to Beijing in the beginning of the twentieth century recorded both female prostitution and the practice of *xianggu* (young boy actor/entertainer) in the city. See Ogawa Umpei, *An Overview of North Qing* (Tokyo: Shin-ashia Books, 1904), 92–96.

36. Xu Ke, *Qing bai lei chao* (Collection of Qing miscellany) (reprint, Taibei: Shangwu yinshu guan, 1916), 5153–55.

37. Hou Xisan, *Beijing lao xiyuanzi* (Old theaters in Beijing) (Beijing: Zhongguo chengshi chuban she, 1996), 48.

38. *Zhongguo jingju shi* (A history of Peking Opera in China) (Beijing: Zhongguo xiju chuban she, 1990), 242.

39. Hou, *Beijing*, 48.

40. The sociologist Niu Naie commented that the practice went underground after it disappeared from public view. See Niu Naie, "Beiping yiqian erbai pinhu zhi yanjiu" (A study of 1,200 poor households in Beiping), *Shehui xuejie* (Sociological world) 7 (1933): 187.
41. Sidney Gamble, *Peking: A Social Survey* (New York: Doran, 1921), 246; John S. Burgess, "The Problem of Prostitution: Address Given at the Y.M.C.A. in Peking, November 18, 1923," *Chinese Journal of Sociology* 2, no. 4 (April 1925): 3.
42. "Statistics of Number of Brothels in Beiping," Beijing Municipal Government, Department of Social Work, March 1930.
43. Burgess, "The Problem of Prostitution," 3.
44. Mai Qianzeng, "Beiping changji diaocha" (A survey on prostitution in Beijing), *Shehui xuejie* 5 (June 1931): 115.
45. *Da ziyou bao*, October 4, 1912, 11.
46. *Da ziyou bao*, October 18, 1912, 7.
47. Gamble, *Peking: A Social Survey*, 252.
48. Gamble, *Peking: A Social Survey*, 258.
49. Mai, "Beiping changji diaocha," 123.
50. Gamble, *Peking: A Social Survey*, 255.
51. *Da ziyou bao*, December 10, 1912, 7.
52. See "Jianzhi jinu guize" (Regulations on examining prostitutes), *Beipingshi shizheng fagui huibian* (A collection of regulations of the Beiping Municipal Government), Di qi lei, weisheng (Category Seven, Hygiene), 20–21; and *Jingshi jingcha faling huicuan*, 383–86.
53. Cai, *Minguo yanyi*, 2:102.
54. Cai, *Minguo yanyi*, 2:102.
55. Xu Jichuan, *Xu Jichuan*, 47.
56. Xu Zhuodai, "Xu" (Preface), in Tao Hacui, *Minguo yanshi yanyi* (Erotic history of the Republic) (Shanghai: Shihuan shuju, 1936), vol. 1.
57. Xu Chihen, "Xu" (Preface), in Tao Hancui, *Minguo yanshi yanyi*, vol. 1.

8

Gender and Maoist Urban Reorganization

Wang Zheng

STUDIES OF THE PEOPLE'S REPUBLIC OF CHINA have usually discussed the functions of residents' committees in socialist transformation without a gender perspective, although they have sometimes noted the high percentage of women in urban neighborhood work (*linong gongzuo*). This chapter integrates gender into the study of socialist state building, drawing on interviews with former members of residents' committees as well as the rich, recently opened government archives in Shanghai in order to examine the emergence of residents' committees in Shanghai in the early 1950s, and the meanings of urban women's neighborhood work. Social transformation and state formation intertwined with changing social spaces and gender boundaries. Located in the core of the spatial hierarchy, the urban women examined here were in the whirlpool of socialist transformation, contrasting sharply with women in the rural periphery, described in Gail Hershatter's chapter.

Socialist state building was replete with gendered conceptualization and practice. In the Chinese Communist Party's (CCP's) reorganization of Shanghai, residential areas were envisioned as the rear where women were supposed to provide services to male workers in the industrial production front. Housewives (*jiating funü*),[1] valued for their "political purity," were mobilized to work in residents' committees, replacing male *baojia* heads and gangsters to become prominent figures in local administration. With housewives moving into neighborhood work, the *nei–wai* boundary blurred. Residential areas, once considered *wai* in relation to individual households, would be turned into a "women's sphere." The CCP-created women's sphere represented a murky domain where domestic women crossed boundaries of household and gender, worked for the government within their communities, and brought state issues directly into individual households. The success of state penetration of urban families, in other words, was inseparable from the feminization of this public arena. And women neighborhood cadres were at the forefront of practices that created a socialist state effect in residents' daily life.[2]

The reshaping of gendered social spaces, however, was not accomplished by a coherent state entity detached from social practices but rather was itself part of a gendered process of state formation. It was the women in the CCP that initiated mobilization of a million housewives for the dual goal of liberating them from the bondage of the old "feudal society" and making them qualified citizens for the new socialist state. The grassroots organizing efforts of the Shanghai Women's Federation (SWF) were utilized, and then contained, by Shanghai government branches that were exploring ways of managing local society. Neighborhood, therefore, became a site for gender contention and negotiation not only among residents but also between the SWF and other government branches. Boundaries within the emerging new political order were drawn when such gendered power struggles played out in the social realm, marking the reproduction of gender differences within the processes of the state.

Gendered Conceptualization of Urban Space

Social reorganization began as soon as the communists gained control of Shanghai on May 25, 1949. The new communist government, struggling to overcome the social problems and legacies of a war-devastated economy, was also confronted with the pressing task of "establishing democratic government" (*minzhu jianzheng*).[3] Military victory alone did not give the CCP legitimacy. The new state needed "democratic government" to set it apart from and surpass the Nationalist "reactionary dictatorship." The official vision of democratic government centered on creation of a new power structure that would link people and government. This connection was to be achieved by creating institutions that would enable Shanghai residents to convey their concerns to the government as well as to assure that the government's decrees reached every corner. The key concept that emerged from their discussions is "organizing" (*zuzhi*), a positive word that was never equated with the negative word "control" in their usage (even if, in practice, the two went hand in hand). Cadres viewed grassroots organizing by communist vanguards as a democratic process at the heart of communist revolution. Hardly anyone paused to think of the implications of continuing this organizing practice when the party already became the state power holder.[4]

Of the five million Shanghai people, industrial workers, the trade union constituency, constituted one million, including 170,000 women workers. Several hundred thousand others could be organized in students, professional women, merchants, and trade organizations. The rest were self-employed or unemployed, including one million housewives. This majority of Shanghai's population lived their diverse (and, for more than a few, criminal) daily lives in various residential areas. This messy majority posed a special challenge to communist organization, especially when the spatially based *baojia* system, in place since the Japanese occupation, was abolished by the CCP as "the basis of the Nationalist reactionary dictatorship."

How to sort out who were friends and who were enemies among this diverse majority? What mechanisms could address urgent needs of public facilities, public health, security, and social welfare in poor residential areas where working-class people and urban paupers concentrated? The two questions, central to urban reorganization, suggest different tasks for the Public Security Bureau (PSB) and the Department of Civil Administration (DCA), respectively. Mapping the social topography of residential areas where different classes mixed and population was in constant flux was crucial to the new power holders, who were determined to organizationally penetrate society and turn it towards a socialist planned economy. The second question was also pressing, given that in shantytowns numerous unpaved mud roads flooded after rains, public lavatories overflowed, makeshift homes were subject to frequent fires, running-water stations were controlled by local despots who ripped off the poor, unlit streets bred crime, and many newly unemployed were hungry and grouchy because communists had driven their bosses away. Official internal reports, most based on firsthand investigations, expressed serious concerns about urban underclass living conditions and their sentiments toward the CCP. One such report, emphasizing the urgent needs of the poor, quoted unemployed workers: "Communists say *fanshen* (turnover). . . . Yes, we now turn over into the coffin!" Fundamentally, the legitimacy of the self-styled "people's government" would rest on its ability to effectively address the myriad problems emerging daily at the local level in this large city.

In the early days, the top party echelons remained unsure about the form of local urban administrative structures, but they maintained a principle not to set up formal administration below the district level, expressing a vision that all the residents would be absorbed in the workforce in industrialization. Shanghai government leaders, conscious of their pioneering role in creating a new form of urban governance, devoted much attention to the reorganization of local society. The debates within the leadership expressed two views. One followed the Soviet model, organizing people by trade and profession.[5] The other, based on the realization that the majority of Shanghai people had no stable trade or profession, sought to organize spatially by residence, a clear reflection of the *baojia* concept. Those who preferred this "spatial organization mode" to the "trade organization mode" did not argue against the Soviet model or dispute the top leaders' vision of industrialization. Rather, they emphasized that support for industrial workers required attention to their home life. Spatial organization was needed to improve the workers' living environment and thus further support the production sector. The director of the DCA of Shanghai, Cao Manzhi, discussed Shanghai leaders' views on urban reorganization at a national conference on August 17, 1950. He assured his audience that "the production principle is primary, and the residential area principle is secondary."[6] Articulating a hierarchical division between production and residence/consumption, Shanghai leaders deftly catered to the CCP leaders' preoccupation with industrialization while addressing the needs of urban governance.

Regarding residential areas as auxiliary or rear to the production front not only reflects the imprint of communist wartime experiences in which rural women in the rear were mobilized to support the front but also reveals a gendered conceptualization of urban space. It certainly was not a reflection of social reality in that the "rear" was actually the front for millions of men and women who made a living in the residential areas. But it dovetailed with the image of "family dependents of workers" (*jiashu*) who were supposedly unproductive but provided necessary services to male workers. In reality, many men also belonged in the category of "family dependents of workers," considering the large number of female textile workers in Shanghai.[7] Many wives of workers also engaged in work outside the home. However, in most documents when "family dependents of workers" are mentioned, the term refers to women (as proved by the occasional use of "male family dependents of workers"). Reorganizing Shanghai according to the dichotomous division of productive and nonproductive sectors, the government soon envisioned women's utility in the new socialist society. Instead of simply serving their individual households, women were called on to serve the production sector in residents' committees.

Gendered Reorganization of Social Space

Women's massive organizational participation did not occur immediately although the need to recruit women was recognized by the government early on. In 1950, when the cadres in the DCA were still exploring the form and constituency of neighborhood organizations, they complained about housewives' indifference to any organization. The emerging new activists included workers, students, small business owners, and even "rogues and hustlers" (*baixiangren*), but few housewives.[8] The change of political power did not automatically enable women to step out from domesticity. The neighborhood space in this initial stage remained masculine even though the male dominated *baojia* system was recently abolished. As a DCA report emphasized:

> It is necessary to rely on student and worker activists to take the lead. But they usually do not have time to care about residential matters. Therefore, training family dependents of workers, housewives, small business people and enlightened people can make a more constant force. . . . We must mobilize and train women activists. In the beginning we can train more progressive intellectual women with blue or white-collar family background and without children. Then we can include backward housewives.[9]

Transforming housewives thus became an integral part of urban reorganization.

Before the DCA eyed housewives, the Shanghai Democratic Women's Federation (SDWF) had already begun to mobilize a million housewives, its largest constituency in the city. Shortly after the establishment of the preparatory committee for the SDWF on June 26, 1949, it decided to combine six existing women's organizations to form the Shanghai Housewives Association (SHA) on August 22, 1949. The six organizations had either been peripheral organizations of the CCP or were newly formed by the CCP.[10] The SHA, working under the leadership of the SDWF, set out to "liberate housewives and prepare them for social production."[11] The decision to organize housewives was not an easy one. The party emphasized a class line. Previously housewives (an urban category) had never been included in women-work (*funü gongzuo*). But since organizing Shanghai women workers was the job of the Women Workers Department of the Trade Union, the SWF sought its own constituency. The director of the preparatory committee of the SWF, Zhang Yun, who had been an experienced leader of women-work since the 1920s, envisioned organizing housewives as a crucial part of the SWF's institutional development. By December 1950, twenty-one branches of the SHA were set up at the district level to reach housewives in residential areas. A report of the DCA that discussed neighborhood organization in 1950 assessed the work of the SHA: "Chinese housewives are usually influenced by the poison of old ethics of ritual and lack understanding of society and politics. But after joining the Housewives Association, some enhanced their understanding and reformed their mentality. This organization should continue to exist in order to protect women's rights and raise women's status."[12] The positive evaluation of the SHA revealed the DCA's recognition of the effectiveness of the SHA's work with housewives. Its problematic language, saturated in the May Fourth representation of the backwardness of women in domesticity, claims that it was through interaction with the SHA that some housewives began to express interest in affairs outside their households.

In December 1950, parallel to the DCA's exploration of resident organization, the SWF decided to establish grassroots organizations in the jurisdiction of each public security station. In less than one year, women in 10,009 lanes elected 42,900 representatives and 6,000 chief representatives, and 120 housewives' committees were set up with 1,300 members. In 1952, following the call of the All-China Women's Federation to establish Women's Congresses in urban areas, the SWF replaced chief representatives and housewives committees with a Women's Congress. Women representatives elected by neighborhood women formed the Women's Congress. They in turn elected a women's committee that paralleled the emerging residents' committee.[13] The neighborhood-based Women's Congresses assured close contact between the municipal and district women's federations and women in residential areas.

The district women's federations hosted frequent meetings and workshops to train women representatives as grassroots activists. Women activists identified and trained by the SWF began neighborhood work. Moreover, the gender-specific Women's Congress, with its emphasis on women's special needs, was much more attractive to women than the early neighborhood organization dominated by men. If a resident meeting was called by the winter protection brigade (an early form of neighborhood organization), few housewives would attend. But if the meeting announcement was signed jointly with the Women's Congress, many would attend.[14] The DCA leaders immediately recognized the strength of the SWF in mobilizing housewives. Many internal reports emphasized the importance of "working closely with *Fulian* (Women's federation [WF])."[15] The municipal leader even instructed that the SWF should concentrate on neighborhood work, stressing the pressing demand for developing neighborhood work as well as confirming the crucial role of the SWF in residential areas.[16] Supported by the city authority, however, women's organized neighborhood activities quickly encountered men's hostility. A DCA report described the interaction of the male-dominated neighborhood organization and the women's organization:

> Some leaders of the neighborhood organization hold an old mentality. . . . They think housewives are neighborhood residents and should be under the unified leadership of the winter protection brigade [WPB]. But since housewives have had their own organization and raised their understanding, they cannot accept the bureaucratic arrogance of the WPB. In some areas disputes have occurred and each organization has gone its own way to carry out work.[17]

Local WF cadres complained that men in the winter protection brigade "looked down upon housewives and displayed bad manners." When the two organizations worked together to put up slogans and information in neighborhoods, the WPB would refuse to acknowledge the Housewives Association (HA) by not allowing them to sign the propaganda pieces. When the neighborhood HA wanted to run women's literacy classes, the WPB insisted that its members be the teachers; otherwise it would not allow the HA to run classes. When both were supposed to collect donations for the Korean War, the WPB rushed out to collect donations for a six months' quota for a neighborhood, immediately sending them to the bank in its name alone. "Such competitive mentality led to frequent disputes. The situation is serious."[18] Although gender conflicts emerged as women "intruded" into male space, cadres in both the DCA and SWF tended to downplay gender tensions, describing instead organizational conflicts. Both sides emphasized the need for organizational cooperation. However, the spirit of equal cooperation did not last. Gender conflicts would soon be played out between the SWF and the DCA.

While the SWF was effectively organizing housewives in Shanghai, the DCA, in collaboration with the PSB, was busy setting up neighborhood organizations as a new form of democratic governing. Among the various quarters, residents in the poor areas expressed strong interest in an organization with resources and attention from the government to address their welfare needs, and many men actively collaborated with the organizing efforts of government cadres. In April 1951, the DCA hosted a conference of the representatives of streets and lanes with 1,561 participants from all the districts in Shanghai, and it declared the official decision to form "street and lane residents' committees." By mid-October 1951, 1904 residents' committees had been established.[19] To provide better leadership to the "autonomous" residents' committees, 129 street offices were set up, each managing ten or more residents' committees in the precinct of a public security station.[20]

The residents' committee proved an effective vehicle for the government to "penetrate the masses." By connecting to most urban dwellers (by the end of 1952, 3,891 residents' committees managed 4.21 million residents, 85 percent of Shanghai's population), it was the most widespread grassroots organization. Any government branch that wanted to reach the people would go to the residents' committees for help. The committees were quickly overwhelmed, as attested by a 1953 report.

> The various branches of the municipality and districts all need to reach residents in lanes, and the street offices are the ones directly facing residents. . . . Each government branch tells the street offices to carry out their work. . . . We investigated the tenth street office in Songshan District and here is its situation:
>
> Its major work is the campaign. After the campaign concludes, there is much work to finish. Besides that, the civil administration section requests it to work on relief and help families of military personnel and martyrs. The health section

> asks it to work on street sanitation, public hygiene and immunization. The culture and education section asks it to run literacy classes and investigate the situation of school age children. The district people's court asks it to work on accumulated cases. The district political consultative committee asks it to send out meeting notices and to report on how representatives to the People's Congress connected with residents. . . . Besides these demands from district branches, there are also demands from the municipal government. The Land and Property Bureau asks it to persuade residents to pay more rent. The Revenue Bureau asks it to mobilize residents to pay property and land tax collectively. The Culture Bureau asks it to organize residents to participate in group dance. The insurance company asks it to investigate residents' financial situation and mobilize residents to buy insurance. Cooperatives ask it to help collect scrap bronze. The local products company asks it to help sell all kinds of local products. The Telephone Bureau asks it to popularize long distance service and public phone booths. The film company asks it to sell movie tickets. The people's bank asks it to investigate residents' pre-war savings and current financial situation, and to promote patriotic saving so as not to leave any resident out. The Public Utilities Bureau asks it to fix hazardous houses, to dredge sewers, and to repair street lamps and wires.[21]

Evidently, the residents' committees were expected to manage everything in urban life except producing commodities. The perceived auxiliary nonproductive sector, suitable for "family dependents of workers" to manage, was a complicated miniature city in its own right. Within the boundary of the miniature city, tens of thousands of housewives stepped out of their domesticity and broke gendered boundaries by engaging in all sorts of work in civil administration and public security. Many parts of the city saw an increasing physical presence of women who were "running" neighborhoods as literally "domesticated" social spaces, spaces that a few years earlier had been associated with gangland violence.

Drawing Gender Boundaries in State Formation

In 1953, the Shanghai government launched a citywide employment survey combined with a campaign for "rectifying residents' committees." The benign employment survey camouflaged a new stage in the campaign for suppressing counterrevolutionaries that had begun in 1951 and was now to enter residential areas. The DCA instructed cadres to use unemployment registration to thoroughly investigate Shanghai lanes where fugitive landlords, hidden counterrevolutionaries, and other dangerous elements took refuge. All residents' committees were to be rectified and reorganized so as to ensure working-class leadership in neighborhood work.[22]

The conscious class line was supplemented with an explicit "gender line." The DCA directives emphasized the need "to mobilize and rely on women."[23] Housewives were not expected to confess their past history as other members of the residents' committees were. The reason was explained by a report of the SWF that also participated in the rectification work. "Having been unable to participate in social activities, housewives had a limited social circle in the old society. . . . Generally speaking, therefore, they have few historical problems and they are not the major targets of the rectification."[24] Thus, political purity and reliability were added to the earlier pragmatic rationale for recruiting housewives as a permanent neighborhood workforce. Housewives became more desirable than ever in the eyes of the party. By the end of the rectification over ten thousand former residents' committee members were purged, nearly all of them men. Many women activists were selected to residents' committees, replacing men with a shady past (former *baozhang*, landlords, rogues, and Nationalist Party members), men who abused their power in residents' committees (these two types sometimes overlapped), and men with an occupation that did not allow them to function well in neighborhood work. When rectification ended in 1954, women constituted 54.6 percent of 103,931 residents' committee members, a significant increase from 37.3 percent in 1953.[25] Incorporating a "gender line" into its class line, the CCP transformed the social space of the resident organization into a women's sphere within five years.

The women's sphere, however, was not led by the SWF. The rectification enabled the DCA to stake its claims in the new territory. Investigative reports in the DCA described the Women's Congress and the residents' committee as competitors who "vie with each other for cadres, for the masses, and for work."[26] But women in the Women's Congress did not see themselves or their organization as secondary to the residents' committee. As one WF cadre complained, "The public security station gets the upper hand of the street office, and the street office gets the upper hand of *Fulian*."[27]

The SWF's strong neighborhood presence was no longer appreciated by the DCA. DCA internal reports began to call for a "unified leadership" as a solution to the competition in neighborhood work.[28] Earlier the neighborhood organization's male leaders used the term *unified leadership* to control the women's organization. Now the same term used by the DCA officials had the same connotation. Worse still, officials in the government began to suggest that since residents' committees were established, the Women's Congress should be eliminated. The threat to the existence of its grassroots organization posed a major crisis to the SWF. The SWF appealed to the All-China Women's Federation, which succeeded in retaining the Women's Congress with a compromise.[29] In late 1954, the DCA issued regulations that defined the Women's Congress as an integral but subordinate part of the residents' committee. The chair of the Women's Congress should be the deputy director of the residents' committee, an arrangement confirming the importance of the Women's Congress, or a conciliatory gesture to the SWF. However, the Women's Congress was no longer allowed to conduct any concrete work on its own initiative, but only to convey women's demands to the residents' committee and to carry out the tasks assigned by the residents' committee. In February 1955, the municipal leading body Shanghai Neighborhood Work Committee issued "tentative regulations on the organization of Women's Congress in Shanghai neighborhoods." It formalized the Women's Congress's subordinate position to the residents' committee while confirming the importance of women-work in neighborhood work.[30] The central stage of residential areas was now dominated by the residents' committee, an organization created and managed by the DCA and the PSB.

By drawing a new boundary between neighborhood work and women-work, the containing regulations of the Women's Congress drastically reduced its power and imposed on the SWF a narrower definition of women-work to legitimate its subordination to neighborhood work. In reality the Women's Congress was continuously called on to do all kinds of neighborhood work. Drawing gender boundaries thus was practiced at multiple levels in the process of state formation. The DCA maneuvered to maintain its dominant role in local society by marking institutional differences. Demarcating the boundary between the "mass organization"—the Women's Federation—and the "government," the latter succeeded in institutionalizing the WF's subordinate position. It epitomized a classic irony in the history of the CCP that mobilizing women at the grassroots to break gender boundaries went hand in hand with creating or reproducing gender boundaries within the party power structure.

The WF's involvement in neighborhood work had another ramification. Working with housewives, the WF unwittingly devalued itself even in the eyes of many urban women who had opportunities to move out of domesticity. The WF's *funü gongzuo*, women-work, came to be understood as *jiating funü gongzuo*, housewives' work. The hierarchical division of production sector and living quarters, and corresponding feminization of the latter, placed those who worked in this new women's sphere as secondary. The Engelsian emphasis on women's participation in social production as an index of women's liberation, and the dominant gender ideology of breaking gender boundaries in work as a sign of modernity, further degraded and marginalized millions of housewives in the Mao era. The association between the WF and housewives, as a result, disqualified the WF from representing the vanguard of urban women, a predicament that the WF would try hard to remedy in the post-Mao era.

Similar to the experience of the WF, the residents' committee constituted mainly by housewives could not reach an elevated status, either. In subsequent years, the term *juweihui* (residents' committee) would connote a social space occupied by women with a low level of education, preoccupied with trivial activities. The nature of their work in a gendered social space contrasted with the glamorized subjects of state propaganda, such as women flying airplanes, operating locomotives, or climbing power poles. Except in the early years of mobilizing housewives, "neighborhood cadres" remained one of the least noticed groups in state representation. The following section introduces two of these discursively obscured women who served their urban communities in the 1950s. Why did these women respond to the CCP's call? What did neighborhood work mean to them? To better understand the local dynamics of socialist transformation, it is important to examine some of these women's lived experiences.

From Housewives to Neighborhood Cadres

This section draws on interviews of women in a neighborhood where I grew up, located in the former French Concession, and composed of mixed classes. Composed of many upscale apartments and townhouses, the neighborhood was a desirable residency for professionals and business owners. In 1949, before the communist victory, many wealthy residents moved to Hong Kong, Taiwan, or other parts of the world. Newcomers were still mostly members of the middle and upper-middle classes from other parts of China, but many had experienced displacement because of the wars. Lower-class residents lived in the same lanes or buildings, working as maids, washerwomen, gatekeepers, vendors, and so on. They lived in servants' rooms, garages, or makeshift structures. The crowded neighborhood had over twelve hundred households and about six thousand residents on one block in early 1950s. The seven-member residents' committee was to manage the life of this community, with the help of several subcommittees and many small-group leaders.

Of many neighbors interviewed from 1996 to 2001, five were among the first cohort of neighborhood cadres. My discussion will focus on two of them, Zhang Xiulian and Gao Wenling, while drawing on information provided by other neighbors.[31] In the early 1950s, except for a retired man in the initial stage of neighborhood organization, the residents' committee was staffed by housewives in their late twenties to mid-thirties, young mothers with children. The high female participation reflected the class composition of this neighborhood in which women with a secondary or higher education were not rare. Archival documents show that many housewives worked for the residents' committees hoping to gain employment through connections with government officials.[32] But in this neighborhood, the majority of first cohort neighborhood cadres stayed, mostly because of family responsibilities or no financial need for another income.

Zhang Xiulian became involved in neighborhood work when the government began to organize winter protection brigades in 1950. A daughter of a dockworker, Zhang was twenty-nine years old with a middle school education, married with four children. Two additional children in the early 1950s kept her family in poverty until her older children entered the workforce. Her husband was a white-collar worker in a foreign company and a Communist Party member. Fitting well the profile of "family dependents of workers," she was visited by a cadre from the district public security bureau. "Please come out to work; you are from a worker's family." Zhang recalls the phrase the cadre used to persuade her. Initially unwilling to "come out to work" because of heavy demands of child care, Zhang was persuaded by her husband to do voluntary work for the new government.

The term "come out to work" indicates that in 1950 the neighborhood was seen as *wai*—outside to women's domesticity. But a few years later some men who did not allow their wives to work in factories would let them do "neighborhood work" as it became regarded as *nei*—inside, where women belonged. Women managed community life as devotedly as they managed their own households and equally without payment. But while the neighborhood became *nei*, or female space in the public mind, neighborhood work was qualitatively different from domesticity in the minds of these women. Crossing the boundary of domesticity would entail unexpected social and political meanings that eventually transformed these housewives.

Once she became involved in neighborhood work, Zhang fell in love with it. She was appointed director of the security and defense committee because of her good class background. Her work was to provide information about residents to the public security station in the neighborhood precinct or directly to the district public security bureau. Who were the permanent residents, and how did they make a living? Who were the temporary residents, where were they from, and why were they there? This was basic but crucial information for a PSB that was eager to map the complex social landscape of Shanghai neighborhoods. To know each household, Zhang participated in all kinds of work run by other branches of the residents' committee. She joined sanitary teams to check the household cleanliness. To make friends with the residents and to win their hearts, she helped clean dirty hallways and spray pesticide on bug-infested bed frames.

Knowing all the neighbors personally, she proved to be extremely valuable to the public security station. "One day the policeman Chen came to ask me,

'A counterrevolutionary from the West Gate [a residential area in Shanghai] has come to hide in this neighborhood. Have you seen such a man?' I answered immediately, 'Yes, I know where he is. Is he in his mid-thirties?' Chen was stunned." She had seen her classmate's mother-in-law chatting with a man selling loquats in the neighborhood. The mother-in-law had told her that the man was her neighbor in the West Gate. She told the story of her discovery of the counterrevolutionary in great detail, revealing not only an excellent memory but also apparent pride in her past perceptiveness as director of security.

Zhang's exuberant accounts of catching "counterrevolutionaries" and other dangerous elements surprised me. Knowing that her collaboration with the public security system had given her a notorious reputation in the neighborhood, I had assumed that she would refuse to grant me an interview. When she delightedly agreed to meet me in 2001, I thought that she would avoid such stories. Her unexpected openness expresses an unchanged identification with the CCP, though she never gained party membership. Understanding the meaning of such identification became the core of my investigation.

Zhang's proud recollections included more than security work. She was selected as a jury member of the district court and as chair of the Women's Congress. Because of her close relationship with officials in the street office and the public security station, she had tremendous informal power. She helped unemployed residents get jobs, and her words counted in determining whose grain rations should be reduced and who should get subsidies. She emphasized that she based her decisions on each household's actual needs. "The other day I went to buy a cake at Laodachang [a bakery]. A Shandongese who worked there said to me, 'Auntie, thank you so much. If not for you, I would have starved in the period of reduced grain rations.'" Her anecdote was a tribute to her past, suggesting that neighbors continually reminded her of her former good deeds that she would otherwise have forgotten.

Zhang's intimate knowledge of her neighbors worked two ways, helping establish effective state control over local society and also making the socialist state appear humane in the eyes of residents. The two facets of her work were often felt along class lines in the mixed-class neighborhood. For neighbors of comfortable families who had no welfare needs from the government but real worries about state control, Zhang was a nuisance who meddled in residents' lives to please the authorities. Zhang once brought the PSB to a middle-class family to investigate allegations that the family's five-year-old daughter had shouted counterrevolutionary slogans. This notorious case added to her unpopularity among middle-class neighbors. Many poor families that had no fear of Zhang's reports to the public security gratefully remember her crucial help when they were in need, such as finding a hospital space for a sick neighbor or giving a job opportunity to the wife of a poor family with many children. Stories told to me by neighbors of different classes suggest that Zhang identified with the poor and had a grudge against the rich even before the CCP raised her class consciousness. The state effects along the class line were created not only by the party's differential policies, but also by many women like Zhang who expressed their own class-based sentiments through their daily work.

But class was not the only dimension in this woman neighborhood manager's life. It was quite telling that while Zhang was disliked by most middle-class neighbors, it was the men who felt her presence in the neighborhood intolerable and attempted to curb her power. In the early 1950s, three men gathered signatures from male residents on a letter to the PSB, denouncing her for various crimes. They soon learned that her relationship with the PSB carried more weight than their accusations. The government's reliance on such women in local society thus disrupted gender norms and generated new gender dynamics, which might have caused unintended animosity among many men who resented being subject to women's authority in neighborhoods.

The new government supported women like Zhang in a deeper sense. In the interview, Zhang's animated tones revealed clearly the moments most dear to her. "Oh, the happiest moment was when I organized residents to tour the newly built China-Soviet Friendship Palace. I was truly exhilarated! I organized several hundred residents, all housewives!" Leading housewives to appear in a prestigious public space had deep symbolic meanings for her. Both her class and her gender could no longer exclude her from entering the social space to which she could not have belonged a few years before. Such experiences stimulated her most euphoric recollection. She also emphasized the big meetings at which she was the honored speaker. "My husband went to a conference held by the East China Bureau. I was invited to give a talk about women's liberation. . . . Many of the attendees at the East China Bureau conference were quite-high-ranking cadres. . . . I only had an outline, first point, second point, and third point. I did not have a draft." In the talk, she recalled her life in the old society:

> My father worked on the dock. When foreign ships came, they used a sampan to send the cable to the dock. My father rowed the sampan. How dangerous it was! A big wave could overturn the sampan. One night he did not come home. I was scared to death. I took his cotton coat to the dock to look for him. It was extremely cold. I experienced all this. That is why I was able to tell my stories without a draft. You cannot make up those stories.

As a woman, being able to tell her working-class father's bitter life to a prestigious audience meant more than demonstrating a clear identification with the party. Explaining her devotion to neighborhood work, Zhang emphasized,

"I never thought of quitting, because I felt extremely happy. We women have power now. We can speak. In the old society, other people would say, 'You get to the side! I want to talk to your man! Go back into your house!' Women had no status. No one wanted to talk to you. . . . Thinking I can speak to the leaders, I can attend all kinds of meetings, how happy I was!" The euphoria of being able to speak in public still persists for Zhang. It was the CCP, including male officials, that provided her with the opportunity. Transformed from a voiceless working-class housewife who was brushed aside rudely by men to a vocal cadre who had a public presence, Zhang regards those early years in 1950s as the most cherished time in her life.

Women like Zhang played an important role in helping the CCP create a fresh image of a "people's government" that declared the public space in socialist China to be a space of the "new masters"—previously downtrodden classes, including women. Speaking subaltern women, laden with signification, were both created by and creating a new political order.

Gao Wenling, who lived in the same lane with Zhang Xiulian, was thirty-four years old in 1949, with three children in middle and high schools. Her husband, assistant to foreign CEOs of postal services in China, had a high salary (about five hundred yuan per month). She was content with her comfortable domestic life and worked toward sending three children to college. Participating in socialist construction was not on her agenda. But her son, influenced by her brother, an underground communist, joined the army when he was in college. Heartbroken by her son's choice, Gao nevertheless became a glorious "military dependent," a prime candidate for neighborhood work. Government officials came to talk to her "with flattering words, such as 'This is revolutionary work; you are a glorious mother; you will answer the call of the state.'" It was difficult for her to refuse since the work simply involved helping register voters for the People's Congress. But one task led to another. Gao was soon recognized by the officials as a capable woman. When the next election for residents' committee members came, the officials put her name on the ballot and she got the majority of the residents' votes. She worked in the neighborhood for over thirty years until her retirement, serving as chair of the Women's Congress, director of the security and defense committee, and director of the culture and education committee, among many of her titles. Like all neighborhood cadres, Gao, previously addressed as Mrs. Pu, became known by her own surname. The new form of address suggested an identity change from a wife to an independent working woman, a feminist practice with a long history in the CCP, although in this case the neighborhood cadres still rely on their husbands' income.

Gao's recollection emphasizes the scope and complexity of her work. A list of her work includes finding piecework for poor women with children; helping with the census conducted by the public security station (collecting and verifying household registration pamphlets); mobilizing residents to do public hygiene work and doing it herself (sterilizing sewer lids to prevent disease, setting up medicinal bonfires to kill mosquitoes, leading inspection teams to check residential cleanliness, etc.); writing signs for campaigns and blackboard articles (on political events or public health); organizing weekly residents' group meetings to read newspapers or government documents (few families had a radio or TV set in those days); distributing coupons for grain, oil, cloth, and any other rationed items to each household; collecting utility fees, milk fees, land taxes, and "patriotic" savings; setting up neighborhood canteens, day care centers, elementary schools and persuading residents to donate part of their housing for such purposes; and mediating disputes among residents, including court appearances.

"People would come to the residents' committee for everything. . . . That is why we knew many people. Even now those people are old, I still know their names, their buildings, what jobs they had. It was like being an old ancestor who had to manage everything." She stressed that residents still look to her for help long after her retirement. "Just recently, an old man of over ninety years old climbed up three stories to my home, calling me 'director, director.' He wanted me to mediate a dispute with his neighbor."

Skillfully and shrewdly managing conflicts among residents or between residents and the government, Gao was a respected neighborhood authority figure, whom residents addressed as "Sister Gao" or "Auntie Gao," depending on their age. Neighborhood work provided women activists a space where they formed lasting personal relations with residents. Aided by the state-enforced mobility control and through their work organizing residents' collective actions, neighborhood cadres turned urban anonymity into semikinship. Expanding the boundary of *nei*, women managers helped Shanghai lanes acquire certain qualities of rural villages in the course of socialist industrialization. In the murky domain of the neighborhood, *nei* intersected with *wai*, the public mixed with the private, and state control blended with state welfare. It was a "socialist big family" that embodied the communists' vision of the state and relied on women's expanded "domesticity."

Working diligently at her post, Gao did not experience her role in the same way as Zhang. For an upper-middle-class woman, taking on neighborhood work did not mean a radical boundary change or shift in social status. In her class position, she had not experienced the same gendered spatial boundaries as Zhang. She had traveled many places with her husband, including Japan, and had mingled with elite foreign residents. For her, 1949 marked a decline in her family's social status. Compared with her past experiences the neighborhood was a small mundane world with little excitement beyond the headache of daily management. Except for the early days when the government was wooing her and Gao was elected to be a member of the district People's Congress, Gao's long tenure lacked elevated moments. Gao's account, though at times expressing pride, satisfaction, indignation, and humor, does not contain the excitement characteristic of Zhang's narration.

Gao reveals her reason for continuing at her post when she mentions talking with her friend Ma, who was chosen to be the director of the residents' committee. "I asked her, why accept such misfortune? The work is so much trouble. The work is such that only they can fire you and you cannot quit. . . . Otherwise people would think, oh, how come she went home? She must have some problem." In the countless political campaigns of the Mao era, numerous people lost the trust of the party. To be selected as a neighborhood cadre signified a political status and served as a badge that one was problem-free. Although Gao was protected by her identity as a military dependent, her class background meant that she was not trusted as much by officials as Zhang. To maintain the aura of being problem-free was thus extremely important. "I felt that I had simply been a housewife. Now I worked in society. It was impossible for me to have a [political] problem!" Working as a neighborhood cadre for Gao, therefore, was in part a statement of her refusal to be marginalized. It was a conscious effort by a woman who had previously enjoyed high social status to maintain a respected political status in the socialist society.

Gao and Zhang had been close to each other in the early days of working together, but their relationship turned sour. In interviews each had different perceptions of the tensions between them. In Zhang's view, Gao was a caring person who had been initially kind to her. It was improper handling of officials that created tension between them. Because cadres from the street office and the public security station always came to her (Zhang) to get information, instead of talking to the director, Ma (also an educated middle-class woman), or Gao, who was the deputy director, Gao and Ma became unhappy. Gao's version confirms that Zhang had very close interaction with the public security station. But this was not the source of her envy but rather of her aversion to Zhang. Gao contemptuously indicated the negative consequences of Zhang's behavior. "Although the residents' committee is only a grassroots organization, to residents, to friends, on the issue of political identity, your one sentence could make people suffer. That is the reason many people hate her. Why did she go to the public security station all the time?"

The tension between the two women neighborhood cadres *was* created by the officials, or more precisely, by the CCP's class line. Zhang frequented the public security station more than other neighborhood cadres because she was the most trusted. Often she was the only one selected to attend special training workshops or meetings hosted by the PSB. Many tasks she received from the PSB were confidential, which prohibited her from explaining to other cadres what she was busy doing. The differential treatment certainly made the experience of neighborhood work different for women of different class backgrounds. It helped consolidate Zhang's close identification with the "people's government" and Gao's detached stance. From their different political identifications, Zhang could not understand that other neighborhood cadres might not want to help the PSB as wholeheartedly as she, and Gao could not see that the business of the PSB *was* Zhang's business and that Zhang was proud of being part of the political game. Although the two women never mentioned their different class backgrounds, a factor that did not initially affect their closeness, the party's class line eliminated the likelihood that these women would feel sisterhood in neighborhood work. The gendered space in the neighborhood of mixed classes was undoubtedly divided by party-defined class identities.

Conclusion

Defined by the CCP as an autonomous mass organization, the residents' committee was a form of local governance mixing the heritage of the *baojia* system and innovations of the CCP. Public facilities, public health, public order, and social welfare are costly. The Communist Party found the most economical and effective way to address these issues early in its experience with urban governance. Urban women's unpaid work became part of the "infrastructure" for the central planning apparatus that the party sought to put in place. The story presented here, however, is not only about women's indispensable economic utility to the state. Women's participation in neighborhood work involved spatial rearrangement and social reorganization in the process of socialist state formation.

Gender, central in this process, functioned at multiple levels. It was expressed in communist male officials' conceptualization of a gendered urban space with unemployed women in a residential "rear" providing service to the production "front." It was demonstrated in the Women's Federation's effort to build its urban grassroots base by including housewives in its work, an effort that resulted in its rapid organizational development and collision with male-dominated branches of the government that were establishing their control of local society. Mobilizing women in local communities, in this sense, was a practice staged by communist women and men with different goals and understandings. Conflicts between communist men and women led to the demarcation of distinctions between the residents' committee and the Women's Congress. This practice should be seen as part of the process of drawing boundaries between the "government" and party-led "mass organizations" in the formation of the party-state. In this case, the unequal gender relations in the party were naturalized, consolidated, and legitimized by the internal distinction between the "government" and the CCP-led "mass organization," a distinction full of ambiguity but nonetheless taking on "the appearance of structure" of a communist state.[33]

Gender was also expressed in local women's involvement in the state project. As Zhang Xiulian's story illustrates, participation in local governance was experienced by many women as breaking gender boundaries, moving from domesticity into public space. For women like Zhang, who had been marginalized by both gender and class, neighborhood work enabled them to ascend to the core of community life and become speaking subjects. However, this is not a simple empowerment story in a newly created women's sphere. This "women's sphere" was not autonomous but was closely supervised by the public security station and the street office, and permeated not with gender consciousness but "class consciousness." The estrangement between Zhang Xiulian and Gao Wenling provides a glimpse of a political environment in which the party's class line had a divisive function in the women's community.

Diversely experiencing neighborhood work, women of different backgrounds and motivations all participated in producing the socialist state while being produced as new state subjects. The residential area as a social space was a prime site for the party to develop its state project. Running each block of the city, minutely taking care of myriad tasks assigned from top down, women neighborhood cadres transmitted the daily message that the new state was at residents' doors. An all-encompassing social organization envisioned by the party was accomplished by these diligent women who brought each household into the "socialist big family." The patriarch still resided in this "big family." But by reducing the power of patriarchs in individual households through state planned economy, and by replacing male *baojia* heads with women neighborhood cadres in local administration, the party inadvertently changed gender power dynamics in urban society.

Notes

The author thanks Luo Suwen, Xiong Yuezhi, Chen Zai, and Sun Weimin for help during fieldwork in Shanghai, and Gail Hershatter, Elizabeth Perry, Bryna Goodman, Wendy Larson, and Mark Selden for comments on early versions of this chapter. A 1999 American Council of Learned Societies Research Award made fieldwork possible, and a Stanford Humanities Center fellowship enabled me to conduct further research and writing.

1. The term *jiating funü*, literally "family woman," emerged in the Republican era referring to married women without employment, as a contrast to "career woman."

2. I draw on Timothy Mitchell's insights on the elusiveness of the boundary between state and society in "Society, Economy, and the State Effect," in *State/Culture*, ed. George Steinmetz (Ithaca, N.Y.: Cornell University Press, 1999), 76–97; and on Gail Hershatter's discussion of Mitchell's concept of the "state effect" in "The Gender of Memory: Rural Chinese Women and the 1950s," *Signs* 28, no. 1 (2002): 43–70.

3. Shanghai Municipal Archives, B168-1-742 (preliminary summary of administrative work); B168-1-497 (summary of Civil Administration Takeover Department's July work).

4. B168-1-742.

5. B168-1-756 (directives and reports on establishing democratic government, Political Council, Ministry of Internal Affairs, and Civil Administration Department of Shanghai).

6. B168-1-745 (talk outline by director Cao Manzhi, Department of Civil Administration of the Shanghai People's Government at a national conference of civil administration on constructing district power structure in big cities).

7. B168-1-782 (investigation of families of workers' committee, No. 7 Textile Factory), 1955.

8. B168-1-751 (DCA summary of neighborhood work in nineteen districts), 1950.

9. B168-1-751.

10. *Shanghai funüzhi* (Shanghai women's gazetteer), ed. Shanghai Women's Gazetteer Compilation Committee (Shanghai: Shanghai Academy of Social Sciences Press, 2000), 258. In January 1952, the SWF and SHA set up joint offices at municipal and district levels. The SHA disbanded in April 1955, having "completed its historical mission."

11. C31-1-2 (summary of work in the first four months of SDWF preparation), July–October 1949.

12. B168-1-751.

13. *Shanghai funüzhi*, 265. In 1996 there were 2,809 Women's Congresses in Shanghai.

14. C31-2-57 (on future organization of residents' committees), 1951.

15. B168-1-749 (provisional methods of organizing residents' committees), 1950.

16. C31-1-37 (report to the municipal party committee), September 13, 1951.

17. C31-2-57 (investigation of relationship between neighborhood organizations and the Housewives Association), June 14, 1951.

18. C31-1-33 (summary of SWF work), 1951.

19. The jurisdiction of committees varied from a few hundred households to a thousand, depending on the population density of a residential area. Boundaries were usually drawn along lanes or blocks.

20. B168-1-756 (work establishing democratic government), April to October, 1951.

21. B168-1-772 (briefing on the street office's organizational structure and suggestions for future work), July 20, 1953.

22. B168-1-772 (combining employment work with rectifying residents' committees).

23. B168-1-14 (summary of neighborhood rectification), 1954.

24. C31-2-259 (report on rectification work in lanes), No. 52. May 22, 1954.

25. B168-1-783 (Shanghai residents' committees' organization work), May 28, 1954. The percentage of women continues to increase. Currently it is over 80 percent.

26. B168-1-14 (report on rectification work of Shanghai residents' committees), October 23, 1954.

27. B168-1-772 (the problem of grassroots organizations), 1953.

28. B168-1-14.

29. The contention over the Women's Congress is the subject of "'State Feminism?' Gender and Socialist State Formation in Mao's China," forthcoming in *Feminist Studies.*

30. B168-1-30 (tentative regulations on Women's Congress organization in Shanghai neighborhoods), February 26, 1955.

31. I use pseudonyms for the neighborhood cadres presented here.

32. By 1952, more than forty thousand housewives in Shanghai entered gainful employment, most of whom had a secondary education or above.

33. Mitchell's analysis of internal power relations and the appearance of external "structures" of the state is borrowed here. The distinction between the "government" and the "mass organization" by the CCP has been seen as intended to keep a firm control of society via "mass organizations." My emphasis here is that the distinction also results from internal power relations. The distinction did not create an appearance of state-society separation but rather a party-state that penetrated all social spheres, "producing and maintaining the distinction between state and society is itself a mechanism that generates resources of power." See Mitchell, "Society, Economy, and the State Effect," 83.

9

He Yi's *The Postman*

The Work Space of a New Age Maoist

Wendy Larson

> Today, who can imagine people giving up their negative freedom to follow a charismatic leader advocating a people's democracy? . . . The age when people would sacrifice their secular happiness for utopian ideals is gone. Now, the opposite holds true: People are willing to abandon any and all ideals in the name of realism.
>
> —Gan Yang[1]

Work in New Era Culture

IT SHOULD NOT BE SURPRISING that Maoist concepts of work have been prodded and poked, renegotiated, and even thoroughly dismantled in New Era fiction and film. The worker loyal to the state and motivated by ideas of self-sacrifice for the common good has been replaced by all kinds of self-centered or simply disengaged working people. The very idea of the *worker* does not really fit the new image that has appeared because work, which under Maoism was at the core of the central notion of *serve the people*, in more recent representations is not necessarily at the crux of social or personal identity production, but rather simply a site among many—and not necessarily the most important one—where the self is formed. In many cases, emphasis moves from the work and its results to this self and its formation and existence in relation to work.[2] In the post-Mao period, this self often is highly gendered, and the Maoist (theoretical) emphasis on non-gender-specific labor is rejected.

After Mao's death, writers and filmmakers immediately set out to deconstruct the revolutionary worker and the idea of work itself. In the literature of the wounded (*shanghen wenxue*) of the late 1970s and the early 1980s, we still see the Maoist worker represented, but the idealism that sustains him or her has been gutted by the violence of the Cultural Revolution and the corruption of the state. In Wang Meng's 1979 *Buli* (Bolshevik salute), Zhong Yicheng actively looks forward to his late 1950s rehabilitation through labor and gushes romantically about the pleasure and value of hard work:

> Work, work, work! Millions of years ago labor turned monkeys into humans. Millions of years later in China, physical labor was exercising its great strength to purify thinking and create a new soul. Zhong Yicheng deeply believed in this. . . . He scooped feces out of latrines. The smell of feces made him feel glorious and peaceful. One bucket after another, he mixed the liquid with earth, feeling from his heart that it was really and truly delightful.[3]

Zhong recalls the morning struggle, afternoon struggle, and evening struggle—political/military terms used to describe the extra labor heaped on bad elements. He experiences some success in a system that uses categories to rank the elements based on their work. Wang Meng shows that the basic idea of reforming intellectuals through labor works, so to speak: Zhong's positive attitude and unstinting effort succeed in forging an emotional link between him and the peasants, and his labor gives him a new awareness. Zhong's disillusionment comes only when party hacks purposefully misinterpret his heroic fight against a fire. If only the party were more honest and less corrupt, Wang Meng implies, work would indeed cure intellectuals of real or imaginary attitude problems. The significant intellectual questioning that Zhong undergoes as he passes through various phases of contemporary Chinese history exists only for the male protagonists, and the female characters function in subservient roles that the male can use to contextualize his own intellectual journey.

Another similar example that deals with elite rather than strictly manual labor is Shen Rong's novel *Ren dao zhongnian* (At middle age). Ophthalmologist Lu Wenting devotes herself heart and soul to her job, eventually suffering a heart attack because of overwork and bad conditions. The author points to party corruption as contributing to the situation, but most of the blame falls on the lack of modernization that party control has produced. In this novel as in *Buli*, the protagonists are true believers in the value of work, and their identities are formed largely within their practice and conception of work. While Shen Rong portrays some work-related problems as gender based, she does not bring out these issues as much as does Zhang Jie, who in her long novel *Fangzhou* (The ark) shows a highly gendered work environment in which women are subject to any number of abuses. Although her three female characters work hard and hope to achieve worthwhile accomplishments, there is little chance that they will be able to function successfully in the masculine power context that work really is. Far from being an idealistic realm where the people can be served, work is an arena where male bias against women and general social prejudice can flower.

In his writing about intellectuals sent to work in the countryside, Zhang Xianliang pushes aside the lyrical qualities associated with hard labor that Wang Meng exploits, drawing a stark line between physical work and intellectual endeavors, which he portrays as much more profound and pleasant. Basically rejecting the Maoist work-cure, Zhang also shifts the locus of identity construction out of labor and into sexual relationships and philosophical thought, expanding a trend that only deepens in the next twenty years. For Zhang, however, the agency in this redefinition always is ascribed to men; women function as convenient sexual or intellectual catalysts that allow the culturally important males to proceed along their road to self-understanding. Furthermore, the entire process whereby males figure out a way to gain power through sexuality and intellect is presented as crucial for national renewal. As for Zhang Jie, work is gendered at its most profound levels, but Zhang Xianliang promotes rather than critiques this gendering.

The most radical deconstruction of work came with the experimental writers—Yu Hua, Can Xue, Su Tong, Mo Yan, and others. In Can Xue's enigmatic *Huangni jie* (Yellow mud street), a disturbing shell of socialist work structures remains in place to prick the reader's expectation that some ordinary narrative and social progress may occur. Although committees meet, leaders convene, and typical work strategies of procrastination or indecision are in full effect, the point is not so much that nothing is accomplished as it is that these strategies are part of a larger set of unrealistic but strangely logical and real relationships between people in all aspects of life. Yet with the significant exception of the writing of this one famous female experimental writer, the important actors in the experimentalists' stories are usually male. For example, Mo Yan's short *Shenpiao* (Divine debauchery), which is a direct attack on socialist working mores, features wealthy landowner Master Ji, who, through his aesthetic and spiritual immersion into flowers and his complete disregard for common morality or any kind of productive labor, accomplishes what the socialist system never could completely do: the redistribution of wealth to the poorest in society.[4] The main character in Yu Hua's *Hebian de cuowu* (Mistake on the riverbank) is a dedicated policeman who begins to investigate a crime only to slowly lose control over his internal narrative of clues, guilt, cause and effect, and social responsibility. Eventually the idea of work in its entirety disappears from the policeman's mind, which is taken over by a mysterious internal process. In Su Tong's *Qiqie chengqun* (Wives and concubines) and the Zhang Yimou film, *Dahong denglong gaogao gua* (Raise high the red lantern) based on it, work recedes in importance until it virtually disappears, replaced by a sexualized and male-controlled, performance-based, and culturally inherited structure of power and oppression.

In recent years, critiques of work under capitalism have sprung up alongside those of work under socialism. In Zhou Xiaoming's film *Ermo*, a peasant woman extracts herself from traditional village noodle making to set up a modernized noodle factory in the city. Her work, originally fully integrated into the rural community, becomes focused on one goal—that of buying the biggest television set in the village—and in a symbolically significant act, she sells her own blood to get extra money. In this narrowing of work to its exchange value, or the capitalization of work, Zhou exposes the emptiness of the process and the impossibility of Ermo ever really catching up with the images that motivate her: another neighbor instantly proclaims that she will buy a set bigger than Ermo's.[5] Because Ermo's husband is disabled, she takes over the entrepreneurial work, and at the end of the film we see a brief but disturbing image of Ermo awake while everyone else in the room has fallen asleep. Her dull stare at a screen that produces only static implies budding self-knowledge and an intuitive understanding that something has gone wrong. Here the director continues a twentieth-century tradition of granting heightened awareness to women and other characters on the margins of cultural creation.[6] However, although women can identify problems, social gender restrictions constrain their ability to act effectively on behalf of constructing a viable future.

Recently, young writers also have incorporated work into their projections of a contemporary global lifestyle. For Chen Ran's ubiquitous female character Dai Er, work is something of a distracting nuisance that gets in the way of her sensations and thought processes—unless, of course, it can be refashioned as part of the new way of living. Generally Chen Ran presents long-term salaried work as restricting: the requirement of set hours, a regular schedule, and, most important, the elevation of work goals above those of lifestyle prevent her characters from achieving the freedom and independence that are the unspoken conditions to which they aspire. This limitation, however, is more serious for men, who cannot escape the strictures of responsibility and thus are not as capable of the floating existence as are women.[7]

The Postman

One topic of the 1995 film *Youchai* (The postman) by sixth-generation director He Yi (He Jianjun) is urban labor and its gendered meanings.[8] Although like many post-Mao cultural works, *The Postman* presents a world quite different from that in which concepts—not to mention practices—of *nei* and *wai* were clearly delineated, in subtle ways both the theme and the aesthetics of the film depend on a gendered narrative of labor. One important aspect of this gendered story is the film's perspective on generative social space, which is not overtly but rather covertly marked as male.

In a seemingly contradictory way, the film presents two takes on work. On one hand, it relegates work to a nonidealized sphere that is no different than that occupied, both mentally and physically, by the innocent but alienated city dweller. In this kind of work, women and men inhabit the same world and are separated only by different levels of skill, strength, and normative hierarchy. Work becomes a repetitive sensual experience of sound and motion, a cynical consciousness, and an attitude of detachment, just as those attributes are part of city life in general. At the same time, work and the workplace carry with them a trace of possibility reminiscent of the idealized work concepts of revolutionary culture. Although work is mandatory for everyone, the ability to conceive of and bring out its utopian side belongs only to the male protagonist, who through this identification takes on the weighty burden of helping others live a correct life.

The film's plot is confusing, and it is not always immediately clear who is speaking or acting, a technique that, we eventually realize, puts us into a position similar to that of the main character. The film demands some mental detective work on our part since we must put various apparently unrelated scenes, people, and words together to form a meaningful narrative. Xiao Dou, a young postal worker, is assigned to replace Lao Wu, who is removed from his position as letter carrier in Xingfu (Happiness) district because he has opened and read other people's letters. Shy and awkward, Xiao Dou lives with his sister in a large rundown house passed on to them by their parents, who died when he was young. His sister has a boyfriend who frequently visits and complains that she must give up this old house so they can get married and move into a modern apartment. The sister is reluctant to follow this plan as it will leave Xiao Dou behind alone. As Xiao Dou prepares to take over the route, a young and attractive female coworker, Yunqing, assists him and, not long afterward, seduces him.

Xiao Dou immediately follows in Lao Wu's footsteps in more ways than one, opening and reading letters he is supposed to deliver.[9] He goes farther, however, and tries to intervene in people's lives in four instances. The first is that of a woman (Qiu Ping) and a man (Zhao Zeren) married to others but involved with each other. Xiao Dou anonymously writes to Zhao, threatening him with serious but unnamed consequences unless he ends the relationship and leaves all of their correspondence at a prearranged spot for pickup. The second is the case of a prostitute, Wan Juan, who gets introductions to clients from a doctor, Qian Yuzi. Xiao Dou visits the doctor after he sees Wan Juan go in and then goes to see Wan Juan, claiming the doctor sent him. He says almost nothing and rushes out before any intimacy takes place. The third involves two young people, most likely a married couple, who have written suicidal letters to the man's parents. Xiao Dou writes a new letter that describes in sunny terms how everything is fine and sends it with the pictures originally enclosed in the suicide letter. The fourth is the drug addict Zhang Xin, who is melancholy and violent over lack of news from his homosexual lover, Chen Jie. Xiao Dou, who has withheld the letters from Chen Jie, goes to Zhang Xin's apartment, pays the rent so the landlady will allow him to enter, listens to Zhang Xin talk about his relationship with Chen Jie and what it is like to be high, and removes some drug paraphernalia when he leaves. He later sees Zhang Xin taken out on a stretcher. Previously, Xiao Dou confronted Chen Jie when the latter asked if there were any letters for him. Xiao Dou said, "You're Chen Jie, aren't you? A writer?" but did not respond when Chen Jie asked him how he knew this.

The film presents a depressing society chopped into small, isolated, reified units spatially and materially, and therefore psychologically, a situation experienced equally by the male and female characters. The only healthy way people living in this environment can connect is through organic links developed when they were children—and these eventually fail them—or through the indirect method of letter writing. Barriers in architecture, work styles, and social habits and at the very level of consciousness are rigidly enforced by various normative structures, and these are what prevent face-to-face communication. Yet people retain a desire for emotionally satisfying relationships with other human beings.

Although the film's portrayal of work is, on the surface, almost opposite to what we find in ideal Maoist images, in Xiao Dou's attempt to right what has gone wrong we see idealism underlying his concept of what work should be. The seemingly blasé work environment that has replaced the Maoist vision of passion and positive social change is actually a physical and mental *space*—the only one in the film, and one presented with both irony and hope—where positive social change can be conceptualized and put into action. This vision of what work should be, diluted though it is, is inherited as a residue from a long contradictory discourse of labor under Maoism that includes first a glorification, and second a political relationship to authority that demands a challenge to inappropriate power.[10] The nature of this authority, however, has radically changed and is dispersed into the surroundings, also drawing the viewer's attention to the issue of space. Space, I argue, is none other than this diffusion of authority.

Xiao Dou's job as a postman gives him the opportunity to intervene in personal relationships, strike at the heart of what he finds wrong with society, and help forge *proper connections* between people. Although Xiao Dou cannot find a clear authority to challenge, his intervention, ideological in nature, proceeds as if there were one and replaces letter delivery as his real work. The letter becomes a double-edged representation of the spatial segmentation and inability of people to communicate and of the hopes that Xiao Dou invests in his work. As the film progresses, Xiao Dou refines his activities, which eventually meet with failure.

The opportunities offered by this special work space, which is both partially imagined and partially remembered by Xiao Dou, are part of a gendered cultural sphere. Xiao Dou is a contemporary antihero, now diminished in his abilities and sensibilities, who still takes on the burden of cultural construction and directs his actions toward positive ends. His goal is to act within the space that is the diffusion of authority and find a place where he can intervene. Women stand in a familiar position, representing, first, the possibility of a natural life of honest human affection and, second, a sexual route that also offers Xiao Dou a path toward increased understanding of his personal and social role. The women themselves have no ability to transcend or even imagine transcending the deadening social limits against which Xiao Dou struggles. The film takes a position on the contemporary debate about Chinese modernity, holding that there is little—but still some—hope for a social life based on revolutionary values to emerge, as long as at least one male actor within this sphere can retain a grasp on his ability to move others toward a positive goal.

The World Doesn't Seem to Need Us Anymore

The film portrays contemporary Chinese society as a visually and more generally sensually oppressive set of small boxes. What we first see are slow and gritty shots of rundown apartment buildings as they actually exist in many cities in China. Doors and entryways—foregrounded throughout the film—are blocked by old bicycles, trash, and other items. Paint is fading and falling off, the ground is grimy and dusty, and smog hangs in the air, with four industrial towers in the distance taking up the screen now and then. Colors are brown, beige, dull olive green, and gray. The urban environment is almost completely without charm, and there is not a shred of romanticism in these images.[11] We see Xiao Dou working with a chain and hoist to install a new post office box, a scene that also reappears at the end and anchors the preoccupation with work—physical and mental—that structures the film. Many shots in the post office are close-ups of hands doing their regular work, stamping letters, sorting, and filing.

Although Xiao Dou's job at this point is manual labor, when I say "preoccupation with work," what I mean is not only the actual job of setting up post boxes and delivering letters but also the more abstract cultural work that lies behind Xiao Dou's actions: the ideological work of social change and the demand for cultural improvement directed at males and taken up by Xiao Dou despite his obvious unsuitability for the role. The close-ups of Xiao Dou heaving the box into place, of chains, the weight of iron, and the difficulty of moving the box appear at the beginning and end of the film and form a frame for the plot. Although here what we see is the resistance of matter in work, we soon discover that the post office box is not only physically heavy but also endowed with special metaphorical meaning as a spot where a once-removed (not face-to-face) exchange between people takes place.[12] This world-space of human relations in the film has shriveled, it turns out, to the space occupied by this small circular container. The scene thus highlights both the physical labor of work and also its symbolic meanings; furthermore, we see that ideological work is also hard work. The sharply material images place Xiao Dou's efforts and achievements, questionable though they are, within the context of a long discourse of ideologically meaningful manual labor.

He Yi's approach, a kind of dirty realism, shows the grimy city and its dense structures at several points, but never directly implies that it once was otherwise, at least for adults. The camera tends to pan slowly from side to side or top to bottom over blocks of living quarters, lingering there and drawing our attention to their poor condition and deadening regularity, and there are many references to city life as ruins. For example, Xiao Dou's sister lives in a large but dilapidated house that—judging from her constant attempts to get her brother and boyfriend to put on warm clothes—does not have central heating or adequate plumbing and bathing facilities. In the letter Xiao Dou writes to the old couple in their son's name, he inquires about plans to tear down the neighborhood in which the parents live. And Xiao Dou's sister's boyfriend insists that the furniture in her house is too old and must be replaced with something modern, even though much of it is real wood, the sister protests.

Although He Yi does not present us with a vibrant world of human connections that once existed in older buildings and the social activities that took place in them (as, for example, in Zhang Yang's 1999 film *Xizao* [Shower]), in his frequent straight-on pans across apartment blocks, in his centering of doorways leading from one space to another, and in the thematic elements discussed above, he brackets the division of space into unconnected units and replacement of the old by the new as an unsettling and unsatisfactory aspect of urban life. However, because the past exists not as any clear history or unified memory that can be manipulated into romance but rather as traces and remnants—the repetition of the orchard story (described below), the orchard keeper turned fortune-teller, the all-wood furniture inherited from parents, and the soon-to-be destroyed neighborhoods—we can hypothesize that at some point there either was a past different from the present, or that minimally, there now exists a rapidly fading memory of a time when everyone thought things could, should, or would improve.

Another aspect of this urban fragmentation and disintegration is a mysterious underlying violence that sometimes breaks through the surface. Our first glimpse of this violence is Lao Wu being forced roughly into a car and taken away after he confesses to opening mail. Following shortly is a scene of a man running with several others chasing and yelling at him. Xiao Dou is an observer who makes no move toward intervention and expresses no emotion. At Xiao Dou's home, we see the unhappiness of his sister's boyfriend, who is adamant that they must move into the new apartment that is waiting for them. Lack of privacy is obvious, as the doors in the old house even when shut are effectively kept open by windowpanes in the top half. It is awkward for the couple to interact sexually with Xiao Dou in the house. Noises travel freely and quickly, and we see Xiao Dou listening to his sister and her boyfriend as they make love, and even peering through the window blinds. At the end of the film, a mysterious scene with Xiao Dou's sister crying in the background and her boyfriend yelling, "Cry! Cry! Can you ever stop crying!" as he kills and chops up a chicken for a meal again reveals a barely covered hostility and aggression, with no clear explanation.

Other than the relationship between Xiao Dou and his sister, we see very little warm human interaction, implying that the depressing environment has infiltrated the consciousnesses of the people who inhabit it and violence is most likely far from unusual. Yunqing seems to be more interested in sexual satisfaction than in any long-term emotional relationship and calmly tells Xiao Dou that her sexual encounter with post office manager Lao Liu half a year before was the same as her encounter with him.[13] Lao Liu compliments Xiao Dou on his work but maintains a distance. Xiao Dou's sister's boyfriend offers him a cigarette, but otherwise there is almost no interaction between them. Xiao Dou fails to make a real connection with any of the people whose letters he intercepts, although he desires communication. Even the party for Xiao Dou's sister and her boyfriend as they are preparing to get married, which should be boisterous and fun, suffers from stiltedness, and the partygoers complain of a lack of liveliness. Their solution, to take a picture, only reifies the awkward relationship between Xiao Dou, his sister, and the boyfriend; the shot shows the sister and her fiancé standing next to each other with Xiao Dou as a shadowy presence between them.

The isolation of the characters is obvious, yet there is no clear cause presented within the film, nor does the film point to any authority responsible for the situation. Although we observe a few examples of the law stepping in to enforce social stability, for the most part what we see is a system of normative regulation that, like the repetitive pounding of cancellations that is the overwhelming sound of work at the post office, simply reproduces itself. The beauty within human society, the film implies, has been overwhelmed and subdued; the routines of daily life and the demands of a large population within a small space could be at fault, but the film does not exactly make that connection either.[14] This portrayal is not unusual in modern film or literature. To bemoan, even subtly, the effects of modernity on human society has been a major cultural theme in the twentieth century and today.[15] Yet one thing that makes He Yi's film interesting and unusual is its implied connection with and commentary on the Chinese revolutionary past in the pinpointing of work as a site where idealistic action can still be imagined and even, to a small degree and with questionable success, undertaken. The agent best suited to continue the positive aspects of the revolutionary past does not need to be a strong role model, but, as I discuss here, he must be male.

Latter-Day Confucian, New Age Maoist

What rather quickly becomes clear about Xiao Dou is that by contemporary standards he is almost dysfunctional. Bereft of friends, the only person Xiao Dou is able to talk to is his sister.[16] This link, which often consists of chatting about a peach orchard that they frequented as youth, their fear of the orchard keeper, and their failure to taste a peach despite many attempts to steal one, borders on incestuous. Indeed, toward the end of the film we see Xiao Dou and his sister making love in a bed with the "double happiness" characters on the wall above; clearly this is the marriage bed of Xiao Dou's sister and her husband. As they lie in bed, a shocking admission floats out: although we are too far away to see moving lips, we hear the sister's voice as she states that she once was in the orchard without Xiao Dou and did taste the peaches after all. The comment about the orchard comes after several similar references at different parts of the film and the repeated statement that neither of them ever tasted a peach.

The meaning of the orchard is unclear, although the mysterious, exciting, and forbidden context, the reference to a torn skirt and blood running down the girl's leg, the constant desire for a peach that underlies their visits to the orchard, and the admission of a secret taste imply a sexual significance. At the same time, the tale of the orchard is the one Xiao Dou and his sister love to share, suggesting that the orchard represents a private, preadult, idyllic childhood relationship. These idyllic childhood days are over, their close relationship is about to be terminated (she is about to get married), and now the pleasant memory of those times also is destroyed through this new revelation (that the sister did indeed taste a peach). Her admission of previously undisclosed experience could be interpreted as a statement that she has had other sexual experiences and also as a betrayal of their special past together.

We do not discover with whom, if anyone, Xiao Dou's sister had a sexual relationship, but another mysterious character drawing Xiao Dou's attention is the orchard keeper, who now has become a fortune-teller and banana vendor on the street. When Xiao Dou sees the man telling a fortune, he brings himself close and studies the man's face, and later the camera focuses on the fortune-teller's impassive expression as he reorganizes the bananas in front of him. Because Xiao Dou's sister did taste a peach after all, and because it was the orchard keeper who supposedly had prevented her and Xiao Dou from taking a peach, a vague and imprecise connection is proposed: as a child, was Xiao Dou's sister bribed with a peach to have sexual contact with the orchard keeper?

Thus, Xiao Dou's relationship with his sister, although deeply emotional for both of them, joins the other modern relationships as abnormal by ordinary social standards. In its many sexual references and sense of scurrying around the issue of sexual relationships, the film picks up a commonly heard complaint in the post-Mao days: under Maoism, sexual desire was suppressed by the state and repressed in each person, and this long-lasting suppression is still influential in affecting attitudes toward sex. He Yi participates in this interest by highlighting sexual motivation behind many events. His main character has sexual difficulties that within psychoanalytical theory may appear to be perversion or repression. For example, Xiao Dou watches his sister bathe through a window, and although he is first afraid when Yunqing kisses him, it does not take him long to respond actively and almost violently. Furthermore, three of the four situations in which Xiao Dou becomes involved—an affair between two people married to others, prostitution and pimping by a doctor, and a homosexual relationship between a drug addict and a writer—are concerned with so-called illicit sexual relationships, although in the case of the drug addict it is unclear whether Xiao Dou intercedes to "correct" the homosexual liaison or the drug use.[17] The relationship between Xiao Dou and his sister, therefore, is not any different than the others.

My point here is that although sexual desire seems to be behind much of the action and clearly is important in some way, I do not see it as the main target of the director's concern. He Yi is not castigating sexual behavior as something that in itself has caused the dilemma, nor is abnormal sexual behavior a clear result of excessive state control either now or in the past. Even more important, bringing sexual desire out into the open or centering it as a mandatory part of personal identity is not presented as an implicit solution to any problem presented in the film. We see no positive sexual models to which we as audience could imagine the characters aspiring, and the sexually "progressive" characters are as disturbed as anyone else. The director gives sexual repression as a concept pride of place, but not the power of origination, and it is here that his approach differs from that of many other films and novels that center sexual identity as something to be damned or praised.[18]

However, although the director is not making a statement about sexuality that corresponds to these more common interpretations, sexual relations clearly are of consequence in the film. Their importance lies, I believe, in several areas. First, sexual relationships are easily invoked as expressions of a more general desire that can transcend sexuality. What this film shows is that if anything has been repressed, it is not sexual desire but the idealism associated with a prior social life. Indeed, Xiao Dou's tryst with Yunqing shows us what a simple task it is to become sexually involved, and Yunqing's blasé comment about her sexual involvement with Lao Liu indicates no worry about sexual morality or fear of social condemnation. Yet achieving sexual pleasure does not make Xiao Dou any more content, and aside from Yunqing's oddly expressed comment about how good she feels after sex with Xiao Dou, no character expresses the enthusiasm and excitement frequently associated with sexual desire and behavior. From the perspective of symbolic desire, we must place sexual desire within the larger concern of Xiao Dou's social role and work before it makes sense; desire has been not only repressed and thwarted but also gutted of significance, and sexual desire can visually express and encapsulate that basic condition.

Second, from the larger viewpoint of gender relations, the film repeats and confirms a very conventional aspect of male-female sexual involvement. The relationships that Xiao Dou has with his sister and with Yunqing are similar to the relationships between central male characters and women in the films of Chen Kaige (with whom director He Yi has worked). For Chen, women always offer redemptive qualities that can help cure personal and social alienation in the forever-seeking male protagonists. To accept this comfort, however, means rejecting the most important male endeavor of cultural reformation and accepting a degree of social feminization, which is partially defined by freedom from this responsibility (and a corresponding lack of social importance).[19]

Along those lines, both Xiao Dou's sister and Yunqing offer him a symbolic and practical way out of his predicament. The sister embodies an emotional connection that predates adulthood; it was set up before the uncomfortable difficulties so obvious in adult relationships were in place. As a readily available source of labor to help with the tasks of cooking, eating, and wearing proper clothes, the sister structures daily life. This labor is significant not only in itself but also in that it presents a larger framework for work, which needs "something to come home to" as a counterbalance. Through her defining contribution, work is circumscribed and limited: it is not socially important so much as it is for the purpose of sustaining another life, that of family relationships. But if the sister wants to take up her own social role as a wife and transfer these services to her new husband, her relationship with her brother cannot be continued. However, she offers a replacement for all of her work when she finds an appropriate mate for Xiao Dou. As she brings in a sweater she is knitting for him to see if it is the right size, she broaches the idea of Xiao Dou going to meet a girl she has chosen. Her physical awkwardness and linguistic hesitation as she tests the sweater against Xiao Dou's body show that she is fully aware of the profound bond her action is breaking. She experiences great difficulty making the offer.

Yunqing, on the other hand, virtually throws herself at Xiao Dou, but her involvement lacks the deep emotional link inherent in the sister. What Yunqing offers is another balance that has the potential to redefine labor, possibly even more significantly than does the presence of a loving sister or wife at home. If Xiao Dou were to stay in Yunqing's world, work would not be just something to get away from as one goes home to a warm and caring environment, but it would itself become a site where new physical relationships can be negotiated. The office, in other words, would be redefined as a playground. Physical proximity allows sexual relations to be smoothly hidden under the movements, gestures, and language of work, which turn into both their cover and their necessary condition. In fact, in this model such actions are no longer simply labor, but become sexual in and of themselves. Negotiations and transactions do not have to proceed directly but can be carried out covertly, through the speech and acts that ostensibly are part of work. Even though Xiao Dou does not know Yunqing is attracted to him until she actually approaches, his lack of understanding comes from his innocence. If he were to accept this vision and become experienced in this form of work, he would notice another Yunqing's interest much earlier. This vision of work could easily displace both the family-life narrative and the alternative story that he eventually concocts and plays out through his efforts.

The fact that Xiao Dou has to be torn away from his sister, first by her agency and his passivity in finding him a mate and second by her admission that their past together has been based on a lie, shows that he is a severely weakened cultural hero. However, he is strong enough to realize that Yunqing does not offer him what he is seeking, and he is also strong enough to take the crucial first step toward putting his idealism into motion. As in Chen Kaige's movies, although the film is informed by a basic misogyny that insists its conditions are mandatory, investigation of gender meanings is not central to its goal. The sex of the troubled agent in this fallen utopia is taken for granted; men hold in their hands and minds the power of cultural renewal, and women not only are excluded from this crucially important endeavor but also offer, in various forms, a dangerously alluring temptation that can cause the hero to veer from his track.

So the hero, surrounded and buttressed by, and even created against, tempting female-based alternative narratives, must be male. But what kind of a man is Xiao Dou? In many instances in the film, Xiao Dou's lack of basic social skills and fundamental inability to articulate his concerns are apparent. When Yunqing invites him out to eat and chat, he replies antisocially, "What's there to talk about?" His response to his boss's compliments on his good work is to look down silently. He runs off without doing anything after entering the prostitute Wan Juan's apartment, and he says almost nothing. And when he visits drug addict Zhang Xin, Xiao Dou cannot get a word out of his mouth. Yet within the context of the film, Xiao Dou's dysfunctional nature does not seem too extreme, because the camera work, slowly moving across cold, gritty streets and shabby rundown apartments, implies that the entire society is spatially depressing and mentally alienated. Such an idea comes across well in the sexual encounter between Xiao Dou and Yunqing; Xiao Dou's response to Yunqing's comment about sex being the same with him or with Lao Liu is to pick up a toy windup elephant in her apartment, wind it up, and watch it go through its mechanical movements, an exact expression of unthinking and unfeeling repetition.

Socially, what identifies Xiao Dou as a male hero is that despite his dysfunctionality, he is motivated by some notion of how things should be. He in no way directly expresses this desire, but we can intuit it from his actions. We see little hope for social improvement, or even any such concept, in the surroundings or the people who live in this society. Yet in all four cases in which he tracks people down through their letters and attempts to understand their lives, Xiao Dou creeps—or leaps—out of his observer status to get involved and set right certain perceived wrongs.

In the case of Zhao Zeren, the married man who is having an affair with Qiu Ping, Xiao Dou acts directly, writing to Zhao and urging him to consider several things: the cost of maintaining Qiu Ping's lifestyle, whether or not he could actually make her happy, and other vague but threatening consequences of their relationship. Although the letter is written anonymously, compared with his ability to voice (or write) his concerns in the other cases, here Xiao

Dou is fairly expressive. It is from this case that we can most directly see Xiao Dou's desire to intervene. His ability to articulate his concerns exists only when he does not confront his targets face-to-face, however, and diminishes as the film goes on. As Yunqing states, it is hard to understand why people feel comfortable writing to each other but cannot directly state their feelings. Indeed, when Xiao Dou is with the prostitute Wan Juan, the elderly couple, the drug addict, and the novelist, because he cannot speak out, we cannot discern his rationale for visiting them.[20] Without the first case to clue us in, we would not be able to tell what Xiao Dou is after.

Although he is weak and inarticulate, Xiao Dou uses the sterling opportunity presented by his work to straighten a society gone awry. His focus on proper relationships—of married adults (Zhao Zeren and Qiu Ping), of children to parents (the suicidal couple and their elderly parents or parents-in-law), between men and women (Wan Juan and her customers), and between (male) friends (Zhang Xin and Chen Jie)—makes his concerns strongly reminiscent of Confucian values, where these relationships anchor the morality of an entire society. Because Xiao Dou never explains his discomfort directly, we cannot fathom his exact objections to these relationships, but minimally we can see that all of the situations in which he has chosen to intervene to some extent fall outside conventional social morality. His own life is also in this category.

Xiao Dou's sexual interest in his sister would make him only a very troubled Confucian. Regarding him as a New Age Maoist, however, illuminates the film's strange and contradictory notion of gendered work and the relationship of work to social improvement. Anything attractive about work or labor has now been subdued both by the same forces that have produced an alienated population and by the disappearance of its glorification as a backbone of social morality in revolutionary culture. Yet with other social realms—family and sexuality—offering nothing other than diversion, it is work that retains for Xiao Dou the ember of revolutionary values. Another way to describe this situation is to say that when sparked by the efforts of a male cultural hero, labor's lost ability to embody social improvement is restored. This narrative of work may have been open to both women and men when it was a strong revolutionary discourse, but now that it has faded to the point of disappearing, a male trigger must bring it back to our consciousness and present it to us as a social option. It also is worth noting that the new capitalist entrepreneurship, with all of its chaotic energy, does not so much as make an appearance—unless we consider the orchard keeper now turned into a street-side fortune-teller and fruit vendor, who does not in any way represent any redemptive possibilities. The traditional old post office, which has not mechanized or benefited from even the most basic modernization, surely evokes an earlier period when state-owned industries based on the concept (if not necessarily the reality) of workers and the workplace serving the people was the norm.

The actual situation of workers in China is complex and a great deal has been written about their savvy and practical understanding of the highly romanticized discourse of the worker under socialism.[21] The attitude of Yunqing, for whom work seems to be nothing more than a way to sustain her life and a space where she can find sexual partners, may illustrate the post-Mao inheritance of decades of worker suspicion toward socialist labor fantasies. In this respect, Lao Liu also is an interesting character, for his attitude toward the workers under him contains a somewhat fatigued vestige of socialist paternalism. For example, Lao Liu responds in a semisympathetic fatherly way toward Lao Wu's transgressions and urges him to accept the consequences. He uses concerned flattery to get Xiao Dou to help him set up the new mailboxes on a weekend, telling him that he is the only one around who knows how to do it and his services are indispensable.

With the near-total contemporary disillusionment of worker belief in the glory of labor, it is surprising to find a character motivated by altruistic social improvement. I believe Xiao Dou and his social improvement program derive from revolutionary culture, especially from the values associated with the model worker. One of the Communist Party's most famous model workers, Lei Feng, now has a website (www.leifeng.com) with articles about the Lei Feng spirit, selections from Lei Feng's diary, stories about Lei Feng's life, and much more.[22] The qualities of wholeheartedly serving the people and the party, of being a mere screw in the huge enterprise of revolution, the emotive intensity of loving and respecting one's job all are listed. But it is selections from Lei Feng's diary that most clearly depict the spirit of the socialist worker:

> [I]f you were a drop of water, did you moisten an inch of soil? If you were a ray of sunlight, did you brighten a patch of darkness? If you were a single grain, did you nourish a useful life? If you were the tiniest screw, did you maintain your position in life forever? If you wanted to tell me about certain ideas, did you night and day spread those most beautiful ideals? Since you were alive, did you labor on behalf of those in the future, day by day making life more beautiful? I want to ask you, what have you done for the future? In the reservoir of life, we should not be just endless followers. (June 7, 1958)

> Ah, youth, it always is beautiful and good, but true youth belongs only to those who struggle to swim against the current, who labor forgetting the self, who are forever humble. (October 25, 1959)

I must remember: "In work (*gongzuo*), we must learn from the comrades who have the highest enthusiasm; in life, we must learn from the comrades who have the lowest living standard." (June 5, 1960)

Those who have no thought of themselves but only hold the People in their minds can surely obtain the highest glory and trust. And on the contrary, those who have only the self and not the People in their minds shall sooner or later be spat out and rejected by the People. (March, 1961)

The most glorious thing in the world—labor (*laodong*).
The most thoughtful people in the world—laborers. (March 16, 1961)

[T]he People's problems are my problems, to use a bit of my strength to help the People solve their problems is my responsibility, the place where I concentrate my efforts. I am a master, one of the great laboring masses, and conquering any bit of difficulty for the People is my greatest pleasure. (September 11, 1961)

One salient aspect of the Lei Feng myth is the intensity of emotions behind Lei Feng's feeling for the people, brought out in a scene from the 1965 film *Lei Feng*: "At that time the sky was dark, it was pouring rain, the road was sticky with mud, and there was a long way to go, but Lei Feng first and foremost did not think of his own difficulties, but of those of others. He was full of limitless, burning love for the People, and without any hesitation carried the child for the woman and took them to their door."[23]

The familiar qualities of selflessness and self-denial, serving the people, hard work with no consideration of personal gain, exhaustion, or reward, identifying problems that others have and working to solve them, no concern with one's own living standards, and faith in a better future and one's own ability to contribute to it all have a resonance in Xiao Dou's life. Like an overworked contemporary CEO or a tireless, earnest party cadre, Xiao Dou takes the office home with him, stuffing his drawers with letters to scan for people who need his help. He directs his own activity toward solving the problems he perceives others to have. Rejecting his sister's attempts to find a girlfriend for him and initially, at least, showing little interest in getting involved with Yunqing, Xiao Dou appears to have no desire to improve his own standard of living or to strive for his own pleasures. As he tries to right the incorrect relationships he reads about in others' letters, Xiao Dou is working for a better future for society at large. Xiao Dou's latent idealism is expressed in the film not only thematically but also in a mystical ring of bells that occurs several times throughout the film and stands in marked contrast to the cold and unattractive daily-life reality that we see.

Gendered Work Space and Revolutionary Desire

Lei Feng and Xiao Dou are both cultural figures who embody the male responsibility of social improvement and who show how work can—and must—be modeled and configured to meet that lofty aim. Compared with the historical Lei Feng and the image he projected, Xiao Dou has no visible passion or any clear ideological goal, yet his activities reveal similar ideals. The hidden nature of Xiao Dou's urges has a counterpart in Lei Feng as well; indeed, Lei Feng would never have been "found out" had it not been for his diaries, nor would Xiao Dou have been but for the film. The performance of political virtue, although criticized widely, appeared in this diary-losing form after Lei Feng's death as activists wrote and purposely lost diaries that they hoped others would find.[24] Xiao Dou's activism likewise is hidden in his work, and he even receives praise from his boss for his excellent performance much as did Lei Feng—although Xiao Dou's ideological work is not what Lao Liu recognizes.

The film steers clear of several current approaches to culture. Critics have written about the nostalgia of recent years, when the ideals and passions of the revolutionary era are becoming disassociated from the violence and fear of the period and taking on a glossy veneer of attractiveness.[25] The slogan "Make a revolution in the depths of your soul," the deep love for the people supposedly felt by model workers such as Lei Feng, the heartfelt loyalty expressed toward Chairman Mao in dances, declaration, and badge collecting all speak to an ethics of emotion, desire, and hope, qualities that may be somewhat more difficult to find in a consumer society where irony and self-consciousness are of paramount importance. Some believe that this lack has produced nostalgia for what many now imaginatively remember as pleasant and morally simpler days.[26] However, it is difficult to envision He Yi's film as a nostalgic enterprise, because its relentless critique of contemporary culture never cracks open to allow that ray of escapist pleasure to emerge. The film's presentation of the past as a trace rather than as a fully imagined and embodied presence also does not lend itself to an interpretation of nostalgia as its primary motivation.

Another common topic is the moral decrepitude that comes with capitalist practices.[27] Yet we can see that the lure of money and the decadent lifestyle does not entice Xiao Dou or anyone else in the film. Moreover, although we do see in the letters the strong need for human connection, the film is not suggesting that some recognizable aspect of society—corruption, greed, power manipulation—has caused people to lose a human essence, nor proposing a new humanism and subjectivity similar to that debated so actively in the 1980s.[28] Although people have trouble talking to each other directly, in their letters they are full of easily described passion.

Xiao Dou's social intervention cannot be carried on face-to-face because the space available for this kind of direct action no longer exists. Likewise, the space available for any direct human interaction has shrunk, for reasons unclear. Although Xiao Dou has inherited a moral stance and a faint belief in his responsibility to act, the film presents no authority, reason, ultimate cause, or even suspicion of a spot against which he can organize his struggle. In place of the usual bogeys of evil, He Yi proposes this restricting spatial logic of human subjectivity, or the diffusion of inhibiting authority into the spaces in which people live. Although this filmic presentation of a problem has obvious relevance to actual urban society in China where space is at a premium, it is not precisely a realistic portrayal. Indeed, from the point of view of people taking pleasure in their lives and each other's company, and from the perspective of people talking to each other and communicating, the film presents things as much worse than they actually are. The attractive human energies of urban spaces—malls, discos, bookstores, department stores, sidewalks, theaters, food stalls, restaurants, stadiums, and so on—are always in full swing in reality but do not so much as appear in the film. The filming techniques, with their minimal camera movement and close-up attention to the disjointed movements of work, also do not project a sense of realism. The spatial dilemma is shown in the real-life separated living units and in consciousness that repeats in images of newly constructed apartments at the end of the film, but even more so it exists as a theoretical inquiry.

To imply as He Yi does that spatial organization has determined human consciousness and limited agency or even any thought of agency guts traditional ideas of authority, diffusing it into buildings, the ground, images in the sky, and the environment in general. As in many of the writings of the experimental writers, a specific history is no longer directly to blame; going a step farther, this director also portrays a material structure that weighs heavily against Xiao Dou's lingering idealism and dooms his project to failure. For Xiao Dou the body is culturally inscribed and the mind and heart are culturally inscribed; even worse, however, there is almost no place that is not inscribed by this diffusion of authority.[29] When Xiao Dou's actions fall short in helping any of his targets, and when his own relationships with his sister and with Yunqing do not present him with either motivation or self-understanding, we see that the film gives us not only no authority against which to fight, but also no forcefully presented solutions.

The film offers two ways to think of the work space and the worker—even if hidden, unarticulated, and dysfunctional—as a barely functioning site of social hope. On one hand, to propose a place so seriously compromised in recent Chinese history must be taken as an ironic smile, the gesture of someone who wants to believe but cannot find a thread on which to hang his faith. By muddying Xiao Dou's idealism with murky issues of sexuality and the ideals of childhood, incest and revolutionary heroism, He Yi hedges his bet and plays to the knowing viewer. No one who has been through the Maoist period and the Cultural Revolution or even heard firsthand the stories of parents and relatives who labored in May Seventh Cadre Schools to improve their political standing would be able to transparently and instantly believe in the curative power of work. On the other hand, by undermining recent approaches to understanding the self and society common in film and literature, and particularly by placing at the film's center his studied investigation of authority and resistance—so central to twentieth-century Chinese cultural discourse—He Yi carves out a space that demands that Xiao Dou's moral activism be taken seriously. Common sense tells us that the shy and bumbling Xiao Dou, who can almost never directly approach the targets of his altruism and calmly discuss with them the details of and reasons for their situation, should take up his concerned sister's offer of an introduction to a suitable mate and get on with a regular life. Yet he rejects this road, turning his work into a sly new form of *serve the people.*

In beginning this chapter with a quote from Gan Yang critiquing Chinese conservatism in the 1990s, I inserted *The Postman* into the contemporary debate on intellectual politics. As Gan Yang details, the debate can be simplified into procapitalism and prorevolution poles that are argued theoretically, historically, culturally, politically, and economically, although the various arguments hardly fit together in a seamless whole. As Gan Yang states, the multiple aspects of the procapitalist line "do not even coordinate well with one another. Rather, *they betray a social mood that relies on tacit agreement*" (italics added) (47). With *The Postman* in mind, I would like to quote a section of Gan Yang's text that could easily be taken to describe the film rather than the intellectual atmosphere at large:

> In my view, this conservatism is bound to devitalize and suffocate Chinese intellectual life, leaving it epistemologically torpid and regressive. In fact, intellectual ossification, stagnation, and cynicism may already have set in, as evidenced by the publication of *The Last Twenty Years of Chen Yinke.* Full of cultural narcissism and fatalism, this biography evoked widespread resonance and self-pity among Chinese intellectuals. It looks as if Chinese intellectuals have collectively reached a dead end, and all they can do now is to intone mournful elegies for dead masters.[30]

Although *The Postman* is not about intellectuals, it is an intellectual film that makes a proposal about everyday life, work, and the possibility of revolutionary idealism. Projecting a world in which all are resigned to their bleak lives to the point of unawareness of any possible other option, He Yi does indeed project "a social mood that relies on tacit agreement." The film's suffocating editing recognizes this resignation as absolutely pervasive, but Xiao Dou offers some small relief.

The debate on a possible Chinese alternative modernity often centers on the question of to what extent the revolutionary period should be thought of as integral to the Chinese modern. One approach, promoted by Leo Ou-fan Lee in his book *Shanghai Modern: The Flowering of a New Urban Culture in China, 1930–1945*, identifies a modernity developing first in Shanghai, later in Taiwan and Hong Kong, and then once again in Shanghai as the concept leaps over the revolutionary period entirely.[31] Another approach has been developed directly by Liu Kang and more indirectly by a number of scholars working in literature, economics, political theory, and cultural theory.[32] Arguing that revolutionary thought emphasizing equality, engagement, community, and cooperation has had a significant influence on the creation and experience of modernity in China, Liu Kang and others promote more intellectual awareness of this history and a commitment to its values. According to Zhang Xudong, the discourse of an alternative modernity or the "Chinese way" "keeps alive the suspended historic promise of bourgeois revolution and modernity, namely, the liberty, equality, and self-realization of mankind" and "the continued effort to extend the benefits of freedom (from oppression, deprivation, and coercion) and democracy to a perpetuated national and international underclass." As such, this vision does not stem from a "utopian notion of History" but remains critical of the "disengagement from the commitment of the Chinese Revolution to the masses" that the economic reforms have put into place.[33]

The Postman presents us with an example of a bizarre hero who cannot think or act collectively, politically, or even with any clear vision of social improvement or moral right. Yet he develops a plan, and he acts on behalf of the social good and without thought to his own self-benefit. Within the context of the debate on Chinese modernity, what perspective does the film provide? Clearly He Yi is very critical of the society that has emerged in the mid-1990s. The reforms have produced not prosperity but a devastated urban environment populated by a people who are almost numbed into dullness and routine. It would never dawn on the characters to resist or even criticize the degradations of their social lives; for them, it is just daily life, and the masses have no awareness of anything else. The possibilities for change have almost evaporated, but they live on in an unlikely hero.

Whether this change should embrace gender equality at its most basic and generative level, however, is a question the film steadfastly declines to consider. *The Postman* takes for granted the belief that although all have been crushed into the same alienated and un-self-aware routine that has narrowed their lives and robbed them of meaningful human communication, the power to break through this monotonous worldview resides only in men. Xiao Dou is not as well-developed a hero as Lei Feng, but he still retains an ability to perceive and act out a story of social improvement. Although this narrative once may have been open to everyone, it now requires not merely following a set role but actually conceiving and creating, as if for the first time. Whether the social conditions are so desperate as to disallow the radical move of placing cultural creation in the mind of a woman or whether the director simply cannot conceive of such a thing is unclear. While presenting an original and thought-provoking vision of contemporary social life, *The Postman* has little to offer women who envision for themselves a central role in social construction.

Notes

1. Gan Yang, "A Critique of Chinese Conservatism in the 1990s," *Social Text* 55, vol. 16, no. 2 (Summer 1998): 45–66.

2. It is important to note, however, that the Maoist model contained an inherent contradiction between valorizing work, society, and others, and valorizing the self. As the story of Lei Feng well shows, it was all too easy for the revolutionary worker to be put forth as a model in diaries, poems, and images, and the following that Lei Feng generated illustrated the fine line between promoting the socialized self and promoting socialism itself. This contradiction was investigated in Cui Wei's 1959 film *Song of Youth*, where the protagonist fights an internal battle that wages true self-sacrifice against self-glory in the name of sacrifice.

3. For this translation, see Wang Meng *Bolshevik Salute: A Modernist Chinese Novel*, trans. Wendy Larson (Seattle: University of Washington Press, 1989), 100–1.

4. Published in *Lianhe wenxue* in 1992, Mo Yan's *Shenpiao* was translated by Andrew F. Jones with Jeanne Tai in *Running Wild: The New Chinese Writers*, ed. David Der-wei Wang with Jeanne Tai (New York: Columbia University Press, 1994), 1–12.

5. For a detailed analysis of this film, see David L. Li, "What Will Become of Us If We Don't Stop? Ermo's China and the End of Globalization," *Comparative Literature* 53, no. 4 (Fall 2001): 442–61.

6. See Wendy Larson, "The Self Loving the Self: Men and Connoisseurship in Modern Chinese Literature," in *Femininities and Masculinities in China*, ed. Susan Brownell and Jeffrey N. Wasserstrom (Berkeley: University of California Press, 2002), for a discussion of the position of the marginalization of being female.

7. See Wendy Larson, "Women and the Discourse of Desire in Postrevolutionary China: The Awkward Postmodernism of Chen Ran," *boundary2* 41, no. 3 (Fall 1997): 201–24. For an example from Chen Ran's stories, see "Ling yizhi erduo de qiaoji sheng" (The sound of another ear knocking), *Qianxing yishi* (Hidden natures, lost affairs) (Shijiazhuang: Hebei jiaoyu chubanshe, 1995), 20–77.

8. Starting in 1982, He Jianjun worked with Chen Kaige and other fifth-generation directors on a number of films. In 1988, he began study in film directing and, in 1991, directed the short documentary *Self-Portrait* (*Zi hua xiang*) about painter and intellectual Qiu Sha. In 1993, He directed *Red Beads* (*Xuanlian*, also known as *Hongdou*), *The Postman* in 1995, and in 2001 *Butterfly Smile* (*Hu Die de weixiao*). For information about and a short interview with He Jianjun, see www.msgp.org/director/hejianjun/intro.htm.

9. Xiao Dou, a damaged social innovator, has little agency of his own unless a door is opened a crack on his behalf. The first opening is Lao Wu's departure, and the second comes when Yunqing hands him a letter that has come open and asks him to reseal it. He puts it in another envelope and rewrites the address on it. This letter turns out to be the first one that he opens and reads. By calling his attention to the letter, Yunqing has given him an opportunity to think of reading the letter and then to open it without detection and without direct deceit, since it was open anyway.

10. In her study of contemporary workers and their concepts of work and of themselves, Lisa Rofel comments that those raised on Cultural Revolution ideology believe that "struggle against improper authority is the singularly most important activity in life" (176). See *Other Modernities: Gendered Yearnings in China after Socialism* (Berkeley: University of California Press, 1999). The Red Guards are perhaps the most extreme example of a group motivated to fight against both conceptual authorities, such as feudal ideas and backward daily habits, and against those who represent authority, such as teachers or local leaders.

11. The only romantic image I could see was the older couple going out to take their birds for a walk. As we soon discover, however, their happiness is based on an illusion.

12. Several times we see people hesitantly approaching the box to mail letters and pausing, full of trepidation, before they drop a letter into the box.

13. In this scene, the camera is focused on Xiao Dou sitting on the floor in his underwear next to Yunqing's bed. He yells out his question, "What was it like that time?" and we hear her disembodied response from a distance. The scene emphasizes Xiao Dou's isolation and Yunqing's lack of emotional connection. Although later in her bedroom she looks at Xiao Dou and comments about how good she feels, and then moves to caress and kiss him, we are unsure if Yunqing feels good because she is with Xiao Dou or because she has had a satisfactory sexual experience.

14. Such a sentiment is put into words by the letter from the young suicidal couple: "The world doesn't seem to need us anymore" expresses their lack of a sense of positive social or physical space.

15. See Charles Taylor's *Sources of the Self: The Making of the Modern Identity* (Cambridge, Mass.: Harvard University Press, 1989); also Henry Sussman, *The Aesthetic Contract: Statutes of Art and Intellectual Work in Modernity* (Stanford, Calif.: Stanford University Press, 1997). As Sussman writes: "[M]odern Western ideology heightens the moral dilemma, isolation, and play accruing to the self. An increased leeway opened through a more direct engagement with the sources of authority implies greater moral responsibility and added participation in the scenario of an 'ultimate' moral outcome" (81).

16. A lengthy shot of Xiao Dou and his sister talking as they eat is taken from a distance away and a little below, with the camera not moving during the conversation. The monotonous angle contributes to the general lack of liveliness in relationships, even in this one that is portrayed as more profound than others.

17. The voices of Zhang Xin and Chen Jie, which come out as Xiao Dou reads their letters, refer mostly to their love for each other, and thus it would make more sense that Xiao Dou is intervening because of the sexual relationship.

18. For a brief but illuminating discussion of the role of sexuality in the construction of the modern self, see Sussman, *The Aesthetic Contract*:

> Eroticism will became a major metaphoric field for the exploration of a newly founded personal freedom. There is nothing "new" about assigning sexuality a certain centrality or essentiality in the unfolding of experience, as an ample body of poems deriving from Western antiquity attests. But there is a concentration of language in "The Canonization" and in others of Donne's lyrics that places eroticism and aesthetics in diplomatic, legal, and commercial contexts with specific nuances within an emerging modern age with an ideology of heightened personal experience. (81)

For a discussion of one aspect of erotics in contemporary Chinese literature, see Zhang Weimin, "Aiyu yu wenming de chongtu: Tan Shu Ping de xiaoshuo chuangzuo" (The conflict between desire and civilization: On the creative works of Shu Ping), *Dangdai zuojia pinglun* (June 1995): 12–16. See also my article "Never So Wild: Sexing the Cultural Revolution," *Modern China* 25, no. 4 (October 1999): 423–50.

19. I have elaborated on these ideas in "The Concubine and the Figure of History: Chen Kaige's *Farewell My Concubine*, In *Cultural Critique to Global Capital: Transnational Chinese Cinema*, ed. Sheldon Lu (Honolulu: University of Hawaii Press, 1997), 331–46.

20. Xiao Dou also writes to the elderly couple, but only in the name of their son.

21. Jackie Sheehan's *Chinese Workers: A New History* (New York: Routledge, 1998) details a long history of worker activism and an uneasy relationship between workers and authorities that spans the entire century. Sheehan also finds that although workers had to negotiate a position for themselves within socialist rhetoric about duties and their vanguard position, they generally took the concepts and ideas with a large grain of salt. Practical concerns such as working hours and conditions, wages, living and health issues, and access to various benefits were the motivation behind conflicts between workers and cadres, rather than ideological issues. In his analysis of *biaoxian*, or self-presentation, Andrew G. Walder (in *Communist Neo-Traditionalism: Work and Authority in Chinese Industry* [Berkeley: University of California Press, 1986]) finds that, ironically, "it is the truly committed who must be the most calculating in their display of commitment" (146) and that there generally is deep resentment against "activists" who constantly try to present themselves as politically correct (166–69). Lisa Rofel finds that the group of workers who used "foot-dragging techniques" of resistance, or indirect techniques of subversion, were those who came of age during the Cultural Revolution, because those workers had developed a politics of authority that encouraged them to challenge improperly used power (*Other Modernities*, 174–75).

22. The website is hosted by the *Wuxun dazhong zixun chuangbo youxian gongsi* (listed in English as the Public Information Company): address, Yongan lu #1, Xinwu qu, Xuxun shi, Liaoning sheng; telephone, 0413-2628233; fax, 0413-2638730; e-mail, leifeng@www.leifeng.com. All translations here are by Wendy Larson.

23. Yang Guisheng (Beijing iron factory worker), "Guanghui de xingxiang" (Glorious image), *Dianying yishu* (January 1956): 3–4.

24. See Walder, *Communist Neo-Traditionalism*, for a discussion of the anger that the blatant activist approach generated in other workers. It would be much safer to gain political recognition through a chance finding of a lost diary than through the daily performance of political virtue that angers colleagues so much.

25. See Dai Jinhua, "Imagined Nostalgia," *boundary2* 24, no. 3 (Fall 1997): 143–62; Leo Ou-fan Lee, *Shanghai Modern: The Flowering of a New Urban Culture in China, 1930–1945* (Cambridge, Mass.: Harvard University Press, 1999), 307–41; Ann Anagnost, *National Past-times: Narrative, Representation, and Power in Modern China* (Durham, N.C.: Duke University Press, 1997), 54–56 and throughout; and Zhang Xudong, "Shanghai Nostalgia: Postrevolutionary Allegories in Wang Anyi's Literary Production in the 1990s," *positions* 8, no. 2 (Fall 2000): 349–88.

26. For a reference to this slogan and a discussion of the "Maoist utopian longing for a full and complete life," see Xiaobing Tang, *Chinese Modern: The Heroic and the Quotidian* (Durham, N.C.: Duke University Press, 2000), 278–80 and throughout.

27. A popular example would be Chi Li's 2000 novel *Lailai wangwang* (Busy life) and Tian Di's television series of the same name and based on the novel, which trace the moral downfall of a formerly upright man who once worked as a butcher and studied Mao's writings in his spare time. Jia Pingwa's famous *Feidu* (Abandoned city) also works along these lines.

28. For discussion of humanism and subjectivity in China, see Liu Zaifu, *Xingge zuhelun* (On the composition of personality) (Hefei: Anhui wenyi chubanshe, 1999); also see Wang Jing, *High Culture Fever: Politics, Aesthetics, and Ideology in Deng's China* (Berkeley: University of California Press, 1996), chap. 1 on voluntarism and chap. 5 on romancing the subject; also see Kalpana Misra, *From Post-Maoism to Post-Marxism: The Erosion of Official Ideology in Deng's China* (New York: Routledge, 1998), chap. 5. Humanism was proposed as a correction to Maoism throughout the 1980s and into the 1990s. The previously mentioned *Buli* by Wang Meng, although still professing belief in socialism, has an underlying humanist message; Dai Houying's *Ren a ren* (People, ah, people) (Hong Kong: Xiangjiang, 1985) is a key literary text in the promotion of humanism.

29. Wang Jing describes the preexperimental roots writers thus: "The body is culturally inscribed but the mind and heart are free" (*High Culture Fever*, 216).

30. Gan Yang, "A Critique of Chinese Conservatism," 47. The book referred to is *Chen Yinke de zuihou ershi nian* (The last twenty years of Chen Yinke), Lu Jiandong (Beijing: Sanlian shudian, 1996).

31. Published by Harvard University Press, 1999.

32. See Liu Kang, "Is There an Alternative to (Capitalist) Globalization? The Debate About Modernity in China," *boundary2* 23, no. 3 (1996): 193–218. See also Zhang

Xudong, "The Making of the Post-Tiananmen Intellectual Field: A Critical Overview," in *Whither China? Intellectual Positions in Contemporary China*, ed. Zhang Xudong (Durham, N.C.: Duke University Press, 2001). This volume contains a number of contributions from the "neoleftist" position that argues that "only by including the masses can the success and political-moral meaning of the Chinese Reform be assured" (Zhang, "The Making," 68).

33. Zhang, "The Making," 67–68.

III

BOUNDARIES

10

Women's Work and the Economics of Respectability

Kenneth Pomeranz

A PRINCIPAL FEATURE OF THE LATE IMPERIAL and Republican economy was the growth of rural handicrafts, particularly textiles. It is generally agreed that the increase in textile production meant a significant increase in production for the market by women, especially in the Yangzi Delta. But scholars have disagreed sharply about the implications of this work for women and their families.

The relevant scholarship presents a confusing, often contradictory, set of claims. For example, some have insisted that the cotton economy raised the living standards of those involved. As women increasingly specialized in textile work, scholars argue, they left the farming to their husbands while their husbands left spinning and weaving to them. Although according to this scenario women stayed indoors more than ever, the meaning of that confinement is debatable. Some see the status of peasant women improving as they became able to reconcile a larger economic contribution with conforming to culturally prestigious near seclusion. Others argue that greater seclusion, coupled with increased labor for the market without an equal decline in domestic responsibilities, made women's lives harder.

For some, textile work was part of a desperate, highly labor-intensive effort to maintain subsistence as population rose and farm sizes shrank. Toil increased for everyone, but household income stagnated, and nobody reaped significant benefits. Women might have gained some "freedom" as their families were increasingly unable to afford a strictly gendered division of labor, but this freedom consisted mostly of greater exposure to an exploitative world.

Evaluating these claims requires first combining the research together for comparison, and then disaggregating Late Imperial China. By bringing scholarship pertaining to different regions and times together, we can see that some of the apparent contradictions may be nothing more than geographic and historical difference. No single "larger picture" emerges because, in fact, a variety of situations existed. A different problem is that the economics of textile production are not completely understood, and scholars have not sufficiently tracked the differences between more skilled tasks, often done by women in the prime of their lives, and other tasks taken on by girls or the elderly. It is also worth remembering that textiles comprised only part of women's work; understanding the lives and labor of rural women will eventually require far more attention to food processing and other activities.

Another difficulty arises when we consider the relationship between cultural norms, cultural change, and economics. When we find that work traditionally considered appropriate for women was also the most lucrative work available for women, the robustness and continuity of those norms become easier to understand. But in some ways those cases frustrate the historian: we learn more about people from the choices they made when economic rationality and accepted values pointed in different directions, and families made painful sacrifices in their economic well-being or their cultural norms. When large numbers of families cannot afford to uphold established norms, social change results, although its progress and meaning also is unclear. One can imagine either that people might abandon norms they could not afford, experiencing some degree of liberation in the process, or that they might continue to care about those norms enough (either for their own sake or because they knew that others would measure them by their failure to uphold them) that a sense of degradation would be added to their economic woes. This psychological aspect of economic and cultural change is important but difficult to pinpoint.

While this chapter looks at a variety of relationships among (relative) freedom, income levels, quality of life (including leisure or the lack thereof), and respectability in different regions and periods, the general picture is one in which the relative economic value of different tasks changed much more rapidly than accepted gender roles. On the whole, the growth of the textile economy seems to have been part of a slow but perceptible ratcheting upwards of living standards, labor inputs, and expectations for female propriety over the course of the late empire, changes that were only partly reversed by the economic decline that afflicted large parts of the country in the nineteenth and (in some cases) early twentieth centuries.

Finally, many of the dynamics we need to look at are obscured if we use a simple binary of family versus individual. Such a stark opposition, which tends to see increases in the economic value of women's work as either compensated by increased autonomy *from* the family (e.g., see the following discussion of Stockard's work) or indicative of increased exploitation *by* the family,[1] may suffice for some cases, but it tends to break when we consider a broader range of time, space, and possibilities.

Two Contrasting Visions

In two provocative essays, Mark Elvin has argued that the Yangzi Delta prefecture of Jiaxing experienced continuing growth and a rising material standard of living in the late empire, but at the cost of increasing environmental fragility and overwhelming work burdens for women.[2] He also suggests that under the stress of ecological/economic necessity, the "traditional" gender division of labor broke down. Women, he argues, became increasingly heavily involved in farming as part of highly labor-intensive strategies to cope with an environmental and demographic crunch; they also became more involved in buying and selling, and various other activities in public. They paid for this, however, with work lives so demanding that their mortality rates increased. By contrast, Elvin considers two frontier prefectures—Guiyang in Guizhou and especially Zunhua, near the Great Wall in northern Zhili—where people pressed less heavily on the environment, material life was more spartan, and women were much more confined but lived considerably longer.[3] Using two different methods, Elvin comes up with life expectancies for Guiyang women of 32.0 or 30.4; a remarkably high 50.0 or 48.1 for Zunhua; and a dismal 24.5 or 18.3 for Jiaxing (Elvin himself says that the last number is implausibly low).[4] These estimations are subject to large errors, but there is no particular reason that those errors should affect relative longevity across these prefectures.

Li Bozhong sees a very different Late Imperial Jiangnan, in which an improving material standard of living went along with generally improving or stable life expectancies for both males and females (except perhaps for newborns, given the importance of infanticide for population control in his story). Both men and women worked more, but this represents a benign decrease in "underemployment." And where Elvin sees the "traditional" gender division of labor breaking under new stresses, Li argues that it was not *until* the Qing (and at first only in Jiangnan) that "man plows, woman weaves" came to describe the lives of ordinary families as well as their aspiration. Consequently, though the phrase "husband and wife work together" (*fu fu bing zuo*)—a term elastic enough to fit almost any work routine—had once been as proverbial as *nan geng nu zhi*, rhetoric now shifted to match changed realities, and *fu fu bing zuo* largely disappeared.

I have suggested elsewhere that such a shift might have been partly a matter of more families feeling they could "afford" to keep women sequestered amidst the rising incomes of the high Qing,[5] but Li emphasizes economic efficiency, arguing that improved techniques for farming, sericulture, and rural textile production made all three kinds of work more skilled and more specialized. As quality requirements for marketable cloth increased, and as more silk reeling moved from homes into specialized sheds near market towns, the women involved ceased to help in the fields.[6] Thus, economic growth was associated with better lives, greater skill levels, a *sharper* gender division of labor, and a mixed picture for sequestration (more women working away from home, but also more working indoors instead of in the fields, and probably more foot binding). And while Li focuses on Jiangnan, he suggests that as several other areas of China began their own "proto-industrialization," they moved in similar directions. Interestingly, although the early Qing references to rural cotton textile production in Shandong collected by Xu Tan often refer to both men and women spinning and weaving, later quotations mention only women.[7] This cannot represent the literal truth—we know that some North China men wove and even spun during slack periods even during the Republic—but it may indicate a trend in *normative* gender roles that tracked what Li describes for Jiangnan in an earlier period.[8]

Despite their differences, these competing perspectives both rely on a transcultural logic of income maximization under largely physical constraints and ground at least partial explanations of cultural change in that logic. Both agree that labor effort per person increased, and that women's work producing for both local and long-distance markets became more important—though in different ways. Li argues that women's earnings increased; Elvin does not address that point, but argues that every bit of income became increasingly essential as nonmarket safety valves disappeared. Both assume that deliberate fertility control was important, though they differ on how much "population pressure" there was. And both agree that the rigidity with which male and female spheres were separated (understood both in terms of space occupied and tasks performed) is a separate matter from the material welfare of women. Indeed, both suggest that these things moved in opposite directions. While we might expect that women's material welfare and the flexibility possible for them would move together—either because greater freedom to move across space and undertake varied tasks will enable people to help themselves, or because an increase in the importance of somebody's earnings to their family will make others more solicitous of their interests—a different logic seems to have animated the Late Imperial Chinese family system.[9] Apparently norms of female seclusion were powerful enough to demand adherence when a family's resources allowed them to do so, thus corresponding with increased wealth and material benefit for women.

Men, Women, and Household Economy in Late Imperial Jiangnan

Some Chinese women have produced for the market since ancient times, but a distinct female role in production for use beyond the household began receiving more attention with the rise of the midimperial textile economy which often emerged from state demand for specific in-kind contributions.[10] (In other cases, estates forced the wives and daughters of their bondsmen to weave, so that the demand was again involuntary and in kind;[11] for many formerly bound households that became tax-paying free commoners after 1500, it may have seemed natural to instead render cloth to the state.) By the end of the Ming, state demand for rural cloth had been largely absorbed into cash taxes, but selling silk and cotton textiles had become crucial for many rural households, especially in Jiangnan; these households ranged from very poor families who sold cloth to eat through the much more prosperous for whom "survival" meant maintaining certain appearances and behavioral standards.

A crucial, often overlooked point is that women's earning power appears to have been particularly volatile, but became less so over the Late Imperial period. In good periods, rural textile producers might even outearn their farming husbands, and if one smoothes out short-term fluctuations in prices, it appears that in the eighteenth century, their earnings came surprisingly close to men's. Even a woman who transformed raw cotton into cloth completely on her own outearned male agricultural laborers, though not tenant farmers. A woman who could mostly weave while her children or an elderly mother-in-law handled less demanding tasks would earn much more, though precise figures depend on how we value the labor of young or elderly family members.[12] On average, rural women making cloth were certainly closer to matching their husbands' earning power than they had been when farms were larger and women had helped cultivate them,[13] and they were much closer to their husbands in earning power than were English women of the same period.[14]

But people—especially poor people—did not live "on average" in "the eighteenth century" but from year to year. Consequently, I have estimated the rice-buying power of a piece of middle-grade cotton cloth for selected years; the results are *very* crude but give some sense of how volatile women's earnings were (1750 = 100):[15]

1634	110
1644	50

1654	20	
1664	300	
1674	67	
1684	77	
1694	47	
1750	100	
1780	88	
1800	133	(see note 17)
1835	44	

Even these shaky data yield some reliable inferences. First, the rice-buying power of cotton cloth did not track that of silk (which rose modestly in the eighteenth and early nineteenth centuries, and sharply after 1860);[16] thus, my conclusions here do not necessarily represent all textile work, much less all women's work. Second, changes in the rice-buying power of cotton cloth were largely driven by rice prices, which fluctuated much more than cloth prices until about 1700 and were still somewhat more volatile thereafter.[17] Raw cotton prices were also volatile and would complicate the picture further, since some weaving families produced their own raw-cotton while others bought it. For the most part, though, raw-cotton prices seem to have moved enough in sync with rice that they would usually reinforce both the long-term trends and the short-term fluctuations.[18] Third, because rice prices were more stable after about 1700 (because growing long-distance imports made local harvest fluctuations less crucial), so were female earnings. The volatility of real earnings from cotton textile work probably also declined over the very long haul, beyond the two hundred years reflected in these data, as markets became better developed. This would be consistent with recent literature suggesting that rather than a "Song economic revolution" followed by long years of stagnation or decline until the late Ming boom, the Song-Yuan-Ming period may have seen a much more gradual diffusion and elaboration of institutional and technical changes that first emerged in the Song.[19] If we accept this, at least provisionally, it might also offer another perspective on the changing role of textile earnings in the family budget. Insofar as a great deal of rural textile production was originally either for home use or to meet an in-kind demand from tax collectors or estate owners, even huge fluctuations in the rice-based value of that cloth would not have affected the producers much. But once many rural families sold their cloth, prices became crucial, making economic life painfully unstable until markets became more predictable.

Interestingly, a recent book on North China suggests in passing (and, unfortunately, with limited evidence) that that region also experienced an intermediate stage: one in which earnings from marketed textiles were particularly important in funding rural families' ceremonial expenses.[20] This would be interesting in the present context because ritual expenses were large but irregular and thus perhaps well matched to an unstable income source, at least to the extent that one could wait for years in which cloth sales had been lucrative to hold weddings. Such a deployment of women's textile earnings would have kept them culturally distinct from men's—as some have suggested they were when textile production was tied to state demand.[21] There might also be some continuity here with the observation that women continued to produce at least some of the textiles they brought with them into marriage, even once such goods were easily purchased for cash.[22]

It is also interesting in this connection that documents referring to female infanticide in Ming/Qing Jiangnan (and other parts of East and South China) all emphasize the high price of marrying off daughters, rather than the cost of supporting children more generally.[23] But for now we can only speculate that Jiangnan also experienced such a transitional period in which textile sales became crucial to rural families' *social and cultural* reproduction/subsistence, but not yet to their biological survival. At any rate, many rural families had become dependent on textile earnings to purchase food by the end of the Ming, when those earnings were still highly irregular. Given this instability—and since new farming techniques required precise timing[24]—it is not surprising that Li and Elvin see a late Ming "degendering" of work, with both men and women switching among tasks in response to rapidly shifting market conditions.

Indeed, one would hardly expect a stable gender division of labor (except perhaps among the rich) while economic returns to the epitome of approved "womanly work" varied as wildly as they did in the sixteenth and seventeenth centuries. Rigidity about male and female tasks was dangerous, in that there was too much to lose. The more predictable textile earnings of the eighteenth century would have made a firm division of labor less risky, while smaller farms meant that losing women's farm labor involved little sacrifice. Forgoing potential income from peddling and so forth, however, would have remained a genuine sacrifice to cultural respectability, though a generally affordable one during this relatively prosperous period. Thus Elvin's claims about a "degendering" of work and technology amidst economic and environmental stress may hold for late Ming and very early Qing Jiangnan, while Li's picture of greater investment in specific skills and a sharper gender division of labor would hold for the high Qing. While Elvin cites material from late-nineteenth-century gazetteers saying that in Jiaxing and Shanghai even young married women conducted many transactions in public (much to the consternation of the authors), he notes that most of these materials are copied from earlier editions; they probably refer to the seventeenth century.[25]

There are thus grounds for thinking that while the late Ming breakdown in the Confucian *sexual* order was probably limited to specific elite circles, as Matthew Sommer has argued,[26] other parts of the gender system may have been visibly breaking down even among peasants, at least in the closely watched delta region; this may well have led people not used to seeing respectable women in public to infer a broader breakdown of mores. At the same time, a firmer gender division of labor in the high Qing suggests that commercialization per se need not erode "traditional" gender roles. There are parallels here to Richard Von Glahn's observation that in fifteenth- to seventeenth-century Jiangnan, the god of wealth was seen as subversive of the sexual order—being not only a prolific seducer but a rapist—and his economic favors as huge but fleeting, while in the eighteenth century, he assumed a stabilizing and beneficent guise. Von Glahn himself links this to the greater stability of Qing markets, though his focus is largely on monetary affairs.[27]

Meanwhile, increased commercialization may have meant that in the Qing the sale of sexual services, and of women themselves, became more common, with some relatively poor men becoming purchasers for the first time. Because these irregular relationships among the poor became more common and visible, some scholars have inferred that poverty must have been increasing, but the increase in such transactions could equally well reflect increased use of money among the poor, independent of trends in living standards. It could even indicate improving living standards, as the survival strategies of those at the *very* bottom (a large number of Sommer's wife sellers, for instance, were not merely poor but chronically ill or disabled[28]) not only were increasingly visible in a more mobile society but stood out more sharply in contrast to able-bodied and respectable poor tenants, who increasingly kept "their" women at the loom, away from the gaze of others.

But can we describe eighteenth-century textile producers as relatively prosperous and secure, except in contrast to the undoubtedly wild seventeenth century? Some historians, on the contrary, see this as an era of painful population pressure, in which the returns from women's labor were extremely low, perhaps even below subsistence. Relative predictability at those levels would hardly seem likely to support a more rigidly gendered division of labor (unless all other female activities earned even lower returns). My other scholarship addresses this question; some important points now seem well established.

First, it is no longer possible to claim that the returns from textile production in eighteenth-century Jiangnan were at a bare subsistence level. The case for that proposition turns out to rest on faulty math and other errors, and at least three different methods of calculation converge on a common result: one that suggests that women in mid-eighteenth-century Jiangnan who engaged proportionately in all parts of the process of turning raw cotton into cloth would earn about enough per day to provide rice for a bit over four adult person-days.[29] To the extent that an adult woman could delegate spinning, cleaning, and other tasks to others and concentrate on weaving, she could make much more, since weaving paid over thirty times as much as those tasks. But—probably because weaving paid rather well and spinning quite poorly—there appears to have been relatively little yarn for sale; concentrating on weaving generally required having kin who would provide yarn. Despite some exceptions,[30] the market did not generally replace the family (or extended family) in organizing this part of the division of labor. Thus, it is somewhat misleading to think of the value of "a woman's labor" outside her particular family structure: teenage girls or an elderly mother-in-law, for instance, might be economically quite valuable insofar as they could supply yarn for their thirty-five-year-old mother/daughter-in-law to weave, but they become liabilities overnight if the family suddenly lost its weaver.

Sometime after 1750, the rice-buying power of low- and medium-grade cloth began to decrease. But this was decline from a fairly high level, and it was probably quite some time before it affected women's earnings enough to undermine Jiangnan's basic pattern of relative prosperity and a sharply gendered division of labor.

The average quality of both the cotton cloth and the silk produced in Jiangnan appears to have improved over the first two-thirds of the Qing.[31] Thus, the aforementioned downward trend in the rice-buying power of a fixed quality of cloth after 1750 does not necessarily represent the earning power of actual weavers; to the extent that they switched to higher qualities of cotton cloth (which often sold for roughly twice as much as middle-grade cloth, without taking twice as long to make), rural Jiangnan weavers would have maintained more of their earning power—both absolutely and relative to those doing other tasks—than these numbers suggest. "Higher quality" did not always refer to more durable or comfortable cloth; often this designation was more a matter of styles, colors, and fashion trends. The important point is that they fetched a higher price and to the extent that weaving in each style was a local specialty, these gains may represent an investment in highly specific skills. On the other hand, it leaves us in some doubt about how much of the higher prices were actually captured by dyers and other male townspeople. And to the extent that this proliferation of market niches increased control of the cloth trade by outside guest merchants who tied producers to style-sensitive markets, the increasing marginalization of local marketing (some of which, as we saw, had been done by women) might represent another instance of earning power being at odds with flexibility in roles.

Meanwhile spinners, whose product was much more generic, had less chance to buffer unfavorable price trends. While price data for yarn is extremely fragmentary, it seems very unlikely that prices could have risen enough for spinners to maintain their real incomes between, say, 1750 and 1850. Thus, while Li may be right that mid-eighteenth-century spinners were somewhat better off than some other scholars have suggested,[32] I am skeptical of his claim that spinning was a consistently viable way for adult women to support themselves. Yet there still needed to be almost four hours of spinning for every hour of weaving. Who did it and why?

Some answers are clear. Many Jiangnan spinners were young girls (or elderly women, no longer strong or dexterous enough for the loom), who had no other way to add to the family income but consumed food. Moreover, most of these girls were providing yarn that their mothers wove (not selling the yarn) and so were maintaining an integrated household enterprise that was reasonably remunerative; separate calculations of the value added by each person involved may be somewhat beside the point. When women in their prime spun, it was often for the same reason: to supply themselves with yarn needed for the more lucrative project of weaving. Relatively little yarn was sold, it appears, though more evidence on this point may yet surface.

The small size of the yarn market is somewhat puzzling. Since a woman could make much more money by freeing herself from spinning and doing more weaving, even if she had to pay well above the apparent going rate for yarn,[33] why didn't the price of yarn rise and the amount sold increase? Surely some families—such as those of widowers with teenage daughters—could produce yarn but not weave it and needed extra income. Explaining why such households did not sell yarn is particularly difficult for those scholars who assume that women had few other ways of earning any money and that most households needed every dime just to survive, but even those of us who take a more sanguine view would have reason to expect a larger yarn market than we have found so far.[34]

Recently, however, Li Bozhong has argued that spinning was indeed increasingly common and viable as an independent, specialized occupation. Li finds sources indicating that some entire villages only spun, and it is hardly plausible that there would be villages where every household lacked women capable of weaving and/or with access to enough cash for a basic loom.[35] Li explains the spinning villages by arguing that what happened instead was that as quality and thus skill requirements rose in the fiercely competitive cloth market, households that could not compete instead specialized in spinning.[36] Because merchants needed reliable supplies of fabric with very particular specifications, they increasingly focused their buying on specific communities. The production of different kinds of fabric thus became local specialties, with the required skills taught and retaught in that area. Nearby areas that were excluded from these niches then concentrated on the complementary activity of spinning. Logical though it sounds, this story leaves much to be explained.

Such a division of labor could be relatively stable if the women in spinning-only villages made reasonable amounts of money (even if less than those who also wove). But since there were long periods in which the returns for spinning were very low (and the potential gains for any merchant who got impoverished spinners involved in weaving correspondingly high), it becomes harder to see how such a system could be stable. Certainly if the price of yarn in rice had declined as much as that of cloth for 1750–1850, by the latter date women who only spun would have been completely destitute. Unless spinners were almost completely insulated from the price shifts of that century, it is hard to see how they could have done well enough to reproduce a stable division between spinning only and spinning/weaving villages. Nor is it easy to see how particular villages could keep a monopoly on weaving knowledge in a world of village exogamy. Thus, the apparently tiny yarn market remains puzzling.

With yarn hard to buy, it is somewhat artificial to speak of the earning power of an individual textile producer without specifying not only the date and the woman's skill level but also the familial context. A skilled weaver, for instance, contributed more to her family's income than her thirteen-year-old daughter could, and everyone must have known this; but it must have been equally obvious that this daughter's presence roughly doubled how much weaving her mother could do and thus added to the family's income almost as much as a second adult woman could contribute. This is one more reason to take to heart Skinner's observation that a given family system (and economy) does not simply make sons more valuable than daughters, or vice versa; it generates an optimal mix of family members of particular ages and sexes.

Beyond Jiangnan—and beyond 1850

Jiangnan not only traded with a larger Chinese economy but also often was seen as a model region, not least in having so much of the female population involved in the "womanly works"[37] of textile production. Efforts were made to encourage fiber production and female textile work elsewhere in the empire. Those making these efforts envisioned moral improvement, increasingly reliable tax payments (thanks to the diversification of families' incomes), and greater economic welfare for the families themselves. Whether because of this or not, a great diffusion of commercialized rural cloth production occurred during the Qing, which was still work done mostly by women.[38] There are reasons, then, to expect a recurrence of Jiangnan's evolving gender division of labor, but also reasons to expect differences.

First, in no other area (except perhaps parts of the Pearl River Delta) did commercial textile production become as important to the family budget as in Jiangnan. Nor, I suspect, did any other place rely as heavily on the reputation of its textiles for high *quality.* Moreover, the exceptionally small size of most farms in Jiangnan meant that there was much less reason for women to do agricultural work, in which they could not rival male productivity. Jiangnan may also have been unusual in the extent to which earnings from the production of *low-grade* cloth lagged behind those in farming, since the methods (and thus labor productivity) involved in producing coarse cloth seem to have been fairly uniform wherever this production appeared, while the labor productivity in Jiangnan agriculture was considerably higher than elsewhere. For all these reasons, families in other regions would have fewer economic reasons to focus on very specific female skills and develop as rigid a sexual division of labor as in Jiangnan.

At the opposite extreme from Jiangnan would be frontier zones: sparsely populated areas, often including many non-Han, where woods, marshes, and other unfarmed lands (Elvin's "environmental buffers") could still provide extra resources when crops proved inadequate. Most migrants to these areas, whether on the edges of the Han world or in internal highland areas, were males. The Chinese family system did not allow much migration by single women, either to cities or to peripheries, until twentieth-century factories with tightly supervised dormitories made this possible within the bounds of respectability.[39] The importance of male-only occupations (e.g., logging and mining) on some frontiers and the real or perceived dangers from restive minorities would only have reinforced this tendency. As some frontiers became more securely Han (or more securely settled, in the case of some steep, previously unpopulated highlands), sex ratios would have gradually declined, but one can easily imagine reasons why even frontiers that were filling up quickly would maintain the sharp gender divisions of labor and strong tendencies toward female seclusion that Elvin sees in Guiyang and Zunhua. Where minerals or forest products dominated the cash economy, female production would be largely for home use. Highlands were often first settled during economic upswings by people selling forest products or cash crops to satisfy booming demand in core regions; when the economy slumped, such people often either left or, if they stayed, shifted to subsistence production (much easier once corn and potatoes became widely available).[40] In such situations, so-called normal family life might have taken root just as the local economy was becoming less commercial, leaving women focused on domestic production and with relatively little reason to go out. Frontier families (including, or maybe even especially, recently assimilated minorities) may also have favored female seclusion as a way of demonstrating that they were on the right side of the ethnic/civilizational line.

One interesting exception to such frontier patterns, though, would seem to be the extension of tea planting in the highlands of Fujian and Hunan. Women frequently worked growing tea, often for wages and under the supervision of nonkin. They also breached seclusion in other ways. Robert Fortune reports seeing women, along with children and old men, selling tea seeds at temple fairs and seeing "housewives"—presumably respectable adult women—selling cloth in Fuzhou markets. Shigeta Atsushi cites a gazetteer saying that in the early Qing, both men and women worked as local tea merchants (not just cultivators) in Anhua, Hunan. There is no mention of such activity later, when outside "guest merchants" took over the trade, perhaps paralleling the earlier disappearance of women trading in Jiangnan cloth markets.[41] Moreover, cultural diffusion went both ways. In some places, minority customs that gave women more scope for activities outside the home seem to have influenced regional practices even long after the Han had become dominant.[42] But, in general, it seems likely that most Late Imperial frontier zones were indeed areas of particularly sharp gender segregation and division of labor, at least for Han[43] families. This is quite logical once we see these areas not as zones of particularly intense necessity and pragmatism (on the model of an ideal-typical American "frontier family") but instead as areas where families could meet their limited cash needs from the proceeds of male labor, where the absence of some laborsaving goods available for purchase in core regions might have made women's work within the home particularly time consuming, and where the continued presence of large numbers of single (and sometimes non-Han) males commonly deemed dangerous might have increased pressures for female seclusion.

More important, though—at least numerically—are the long-settled lowland regions that underwent rapid population growth (and/or regrowth after depopulation in the Ming-Qing transition): large parts of Hunan and Hubei, Sichuan, Jiangxi, Guangdong, Shandong, Hebei, and Henan, and so on. In many of these places continued population growth in the latter half of the Qing went along with trends that are not easily categorized: trade across macroregional lines (particularly along the Yangzi and the Grand Canal) often decreased, while *within* some of the same macroregions, the regional economy diversified and internal trade increased.[44]

In many such regions, cloth production increased sharply as people within the region produced first low-grade and then middle-grade cloth that substituted for goods once imported from Jiangnan. As the process continued, some regions not only substituted local cloth for Jiangnan imports, but also began to sell cloth elsewhere. Yamamoto Susumu has traced this process for Sichuan from the mid-Qing into the Republic. He shows a leapfrog pattern in which areas that began importing cloth from Northern Hunan/Southern Hubei (which used to buy from Jiangnan before its cloth production increased) subsequently began to produce their own cloth instead, and in some cases then began exporting to other parts of Sichuan, which later engaged in its own import substitution and began exporting to still more remote regions, and so on.[45]

It is worth noting that the opening of treaty ports, though it interrupted many other processes in Late Imperial history, only accelerated this one. Qing efforts to promote cotton cloth production were, so far as I know, limited to areas in which it was possible to initiate or extend cotton *cultivation*, creating the needed raw material on the spot; while a few fairly prosperous areas, particularly in Guangdong and Fujian, traded for raw cotton (mostly with sugar) and so began extensive cloth production without cultivating cotton, most of China's poorer regions (where the big population growth was after about 1750) did not. However, imports of foreign yarn in the late nineteenth and early twentieth centuries allowed areas that did not grow cotton to begin making cotton cloth, spreading the import-substitution process still further.[46]As best we can tell, interior regions that lost cloth markets through these mechanisms did not find new niches by producing higher-quality cloth the way Jiangnan had; instead, these regions (and particularly their women) lost an important source of income, sometimes with very serious results.[47]

In some cases, we can explain increased local cloth production in economic terms, as the most lucrative available employment for women (and some men). Most places in the empire were far less productive in agriculture than Jiangnan was, but many, once they began, could catch up quickly in the efficiency with which they produced the cheaper grades of cloth. Thus, it quickly became advantageous for them to make cloth themselves, rather than buy it in exchange for grain or raw cotton. If this point is correct, rural textile workers outside Jiangnan might have been quite close to their husbands in earnings *per day*, though smaller supplies of cotton and smaller markets (due both to lower incomes and less transportation) would have meant that they worked for money far fewer days than their husbands did (while Jiangnan women probably worked almost as many days for income as their husbands).[48] In such an environment, it would also often make sense for men to both farm and do some weaving (unlike in Jiangnan), and this seems to have occurred fairly often.

In other cases—such as parts of Hunan, where the profit-maximizing use of additional labor might have been increasing the double-cropping of rice—economics may not explain the growth of cloth production. Instead, cultural preferences may explain why women were kept indoors: foot binding could be practiced without decreasing women's earning capacity, and textile work supposedly cultivated diligence and other positive values in women.[49] It is tempting to think that at least in the Middle Yangzi, the spread of such social ambitions was originally stimulated by rising prosperity during the eighteenth-century export boom, but it certainly seems to have transcended that rationale. In much of North China, for instance, it is likely that there was a long-term decline in living standards from the high Qing to the Republic, yet female seclusion certainly was prized there.

In all likelihood, then, the general path we see in these densely settled regions differed both from that of Jiangnan and the frontiers. Certainly the growth of population density and of textile production coincided with increased ecological stress. Various "environmental buffers" disappeared as lake sizes decreased and forests disappeared, and, in at least one North China case, fuel gathering—usually a job for women and children—became much more difficult.[50] Some people in these areas brought new resources into play—growing peanuts or opium on previously useless land, making "black salt" and related products on the saline old beds of the Yellow and Huai rivers—but they did so by *commercializing* these previously unclaimed resources, not appropriating them for home use, as Elvin argues that people did with the forest and hillside plants of Guiyang and Zunhua.[51] The gendered division of labor seems not to have become as sharp in other densely settled areas as in Jiangnan; in North China, as we have already mentioned, men wove and occasionally even spun during the long agricultural slack season.[52] The new kinds of production women engaged in mostly involved skills that could be learned very quickly and so did not promote a sharp division of labor. North China probably also saw less increase in the consumption of goods that might have decreased domestic work than did pre-1850 Jiangnan—and certainly less than more prosperous twentieth-century areas that increasingly purchased kerosene, matches, and machine-spun yarn.

But neither do we see the degendering of previously marked tasks that Elvin sees in Yuan and Ming Jiangnan. Married women may have cut opium plants, cleaned peanuts, and so on, but I know of no references to them personally marketing these or other products in the north. Other new ways that women earned money (e.g., making straw hats and hairnets for export) seem to have been entirely contained within the home. There may have been an increase in female field labor and domestic labor, but not, it seems, in public visibility, except perhaps in places (e.g., Northeast Shandong) where large numbers of men were becoming migrants.[53] Interestingly, back in Jiangnan, the unusually sharp gendered division of labor endured and may have deepened between the Taiping and the Revolution, even as the specific tasks and economic dynamics involved shifted. The post-1860 rise of new silk districts in the Western part of the delta (particularly around Wuxi) brought many more women out of their homes into centralized filatures, a process that already had been evident in the silk-reeling sheds that grew up in and around eastern delta market towns during the previous century.[54] Yet while premechanized silk reeling had involved special skills and seems to have been practiced by women for as long as they could keep it up, working in the mechanized filatures required less skill (though significant endurance); young women did most of this work and usually abandoned it after marriage.[55] The actual tending of silkworms was also overwhelmingly female, but this job remained home based and involved both married and unmarried women. These women may have had even less contact with nonkin males than pre-1850 cocoon producers; those women had often reeled the silk as well, and in some places that process had been supervised by skilled workmen hired in from outside.[56] While the Guomindang state tried to establish direct contacts with women engaged in twentieth-century sericulture, it did this through agricultural extension workers who were almost exclusively female.[57]

While returns from sericulture varied wildly—due not only to price fluctuations, but even more to the inherent risks of total crop failure—this does not seem to have encouraged a diversification of women's efforts, as the instability of cotton returns in the late Ming apparently did. On the contrary, many women in this region intensified their commitment to sericulture during the 1920s, rearing two crops of silkworms.[58] From the 1860s to at least 1900 was a lucrative time, to the point that there is no puzzle about women concentrating on silkworm cultivation, even with its fairly high risks. However, estimates for the 1920s onward vary enough that one may need some explanation besides simple profit seeking to explain what seems to have been an ever-greater degree of concentration on this one economic activity by women in silk regions.[59] The concentration on one activity was such that when the silk industry in Kaixiangong village collapsed in the 1930s, the women became largely idle, rather than moving into any other kind of work.[60] At least in Bell's account, rural Wuxi women who did not work in sericulture were mostly women who lived on particularly small farms that were far from the area's urban core. Their husbands often left for jobs in cities (they lived too far out to commute and had too little land to focus their labor on it), leaving the family's women to tend the microplot. Thus they were doubly disadvantaged and perhaps doubly isolated: their move into farming can hardly be seen as breaching traditional gender barriers, but was akin to what women left behind by migration (or death) and unable to hire a farm laborer had done for centuries, with the difference that many received remittances from their husbands.[61] From another perspective, the situation of these women foreshadows the feminization of agriculture in parts of contemporary China (and earlier in Taiwan) as men moved into better-paying jobs. Since this has occurred at the same time that farms again often become single households, many of the women taking over farming have not only fallen further behind their menfolk in income, but also in the range of their extrafamilial contacts.

Looking at cotton-growing Tongzhou just north of the Yangzi across from Jiangnan, Kathy Walker describes what may be the closest twentieth-century analogue to Elvin's picture of the late Ming. Once largely a supplier of raw cotton to Jiangnan (an earlier incarnation of its textile industry having been mostly wiped out by southern competition), the Tongzhou region began producing middle-grade cloth for export (especially to Manchuria) after about 1880, using foreign yarn for the warp and homespun yarn made from local cotton for the weft.[62] Most of the producers were tenants or part tenants/part owners on small farms, and both men and women wove in an attempt to fully utilize their looms and compensate for small, not especially fertile farms. The pattern became more firmly established during the Republic.

Walker argues that this rural industrialization did not make Tongzhou any more prosperous, and she criticizes Thomas Rawski's claim that increased cloth consumption indicates an improvement in living standards; at least in Tongzhou, she argues, buying more manufactured cloth (which was less durable than homespun) represented a step *down* for people who were too busy trying to scrape together a subsistence income to make cloth for themselves anymore.[63] Unfortunately, Walker provides almost no more general data on incomes or consumption, and the little she does have is from a wartime Mantetsu survey. But if she is right, her point would be quite important.

Walker also argues that as men took up the loom, Tongzhou women moved into agriculture for the first time, or at least the first time in quite a while. Prior to the twentieth century, she claims, there are almost no references to women in this area doing farmwork except for weeding, yet twentieth-century women often worked in their own fields and even hired out as farm laborers. While this was due to the labor intensity of cotton production and to men beginning to weave, it also reflected a more general, highly gendered process of proletarianization. As peasants' holdings proved increasingly inadequate (due both to the emergence of a new landlordism and to population growth),[64] poor men and women had to hire themselves out more to make ends meet. Men, however, tended to get better-paying nonfarm jobs, either locally or in the cities; if they hired out as farm laborers, it was usually short-term work between other jobs. Women, largely blocked from better jobs, were left to tend the family microplot and/or become hired farmhands. Though women were a minority of hired agricultural laborers, they worked the majority of hired days, in Walker's data. When the women who ran many small farms needed help, they hired other women, whom they could supervise more easily; big farms preferred women because they could pay them less.[65] Cotton production, which involved less irrigation than rice, was also easier to feminize prior to the widespread use of power-driven pumps. Thus, paradoxically, *work* was "degendered" in the sense that women took on tasks once considered exclusively male, but without a concomitant erosion of *spatial* restrictions and seclusion like that of the late Ming. Instead, Walker presents a grim scenario that combines additional work burdens, a stagnant or falling standard of living, and continuing or even increased seclusion. As noted earlier, the evidence for a falling living standards is thin, but this is certainly possible; and while the seclusion may also be overstated—it may be that proximity to rapidly changing Shanghai area blinded people to smaller local changes—Bell and Walker between them certainly give us plenty of reason to doubt that the increased economic importance of female employment outside the home in the twentieth-century Lower Yangzi enhanced their autonomy.

The outcomes that Bell and Walker describe thus differ strikingly, not only from the "common sense" that tells us individual earning power will enhance women's autonomy, but also from the situation that Janice Stockard describes for the Pearl River Delta, China's second most advanced region, where silk played a leading role. While young women's earning power there certainly did not create equality, it gave them considerable power to negotiate the timing and to some extent the terms of their marriages, or to resist marriage altogether. They could also resist certain other kinds of work—as Tongzhou cotton workers, for instance, could not—that might interfere with their ability to reel silk. And while this power was most effectively wielded before marriage, when a natal family eager to hold on to a young woman's earning power might well back her up, spaces that benefited women more generally also appeared.[66]

Some avenues do seem available to advance this inquiry further. There are, for instance, some 1930s county-level data on purchases of imported and manufactured goods for Jiangsu and Zhejiang; it might be interesting to see to what extent these areas were using things that should have made managing the household a little easier for women, such as matches or kerosene, and how much of any growing consumption consisted of goods like cigarettes, which were consumed individually (mostly by males) and so would have done nothing to compensate or offset women's additional labor for the market. This might clarify both standard-of-living questions and issues of what happened to control of the "family income" as it became more easily separated into parts earned by each member.

It may, in fact, turn out that much of the difference between Stockard's relatively optimistic view of women's work and autonomy and the much darker views of Bell and especially Walker can be understood in terms of the geographic and job mobility of *men* during the same period. While men were never as restricted in their mobility as women, neither did they automatically control their movements or earnings, at least as long as they were part of something larger than a simple conjugal household. The degree of that control varied, among other things, with the location of their work. Where men remained on the farm and in the village (as appears to have been the case for most of them in the region studied by Stockard), the movement of women into off-farm wage labor (or even into more remunerative and specialized labor within the household compound) may well have been to their advantage, increasing their perceived importance and sometimes creating a small fund that they (or a more senior woman in the family) could draw on directly. But where men as well as women did more of their work outside the household economy, both geographically and in terms of the mode of production—and men were able to move farther and faster, at least geographically—the erosion of a unified household economy may have actually left men in control of a larger share of the family income than before. In such a situation, particular family configurations would have mattered enormously: a young wife with good relations with her mother-in-law, for instance, would be in a far better position to insure that a large share of the earnings of an absent husband went to immediate household needs than otherwise.

Conclusion

This essay raises more questions than it answers, not only because of missing evidence. I have tried to pull apart certain questions that have often been bundled together, suggesting regional, temporal, and conceptual ways to subdivide them. Beyond such efforts, I think, lies the more complicated challenge of rethinking the categories of "individual" and "family" in a Chinese context, a challenge that only intensifies when we try not only to understand economic trends but also to interpret their cultural ramifications. As my discussion has shown, the degendering of work may or may not indicate spatial and conceptual freedom. The relationship between cultural norms in female work and the autonomy—let alone more complicated notions such as the perception of status or rank—is complex and changing. The shifting patterns discussed in this chapter speak to more specific and complicated trade-offs, in which individual and family can be neither clearly delineated nor set up against each other as discrete units. Both the framework and the internal pieces of that picture are still only partly visible.

Notes

1. This is, for instance, very much the orientation of Hill Gates, *China's Motor: A Thousand Years of Petty Capitalism* (Ithaca, N.Y.: Cornell University Press, 1995).

2. In saying that the material standard of living rose despite these other problems, Elvin differentiates this position from the "involutionist" position, which posits that rising workloads merely insured bare survival, and which now seems untenable. See Kenneth Pomeranz, "Beyond the East-West Binary: Resituating Development Paths in the Eighteenth Century World," *Journal of Asian Studies* 61, no. 2 (May 2002): 539–90, for one refutation; Mark Elvin, review of *The Great Divergence, China Quarterly* 167 (September 2001): 749, for a strong statement by Elvin, who agrees that Chinese living standards were indeed quite high in comparative perspective even as late as the late eighteenth century.

3. Mark Elvin, "Blood and Statistics: Reconstructing the Population Dynamics of Late Imperial China from the Biographies of Virtuous Women in Local Gazetteers," in *Chinese Women in the Imperial Past*, ed. Harriet Zurndorder (Leiden: Brill, 1999), 4, 8–19, 135–222.

4. Elvin, "Blood and Statistics," 142.

5. Kenneth Pomeranz, *The Great Divergence: China, Europe, and the Making of the Modern World Economy* (Princeton, N.J.: Princeton University Press, 2000), 249.

6. Li Bozhong, "Cong 'fufu bing zuo' dao 'nan geng nu zhi'" (From "husband and wife work together" to "man plows, woman weaves"), *Zhongguo jingji shi yanjiu* 11, no. 3 (1996): 99–107; Li Bozhong, *Agricultural Development in Jiangnan, 1620–1850* (New York: St. Martin's, 1998); Li Bozhong, *Jiangnan de zaoqi gongyehua* (Proto-industrialization in the Yangzi Delta) (Beijing: shehui kexue wenxian chubanshe, 2000).

7. Xu Tan, *Ming Qing shiqi Shandong shangpin jingji de fazhan* (The development of a commodity economy in Shandong province during the Ming-Qing period) (Beijing: Zhongguo shehui kexue chubanshe, 1998), 89–92.

8. Francesca Bray has, however, suggested an almost precisely opposite shift on the level of rhetoric and representations: one in which *men* became more prominent in representations of weaving over the course of the late empire. See Francesca Bray, *Technology and Gender: Fabrics of Power in Late Imperial China* (Berkeley: University of California Press, 1997), 239–252.

9. Much of my sense of the logic of that system is drawn from G. William Skinner, "Family Systems and Demographic Processes," in *Anthropological Demography: Toward a New Synthesis*, ed. David Kertzer and Tom Fricke (Chicago: University of Chicago Press, 1997), 53–95.

10. Nishijima Sadao, "The Formation of the Early Chinese Cotton Industry," in *State and Society in China: Japanese Perspectives on Ming-Qing Social History*, ed. Linda Grove and Christian Daniels (Tokyo: Tokyo University Press, 1984), 17–78, 24–25, 30–33; Tanaka Masatoshi, "Rural Handicraft in Jiangnan during the 16th and 17th Centuries," in *State and Society in China: Japanese Perspectives on Ming-Qing Social History*, ed. Linda Grove and Christian Daniels (Tokyo: Tokyo University Press, 1984), 79–100, 87–89.

11. Nishijima, "Early Chinese Cotton Industry," 62; Kathy LeMons Walker, *Chinese Modernity and the Peasant Path: Semicolonialism in the Northern Yangzi Delta* (Stanford, Calif.: Stanford University Press, 1999), 37–39.

12. For the relevant arithmetic, see Pomeranz, "East-West Binary," 548–51, 558–62; and Kenneth Pomeranz, "'Facts Are Stubborn Things': More on Eighteenth Century Jiangnan's Economic Performance in Comparative Perspective," *Journal of Asian Studies* 62, no. 1 (February 2003).

13. Li, *Agricultural Development*, 141–51. Those people who see the move into textiles as a case of decreasing returns per labor day have thus made a basic mistake, confusing a comparison to the returns on grain farming done by men and textile production done by women with the real issue, which is the earning power of the same people (in this case women) as they moved from one task (farming, in which they had been much less productive than men, as reflected in their much lower wages) to cloth making. For examples of male-female comparisons of this sort, see Philip Huang, *The Peasant Family and Rural Development in the Lower Yangzi Region, 1350–1988* (Stanford, Calif.: Stanford University Press, 1990); Philip Huang, "Development or Involution in Eighteenth Century Britain and China?" *Journal of Asian Studies* 61, no. 2 (May 2002): 501–38; and Brenner and Isett, "England's Divergence." I discuss this further in Pomeranz, "East-West Binary" and "'Facts Are Stubborn Things.'"

14. For the China/Europe comparison, see Kenneth Pomeranz, "Women's Work, Family, and Economic Development in Europe and East Asia: Long-term Trajectories and Contemporary Comparisons," in *The Resurgence of East Asia: Perspectives of 50, 150 and 500 Years*, ed. Giovanni Arrighi, Hamashita Takeshi, and Mark Selden (London: Routledge, 2003).

15. Data drawn from Zhang Zhongmin, *Shanghai cong Kaifa dao Kaifang, 1369–1843* (Shanghai from founding to opening) (Kunming: Yunnan renmin chubanshe, 1988); Wang Yeh-chien, "Secular Trends of Rice Prices in the Yangzi Delta, 1638–1935," in *Chinese History in Economic Perspective*, ed. Thomas Rawski and Lillian Li (Berkeley: University of California Press, 1992), 35–68; and Kishimoto Mio, *Shindai Chugoku no Bukka to Keizai Hend?* (Prices and economic change in the Qing dynasty) (Tokyo: Kenbun shuppan, 1997).

16. On ratios of silk to rice prices, see Zhang Li, "Peasant Household Economy under the Influence of International Trade, Industrialization, and Urbanization: A Case Study of Wuxi Peasants' Response to Economic Opportunities, 1860s–1940s" (Ph.D. diss., University of California, Los Angeles, 2002), 111–18; the pre-1860 data are extremely thin but nonetheless suggestive.

17. See Wang, "Secular Trends," 50, for a graphic depiction of annual deviations from the thirty-one-year moving average of rice prices, which decreases markedly after about 1700. This accords with a general sense that this was a period with fewer of the massive disorders that would send prices wildly up or down.

18. For spotty data on raw-cotton prices at Shanghai, see Zhang Zhongmin, *Shanghai*, 205–6. From the late Ming until the late Kangxi periods, general trends in raw cotton prices seem to map those for rice fairly well, so that they would make the fluctuations even wilder, but in the same direction. In midcentury, raw-cotton prices, like

those for rice, seem to have shown far less pronounced swings amidst a general rising trend (stronger for cotton than for rice). After 1790, rice prices were roughly flat for ten years, doubled over the next five, and then fluctuated modestly around that new, higher price until the Taiping Rebellion. Cotton prices hit several extremely high spikes between 1790 and 1810 (as much as six times the usual price), but in general seem not to have shown much of a trend: Zhang Zhongmin says that on the eve of the Opium War, they were roughly double early Qing prices, which is where Kishimoto's scattered data (*Shindai Chugoku no Bukka*, 139) suggest they had gotten by the 1790s. This bump in raw-cotton prices would probably depress the surprisingly high real earnings for weavers estimated above for 1800, bringing that year back into line with the general downward trend after 1750 and strengthening further the point that short-term fluctuations became less important in the high Qing.

19. See Richard Von Glahn, "Introduction" in *The Song-Yuan-Ming Transition*, ed. Paul Smith and Richard Von Glahn (Cambridge, Mass.: Harvard University Press, forthcoming).

20. Xu, *Ming Qing Shandong*, 89–90.

21. For example, Bray, *Technology and Gender*, 186–96.

22. Bray, *Technology and Gender*, 188, 254.

23. For the Ming, see the citations in Chang Jianhua, "Ming dai niying wenti chu tan" (A preliminary inquiry into infanticide in the Ming dynasty) (paper presented at Nankai University Conference on Demographic Behavior and Social History, May 2001), 1–4; for the Qing, see James Lee and Wang Feng, *One Quarter of Humanity: Malthusian Mythologies and Chinese Realities* (Cambridge, Mass.: Harvard University Press), 47–48, 60–61.

24. Mark Elvin, "The Unavoidable Environment" (paper presented at All-UC Economic History Group Meeting, Davis, California, October, 1999), 42–43; Li, *Agricultural Development*, 68–75.

25. Elvin, "Blood and Statistics," 151. Lu Hanchao, "Arrested Development: Cotton and Cotton Markets in Shanghai, 1350–1843," *Modern China* 18, no. 4 (October 1992): 468–99, 481, 483, cites sources from the eighteenth and nineteenth centuries indicating that in this period male household members handled the market transactions.

26. Matthew Sommer, *Sex, Law, and Society in 18th Century China* (Stanford, Calif.: Stanford University Press, 2000), 1–2, 15–16.

27. Richard Von Glahn, "The Enchantment of Wealth: The God Wutong in the Social History of Jiangnan," *Harvard Journal of Asiatic Studies* 51, no. 2 (December 1991): 651–715, 691–94, 697–98, 701–14.

28. See Sommer, *Sex, Law, and Society*, 318, and his chapter in this volume. On customary recognition of married men who became disabled bringing in a second "husband," see Liang Zhiping, *Qingdai xiguan fa: Shehui yu guojia* (Qing dynasty customary law: Society and nation) (Beijing: Zhongguo Zhengfa Daxue chubanshe, 1996), 70.

29. Pomeranz, "East-West Binary," 547–50, 561.

30. Li, *Jiangnan de zaoqi gongyehua*, 63, 71, 76, 82–83.

31. Li, *Jiangnan de zaoqi gongyehua*, 53–57, 60–61, 63–65, 81–82, 84–85.

32. Li, *Jiangnan de zaoqi gongyehua*, 66–71; Pomeranz, *Great Divergence*, 320–22. (The forthcoming Chinese edition corrects some errors in these estimates, but the dif-

ferences do not affect the basic argument.) See also Lu, "Arrested Development," 480. For the best-known statement of the contrary view, see Huang, *Peasant Family*, 84-86; its errors are discussed in Pomeranz, "East-West Binary" and "'Facts Are Stubborn Things.'"

33. Pomeranz, "East-West Binary," 559–62.

34. Note that twentieth-century rural North China had a large market in homespun yarn, despite returns that were probably as bad or worse than those in eighteenth-century Jiangnan.

35. Purchase with cash would of course be preferred, but Late Imperial Jiangnan also had a great deal of small-scale credit available. For evidence that such credit was widely used for production and profitable to use even at very high rates of interest, see Pan Ming-te, "Rural Credit Market and the Peasant Economy (1600–1949)—The State, Elite, Peasant, and Usury" (Ph.D. diss., University of California, Irvine, 1994), 46–72, 78–103.

36. Li, *Jiangnan de zaoqi gongyehua*, 63–65.

37. See Susan Mann, "Household Handicrafts and State Policy in Qing Times," in *To Achieve Security and Wealth: The Qing State and the Economy*, ed. Jane Kate Leonard and John Watt (Ithaca, N.Y.: Cornell University Press, 1992), 75–96; Bray, *Technology and Gender*; and Sommer, *Sex, Law, and Society* for three different but compatible arguments highlighting the ways in which female attention to textile work (as opposed to either "idleness" or various other income-producing activities) was thought to improve their character and help stabilize the society.

38. See, for example, Xu, *Ming Qing Shandong*, 89–92, on Shandong. I discuss various possible reasons for this in Pomeranz, *Great Divergence*, 243–51, and in Kenneth Pomeranz, "Agricultural Labor Productivity in the Yangzi Valley, Japan and England, 1750–1850" (paper delivered at International Economic History Association Congress, Buenos Aires, July 2002).

39. I discuss some of the implications of this in Pomeranz, *Great Divergence*, 248–50. For a very clear treatment of the logic of the Chinese family system explaining this feature in comparative perspective, see Skinner, "Family Systems."

40. See, for example, S. T. Leong, *Migration and Ethnicity in Chinese History: Hakkas, Pengmin, and Their Neighbors* (Stanford, Calif.: Stanford University Press, 1997), 118–23. I discuss one such case in Kenneth Pomeranz, "Re-thinking the Late Imperial Chinese Economy: Development, Disaggregation and Decline, circa 1730–1930," *Itinerario* 24, nos. 3–4 (December 2000): 50–53.

41. Robert Fortune, *A Residence among the Chinese* (Wilmington, Del.: Scholarly Resources, 1972; original publication 1857), 4, 143, 248; Robert Gardella, *Harvesting Mountains: Fujian and the Chinese Tea Trade* (Berkeley: University of California Press, 1994), 103–5; Shigeta Atsushi, *Shindai shakai keizaishi kenkyū* (Research in the social and economic history of the Qing dynasty) (Tokyo: Iwanami Shoten 1975), 217.

42. See, for example, Janice Stockard, *Daughters of the Canton Delta: Marriage Patterns and Economic Strategies in South China, 1860–1930* (Stanford, Calif.: Stanford University Press, 1989), 170–75.

43. Some poor lowland women adopted as "little daughters-in-law" by highland tea pickers might plausibly have been recategorized as "minority" women in the process.

44. Pomeranz, *Great Divergence*, 243–26. The long-term decline in trade along the Yangzi may have been even larger than I suggested. If Ch'uan Han-sheng and Richard Kraus, *Mid-Ch'ing Rice Markets and Trade: An Essay in Price History* (Cambridge, Mass.: Harvard University Press, 1975), 77, are right about the scale of the Yangzi Valley rice trade in the eighteenth century, and Dwight Perkins, *Agricultural Development in China, 1368–1968* (Chicago: Aldine, 1969), 116–24, is right about the 1930s, these shipments had declined by a stunning 73 to 82 percent. G. William Skinner, "Regional Urbanization in Nineteenth Century China," in *The City in Late Imperial China*, ed. G. William Skinner (Stanford, Calif.: Stanford University Press, 1977): 211–49, 713, n. 32, argues that Perkins underestimated the 1930s trade, perhaps quite substantially, but even allowing for that, the decline from eighteenth-century levels would be very large.

45. Yamamoto Susumu, "Shindai Shikawa no chi-iki keizai Hatten" (Regional economic development in Qing dynasty Sichuan), *Shigaku Zasshi* 100, no. 12 (December 1991): 1–31.

46. See, for instance, Huang, *Peasant Economy*, 134, on Gaoyang.

47. See Joseph Esherick, *Origins of the Boxer Uprising* (Berkeley: University of California Press, 1987), 70–72, for examples in North China. The Imperial Maritime Customs in *Decennial Reports of the Trade, Navigation, Industries, etc., of the Ports Open to Foreign Commerce in China and Korea, 1892–1901* (Statistical Series of the Inspectorate General of Customs, 1903), describes a similar pattern for the area around Shasi (in the Hunan/Hubei cotton region), which lost many of its Sichuanese markets to imports of yarn.

48. See Li, *Agricultural Development*, 150–51; Pomeranz, *Great Divergence*, 101–2; and Xu Xinwu, *Jiangnan tubu shi* (History of Jiangnan native cloth) (Shanghai: shehui kexueyuan chubanshe, 1992), 215, 469, 472–553, for some estimates of days worked per year in Jiangnan textiles; data for other regions before the twentieth century are extremely scarce. On the work year in agriculture (probably no more than two hundred labor days per ten-*mu* farm in the mid-Qing), see Li, *Agricultural Development*, 139.

49. See Pomeranz, *Great Divergence*, 249–50. A precise analysis of how profitable it would have been to mobilize female labor for double-cropping rice would depend, *inter alia*, on a careful breakdown of the tasks involved to see how many (e.g., pumping water without the aid of an ox or transporting and spreading manure) were ones in which upper-body strength conferred a large advantage—something on which I have been unable to find good information for the Middle Yangzi in this period.

50. Kenneth Pomeranz, *The Making of a Hinterland: State, Society, and Economy in Inland North China, 1853–1937* (Berkeley: University of California Press, 1993), 123–28.

51. On peanuts, see Pomeranz, *Making of a Hinterland*, 137; on salt and related products, Ralph Thaxton, *Salt of the Earth: The Political Origins of Peasant Protest and Communist Revolution in China* (Berkeley: University of California Press, 1997), 46–49, 63, 86–88, 113–27, 146–48, 168–77.

52. Xu Tan, *Ming Qing Shandong*, 89–90; Sidney Gamble, *Ting Hsien: A North China Rural Community* (Stanford, Calif.: Stanford University Press, 1968 [1954]), 53, 62.

53. Ida Pruitt, *A Daughter of Han: The Autobiography of a Chinese Working Woman* (Stanford, Calif.: Stanford University Press, 1967), is a classic account of a poor woman from precisely this region forced to take on public roles in the very late Qing and Republic.

54. Lynda Bell, *One Industry, Two Chinas: Silk Filatures and Peasant-Family Production in Wuxi County, 1865–1937* (Stanford, Calif.: Stanford University Press, 1999), 97; Li, "Cong 'fufu bing zuo"; Li, *Jiangnan de zaoqi gongyehua*.

55. Bell, *One Industry, Two Chinas*, 103–4.

56. Fortune, *Residence among the Chinese*, 374.

57. Bell, *One Industry, Two Chinas*, 136.

58. Bell, *One Industry, Two Chinas*, 118–20.

59. Bell, *One Industry, Two Chinas*, 110–21, estimates that the returns on labor in sericulture were very low and emphasizes population pressure, cultural opposition to married women working away from home, and various forms of state-merchant power as the reasons why ever more women were ever more involved in this work. On the other hand, Zhang Li ("Peasant Household Economy," 35–63, 119–89) uses the same survey data as Bell to conclude that the returns on women's labor in sericulture represented a considerable improvement over other options and earlier conditions. Zhang's evidence is compelling for the period up to roughly 1920, but the situation is less clear thereafter. On the one hand, Zhang raises several criticisms of Bell's estimates for the 1920s–1940s that appear to be valid (particularly in Bell's use of price data), but there are some gaps in her evidence as well—in part because the survey results generally do not distinguish between male and female labor and seem to count labor inputs in rather idiosyncratic ways—so that the disagreement between her and Bell for this period is hard to resolve without access to the original survey data.

60. Fei Xiaotong, *Chinese Village Close-Up* (an abridged compilation of peasant life in China) (1939), *An Interpretation of Chinese Social Structure* (1946), *Kaixian'gong Revisited* (1957), and *Present Day Kaixian'gong* (1981) (Beijing: New World, 1983), 104.

61. Bell, *One Industry, Two Chinas*, 125–30.

62. Walker, *Peasant Path*, 94–95.

63. Walker, *Peasant Path*, 223.

64. Walker, *Peasant Path*, 176. There are serious risks in basing the conclusion that women worked a majority of hired days on a 1941 survey, since wartime sent many men into armies or into hiding, but Walker sees the feminization of agriculture in Tongzhou as rooted in longer-term processes.

65. Walker, *Peasant Path*, 215–18.

66. Stockard, *Daughters*. On "girls' houses" and married women specifically, see 45–47; on reelers being excused from some other household work, see 152–53.

11

The Vocational Woman and the Elusiveness of "Personhood" in Early Republican China

Bryna Goodman

THE CREATION OF NEW WOMEN was an evolving project of Chinese modernizers. Female exemplars of the Late Imperial period were iconic figures of virtue: chastity, loyalty, and the separation of the sexes. The new woman, first evoked by late Qing reformers and revolutionaries, transposed the virtues of loyalty and service onto the new imagined nation. If, in the late Qing, most reformers conceived of such service in ways that still sheltered women from directly challenging the separation of the sexes (educating women for an improved maternal function as better mothers of new male citizens), revolutionaries went further, envisioning women's engagement in political action.[1] In the iconoclastic New Culture Movement of the early Republican era, traditional women's virtues were caricatured in a critique of patriarchal society. Feminists increasingly called on women to engage in social intercourse with men in the creation of a new society. Like Late Imperial models of chastity and late Qing exemplary mothers of new citizens, the May Fourth–era new woman was still a repository of virtue, but she had to exemplify a more modern kind of virtue. This new virtue was modern personhood, *ren'ge*, an apparently gender-neutral term, which evoked independent thinking, self-reliance, and individual moral integrity.[2]

Women's ability to achieve *ren'ge* was hotly debated. To be fully modern, women had to be employed. To convey personhood, such employment should reflect a meaningful vocation. Even with a vocation, it was difficult for a working woman to achieve *ren'ge*, however, because work in the public realm smeared women's moral purity with the stains of money and men's sexual desires. If elusive during life, fleeting attributions of *ren'ge* could be achieved posthumously through suicide—a contradictory action in modern times to be sure, but one that still reverberated with sufficient cultural capital to command the attention of even leftist intellectuals.[3]

In 1919, Mao Zedong created a modern social issue out of the suicide of a young Hunanese woman.[4] In doing so, he both celebrated *ren'ge* and elucidated its elusiveness. Zhao Wuzhen slit her throat while being transported in a bridal sedan chair to the family home of her fiancé. In his now-celebrated essays on the topic, Mao felt it necessary to address the issue of whether Miss Zhao had *ren'ge.* He acknowledged that she did not entirely have free will, since her parents had arranged her marriage despite her objections. In this sense she was merely a pitiful victim of the evils of the authoritarian family system. Nonetheless, Mao argued, in Miss Zhao's last brief moment of life, when "the snow white knife was stained with fresh red blood . . . , her *ren'ge* also gushed forth suddenly, shining bright and luminous."[5]

Tao Yi, a female member of Mao's New Study Society, developed Mao's discussion of Miss Zhao's *ren'ge* in an article in *Women's Bell* (*Nüjie zhong*):

> Though we should not say that Miss Zhao died "for love of freedom," we must recognize her as "one who sacrificed herself to reform the marriage system." If she were just a passive person trying to protect her own freedom, then why did she not commit suicide at the time she hid the knife, or while she rode in the sedan with her family to her sister's home? Why did she wait till she was in her bridal clothes, and sitting in her bridal sedan, to commit suicide? I doubt that so many people would have known about her suicide or felt so deeply troubled by her death if she had killed herself a day earlier, when she was dressed as a regular daughter, sitting in a regular sedan![6]

Both commentators insisted that Miss Zhao, though victimized by the family system, nonetheless exercised agency and attained *ren'ge* through her carefully premeditated and strategically located suicide. Her action inflicted financial damage upon the families that oppressed her[7] and brought the constrained circumstances of her life and death into the realm of public discussion.

Though intent on endowing Zhao Wuzhen with personhood, Mao and Tao could make only limited claims for her agency because she had no independent existence outside of her natal or conjugal families. Had Miss Zhao been an independent person with a job, one might assume that a carefully executed suicide would not be the definitive mark of her personhood.

In September 1922, a young female secretary named Xi Shangzhen committed suicide in the office of her employer, Tang Jiezhi, after losing money on the stock market. The suicide of a woman who was employed appeared to call into question the project of Chinese modernity. Commentators proclaimed that Xi's death shook the foundations of public opinion.[8] It was widely covered in all of the major Shanghai newspapers: *Shenbao, Minguo ribao, Xinwenbao, Shibao, Zhonghua xinbao, Xin Shenbao, Shishi xinbao,* and *Shenzhou ribao,* as well as in *Crystal* (*Jingbao*) and small-format ("mosquito") papers. Fearing that "scholars of the old school will necessarily use [the suicide] as a pretext for attacking the modern movement," a Shanghai-based Association for Research on Women's Vocations (*Funü zhiye yanjiu she*) published a volume of reflective essays by Chinese intellectuals, highlighting the issue of women's occupations: "Since Miss Xi hanged herself in the office of the *Journal of Commerce* (*Shangbao*), the news has traveled far and near, and everyone has . . . published their views regarding this case in the newspapers. . . . Why is this so? Isn't the reason that, at the dawn of women's vocations, there has been such an extreme setback?"[9]

The link between suicide and *ren'ge* raised in the discussion of Zhao Wuzhen would be reprised, with different emphasis, in public commentary concerning Xi Shangzhen. The major difference, of course, was Xi's work, which (rather than her determined suicide) marked her departure from Chinese tradition and defined her as modern. Xi belonged to a different category of woman than Zhao Wuzhen, who could only travel through public space enclosed within a sedan chair. The different life circumstances of the two women meant that social activists would find different meanings in their acts of self-destruction (though both suicides, characteristically, were attributed broad social significance.)[10] Zhao's suicide was construed as an act of resistance against a feudal tradition. Xi's suicide three years later, in contrast, cast a shadow over the modern working woman and her ability to manifest *ren'ge.*

Personhood and Female Vocations

New Culture reformers and radicals alike viewed the emergence of educated women into a sexually integrated public workplace as crucial to the modern transformation of Chinese culture. Spatial liberation from the confines of women's quarters and economic self-reliance through work were requisites for the formation of the new independent female citizen. The new woman of the early Republican era and the feminist goal of women's vocations (*funü zhiye, nüzi zhiye*) were fashioned in relation to this ideal of modern personhood. In his famous essay "The Way of Confucius and Modern Life," Chen Duxiu argued that the "independence of the personhood of the individual" (*geren ren'ge duli*) depended on the independence of individual property. The two linked principles constituted "the life pulse of modern society."[11] The human bonds of hierarchy and subordination in Confucianism had obstructed "the individual independence of *ren'ge*" (*ren'ge zhi geren duli*), which could not be complete prior to the modern era. The problem of incomplete, or defective *ren'ge*, according to Chen, was particularly characteristic of women, who had been subjected to particular subordination.[12] In this foundational statement of May Fourth feminism, women's *ren'ge* is essential to the modernity that would be heralded by the overturning of patriarchal Confucian society. Nonetheless, the quality of women's *ren'ge* was in question, having been damaged by millennia of bad history. Public discussion of the *ren'ge* issue in the years that followed suggests that achieving *ren'ge* in men's eyes was particularly hard for women, even for those who took for granted that they had it and that it was a universal human attribute.

The left-wing writer Ye Shengtao, considering the question of women's *ren'ge* in *New Tide* in 1919, asserted that women were entitled to *ren'ge* "because they are human beings." More complicated, however, was the question of whether women currently possessed *ren'ge*: "Until recent years, there have been only a small number of independent women. Most women did not have true, firm worldviews, as they were confined to the home. . . . It is no exaggeration to say that these women had incomplete *ren'ge*, or almost no *ren'ge*." Over time, "bound and exhausted women" lost their understanding of the world, their identity, and their ability to reason.[13]

Although some feminists expressed faith in "the theory of the equality of men's and women's *ren'ge*," they voiced this theory in order to encourage women to develop their *ren'ge*.[14] Women's *ren'ge* needed protection. "Safeguarding *ren'ge*," (*baozhang ren'ge*) was one of the central missions of the Association for Women's Suffrage, established in Shanghai in October 1922.[15] Most commonly, however, both male and female feminists recognized that work had to be done to develop or reconstruct women's *ren'ge*. In the words of Wan Pu, representative of the Beijing Society for the Advancement of Women's Suffrage (*Nüzi canzheng xiejinhui*), such societies existed in order to recover women's lost *ren'ge*.[16]

Modern education was a necessary step toward the development of women's *ren'ge*. Although an exceptional woman might demonstrate *ren'ge* in an extraordinary moment of protest and self-sacrifice, it was generally held that without education women could not have independent minds and moral character. The call for women's vocations depended on the prior establishment and proliferation of women's schools in the last years of the Qing dynasty.[17]

Education alone, however, was not sufficient. Only with the economic self-sufficiency and status brought by purposeful employment and engagement in society could women have the freedom to act in public. *Ren'ge* demanded both intellectual training and integration into society through female vocations. In this vocational thrust, despite a common nationalist impulse that linked the new woman to the nation, the Republican-era repudiation of Confucianism necessitated a rupture with the predominant representation of women in late Qing feminism, as mothers of the new citizens of the Chinese nation. In the late Qing, reformers as well as conservatives repudiated the idea of female vocational education, an idea whose time had not yet come.[18] Mainstream May Fourth rhetoric, in contrast, emphasized female vocations, which now only conservatives questioned in print.[19]

The critical role of independent vocations in determining a woman's social value is clear from discussions of female suffrage and participation in government that also appeared in the May Fourth press. Although the appropriateness of female suffrage was by no means generally accepted even among feminists in this period, women's vocations were regularly invoked as a prerequisite for this ultimate achievement of female citizenship. In the words of one journalist identified with *funü zhiye*, suffrage could only be considered for women with meaningful vocations, because only such women could be said to have independent personhood:

> Female doctors, female teachers, female secretaries, female merchants and female restaurateurs—only these count as independent labor, and only these may have the right to participate in government. As for those *taitai* and *xiaojie* who ride in cars, play poker, mahjong, wear gold and diamonds and follow fashion, we absolutely cannot permit them the right to participate in government. They are only parasites on men, not themselves independent.[20]

Such derision of dependent women—*taitai*, *xiaojie*, and also concubines—was common in the progressive press of this period.[21] Not only did these women lack *ren'ge* because of their dependence on men, but, as the passage suggests, they were morally suspect because of their interest in gold, diamonds, and other luxuries. Criticisms of fashionable but morally vacuous women often appeared on the same pages of magazines as commercial advertisements that glamorized domestic women and their modern clothing, furniture, and up-to-date appliances.

If the virtue of *ren'ge* demanded that women enter into work with men, the social conditions of that work also threatened women's *ren'ge*. A 1921 *Shenbao* editorial celebrated the growing numbers of women working in department stores, but questioned their managers' motivations: "If you think that women are rare commodities and hope to attract customers by using them, then you will destroy women's *ren'ge*."[22] Some left-wing writers decried the fact that attractive female workers were advanced over plainer ones. Yang Zhihua, writing a few months after Xi Shangzhen's death, raised concern about the corrupting influence of the power relations in offices that employed women. Yang, who was approximately the same age as Xi Shangzhen, noted that some middle-class women who had benefited from education now held high-quality jobs in banks, telegraph and telephone bureaus, and factories. Nonetheless, she questioned their ability to be independent: "[Today] many women working . . . have no choice but to kiss the asses (*pai mapi*) of the men in charge; otherwise they cannot protect their jobs. If they can't directly kiss ass, then they exert their energies in the direction of those closest and most beloved by those in power."[23] Yang closed her article expressing her hope that, despite the pressures, women might still value their *ren'ge*. Her wistful tone betrays sobering experience of the realities of the politics of male-dominated offices.

Constraints of Class

Just as the realities of office employment threatened women's attainment of *ren'ge*, so did its class bias. The definitions of both *ren'ge* and *funü zhiye*, which emphasized education and freedom, restricted their achievement to a minority of women. In August 1922 a citywide strike of silk filiature workers brought the substantial urban presence and economic plight of female factory workers powerfully to the attention of the Shanghai public. The young workers' strike, poor pay, dangerous work conditions, and long hours were sympathetically reported and discussed in many of the same periodicals that extensively covered Xi Shangzhen's suicide one month later. Though the workers' conditions were deplorable and their activism crucial to the socialism advocated by many of the journalists who wrote for the early Guomindang organ *Minguo ribao*, a comparison of coverage leaves the impression that concern for the office worker's suicide was disproportionately preoccupying. Female factory workers, whose presence and problems were more substantial, were less poignant for the writers and their educated audience because they lacked *ren'ge*.[24]

Female factory workers, more than male factory workers, could not meet criteria for *ren'ge* and could not be considered to have independent vocations. Despite the workers' numbers and their determined mobilization through the *Nüzi gongye jinde hui* (Women's association for the advancement of industrial virtue),[25] commentators noted that, in contrast to the concurrent seamen's strike, which was composed of independent individuals, the women strikers' bodies were not necessarily free. A monograph on female employment published in the year of the strike characterized female factory workers as pitiful slaves of capitalists. The author asserted that because of Chinese culture and China's belated industrialization, Chinese women had only three options: they could sell their labor (*mai laoli*), they could prostitute themselves (*mai xing*), or they could starve to death. There was something about women using their bodies—in any respect—for money that made female workers and female prostitutes comparable and "most pitiful." "The former sells strength; the latter sells sex." It was commonly argued that in practice the sale of sex augmented the sale of labor in the struggle to make ends meet: "If they have children, or if they are widowed, they cannot avoid selling their sex in addition to selling their labor."[26] Left-wing writers, like this author, at times spoke of women's *ren'ge* and women's vocations in universal terms, insisting that the problems of all women were more fundamental than the shortsighted goals of a privileged few who were only concerned for their own educational and professional development. Nonetheless, their characterizations of the young and poor workers reflect victimization only and suggest an absence of both mind and agency. If female factory labor marked a necessary passage in China's modernization process, working conditions would have to change before women workers could become independent, and they would have to be educated before they could possess *ren'ge*.

Political moderates went further in characterizing the exclusivity of *ren'ge*. Chen Wentao explained in a special "female vocations" issue of *Ladies' Magazine* that "[real] vocations must be independent. Occupations not independent in character are only oppressed labor. They cannot be counted as *zhiye*." Chen outlined four categories of female work: household labor, home handicraft production, factory work, and independent occupations, such as female merchants or teachers. The first two types were manifestly under the influence of husbands and family. Chen admitted that factory workers could exercise partial independence, but he only considered the fourth category of employment as fundamentally independent. By Chen's estimate, not even 1 percent of China's women inhabited this category.[27]

If, despite the democratic impulses of New Culture rhetoric, the intertwined ideals of personhood and female vocations were highly exclusive, the conflicting representations of modern women in the May Fourth press suggest the way in which the issue of female vocations—far more than female education in this period—was volatile. Women's education, like modern fashions, could be contained within the home. Most female students married and dropped out of society. In contrast, female employment in society challenged the Confucian separation of sexes, the idea that women must be *nei*, contained within the domestic sphere and separate from what was *wai*, that which was outside, in society and politics. Moreover, because of its class character, the idea of female vocations was preoccupying for the New Culture journalists because it struck directly at the families and personal relations of those who engaged in public writing in this period.

The Vocational Woman Commits Suicide

Catapulted into public view by her suicide at the age of twenty-four *sui*, Xi Shangzhen was immediately recognized by public commentators as a new-style woman. Xi had the prerequisites for *ren'ge*, having been educated in a vocational school, the East City Girls' School (*Chengdong nüxue*). Though her immediate family was poor, an uncle provided for her tuition. Her school embraced a nationalist feminism that stressed political activism and encouraged students to venture into public space. Since only one Chinese woman in ten thousand attended school, to prevent the remaining nine thousand ninety-nine from being "useless people," the school formed student lecture teams to go from the city to the countryside bringing education to poor women. The 1912 issue of the school journal, *Female Student*, included a photograph of female revolutionary soldiers in Shanghai and an essay on the importance of women's participation in government.[28]

Xi Shangzhen was, moreover, engaged in a professional working relationship with men in a modern newspaper office. Office work was a new phenomenon for Chinese women that may be dated to the end of World War I. After teaching at her alma mater, Xi was introduced by a relation to her new employer, Tang Jiezhi, managing director of the *Journal of Commerce*. Press accounts of Xi variously describe her as a female secretary, female copyist, or female clerk, the qualifier *female* appearing before each mention of her occupation because these professions had been monopolized by men and were gendered male. Her desk was located in Tang's office. Her job involved opening incoming mail, showing it to Tang, and distributing it to appropriate individuals at the newspaper.[29] Xi's monthly salary of twenty yuan, though minimal, was sufficient to permit a degree of economic independence. She gave half her salary to her mother, with whom she lived; half paid her own expenses. The *Journal of Commerce* was known for being progressive. The director, Tang, supported the cause of female vocations. Tang had been educated in the United States, and he was a public figure in the May Fourth movement. His newspaper reported on the movement for women's vocations, hailing the appearance of new vocational training programs and the opening to women of various professions.[30]

Xi's modernity and her *ren'ge* were confirmed in the public eye, finally, by the fact that she broke off an arranged engagement and had vowed never to marry. Xi's refusal of an arranged marriage suggests both individual determination and also assurance. Probably both her decision to refuse and her ability to refuse successfully were influenced by her education and facilitated by her money-earning role in her family.

Public recognition of Xi Shangzhen as a new woman is key to understanding media focus on the contradiction her suicide posed for her *ren'ge*, since suicide was associated with weak, old-style women. In the eruption of public concern over the meaning of a suicide by an educated, modern, and employed woman, feminists modeled Xi after their ideal heroine of modernity and found her suicide incomprehensible: "Xi Shangzhen promoted female professional employment and set a standard by her behavior. . . . How can it be that she has died, and not of illness but . . . of suicide by hanging?"[31]

By virtue of the signs of modernity she bore, Xi was presumed to be "someone who experienced women's inequality and wanted to realize liberation and economic independence. . . . In the bravery of her struggle she achieved the position of female secretary at the *Journal of Commerce*."[32] The suicide of a woman who bore the marks of modernity appeared to shatter the image, calling into question the social project of the creation of modern citizens. As Zheng Zhengqiu, the promoter of new drama and pioneer Chinese filmmaker, described the case:

> It was rare that the *Shangbao* was willing to take this step and employ a woman, and it was rare that Miss Xi was willing to take this step. Who would think that the result would be such a tragedy? The future of woman's vocations has been struck a great blow. Doesn't this give the conservatives a good excuse to oppose liberation? Won't most women now see vocations as dangerous?[33]

Some feminists used the fact of Xi's suicide to question her *ren'ge*, suggesting that she had failed to "cast off her traditional woman's mindset."[34] "If one rushes to suicide when one encounters a problem, what kind of independence is this?"[35] Some tried to contain the damage by pointing to individual defects, suggesting that Xi would have been likely to commit suicide at home even if she hadn't worked;[36] nonetheless, her suicide was not generally understood in individual terms. Rather, her shortcomings were emblematic of a broader problem. Conservatives immediately attacked women's vocations, suggesting that feminists "imagined they could draw a tiger but achieved only the likeness of a dog." Women's vocations were socially irresponsible:

> [Xi Shangzhen] was intoxicated with employment. . . . If Miss Xi had not worked at the newspaper office, she wouldn't have lost her money and her life wouldn't have been sacrificed. . . . She could have achieved happiness within women's quarters and today's tragedy would not have occurred.[37]

More than female vocations was at stake. Also at issue were the reputations of the men who publicly advocated female vocations as part of their project of social transformation:

> That [Miss Xi] would commit suicide will influence women's vocations. Many women . . . will see this and experience doubts. But in addition, the average

> stubborn person who opposes modern thinking will use her suicide to attack new thought and people who advocate the women's movement. While Xi's suicide, in terms of her own body, is a small thing, the influence on society . . . is very great.[38]

The promotion and maintenance of modern women were marks of the modern man. The obsessive public concern and, indeed, self-examination in the Shanghai press that accompanied the suicide of a vocational woman suggest that Tang's associates in the densely interconnected world of Shanghai journalism felt their own reputations were at stake. The outpouring of print by primarily male feminists may be interpreted as a mechanism of defense and a means of displaying male modernity.

Exotic and Erotic: Gender Boundaries and Modern Social Intercourse

Although the call for women's vocations was ubiquitous in the May Fourth press, the vocational woman was a rare figure, sufficiently invisible that Lu Xun's exaggerated comment in 1923—that a woman in Chinese society had only two choices—dependence on a husband or prostitution, could still have rhetorical force.[39]

In the male sojourner city, women were a minority of the population, and few women appeared in public. The new woman eroticized the public sphere with her presence and ignited male fantasy. The exoticism of women in general for a large, male, literate Shanghai audience is evident in the copious publication of voyeuristic literature in the city.[40] One popular four-volume compendium entitled *One Hundred Views of Women* is striking for descriptive sections on eighteen parts of women's bodies (hair, eyes, mouths, tongues, ears, necks, bones, skin, eyebrows, noses, teeth, etc.) as well as mundane aspects of women's daily lives.[41]

Professional women were sufficiently exotic in 1927, when this guide was published, that it included a section on women who earned their own living. After outlining women's traditional dependence on men, the author described feminism in Europe and the United States and the appearance of a small number of Chinese women who supported themselves. Anticipating readers' disbelief, he wrote, "If you don't believe [that professional women exist, I have] provided examples." The account details women's emergence into vocations, as teachers, doctors, shopkeepers, and actresses.[42] Another section describes the clothing styles, colors, and shoes worn by female students, female teachers, and other women, as if they were exotic birds that a careful observer of Shanghai streets would want to recognize.

It is not surprising that the novelty of a female secretary's office suicide called forth images of a sexualized workplace. Newspaper commentary involved voyeuristic sensationalism as well as more serious debate over the desirability and morality of having women enter the professional world.

The emergence of young educated women into the male workplace was provocative. Details of the Xi case were titillating. After working for less than a year, Xi entrusted five thousand yuan of family money to Tang to invest in the booming new Shanghai stock market. After the market collapsed and her money was lost, Xi began to attempt suicide. Her first two attempts (by sleeping medicine) were foiled by her married employer, who was either present or in a position to discover her. Her final and successful effort (by hanging) took place in the late afternoon of September 8, 1922, in the office she shared with Tang. At the inquest that followed Xi's death, family members testified that Xi and Tang had argued. Quoting a conversation at which she was not present, Xi's sister-in-law testified that Tang had insulted Xi by crudely suggesting she become his concubine, wounding the educated Xi's sense of virtue. The vulgarity of his desires so exacerbated her anxiety over her financial losses that she took her life.[43]

Fantasies associated with career women and the Xi case's pairing of the images of secretary and concubine—the independent, professional, and forward-looking secretary and the sexualized, dependent, and backward-looking concubine—express the contradiction of employment opportunities for women in male-dominated offices. Secretarial employment offered a means of economic independence but exposed women to their employers' sexual designs.[44] In this respect, the newly valued secretary was more vulnerable to sexual exploitation than the "backward" concubine, who despite inferior status nonetheless enjoyed a socially recognized position and a degree of legal protection.[45] The allure and vulnerability of the new work environment are evoked in a tabloid ditty, "Female Secretary," published a few days after Xi's death: "The female secretary. How stylish! Holding her pencil and pad she enters. She is nicely made up and looks modern and attractive. As soon as he sees her, her employer falls in love. He orders her into his office."[46]

Feminist responses to the Xi case similarly highlight the sexual volatility and purity at risk popularly associated with the May Fourth ideal of public social intercourse for women (*shejiao gongkai*).[47] As if visualizing the screenplay for one of his films, Zheng Zhengqiu decried the vulnerability of women in the workplace, where the "lascivious thoughts [of their employers] would be realized in lascivious actions, seducing the pure white female."[48]

With its suggestions of sexual tension between an employer and his female secretary who committed suicide, the Xi case helped sell newspapers. Love tragedies that intertwined old and new in overwrought female bodies were a trope of contemporary literature, both in "butterfly" writing and new-style fiction, in stories serialized by the same newspapers that reported on the case.[49] The *Xin Shenbao* and the *Shishi xinbao*, published special editions devoted to the suicide. As one observer commented, the case was an "injection of morphine" for newspapers and Shanghai readership.[50]

Such sensationalism was also an issue for intellectuals, who decried the evil Chinese habit of gossip that accompanied the tradition of separation between the sexes, making modern social contact difficult for working women:

> When we see a female working among many men, it is seen as strange and assumes a special character. If we don't say that the woman is shameless, then we say that she has loose morals. If a man who works with her talks informally, it is suspected that they have relations. People smile and gossip. . . . This is an obstacle to women's vocations.[51]

Contaminated by Money

Working women were tainted both by the erotic effect of their appearance in public and the stain of their desire for money. In this regard, the case touched on the frequently linked, morally destructive desires of lasciviousness and greed (*se* and *cai*) and the deep social ambivalence their modern incarnations generated in Shanghai, a city characterized by the impurities of moneymaking.

A two-line "elegy for Xi Shangzhen," published after her death in *Crystal*, blamed the evil workings of the stock market for Xi's death: "It wasn't just five thousand yuan: she was a victim of the stock market. She was just twenty-four *sui*. Whoever is a female secretary should beware."[52] Several months after Xi's death, *Crystal* serialized a novella, *Admonition to New Women*, which melodramatically reprised the theme of new women's susceptibility to the market.[53] The story featured a female secretary who lived with her mother. Rather than marry a student from a propertied family, she chose a new-style man who worked in a stock market. He persuaded her that he would become rich. She reasoned that this was better than marrying a student whose father controlled his purse strings. Unsurprisingly, her choice led to her downfall. Her new-style boyfriend took a sum of money intended for medical research from her office, using her key. Despite his promise to return the "borrowed" money, it was lost on the market. As a consequence of the female secretary's willful acts, her mother died of grief. She herself was sent to languish in jail.

Just as women, to be virtuous, had to resist sexual desire, to which they were vulnerable, it was incumbent on them to resist monetary desires, to which they were also prone. Xi's virtue was imperfect: "Her only flaw was to want to invest."[54] Her decline could be traced to the moment she entered into economic relations with Tang: "She mistakenly wanted to be wealthy."[55] This is a prominent theme in published elegies for Xi written by newspaper readers: "How could she stake everything on a bad venture? He cheated her because of her wish to be in a gold chamber."[56] Or again, "How worthless that she ruined her life through money/being unwise she herself is to blame."[57]

Some blamed the quality of female education, arguing that education had not prevented Xi from acting foolishly:

> Women's education must . . . reduce materialistic desires and promote a serious worldview. Of course this should be required for both men and women, but women are in particular need because they are more susceptible to such desires. If we speak of the case of Miss Xi, both sides testify that she herself wanted to purchase stock. This tragedy was caused by her mistaken thinking.[58]

In the extreme, the impurity of Xi's desire for money opened her to misogynist characterization. Though the predominant rhetorical treatment of Xi was paternalistic, casting her in a passive role, Tang's defenders were not above describing her suicide as a venomous ploy to mask reality and camouflage her own investment follies:

> [Purchasing stock] is a matter of commercial behavior. There will always be success or failure. She took advantage of being a woman to force her loss on others. [In this manner], she receives the benefits and the damage is passed on to others. [This] is a venomous person who must fulfill her desires. Her behavior produces unimaginable results.[59]

The public discussion consistently problematized connections between women and moneymaking. Xi's experience was generalized to all working women and their relations with money. Quoting again from newspaper readers' elegies: "Money is the cause of her misfortune/A hard lesson women's circles will take from your experience." And again, "Making a living damages your life. Money brings a thousand evils."[60]

The exhibition of an educated woman's desire for money made the case particularly shocking: "If Xi Shangzhen were male, her death would not have occasioned a similar social uproar. It is because Xi Shangzhen is a woman and moreover a female secretary within a newspaper office that people take such unusual notice. . . . The *heat of her desire to become wealthy* was not easy to repress."[61]

Xi's defenders, sensitive to the shadows on her virtue cast by work with men and the corruptions of money, loudly protested her chastity: "The jade tablet won't be stained by a trifle of profit/The wonderful secretary Shangzhen will be long remembered/After three years her chaste ghost shall become ennobled/ She died young in Shanghai, and her tomb is fragrant."[62] Such statements suggest that for women there was considerable conflation of modern *ren'ge* with older concepts of female virtue.[63]

Conclusion: Persistent Boundaries and the Ambivalent Morality of the Modern

Just as public discussion of the Xi case reveals a slippage between older and newer notions of female virtue, commentators expressed a persistent faith in the cleansing attributes of female self-destruction.[64] Feminist journalists and newspaper readers determinedly proclaimed Miss Xi a martyr for their cause—however unlikely feminism was as a motivation for her suicide—as a means of redeeming her *ren'ge.* The writer Jiang Hongjiao, for example, hailed the inspirational character of Xi's life and death: "Those who oppose women's liberation will use Xi's suicide as an example [of women's impropriety in the workplace]. I dare to say that Xi Shangzhen's suicide in fact embodies today's [modern] teachings about women. Those with modern social consciousness [will hasten] women's glorious future and eliminate obstacles to women's progress."[65]

Reader poetry published by the *Shibao* after Xi's death echoed this wishful identification of Xi with heroic martyrdom. Repeatedly, within this amateur verse, Xi sacrifices herself "for her *ren'ge.*" She is compared to a host of female heroines, Western and Chinese, ancient and modern made familiar in late Qing reformist textbooks or in Qiu Jin's list of models for emulation, including Madame Roland, Cai Wenji, and, especially, the modern martyr Qiu Jin.[66] The collapse of time evident in these associations of Xi with a variety of women, past and present, suggests the way in which different models of gender coexisted in people's minds, blurring "traditional" and "modern" into a more generalized notion of the exemplary woman.

Through the drama of her suicide and the literary efforts of newspaper readers, the actual, struggling, compromised Xi Shangzhen, embarrassing in her real-life concerns for money, not to mention her likely intimacy with her employer,[67] could be effaced, and a heroine with *ren'ge* constructed. The example of the new vocational woman suggests the manner in which defining modern virtues like *ren'ge* were bonded onto older ones. The new woman was inevitably linked to notions of female purity, to insistently present older figures of exemplary women, and to fascination with female suicide as indicative of moral truths.

How did the progressive urban public of Shanghai, intellectuals, journalists, and educated readers, absorb the new vision of modernity—specifically the vocational woman—into their daily life? We are presented with contradictory images. Recent feminist scholarship insists upon the emergence of real "new women" in the May Fourth era, excavating a history of particularly determined and accomplished women whose lives in the Republican era have been erased or passed over, but whose stories document the existence of successful female lawyers, educators, physicians, writers, and political figures in the 1920s and 1930s.[68]

Public discussion of female personhood and the issue of female vocations indeed included the voices of such new women as well as their public associations.[69] In the debate elicited by Xi Shangzhen's suicide, women's associations that published statements included the Women's Vocational Cultivation Society (*Nüzi zhiye lianxiu she*), the Association for the Advancement of Women's Suffrage, a "company" established to advance women's rights (*Nüzi zhiquan gongsi*), and several women's schools. Such vocality prompted commentators to note the emergence of "women's circles," even as the images of the suicide reinforced public notions of female impotence, inarticulateness, and vulnerability.

Precisely because of the public presence of a growing, if small, number of new women, it is difficult not to be struck by the disconnect between the existence of such women and the tone of public discussion of the issues of female vocations and personhood. In this regard, it is tempting to note the determinedly pessimistic feminist fiction of the May Fourth era. Although May Fourth writers provided a powerful critique of traditional family relations, they portrayed an array of disturbing (and disturbed) bourgeois heroines—tubercular, suicidal, interior, or, if publicly successful, then necessarily chaste.[70] Such heroines were frequently educated but rarely able to transform their intellectual attainments into financial independence, happy marriage, or meaningful public lives. Female authors evoked the troubled psychology of new women. The new women in male authors' stories are often schematic and unpersuasive, or pitiable figures sketched more to reflect the morality of male characters than to be worthy of study in their own right.[71] The media story of Xi Shangzhen fits in well among the anguished heroines of both May Fourth and butterfly literature.

Feminist May Fourth era journalism, ranging from the socialist *Funü pinglun* to the more liberal *Funü zazhi*, contains few portraits of successful new Chinese women, despite volumes of prose dedicated to their creation. Descriptions of the new woman tend to be abstract and formulaic. While dynamic female figures from Japan, the United States, and Europe are periodically introduced, descriptions of living, pioneering Chinese women are more minimal. A persisting ideological disturbance created by the transgression of gender boundaries and the equation of these boundaries with virtue made modern personhood difficult for Chinese women to embody. Advocates of women's vocations noted that even women's vocational schools rarely went so far as to envision women as actors in society. Most such schools, one author stated, promoted home economics rather than independent employment in society.[72] Other articles broadly evoked female employment in society, but focused on women's "special endowments," which made particular forms of employment—such as teaching and nursing, which need not require mixing with men—particularly appropriate.[73]

In the special issue of *Funü zazhi* dedicated to women's vocations only one author provided an example of an actual, that is, named, contemporary Chinese vocational woman. This one example suggests that the imaginative merging of the exemplary modern woman and the female suicide was not aberrant, but rather characteristic, of feminist discourse at the time. The article "Women and Social Work" concludes with an awestruck description of a Chinese vocational woman worthy of emulation. The wealthy Yuan Minfang of Hangzhou founded a private institute to teach poor girls handicrafts and literacy. When her family funds could no longer maintain the school, she appealed for help but was unsuccessful in attracting investors. Yuan swallowed gold and died. Her act inspired Hangzhou local gentry to support the school. The author ended his article with an appeal to readers: "If only our country's women could immediately take action to rival Madame Yuan's claim to fame, that is my greatest hope!" The author's choice of example and language is too striking to go unnoticed. In presenting a model of a socially engaged woman, the author is drawn to the figure of a woman who committed suicide, and moreover one who reputedly swallowed gold (a suicide mechanism of uncertain utility, but familiar to Chinese readers from popular fiction and biographies of chaste widows). Despite the article's evocation of modernity and *ren'ge*, suicide creeps into the portrait, as if the tale of an accomplished woman needed to be balanced by the pathos of her inspiring self-destruction.

The preoccupation of *Funü pinglun* with elite female suicide is even more striking, because of the socialist cast of this literary supplement whose writers rebuked bourgeois women for their elitism and selfish desire to achieve equality simply for themselves, rather than support structural economic reform and working-class women. Although *Funü pinglun* reported on the striking female silk workers in August, Xi's death in September occasioned extended commentary.[74] Subsequent issues featured other poignant sacrifices, illnesses, and suicide attempts of new-style, educated women, whose dramatic deaths embodied *ren'ge*.[75]

My point here is not to focus on the limitations of Chinese feminism or modernity. Instead, I would suggest that the contradictions of May Fourth feminism be understood through twin processes of cultural mapping, both distinctively gendered: The first involves the way in which new cultural programs derived from Western models of modernity were mapped onto deeply resonant notions of gender and virtue. The second has to do with the ways that women, always signifiers of broader social virtue or its absence, were repositories for both the aspirations of modernity and also cultural ambivalence over the social side effects of modernity. For these reasons, women's emergence through vocations into modern economic relations was especially disturbing. By committing suicide for her own reasons, Xi Shangzhen became for the Chinese public a mark of the ambivalent morality of the modern. The modern virtue of *ren'ge* for women was not just more fraught with occupational qualifiers and other explicit limits, dangers, and complexities than for men but in practice less accessible than recognition for chastity in the Late Imperial era.[76] For *ren'ge*, the new woman had to venture across an imaginative boundary so imbued with virtue that it was difficult to overcome the stains of the passage. Marked by her association with men as well as by her desire for money, the new woman was troubling. As one reader expressed the problem of women's ambitions, which conflicted with women's virtue: "When shall we sweep away such empty aspirations/and forever make women trouble-free?"[77]

One might reflect that the most inspiring and trouble-free new women in the early Republican era were those who swept away their ambivalent associations and desires by crossing another boundary, moving from the petty impurities of life to the purity and pathos of martyrdom. The contradictions of this passage, which marked both the virtues and failures of the new morality and the temptations and dangers of modern society, gave Xi a kind of doubled allure for the early Republican public. Nonetheless, as the debates about personhood and the vocational woman that enveloped Xi's suicide suggest, even in death Xi remained troublesome, haunting feminists' dreams with the unlikelihood of their realization.

Notes

I am grateful to Cynthia Brokaw, Wendy Larson, Elizabeth Perry, Mary Rankin, and Ted Huters for comments on earlier versions of this chapter. Research and writing were made possible with support from the American Council of Learned Societies/Chiang Ching-kuo Foundation, the National Endowment for the Humanities, and the Stanford Humanities Center.

1. Hu Ying, *Tales of Translation: Composing the New Woman in China, 1899–1918* (Stanford, Calif.: Stanford University Press, 2000); Joan Judge, "Citizens or Mothers of Citizens? Gender and the Meaning of Modern Chinese Citizenship," in *Changing*

Meanings of Citizenship in Modern China, ed. Merle Goldman and Elizabeth Perry (Cambridge, Mass.: Harvard University Press, 2002), 23–43.

2. According to Cai Yuanpei, *ren'ge* involved four components: physical education, mental training, moral education, and aesthetic education. "Putong jiaoyu he zhiye jiaoyu" (Ordinary education and vocational education), cited in *Hanyu da cidian*, ed. Hanyu da cidian bianji weiyuanhui (Shanghai: Shanghai cishu chubanshe, 1986), 1:1046. Most definitions emphasized individual character. In "The Question of Women's Character," published in *Xinchao* (New tide) 1, no. 2 (February 1919), Ye Shengtao (Ye Shaojun) defines *ren'ge* as "the spirit that distinguishes one from others" and as "a spirit of integrity and independence even when one is part of a group." Achieving *ren'ge* required the individual "to love truth and never follow others blindly." See *Women in Republican China: A Sourcebook*, ed. Hua R. Lan and Vanessa L. Fong (Armonk, N.Y.: Sharpe, 1999), 151. The prominence of the concept of *ren'ge* in May Fourth feminism has been noted in several studies, including Wendy Larson, *Women and Writing in Modern China* (Stanford, Calif.: Stanford University Press, 1998); Wang Zheng, *Women in the Chinese Enlightenment* (Berkeley: University of California Press, 1999); and Tani Barlow, *The Question of Women in Chinese Feminism* (Durham, N.C.: Duke University Press, 2004).

3. The enduring cultural significance of suicide was the focus of papers presented at International Convention of Asia Scholars 2 in Berlin, August 2001: Lyman Van Slyke, "Liang Ji (1858–1918): Elite Suicide in the Early Twentieth Century"; Vera Schick, "Out of the Dark into the Light? The Motif of Suicide in Chinese Literature of the 1920s and 30s"; and Bryna Goodman, "Suicide at the Office: Gender, Cultural Memory and the New Republic." See also Bryna Goodman "The New Woman Commits Suicide: The Press, Cultural Memory, and the New Republic," *Journal of Asian Studies* 64, no. 1 (February 2005).

4. See Roxane Witke, "Mao Tse-tung, Women and Suicide," in *Women in China: Studies in Social Change and Feminism*, ed. Marilyn Young (Ann Arbor: Center for Chinese Studies, University of Michigan, 1973), 7–31.

5. Mao Zedong, *Da gongbao*, November 18, 1919, translated as "The Question of Miss Zhao's Personality," in *Mao's Road to Power: Revolutionary Writings, 1912–1949*, ed. Stuart Schram (Armonk, N.Y.: Sharpe, 1992), 1:423-24. I have slightly altered Schram's translation.

6. Originally published under the name Si Yong. My quote follows the translation in Hua and Fong, *Women in Republican China*, 84–85.

7. The families bore heavy funeral costs and sold their houses. Christina Gilmartin, "Introduction," in Hua and Fong, *Women in Republican China*, xv.

8. *Minguo ribao*, September 17, 1922; *Jing bao*, September 12, 1922; Zheng Zhengqiu, "Cong Xi nüshi zisha delai de jiaoxun" (Lessons from the suicide of Miss Xi), in *Xi Shangzhen*, ed. Cui Weiru (Shanghai: Fünu zhiye yanjiu she, 1922), 1. Chinese interest in the suicide was remarked upon in the Western papers *China Press*, *North China Herald*, and *Millard's Review*.

9. Cui Weiru, ed., *Xi Shangzhen*. The book includes essays by a range of Chinese public figures, including pioneer filmmaker Zheng Zhengqiu, early communist intellectual Chen Wangdao, and writers Hu Yuzhi and Bao Tianxiao.

10. On the Chinese tendency to interpret suicide in terms of social relations rather than individual psychology, see Margery Wolf, "Women and Suicide in China," in *Women in Chinese Society*, ed. Margery Wolf and Roxane Witke (Stanford, Calif.: Stanford University Press, 1975), 117–21; Sing Lee and Arthur Kleinman, "Suicide as Resistance in China," in *Chinese Society: Change, Conflict and Resistance*, ed. Elizabeth Perry and Mark Selden (London: Routledge, 2000), 221–40.

11. Chen Duxiu, "Kongzi zhi dao yu xiandai shenghuo," *Xin qingnian* (New youth) 2, no. 4 (December 1, 1916), reprinted in *Duxiu wencun* (Wuhu: Anhui renmin chubanshe, 1987), 83.

12. Wang Pingling, "Xin funü de ren'ge wenti," *Funü zazhi* 7, no. 10 (October 1921): 10–15.

13. I have slightly modified the translation in Hua and Fong, *Women in Republican China*, 154 and 156.

14. Cheng Wanyang, "Nannü ren'ge pingdeng lun" (The theory of the equality of men's and women's *ren'ge*], *Funü zazhi* 7, no. 8 (August 1, 1921): 14–15.

15. "Nüzi canzheng hui chengli ji" (Women's Suffrage Association Inauguration Record), *Minguo ribao*, October 16, 1922.

16. "Wan Pu nüshi linbie zhi tanhua" (Miss Wan Pu's parting words), *Minguo ribao*, October 25, 1922.

17. By 1908, there were 20,557 female students in primary and higher primary schools. In 1919, the figure had grown to 215,626. Luo Suwen, *Nüxing yu jindai zhonguo shehui* (Women and modern Chinese society) (Shanghai: Shanghai renmin chubanshe, 1996), 135–37, 156; Wang Zheng, *Women in the Chinese Enlightenment*, 130.

18. Luo Suwen, *Nüxing*, 145–55.

19. Some May Fourth radicals imaginatively liberated women from biological reproduction, though their anarchist- and socialist-influenced thinking was nearly as fanciful in the early Republican era as the turn-of-the-century utopian imaginings of Kang Youwei. That even the advocates of female vocations felt the need to address the dangers to motherhood of women's paid employment is evident from contemporary debates on the topic. Yi Jiayue, *Funü zhiye wenti* (The question of women's vocations) (Shanghai: Taidong tushuju, 1922), 100–14; Dongfang zashi she, ed., *Funü zhiye yu muxing lun* (Women's vocations and motherhood) (Shanghai: Shangwu yinshuguan, 1924).

20. Tiesheng (pseud.), "Wo de nüzi canzheng guan" (My views on female participation in government), *Shangbao*, April 7, 1921.

21. See also Yi Jiayue, *Funü zhiye wenti*, 73.

22. Jue Feizi, "Wei nüzi zhiye gao liangzhong ren" (Notice to two types of people for female vocations), *Shenbao*, July 25, 1921.

23. Yang Zhihua, "Tan nüzi zhiye" (On women's vocations), *Funü pinglun* (Women's critic), November 1, 1922. As a Hangzhou Girls' Normal School student, Yang was active in May Fourth protests. She entered radical journalism through her (arranged) marriage to Shen Jianlong, son of radical Guomindang member Shen Xuanlu (who in 1920, with Chen Duxiu, founded the journal *Labor and Women*, in Guangzhou). In 1924, Yang divorced, joined the Chinese Communist Party (CCP), and married Qu Qiubai. Christina

Kelley Gilmartin, *Engendering the Chinese Revolution: Radical Women, Communist Politics, and Mass Movements in the 1920s* (Berkeley: University of California Press, 1995), 39, 103, 231–32; Hua and Fong, *Women in Republican China*, xxxvii.

24. *Funü pinglun*, 53 (August 9, 1922), 58 (September 13, 1922), and 59 (September 20, 1922). The August 9 issue contains one substantial article on the striking women workers by Shao Lizi, "Shanghai sichang nügong bagong ji" (Record of female silk workers' strike).

25. Elizabeth Perry discusses the gang connections of this organization in her brief account of the strike. See *Shanghai on Strike: The Politics of Chinese Labor* (Stanford, Calif.: Stanford University Press, 1993), 171–73. The organization was called into question by sympathetic news accounts—for example, "Sichang nügong bagong ji" (Record of female silk factory strikers), *Shangbao*, August 6, 1922; and Shao Lizi, "Shanghai sichang nügong."

26. Yi Jiayue, *Funü zhiye wenti*, 73–74, 82, 85. Shao Lizi, reporting on the silk workers' strike, similarly noted the manner in which female factory workers were understood to be "loose women" (*dangfu*).

27. Chen Wentao, "Tichang dulixing de nüzi zhiye," *Funü zazhi* 7, no. 8 (August 1, 1921): 7–11.

28. *Nü xuesheng*, 3 (1912): 11–12, 15–16.

29. Chen Wangdao, "Xi Shangzhen nüshi zai Shangbao guan li diaosi shijian" (Xi Shangzhen's hanging at the Shangbao), *Funü pinglun*, 59 (September 20, 1922).

30. For example, "Nüzi zhiye qiantu zhi leguan" (Optimism regarding the future of women's vocations); "Nüzi zai shangjie zhi fazhan" (Women's progress in commercial circles) *Shangbao*, February 22, 1921. See also editorials of April 2, 7, and 11, 1921; August 2 and 6, 1922.

31. Zheng Zhengqiu, in Cui, *Xi Shangzhen*, 1:1.

32. Zheng Zhengqiu, in Cui, *Xi Shangzhen*, 1:5.

33. Zheng Zhengqiu, in Cui, *Xi Shangzhen*, 1:12.

34. Cui, *Xi Shangzhen*, 1:25.

35. Zha Mengci, "Nüzi jiaoyu de quexian" (Defects in women's education), *Zhonghua xinbao*, September 16, 1922.

36. Cui, *Xi Shangzhen*, 2:23, 2:25.

37. Cui, *Xi Shangzhen*, 2:66–67.

38. Cui, *Xi Shangzhen*, 1:18.

39. Lu Xun, "What Happens After Nora Leaves Home," in *Silent China: Selected Writings of Lu Xun*, trans. Gladys Yang (London: Oxford University Press, 1973), 149–54.

40. Shanghai guidebooks and "dark secrets" (*heimu*) literature traded on imaginative connections between the city and a range of desires (financial, sexual, culinary) and focused particularly on the etiquette of interacting with urban women, in brothels and dance halls. Some focus entirely on women in the city. For example, *Shanghai funü nie jingtai* (Shanghai women's mirror of evil) (Shanghai, 1925, reprint of 1918 original).

41. Yun Shi (pseud.), *Funü zhi baimian guan* (Shanghai: Wenyi bianyi she, 1927).

42. Yun Shi, *Funü zhi baimian guan*, 37–42.

43. *Shenbao,* September 10, 1922; *Minguo ribao,* September 11, 1922. Xi's family claimed that Tang defrauded Xi of money, neither giving her stock certificates nor returning her money. In his testimony, Tang denied borrowing Xi's money. He contextualized their financial relations in terms of the market boom. In the 1921 bull market, Tang launched a trust company. Many people in his office purchased stock from him, including Xi. When the market fell, Xi's money was lost. He denied that he had pressured Xi to become his concubine.

44. The 1935 film *Xin nüxing* dramatized a working woman's vulnerability to a sexually predatory employer.

45. Kathryn Bernhardt, "Women and the Law: Divorce in the Republican Period," in *Civil Law in Qing and Republican China,* ed. Kathryn Bernhardt and Philip C. C. Huang (Stanford, Calif.: Stanford University Press, 1994), 209–14; Yi Sheng, "Wo guo falü shang qie zhi shenfen" (The status of concubines in our country's law], *Shenbao,* December 1, 1923.

46. *Jingbao,* September 12, 1922.

47. See, for example, Yang Chaosheng, "Nannü shejiao gongkai" (Public social intercourse for men and women), *Xin qingnian* (La Jeunesse) 6, no. 4, reprinted in *Wusi shiqi funü wenti wenxuan* (Selected May Fourth writings on the woman question) (Beijing: Shenghuo, 1981), 173–75.

48. Zheng Zhengqiu, in Cui, *Xi Shangzhen,* 1:11.

49. Rey Chow, "Mandarin Ducks and Butterflys: An Exercise in Popular Readings," in *Woman and Chinese Modernity,* ed. Rey Chow (Minneapolis: University of Minnesota Press, 1991), 34–83; Tani Barlow, ed., *I, Myself Am a Woman: Selected Writings of Ding Ling* (Boston: Beacon, 1989); Ching-kiu Stephen Chan, "Language of Despair: Ideological Representations of the 'New Woman' by May Fourth Writers," in *Gender Politics in Modern China,* ed. Tani Barlow (Durham, N.C.: Duke University Press, 1993).

50. *Jingbao,* September 21, 1922.

51. Zheng Zhengqiu in Cui, *Xi Shangzhen,* 1:29.

52. *Jingbao,* September 12, 1922.

53. *New Admonition to Women* (*Xin nü jie*), a play on the classical *Nü jie,* by the female scholar Ban Zhao. *Jingbao,* March 6, 9, 12, and 15, 1923. See also Bryna Goodman, "Unvirtuous Exchanges: Women and the Corruptions of the Stock Market in Early Republican China," in *Women in China: The Republican Period in Historical Perspective,* ed. Mechthild Leutner and Nicola Spakowski (Münster: LIT Verlag, 2005).

54. Huang Bingqing, "Xi Shangzhen de zisha shibushi shehui shang zhongda de wenti?" (Is or isn't Xi Shangzhen's suicide a great social problem?), *Shishi xinbao,* September 15, 1922.

55. Cui, *Xi Shangzhen,* 2:8, 2:23.

56. *Shibao,* October 14, 1922.

57. See also *Shibao,* October 19, 1922.

58. Zha Mengci, "Nüzi jiaoyu de quexian." Others explicitly connected financial desire to loss of bodily virtue: "Women lose their virtue for reasons of money. . . . One morning they wake up pregnant." Cui, *Xi Shangzhen,* 1:12

59. *Shangbao* editorial, November 13, 1922.

60. *Shibao*, October 16, 1922, and October 18, 1922.

61. Zheng Zhengqiu, in Cui, *Xi Shangzhen*, 1:2. Emphasis added.

62. *Shibao*, October 19, 1922.

63. For an overview, see Paul S. Ropp, "Passionate Women: Female Suicide in Late Imperial China," *Nan nü* 3, no. 1 (2001): 3–21.

64. Paola Paderni, "Le rachat de l'honneur perdu: Le suicide des femmes dans la Chine du XVIIIe siècle," *Études chinoises* 10, nos. 1–2 (Spring–Autumn 1991), 135–60.

65. Jiang Hongjiao, in Cui, *Xi Shangzhen*, 2:29–30.

66. *Shibao*, October 14–21, 1922; Judge, "Citizens or Mothers of Citizens," 21–23; Qiu Jin's preferred gender models are listed in *Jingwei shi* (Stones of the Jingwei bird): "Everyday I burn incense, praying that women [will follow] in the footsteps of Madame Roland, Anita [Garibaldi], Sophia Perofskaya, Harriet Beecher Stowe, and Joan of Arc." Amy D. Dooling and Kristina M. Torgeson, eds., *Writing Women in Modern China* (New York: Columbia University Press, 1998), 44.

67. Tang and Xi worked together frequently at night; Tang called Xi's home when Xi was ill; Tang stopped Xi's initial suicide attempts; their financial affairs were intertwined; they argued violently. The context of an unequal relationship with her married employer may have led Xi to expect more from Tang and to hold him responsible for her financial losses. Such a relationship would help explain Tang's casual handling of Xi's money and her suicide location.

68. Wang Zheng, *Women in the Chinese Enlightenment*; Christina Kelley Gilmartin, "Introduction: May Fourth and Women's Emancipation," in *Women in Republican China*, ed. Hua and Fong, ix–xxv. Lingling Lien, "Searching for the New Womanhood: Career Women in Shanghai, 1912–1949" (Ph.D. diss., University of California, Irvine, 2001), provides an important new social history of career women.

69. Men still dominated the discussion—just as men dominated Chinese feminism, in this early period. This situation, of course, was not unique to China but characteristic of early feminism—as an aspect of modernity—globally.

70. Examples include Lu Xun, "Regret for the Past"; Ding Ling, "Miss Sophia's Diary"; Mao Dun, "Creation"; Lu Yin, "After Victory"; Chen Xuezhao, "The Woes of the Modern Woman." See also Larson, *Women and Writing in Modern China* (Stanford, Calif.: Stanford University Press, 1992), 7173; Ching-kiu Stephen Chan, "The Language of Despair: Ideological Representations of the 'New Woman' by May Fourth Writers," in *Gender Politics*, ed. Barlow, 13–32.

71. Margaret Decker, "Living in Sin: From May Fourth Via the Anti-Rightist Movement to the Present," in *From May Fourth to June Fourth: Fiction and Film in Twentieth-Century China*, ed. Ellen Widmer and David Der-Wei Wang (Cambridge, Mass.: Harvard University Press, 1993), 221–46.

72. Chen Wentao, "Tichang dulixing," 9.

73. Shao Xian, "Funü yu shehui shiye," 12–13.

74. *Funü pinglun*, August 9, September 13, and September 20, 1922.

75. *Funü pinglun*, October 12, 1922; December 4, 1923; December 11, 1923.

76. On the "democratization" of virtue in Late Imperial China, see Mark Elvin, "Female Virtue and the State in China," *Past and Present* 104 (1984): 111–52.

77. *Shibao*, October 14, 1922.

12

Women's Work and Boundary Transgression in Wang Dulu's Popular Novels

Tze-lan Deborah Sang

FOR FIFTY YEARS, WANG DULU (1909–1977) was forgotten by readers in mainland China and was barely known in Hong Kong and Taiwan. His martial arts and social romantic novels, written in northern China in the 1930s and 1940s, would likely have remained obscure to today's readers had Ang Lee not recently adapted *Crouching Tiger, Hidden Dragon* (*Wo hu cang long*; 1941), the fourth volume of a five-part martial arts series by Wang, into film. Yu Jiaolong (Jen in the English subtitles), a morally ambiguous and itinerant female fighter, occupies the center of Lee's film. While one might be tempted to explain the appearance of such a character in terms of Lee's interest in late twentieth-century global feminism, one must also note that, in the original novel, Jiaolong is every bit as willful, elusive, and vicious as her cinematic incarnation. She is dissatisfied with the gendered nature of work and mobility. She loathes squandering her life away in the idle activity in which upper-class women typically engage—calligraphy, embroidery, reading *The Four Books for Women* (*Nü sishu*) and *The Biographies of Women* (*Lienü zhuan*), and playing with pets. She yearns to venture out into the wide, wide world and prove herself an invincible fighter.[1] Interestingly, the author never condemns her as an evil figure for transgressing female virtue.

What became of Wang Dulu's vision? Since the May Fourth era (1915–1927), China's left-wing critics indiscriminately condemned early twentieth-century writers of serialized commercial fiction as "backward," "feudalistic," and "conservative." Their attack on martial arts fiction and film was especially vehement, criticizing them not only as superstitious but also as a misguided attempt to achieve "national form" in art.

Like many other martial arts writers slightly before him and contemporary with him, Wang's work was contemptuously ignored by literary critics of his time and later even suffered the fate of being eradicated after communists took power, especially during the Cultural Revolution (1966–1976). However, this chapter contends that, although Wang wrote entertainment fiction for a living, he was in fact an aspiring cosmopolitan who was sensitive to the resonance between the so-called progressive new ideas and certain existing elements of China's composite, heterogeneous tradition. Rather than resist the drastic social change and shifting values that occurred in his time, he creatively revised the narrative conventions about chivalrous women in China's long-standing tradition of fantasy literature, thus making tradition relevant for the times, on the one hand, and rendering Western-imported ideas about female independence, profession, and mobility familiar and palatable to ordinary urban readers, on the other. His work instantiates the synthesis of a quintessential national art form—the martial arts fantasy—and transnational ideas of women's liberation.

Specifically, far from producing escapist literature that turned a blind eye to reality, Wang transported the issue of some elite women's iconoclastic search for professional careers and the freedom of love from a contemporary setting (i.e., between the May Fourth era and 1941, the year Wang created the novel) into the premodern, historical setting characteristic of the martial arts genre. The result of this transposition—*Crouching Tiger*—yields a simultaneously romanticized and radicalized portrait of the unorthodox elite woman fighting to emancipate herself from the restrictive roles of the naïve, cloistered daughter and the housewife. This imaginary portrait is a romanticized image larger than life because the novel grants its heroine undefeatable swordsmanship when faced with adversaries—that is, a kind of indomitable ability and resilience in the face of impediments, to which no real woman, no matter how courageous or ambitious, may lay claim. The portrait is also a radicalized image because, by choosing the eighteenth century over contemporary times as the novelistic setting, Wang gained license to represent the Confucian orthodoxy as largely intact and its disciplinary power as entrenched—more entrenched than it might have been in the semicolonial, half-Westernized Chinese cities of his day. The temporal shift from the present (i.e., the early twentieth century) to a somewhat archaic setting thus renders the conflict between a free-spirited woman and the Confucian gender doctrine all the more acute and, in the eyes of the reader, all the more extraordinary, dramatic, and enthralling.

It can be observed, moreover, that while the focus of *Crouching Tiger* is ostensibly the boundary transgression and moral quandaries of an elite woman during the high Qing era and, more implicitly, the self-liberation of the May

Fourth intellectual woman of a privileged socioeconomic background, Wang is keenly aware of class difference among women, especially the extent to which disparate economic standings vary the proper spatial boundaries for women and the kind of mobility that they desire. Gender, in other words, intersects with class in shaping the prescribed fates of women and the particular aspirations they might have to momentarily steer away from, permanently abandon, or even make defunct for those normative paths of life. Such sensitivity to the privileges as well as injustices of class might be only delicately suggested in *Crouching Tiger*, but it forms the moral and dramatic core of the social romantic novels that Wang wrote concurrently with his martial arts fantasies. This particular sensibility, rooted in a profound knowledge of the tacit segregations in his beloved native city, Beijing, renders his work exemplary of "proletarian literature" although they were never admitted by left-wing critics into official literary histories as such.[2]

Crouching Tiger: Hybridization of National Form and Transnational Feminism

Crouching Tiger was serialized in Japanese-occupied Qingdao in 1941, when overtly nationalistic literature was discouraged while other issues—such as gender and sexuality—may have paradoxically been encouraged as material for representation.[3] Partly due to the milieu of the time and partly due to the fact that it was written as an entertainment novel for ordinary readers, there is little trace of an obsession with the crisis of China's survival, which is typical of May Fourth literature. The novel is nevertheless an ideologically loaded work, especially in terms of its depiction of gender norms and their subversion. Wang consciously dramatizes Jiaolong's transgression of female space, work, and virtue as the impetus that launches the narrative into motion. In doing so, furthermore, he radically revises certain common devices in Qing chivalric novels about unconventional heroines, which invariably recuperate valiant women with martial abilities into the discourses of loyalty to a wronged emperor (*zhong*) or filial piety for one's wronged parents (especially father) (*xiao*).[4] Jiaolong defies father, mother, teacher, brother, and husband to search for personal freedom and to test her own prowess. Not even her illicit male lover, Luo Xiaohu, can subdue her and make her surrender to domesticity. After a one-night reunion, Jiaolong leaves Xiaohu. She becomes a single parent who owns a vast ranch in Xinjiang in the sequel to *Crouching Tiger*—*Iron Steed, Silver Vase* (*Tie ji yin ping*), also written by Wang Dulu in the 1940s.[5] For about nineteen years, Jiaolong's main career—if we may describe it as such—consists of eliminating bandits in the southern part of the

Xinjiang, Shaanxi, and Gansu region to ensure the safety of travelers and merchants. Her deeds won her the reputation of being prideful and merciless (*jiaoao henla*); she is both revered and feared. Till her untimely end, Jiaolong remains a sympathetic, if tragic, figure; she is never openly condemned as a tainted woman or one whose honor is irrecoverably lost.

This uncommon characterization of Jiaolong, the beautiful dragon, is significant, for it signals that the moral vision that Wang Dulu constructs through this martial arts series is not the usual kind that upsets an existing Confucian social order only to restore it to perfection. As has been noted by many critics already, the co-optation of roving knights by the political establishment is a common occurrence in Qing chivalric fiction. Especially in the hybrid genre, chivalric-tales-cum-detective-stories (*xiayi gongan xiaoshuo*), fearless heroes cooperate with an upright official to eliminate criminals and uphold the status quo, instead of defying imperial rule.[6] Similar co-opting mechanisms govern the action of masculine females: in several Qing novels where the main protagonists are women with superior martial skills, the heroines either serve the emperor or ultimately become domesticated. For instance, in Lü Xiong's *The Unofficial History of Female Immortals* (*Nüxian waishi*), the female rebel Tang Saier goes to battle not out of her own ambition but rather to reinstate the Jianwen emperor, whose throne was usurped by his uncle.[7] *A Tale of Lovers and Heroes* (*Ernü yingxiong zhuan*) by Wen Kang is an even more striking example, where the chivalrous woman Thirteenth Sister (*Shisan mei*) is expeditiously tamed into a paragon of wifely virtue once her father's death has been avenged.[8] The didacticism embedded in *A Tale of Lovers and Heroes* and the deep ambivalence about female power in *Flowers in a Mirror* (*Jinghua yuan*) have prompted Maram Epstein to argue that these novels create masterful female characters with masculine abilities (intellectual or physical) in order to inject beauty, sentiment, and authenticity into certain Confucian ideals and institutions that have become corrupted by men.[9] The "feminization" of traditionally male spheres in these narratives, in other words, does not so much empower actual women and girls as revitalize and support the moral doctrines of the male authors.[10]

It seems probable that by creating Yu Jiaolong, Wang Dulu is similarly prettifying an ideal, couching it in the terms of the symbolic feminine, thereby making it more compelling. What, however, is this ideal? It obviously is not Confucian orthodoxy, for Jiaolong is neither an obedient daughter, a meek wife, nor a virtuous mother. After Jiaolong successfully delivers a boy in a tavern, she falls asleep in exhaustion, and another woman who has just given birth to a girl swaps the two babies. After pursuing the thief in vain and failing to recover her child, Jiaolong adopts the abandoned baby girl and raises her as her own. Nineteen years later, when she meets her son and discovers his identity by accident, she dares not unveil the truth to him, for she would have to tell him that he is her bastard (*sisheng haizi*). Afraid of being rejected, Jiaolong chooses to be an elderly friend (*pengyou*), rather than a mother, to him. Jiaolong feels ashamed about her illicit love affair (*siqing*) in the past because, after all, she was educated to value chastity. Ironically, her reluctance to restore the mother-son relationship inadvertently disrupts the proper hierarchy of human relationships so fundamental to Confucianism.

Still, the ideal that Jiaolong embodies, if not entirely in agreement with Confucian familialism and propriety, is perhaps not completely in contradiction with it, either. The ideal is plainly announced by her tutor Gao Langqiu (who later becomes the nominal husband of Biyan Huli, the Green-Eyed Fox). He addresses Jiaolong, then a seven-year-old child:

> Jiaolong, you are very intelligent, and you have a lively spirit and natural love for the martial arts. Although you are a girl, if you can be well-versed in the classics and histories, acquire expertise in calligraphy and painting, and, in addition, master the art of war, boxing and swordplay, you can, as much as boys, honor your family and bequeath a miracle to this world (*wei renjian liu yi qiji*). Since antiquity, Ban Zhao is revered as the representative of talented women, and Qin Liangyu is the most renowned female general. A female knight-errant (*nüxia*), however, has never existed. Hongxian and Nie Yinniang are absurd imagined characters in fiction. But if we reason it carefully: A girl does have the chance to become a female knight-errant if she is willing to study sword fighting and boxing diligently under the tutelage of a competent teacher. Now, I would like to spend ten years teaching you reading and writing, the art of war, and swordplay. I want the capabilities of Ban Zhao, Qin Liangyu, and Hongxian to converge in you. You will be an extraordinary woman (*qi nüzi*) that has never before existed, is rare in the present world, and will hardly ever appear again in the future. Are you willing? (1:210)

Such, we might say, is the ambition of Wang Dulu—to be the creator of a marvelous female prodigy, whose accomplishments will one day rival those of Ban Zhao, Qin Liangyu, and Hongxian all combined.[11]

Jiaolong is the brainchild of Wang Dulu, who heralds the amalgamation of multiple legacies in the Chinese tradition as the new ideal in human development. Not surprisingly, she is dazzlingly beautiful. Early in the novel, her appearance is introduced through the surreptitious look of Liu Taibao, a clownish character:

> She was about sixteen. Tall and slender. Covered in a snow blue cape made of some unknown radiant silk lined with silver mink, she wore a red embroidered Manchu robe underneath. Her feet were natural (*tianzu*). She wore thick-soled shoes, the kind that Manchu girls wore, which were made of golden cloth embroidered in

> colorful threads and decorated with tiny glass mirrors. Her hair was combed into a braid. The braid, of course, was hidden by the cape, and only her shiny black clouds besides her ears were shown. A red-velvet phoenix was pinned to her hair and hovered above her ear. A string of dainty lustrous pearls hung from the phoenix's beak. Her face was even more beautiful than her clothes and jewelry: a face shaped like the melon seed, a high nose, big eyes, and handsome eyebrows. If one were to compare her noble and magnificent beauty to flowers, only the peony was comparable, but the peony was not as exquisite as she. (1:5)

Appealing is this personification of versatility, a symbol of composite tradition. By conceiving such a character—who can write as eloquently as Ban Zhao, lead an army as gallantly as Qin Liangyu, and, moreover, perform enigmatic feats like Hongxian, as well as enchant like the most splendid of all flowers—the "old school" novelist Wang Dulu is showing his readers that tradition can be attractive and appropriate for the times. Like a modern girl student, Jiaolong is well educated in all manner of subjects, including physical education and military training.[12] She is, of course, fashionably dressed, but her natural beauty outshines all embellishments. Moreover, her feet have never been bound. Tradition itself is heterogeneous, and if elements are carefully selected, it is not difficult for Wang to find a combination that suits changing "new" sensibilities.

One of the categories of difference that the novel foregrounds is ethnic difference within China. In Jiaolong's adventures, she often dresses as a man, in tight-fitting black tops and pants. However, she has a relatively small frame and a high-pitched voice. Therefore, in her random encounters with other fighters, they are often baffled by her outer appearance and extremely confused about her gender identity. She is repeatedly cursed by her opponents for being "neither female nor male" (*bu nü bu nan*). In their confusion, her opponents always look toward her feet as if the feet are a sure marker of her real gender identity. Time and again, because her feet are of natural size (*yishuang dajiao*), they immediately draw the conclusion that she must in fact be a male. In these situations her opponents' insensitivity or blindness to ethnic diversity within China leads them to make reductive and, therefore, mistaken assumptions about the gender system in China. The novel suggests that a proper awareness of the ethnic and cultural diversity of old China is indispensable to a complex and well-rounded understanding of gender practices in China. Wang's sensitivity to the issue of Chinese heterogeneity is arguably attributable to his own Manchu identity and is very different from the nationalist discourse about a homogeneous China that we see in many May Fourth elite writings denouncing tradition.[13] Even more provocative, in the sequel to *Crouching Tiger*, Jiaolong's desirable capabilities are fully transmitted to her adopted daughter, whose biological origin is Han yet who is raised by Jiaolong in Xinjiang. In other words, while an alternative female ideal—an androgynous or transgendered one, if you will—is epitomized by Jiaolong the Manchu woman fighter, it is not an identity that can be mastered only by girls of Manchu blood. It is, rather, implied to be something that can potentially empower even Han girls and women.

More broadly, the ability of writers of urban entertainment fiction to sinicize—or localize—Western ideas may have been, precisely, the key to their popularity. Their dexterity in utilizing, refashioning, and reinventing tradition radically distinguished them from the "new school" iconoclasts-cum-writers of the May Fourth generation, who generally succumbed to what Theodore Huters calls "the hard imperatives of imported theory" and sought to model their fictional writing closely after European genres.[14] Mao Dun, observing the petty urbanites' (*xiaoshimin*) fanatic love of martial arts novels and movies (*wuxiakuang*) in the early 1930s, bemoaned it as a sign of the remaining hold of "feudalistic thinking" on China's petty bourgeoisie.[15] Mao Dun readily blamed popular writers for stealing readers away from new literature, without ever reflecting on the alienating effects that his own Europeanized diction and syntax and stiff, programmatic "realism" and "naturalism" had on the common reader.

Throughout the 1930s, despite left-wing writers' profuse debate on how to create "proletarian literature and art" (*puluo wenyi*) and "mass literature and art" (*dazhong wenyi*), few were actually able to reach the majority of China's readers. Hence Chen Dieyi, in defense of urban popular fiction, pointedly criticized in 1942 that "writers of new literature" (*xinwenyi gongzuozhe*) since May Fourth made the terrible mistake of refusing to use traditional forms and thus failed to make the populace accept their works. Chen argued, moreover, that the dichotomy between old and new camps of literature set up by the writers of new literature was false: "The division should be knocked down so that new ideas and correct concepts can be introduced to the common reader through popular literature."[16]

It can be argued that Wang Dulu, in practice, was precisely one of the writers who introduced new sensibilities and ideas into entertainment fiction, although communist critics never admitted him into literary histories as such. Not much is known about Wang's life. According to a recent biographical account by Xu Sinian, he was born into a poor Manchu family in Beijing in 1909, lost his father when he was seven, and was self-educated. Wang's home was in the vicinity of Beijing University, so he often audited classes there. This gave him access to May Fourth "new culture" in his youth.[17] More evidence of Wang's interest in modern Western ideas has to be sought in his actual works. *Crouching Tiger*, I contend, not only puts an attractive face on tradition through the wonder girl Yu Jiaolong but is fundamentally revisionist of the chivalric tradition and deeply interested in the changing roles of educated women in early twentieth-century China.

In the story set in the high Qing era, the imperative of domestic confinement and lack of employment primarily applies to upper-class women. By contrast, the "women of River and Lake" (*jianghu nüzi*) of the commoner class can and must work as professional armed escorts, street performers, detectives, and so on.[18] Jiaolong, being born a *mingmen de xiaojie*, or the young lady of a renowned household, does not have to, and she is not permitted to either venture out into society at large or hold a profession. Yet her competitive, adventurous, and imaginative nature does not permit her to be at peace with a quiet languid life at home. The story consists in essence of her gradual metamorphosis into a woman of the River and Lake. Meanwhile, it also tells the trials and costs that Jiaolong must endure.

Perry Link once maintained that Republican urban popular writers show the "absence of disquieting" (a phrase borrowed from Q. D. Leavis)—that is, "a general failure to probe moral questions in any depth." He observes, further, that "China's 'new school' fiction artists of the May Fourth tradition can also be found wanting by such standards, but they did, after all, include a Lu Hsun, and also authors like Shen Ts'ung-wen, Lao She, Yü Ta-fu, and Wu Tsu-hsiang, whose moral insights could be profound."[19] Link calls popular fiction the "fiction for comfort" and avers that popular writers often tried out new ideas in their stories but ultimately confirmed the superiority of traditional values.

However, since no one has yet examined all of the several thousand traditional-style novels of the Republican era, whether the observations mentioned here pertain to all popular writers, especially those writing after May Fourth, is obviously an open question. I argue that in the case of *Crouching Tiger*, there is not an absence, but rather a surplus, of moral disquiet: Jiaolong is confronted with the fact that her own reckless ambition, rebelliousness, and longing for freedom in love cause her parents grief, worry, shame, and illness. Nevertheless, she cannot suppress her own character, and there is no way for her to wholly return to her former existence once she has embarked on the road to the expansive and treacherous world at large.

In the story, after her first chivalric adventure outside the capital, Jiaolong makes a visit home as soon as she learns that her mother has fallen ill of grief. Moreover, not wanting to hurt her father's and brothers' careers in officialdom, she acquiesces to living in her nominal husband's residence. Jiaolong visits her mother daily and tries to console her, but her mother soon dies. Meanwhile, rumors doubting Jiaolong's respectability continue to spread like wildfire in the capital. Consequently, her father also collapses into illness, and it is then that Jiaolong makes the vow that she will make a pilgrimage to the top of the sacred Miaofeng mountain (*Miaofeng shan*) west of Beijing and jump off the cliff to repay the Goddess with gratitude if her father's illness is cured.[20]

These filial and pious sentiments may have endeared Jiaolong to the common Chinese reader of the 1940s, but they certainly would have made anti-traditionalists frown. It is fascinating, then, that the pious girl eventually jumps off the golden summit (*jinding*) not exactly to sacrifice herself in obligation to the merciful Bixia Yuanjun Goddess but to leave her family without causing them shame and harm. It is the fantastic nature of martial arts that saves Jiaolong from her moral quandaries: unconstrained by gravity, she lands at the foot of the mountains unharmed. She subsequently finds her lover Xiaohu and reunites with him, which naturally overjoys him. But the lovers' sweet dreams are fleeting; Xiaohu wakes up the next morning to find that Jiaolong has disappeared without any explanation. The narrator intrudes at this point and informs the reader, by way of conclusion, that Jiaolong, in order to keep her promise to her mother on her death bed that she will never marry a bandit, has no choice but to leave (743–63).

Instead of being decidedly conservative or unambiguously iconoclastic, *Crouching Tiger* presents a moral tug-of-war. The moral dilemma of the woman on the run that it depicts is no less thought provoking and compelling than the May Fourth elite's anti-Confucian slogans and loud cheers for Ibsen's Nora. For most New Women of the intellectual class throughout the Republican period, the emotional and psychological cost of breaking with traditional values and cutting off ties with family was probably high, and quite likely it was difficult for them not to feel guilty for bringing their parents sorrow because of their unconventional behavior.[21] Wang's characterization of his heroine is also refreshing for the fact that, unlike the Chinese Noras in many May Fourth stories, Jiaolong's choice to leave the comforts of home does not hinge on her relationship with a male lover. With or without Xiaohu, she has to leave home, for she can no longer be contented with her prior existence in the cage-like female quarters, nor can she live with a husband whom she does not love. This detail alone of female independence from romantic love amply suggests the ideological complexity and ambiguity of Wang Dulu as a writer.[22] In sum, working with a highly fantastic genre, Wang manages to create a compelling symbolic/allegorical figure to comment on the moral dilemmas confronted by the New Woman of his day, all the while resisting some of the hackneyed agendas circulated by the May Fourth intelligentsia.[23]

Fragrant Buds on a Splendid Market: A Parable of Women's Work

Wang's interest in women's changing place in modernizing China is even more apparent in his novels set in contemporary society. He explores, if not the dissolution of gendered spaces, then women's violation of gender boundaries through spatial movement, and he engages in such an exploration not only in martial arts fantasy but also in what was known as social sentimental fiction (*shehui yanqing xiaoshuo*).[24] In each narrative genre, he presents a somewhat different kind of spatial transgression, however. Whereas his martial arts novels depict women's transgressive movement primarily as a matter of athletic ability, training, and prowess, which disturbs familial hierarchy and matrimonial harmony, his social novels portray female spatial transgression predominantly as enacted in the context of modern urbanism and as intrinsically progressive: women trespass spatial boundaries as they strive for access to new civic, public space and well-paying professions, during which process they aspire to achieve not only financial security but also an independent character. Whereas in *Crouching Tiger*, Wang's most enduring martial arts work, we see an upper-class woman struggle to set herself free from the restrictive inner chambers, gradually take on a degree of resemblance to working-class women, and also suffer particular kinds of humiliation and ostracism because of her fall from her high social station, in his social novels, the mobility-seeking heroine is typically a lower-class girl attempting to enter a new professional sphere dominated by the well-educated bourgeoisie. In Wang's martial arts novels, women's vocations are a by-product of abstract yearnings for personal freedom in some instances and a matter of family tradition in others. By contrast, in his social novels, employment is a foremost concern, a question of survival, that preoccupies his poverty-stricken heroines. Part of the contrast between the two kinds of female spatial movement (i.e., moving from the inner to the outer sphere versus moving from the lower to the middle class) is undoubtedly geared toward an examination of class difference. Here, Wang may have implicitly identified with his lower-class heroines, for anxieties about unemployment plagued numerous men of humble origins like himself as well as lower-class women in economically depressed Beijing of the late 1920s and 1930s. Yet there seems to be also something else at work—a genuine interest in the expanding socioeconomic space for women during the Republican period. And it is in his novels set in contemporary society rather than his martial arts fantasy that Wang could carefully explore the implications of such an expansion.

His social sentimental novels, which stylistically feature an admixture of naturalistic and melodramatic modes of representation, might be understood as a genre in which everyday social problems are exaggerated or dramatized according to a bipolar moral scheme, hence inciting extreme affect and perhaps also a cathartic feeling in readers. In these novels, the issue of women's vocations receives historically grounded consideration as one of the defining problems of modern urban life in Beijing. This modern urban life promised new liberties and also posed hidden hardships for women. On the one hand, ideas for women's liberation and participation in public life were promoted and carried out to some extent. For instance, hundreds, even thousands, of women of elite family backgrounds were admitted to all-women's and coed colleges, and many of these women participated in public agitation for China's political reform and cultural rejuvenation. Women's pursuit of professional careers was widely debated by intellectuals and was encouraged at least in theory. Also, free association and love between men and women became enshrined by youths as civilized norms.

On the other hand, society proved to be a place full of hidden snares for women. The majority of women who entered the workforce (i.e., seeking work beyond performing domestic chores in their homes) were of low socioeconomic status and were confronted with hard, dehumanizing work.[25] Worse still, they might be doomed to unemployment. The lack of proper employment as a women's problem (in the sense that it touched many women's lives) was particularly pronounced in early Republican Beijing. Throughout the early part of the twentieth century, the grand, majestic ancient capital never developed an industrial manufacture sector on the same scale as those in treaty ports such as Tianjin and Shanghai. After the collapse of the Qing dynasty, early Republican Beijing owed its continued prosperity primarily to the presence of the northern warlord government in the city and to the culture and service industries. In this economy, when lower-class women sought work beyond domestic labor, the kinds of work available to them were extremely limited, consisting mainly of handiwork in cottage industries and work in the culture and service industries.[26] A serious blow struck the city and aggravated the situation when the warlord regime was vanquished by Chiang Kai-shek's Nationalist army in 1928 and when Nanjing was opted over Beijing as the seat of the central government of a newly unified China. Beijing lost its prominence as a political center, and the disappearance of a central government as a major employer and the exodus of rich bureaucrats from the city caused a deep economic depression felt through many levels of society. Numerous women from low levels of society as well as men—such as former government employees, new university graduates, owners of small businesses, laborers—lived under constant anxieties about the lack of the means of livelihood.

The pressure of livelihood was undoubtedly felt most keenly by the urban poor, and a considerable number of women belonging to this social stratum entered prostitution, by choice or by coercion, in order to find subsistence for themselves and their families. Women of the middle class—save for those who had large inheritances or married wealthy men—also needed employment, as teacher, secretary, nurse, clerk, and so forth.[27] The pressing question for many women, then, was not whether they could gain the freedom to work outside the home but what professions were open to them and what kinds of structures of reward determined the value of their work.

These issues received extensive treatment in Wang's social novels set in prewar Beiping (Beijing), the majority of which were serialized in Qingdao newspapers between the late 1930s and early 1940s and issued in book form in Shanghai in 1948.[28] Wang's most incisive, and perhaps also most bitter, analysis of women's vocations appears in a novel in two volumes entitled *Fragrant Buds on a Splendid Market* (*Qi shi fang pa*; 1948) and *Cold Waves Threaten Jade-like Flowers* (*Han bo yu rui*; 1948).[29] The plot revolves around an impoverished girl's search for employment in prewar Beiping. Initially, the seventeen-year-old heroine Tian Eryu has to contend with the objection of her conservative father in order to work long hours selling flowers by herself while he is ill. In other words, residual notions about the proper place for women being in the home threaten to obstruct Eryu's work, which she undertakes to earn a paltry sum of money for the subsistence needs of herself and her father.

As the story progresses, an ironic reversal occurs. When Eryu is recruited by a wealthy man, Wu Huiyi, to become a salesclerk in his Oceania Women's Department Store (*Dayangzhou nüzi baihuodian*), Eryu's father, hearing of the (relatively) high pay that Wu promises Eryu, pressures her to accept the job. On the face of it, it seems as if Eryu has overcome traditional prejudices and attained the right to employment, one of the defining prerogatives of a modern woman. However, it is gradually revealed that Wu has opened the women's department store not to promote women's vocations but to devise a complicated scheme to compete with a wealthy male rival and to win back his former lover Lisa, a woman of ultramodern appearance and diabolical manipulative skills. Wu has recruited Eryu not to give her a decent job but to use her as a tool—she is richly adorned to be the quintessential Oriental beauty, whose purpose is to divert the attention of Wu's male rival away from the Westernized, ultramodern Lisa. Indignant at being thus used, Eryu agrees to Lisa's attempt to spoil her traditional look, allowing her old-fashioned long braid to be cut and also getting a perm. A modern-looking Eryu, now sporting a perm and a fashionable silk cheongsam dress, then discusses the prospect of a poor but honest and happy life with her love interest, Wu Wenqi (the cousin of Wu Huiyi). However, her hopes for a love union and a life of moral integrity are quickly dashed, as Wu Huiyi, furious at Eryu's defiance (which has caused his scheme to regain Lisa to fail), fires a bullet into her, causing her death a few days later.

In this excessively melodramatic novel, just as Eryu thinks that she has extricated herself from the grip of old patriarchal prejudices against women's work and succeeded in finding modern employment outside the home, she falls into yet another male trap, which reduces her to an exotic/erotic object and a piece on a chessboard. Wu Huiyi embodies a sinister male skepticism about women's ability to be full-fledged individuals and self-motivated workers. His denial of the meaning of work for women renders Eryu's pursuit of financial security and independent personhood through work futile. When his violence culminates in the act of shooting and fatally wounding Eryu, he physically obliterates the modern woman that she wishes to become and has become. The melodramatic story thus functions as a parable about the deceptiveness of modern employment for women—its reputed modernity is constantly belied by men's attempts to strip women of their control over their own bodies. Eryu's physical beauty is the only prized commodity that she has to offer in the eyes of men. Her physical allure constantly eclipses the other kinds of value (dignity, independence, security) that she wishes to create through her labor.

This novel, while full of surprising twists and turns in the plot, nonetheless contains moments of naturalism in that details of everyday life are dexterously interwoven to give a vivid sense of Beijing as a place. The details construct Beijing's urban form as a particularly heterogeneous space, that is, an especially intense mosaic of contiguous but separate worlds, which appears to nurture spatial crossings and social mobility, but ultimately defeats such crossings and any naïve illusions of class mobility. A logic of segregation belies the heterogeneity on the surface and constantly reinforces class boundaries with tenacity.

Wang is especially masterful at embedding the issue of women's vocations in descriptions of a transforming urban space. For instance, early in the novel Eryu comes to terms with her latent wish to seek modern employment while taking a walk in the Beihai park:

> As she promenaded among the crowd, she did not feel alone this time because, unlike the last time she came to the park, there were many other girls who wore their hair in a single long braid as she did. Then another thought crept into her mind: at that moment, as she tried to decide whether to take the job at the women's department store, she had come to a crossroads—that between squalor and wealth, and between the old and the new. She had been born into an old-fashioned family; her father constantly spoke of "the days when the emperor still existed." . . . What obstinacy! To this day he would not allow her to cut her hair. It upset her. In a few years, she would become just another married woman who wore her hair in a traditional bun. What interesting things could she expect from life then? However, if she were to take the job? Her life would gradually become "new." Even though she did not envy fashionable ladies or want to become like them, she did want a future, and the job promised that.[30]

For Eryu, working at a women's department store promises not only the opportunity to extricate herself from poverty but also the chance to surmount a predictable fate and to enter the sphere of the modern. Here, the amelioration of one's economic standing is imagined in exactly spatial terms: economic mobility impinges on a nimble change in direction—turning away from the road of traditionalism onto a path leading toward modernity.

That desirable forms of employment are associated with novel urban space is further suggested by the location where Eryu's rumination occurs: the Beihai park. This family garden of the Manchu imperial house had, since the 1920s, been appropriated as public grounds, its formerly exclusive, private space remapped as a modern civil institution.[31] It became open to all in theory but, since an entrance fee was charged, was frequented by only the bourgeoisie in reality. Eryu herself, being a poverty-stricken vendor of flowers, can hardly afford the admittance and has visited the park only a few times previously. Nevertheless, it being the fifteenth day of the seventh month on the lunar calendar—the Ghost Day (*guijie* or *zhongyuan*)—a charity organization is hosting folk ritual in the park and has waived the entrance ticket for all. Thus comes Eryu, as do many other old-fashioned young girls and old women who rarely visit the park. And it is in this modern space enjoyed by the leisure class, where Eryu normally would find herself out of place, that she becomes acutely aware of her own desire to fit in the modern world and to eke out a living in it.

That an impoverished girl like Eryu is anxious to find a way to survive in the transforming economy of the city comes as no surprise. However, it is indeed striking how intensely she fears rejection by the new economic/spatial order, considering the fact that she is a native of the city. The space of the city appears to be in flux and divided, and a good part of it appears intimidating and downright alienating to her. She readily classifies places, professions, and people as either new- or old-fashioned. On a previous visit to Beihai, she has been embarrassed by her own appearance, which is defined by a long braid marking her status as an unmarried virgin, a traditional practice/style that has been abandoned by modern girls and women who sport short bobs and fluffy, wavy perms. Sensing the incongruity between her Chinese short jacket and pants and the Westernized suits and high heels of the wealthy middle class, she perceives her visit to the park as a transgression of spatial boundaries. Ironically, one spatial transgression prefigures another. Not long after her first visit she soon makes another to the park. Moreover, soon after her visits to the park, Eryu will actively seek admission to the women's department store, a Western-inspired enterprise that symbolizes capitalist production and consumption, to become a salesclerk.

Eryu's longing for journeying to a world of plenitude is underscored by an overwhelming feeling of alienation. She is haunted by a sense of segregation despite the fact that her home in a little alleyway in the shadow of the Drum

Tower is only a short distance (i.e., within one to two miles) from Beihai, from the women's department store in Xidan, from her employer's mansion north of the Forbidden City, and from the university where her lover is a student. The physical proximity among these worlds may allow the different classes to have chance encounters with one another, yet their borders are not easily crossed by those who have neither material resources nor symbolic capital. As Eryu sees it, mobility and cosmopolitanism are functions of wealth. Robert Park, in theorizing the urban environment, has argued that the city is a "mosaic of little worlds which touch but not interpenetrate," which makes "it possible for individuals to pass quickly and easily from one moral milieu to another, and encourages the fascinating but dangerous experiment of living at the same time in several different contiguous, but otherwise widely separated worlds."[32] In constructing the tragic story of a lower-class heroine who tries to pass into the bourgeois world but ultimately is sacrificed, Wang Dulu seems to argue that the contiguity of the morally separate worlds of Beijing is beguiling and especially dangerous for those who are the least privileged.

Fragrant Buds on a Splendid Market examines the meaning of new forms of employment in new urban space. It argues that new forms of work necessarily transform the cityscape, creating not only new work space in a narrow sense but also new spaces for the leisure needs of a rising bourgeoisie. Its description of the overlapping spatial and social dimensions of Beijing's urban form provides a compelling illustration for the French Marxist Henri Lefebvre's claim:

> Social relations, which are concrete abstractions, have no real existence save in and through space. *Their underpinning is spatial.* In each particular case, the connection between this underpinning and the relations it supports calls for analysis. Such an analysis must imply and explain a genesis and constitute a critique of those institutions, substitutions, transpositions, metaphorizations, anaphorizations, and so forth, that have transformed the space under consideration.[33]

By zooming in on Eryu's feelings of alienation while taking a stroll in the Beihai park, Wang has precisely critiqued the unjust transformation of a public, civic space into an exclusive playground for the bourgeoisie by capitalist work relations. The novel also reveals that access to modern work and its correlative space is not granted to all; rather, many must overcome existing class attitudes and differences to obtain it. There are, moreover, gender-specific obstacles, as remnants of the traditional ideology of male/female separate spheres, and appropriate gender behavior also play a part. Of the questions about gender and work that Wang Dulu poses, the most pressing one seems to be "How should a girl from a poor family make a living in society?"[34] His novel reveals that girls from low levels of society do not have the luxury to be idle and are usually compelled to work outside as well as inside their homes to help support their families. Yet, lacking formal education and high social connections, they are subjected to jobs that are either low-paying or morally corrupting, or both. Such girls' professional options are restricted by their kin and neighborhood networks even when the economy to which they contribute is, in theory, moving away from a household-centered model to one built on the interplay between capital and wage labor. Their work outside the home does not necessarily give them economic autonomy or other forms of independence from the family. On the contrary, many remain prisoners of their family backgrounds and obligations. Written more than two decades after the May Fourth radicals' idealization of women's vocations outside domestic confines as a sign of their liberation and self-reliance, Wang's social novels present a much darker picture of reality, one that exposes the underpinning forces of tradition even as it accords women's vocations the cachet of the modern.

Conclusion

Wang's works—both realistic social dramas as well as his fantastical martial arts stories—reflect the real social tensions that populated the lives of his readers. In localizing transnational ideas about women's emancipation, he displayed a cosmopolitan perspective not normally attributed to popular writers and never lost sight of the pains and problems of modernization. As literally thousands of volumes of popular fiction were written and avidly consumed during the Republican era, one wonders whether Wang's couching of serious issues as entertainment made him a *rara avis* or is simply the tip of an iceberg.[35]

Paradoxically, *Crouching Tiger*, for all its subversion of the political conservatism and Confucian filiality characteristic of Late Imperial martial arts literature and despite its resonance with May Fourth radicalism, neither paints the world lying beyond the feminine domestic realm in a rosy hue nor unreservedly praises the audacity of the female transgressor. On the contrary, a significant part of Wang's narrative is given over to the fact that life outside the upper-class woman's cloistered boudoir is full of challenges and hardships and to Jiaolong's moral quandaries about her own transgressions. These descriptions of personal pains attendant on transgression distinguish Wang's view of the relationship between women and dominant social values from the decidedly antitraditional stance represented by left-wing intellectuals.

Wang's decision to cast dark shadows over Jiaolong's struggle should not be hastily attributed to a certain moral conservatism reputedly shared by popular writers. Rather, his ironic treatment of female mobility and transgression may have been the result of a lower-class standpoint, which was overdetermined by his own experience with poverty and unemployment and, moreover, by his intimate knowledge of the economic predicaments commonly faced by women belonging to the same lower social strata as he. He perceives serenity in the upper-class boudoir and danger in the open world. The perception is intimated subtly in *Crouching Tiger* but is transparent in the dozen social novels that Wang wrote concurrently with his serialization of martial arts novels. In these social novels with modern settings, Wang repeatedly analyzes the lives of poor young urban women, whom he shows to be compelled to seek work outside the home but have very few employment options. Some look for manual jobs that pay a meager wage; others study Beijing opera hoping to become instantly rich and famous upon establishing intimate relations with powerful male patrons. Still others—who are far from a minority—simply enter prostitution. Most tragic of all, those who aspire to transcending their class through the novel forms of work in a nascent capitalist economy—such as Eryu in *Fragrant Buds*—are sorely disappointed or even destroyed. The work environment for lower-class women, Wang thus indicates, is either harsh or morally corrupting. It therefore comes as no surprise that in *Crouching Tiger*, the world of occupations (represented by the River and Lake populated by martial artists) appears infested with strife and danger and that Jiaolong's venture outside the home is portrayed, at least in part, as the loss of privilege, leisure, and protection.

Although a careful reader may not be able to go so far as to assert that *Crouching Tiger* tells the rousing tale of the protected aristocratic woman's exhilarating release from social/physical constraints only to show her to be overburdened with the guilt of having violated the ideal of female virtue proper to women of her class, he or she cannot help but note that the captive chains of patriarchy—here, materializing as Confucian morality—do not cease shackling Jiaolong's body and afflicting it with the shame of the loss of innocence even though that body has been hypermasculinized through martial arts training. Wang's choice to make Jiaolong unable to completely break free of Confucian values is consistent with his pessimistic view—articulated most clearly in his social novels—of the continuing hold of patriarchy over lower-class women in the transforming urban economies of Republican China. He identifies the tenacious and adaptive control of patriarchy not only over the female paupers struggling to survive in transforming Chinese cities but potentially even over women of good breeding, superior financial resources, an education like men's, and seemingly superhuman abilities. Through a combination of allegorical, naturalistic, and melodramatic narrative devices, he suggests that, despite the numerous Westernizing changes occurring in the economy and moral milieu of the city, women born into the privileged classes remain somewhat vulnerable to traditional notions of female propriety, whereas women belonging to the lower social strata are helpless prey to the ever self-adjusting modalities of male domination and exploitation.

Notes

The author acknowledges research funding from the Chiang Ching-kuo Foundation, the National Endowment for the Humanities, and the American Council of Learned Societies that facilitated the research and writing of this chapter.

1. Wang Dulu, *Wo hu cang long* (Crouching tiger, hidden dragon), 3 vols. (Hong Kong: Tiandi tushu gongsi, 2000), especially 1:267. All citations are keyed to this edition authorized by Li Danquan, Wang Dulu's widow. After being serialized, the novel was not published individually until 1948—Shanghai Lili shuju put out an edition in five thin volumes.

2. It is beyond the scope of this chapter to compare in detail Wang Dulu's depiction of Beijing with, say, the work of the a much better-known *jingwei* (Beijing-flavor) writer like Lao She. Suffice it to say here that Wang's focus on the psychological workings of lower-class women is rarely found in Lao She's impressive oeuvre composed of novels, short fiction, and plays, with only a small number of exceptions such as Lao She's "Yueyar" (Crescent moon). Wang's extensive use of interior monologue and the free indirect style (which strongly suggests authorial empathy) to narrate his heroines' thought processes is especially distinctive when compared with the often detached, objectifying, and elliptic descriptions of women by self-proclaimed progressive male writers such as Lu Xun, Mao Dun, and Ba Jin.

3. Literary developments in occupied cities during the Sino-Japanese war have recently attracted a new wave of scholarly attention, although it is still too early to make definitive statements about them. See, for instance, Qian Liqun et al., eds., *Zhongguo lunxianqu wenxue daxi pinglun juan* (Chinese literature in the occupied area during the Sino-Japanese war—The criticism volume) (Nanning: Guangxi jiaoyu chubanshe, 1998), especially 106–60.

4. See, for example, Lü Xiong, *Nüxian waishi* (The unofficial history of female immortals), 2 vols. (Shanghai: Shanghai guji chubanshe, 1991). For a survey of the images of women in Chinese martial arts literature from antiquity to the twentieth century, see Wang Lin, *Weida de tongqing: Xia wenxue de zhutishi yanjiu* (Magnanimous sympathy: A thematic study of chivalric literature) (Shanghai: Xuelin chubanshe, 1999), 179–219.

5. Wang Dulu, *Tie ji yin ping* (Iron steed, silver vase) (Taipei: Yuanjing, 2001).

6. Gender seems to make little difference in how co-optation works in *xiayi gongan xiaoshuo*. Martial heroines, like their male counterparts, are enlisted by the political establishment to defeat those who refuse to obey political authority. See James J. Y. Liu, *The Chinese Knight-Errant* (Chicago: University of Chicago Press, 1967), 117–20. See

also Cao Yibing, *Xiayi gongan xiaoshuo shi* (A history of chivalric and court-case fiction) (Hangzhou: Zhejiang guji chubanshe, 1998). Cao argues that the first tales combining chivalric deeds with court cases appeared in the Tang: "Xie Xiaoe zhuan" (The story of Xie Xiaoe), "Feng Yan zhuan" (The story of Feng Yan), "Tian Penglang" (The story of Tian Penglang), "Pan jiangjun" (General Pan), and "Chezhong nüzi" (Woman in the carriage) (53–61).

7. Lü, *Nüxian waishi*. For a study of the changing images of the female rebel Tang Saier in a wide range of materials including official histories, the literati's collected essays, and popular fiction from the fifteenth century to the eighteenth, see Wu Renshu, "'Yaofu' hu? 'nüxian' hu? Lun Tang Saier zai Ming Qing shiqi de xingxiang zhuanbian" ("Witch" or "female immortal"? On the transformation of Tang Saier's image during the Ming-Qing era), in *Wusheng zhi sheng (I): Jindai Zhongguo de funü yu guojia (1600–1950)* (The sound of silence [I]: Women and the nation in modern China [1600–1950]), ed. Lü Fangshang (Taipei: Jindaishi yanjiusuo, Academia Sinica, 2003), 1–37.

8. Perry Link, *Mandarin Ducks and Butterflies: Popular Fiction in Early Twentieth-Century Chinese Cities* (Berkeley: University of California Press, 1981), 213–14. For an alternative reading of Thirteenth Sister's drastic transformation, see David Der-wei Wang, *Fin-de-siècle Splendor: Repressed Modernities of Late Qing Fiction, 1849–1911* (Stanford, Calif.: Stanford University Press, 1997), 156–71.

9. Maram Epstein, *Competing Discourses: Orthodoxy, Authenticity, and Engendered Meanings in Late Imperial Chinese Fiction* (Cambridge, Mass.: Harvard University Asia Center, 2001), chap. 6.

10. In this light, one might argue that, into the twentieth century, some late Qing and May Fourth male writers depicted women's participation in revolution less to encourage women to become leaders in such movements for saving the nation than to authenticate revolution and make nationalism desirable (granted that revolution and nationalism may not yet have gone bankrupt and hollow as ideals). It is worth noting, nevertheless, that the ideological burden and symbolic meaning of the feminine in fictional representations are complicated questions and that the use of the feminine in early-twentieth-century Chinese literature may not have been uniform across the late Qing and May Fourth periods or across elite and popular writings. For instance, despite the strong nationalistic agenda prevalent in novels published at the end of the Qing, one cannot say that all writers of that period who lauded revolutionary women did so only insofar as their rebelliousness served to revitalize the nation. In fact, at least some women authors put forth sharp feminist ideas that were fairly independent of nationalistic concerns; see David Wang's discussion of Wang Miaoru's *Nü yu hua* (A flower in a women's prison, 1904), in *Fin-de-siècle Splendor*, 170–72.

11. In this regard, Wang Dulu is not unlike other popular writers who portray female knights-errant: such female characters are interesting for the writer (and the common reader) precisely because they are exceptions to the rule; the marvelous is entertaining. See Link, *Mandarin Ducks and Butterflies*, 213–14.

12. For an account of the development of physical education for female students in (urban) China during the first half of the twentieth century, highlighting the tension among the goals of national salvation, women's liberation, and achieving "healthy

beauty," see Chien-ming Yu, "Jindai Zhongguo nüzi tiyuguan chutan" (An initial exploration of views on women's physical education in modern China), *Xin shixue* (New historiography) 7, no. 4 (1996): 119–58.

13. Unfortunately, although there is almost certainly a significant link between Wang Dulu's own Manchu identity and his creation of Jiaolong, there exists too little biographical information about Wang to tell us just how he felt about his Manchu heritage and the extent of his familiarity with Manchu customs and history.

14. Theodore Huters, "Ideologies of Realism in Modern China: The Hard Imperatives of Imported Theory," in *Politics, Ideology, and Literary Discourses in Modern China*, ed. Liu Kang and Xiaobing Tang (Durham, N.C.: Duke University Press, 1993), 147–73.

15. Shen Yanbing (Mao Dun), "Fengjian de xiaoshimin wenyi" (Petty urbanites' feudalistic literature and art), *Dongfang zazhi* (The Eastern miscellany) 30, no. 3 (February 1, 1933), reprinted in *Yuanyang hudie pai yanjiu ziliao* (Research material related to the Mandarin ducks and butterflies school), ed. Wei Shaochang (Shanghai: Shanghai wenyi chubanshe, 1962), 21–28.

16. Chen Dieyi, "Tongsu wenxue yundong" (The movement of popular literature), reprinted in *Yuanyang hudie pai wenxue ziliao* (Material related to Mandarin ducks and butterflies literature), ed. Rui Heshi et al. (Fuzhou: Fujian renmin chubanshe, 1984), 147–61. Chen Dieyi's logic uncannily resonated with Mao Zedong's in his famous talks on art and literature in Yan'an in 1942. One major distinction stands between Mao Zedong's definition of mass literature and Chen Dieyi's conception of popular literature, however: whereas Mao values the language and forms popular among the peasants in the hinterland, Chen has in mind primarily the language and forms popular among the urban population in Shanghai and other major cities.

17. Xu Sinian, "Lun Wang Dulu xiaoshuo yishu zhi sixiang yuanyuan—you 'shehui yanqing' dao 'beiju xiaqing'" (On the ideational origins of Wang Dulu's art of fiction—from "social romance" to "tragic chivalric romance"), in *Xia yu Zhongguo wenhua* (The knight-errant and Chinese culture), ed. Danjiang daxue Zhongwen xi (Taipei: Taiwan xuesheng shuju, 1993), 332. Xu obtained Wang's biographical information from his widow.

18. The chivalrous woman Yu Xiulian runs a professional security/escort firm (*biaohang*), and Cai Xiangmei, daughter of a government detective, helps her father hunt down criminals and performs acrobatics in the streets.

19. Link, *Mandarin Ducks and Butterflies*, 187, 188.

20. Wang, *Wo hu cang long*, 719. The center of the Bixia Yuanjun cult was Taishan in Shandong; local temples were spread throughout North China and Manchuria devoted to her. It was believed that when jumping off the cliff in repayment to the goddess, true believers would be spared of their lives. For an analysis of the cult's popularity in Late Imperial and Republican times and the gender anxieties that may have contributed to the cult's reputation of being *yin* (licentious, supplementary, unnecessary, surplus), see Kenneth Pomeranz, "Power, Gender, and Pluralism in the Cult of the Goddess of Taishan," in *Culture and State in Chinese History: Conventions, Accommodations, and Critiques*, ed. R. Bin Wong, Theodore Huters, and Pauline Yu (Stanford, Calif.: Stanford University Press, 1997), 182–204.

21. The best example of the rebellious May Fourth daughter's guilt and ultimate reconciliation with her "despotic" yet loving mother can be found in Xie Bingying's autobiography, *Yige nübing de zizhuan*, in two volumes, published originally in China in 1936 and 1946. For a translation, see, Xie Bingying, *A Woman Soldier's Own Story*, trans. Lily Chia Brissman and Barry Brissman (New York: Columbia University Press, 2001).

22. One is further impressed by the fact that Wang's heroine's individualism makes her a far cry from the heroines in 1930s leftist literature, who defy traditional families and give up romantic love in order to dedicate themselves to a political collective.

23. The final scene of Ang Lee's *Crouching Tiger* radically departs from the original novel. In the film, Jiaolong does not jump off a cliff in the Wudang mountain until after she has briefly reunited with her lover Xiaohu. And the reason for her leap is left ambiguous by the film—she could be courting death in the hope of reviving her opponent/teacher Li Mubai or moving on without Xiaohu, whom she no longer loves. Whatever the reason, one thing is clear: her leap has nothing to do with religious pilgrimage or with filial piety. Rather, her final act of flying into the abyss has something to do with the triangle of ambivalent attraction among Mubai, her, and Xiaohu. The film, in other words, minimizes the story line of the family and maximizes that of romance and eroticism. It is, after all, a product of late twentieth-century global media culture, where sex and ambivalent love have much more sales value than the struggle between a woman's filiality and her search for the self.

24. Xu Sinian has made a general argument that the tragic social realities depicted in Wang's social romantic novels are the "premise" and "foundation" of his martial arts novels: "Wang's social romantic novels directly reflect modern times; as a result, they contain lots of pent-up anger and indignation at existing society. By contrast, the symbolic structures of his tragic chivalric novels permit the uninhibited release of those strong emotions, allowing him to express his ideals and yearnings" ("Lun Wang Dulu xiaoshuo yishu zhi sixiang yuanyuan," 338, 343). Xu's claim, admittedly inspiring, is also quite vague and does not specifically touch on the issue of women's work and boundary transgression that I analyze in this chapter. Xu also lists the novel *Han bo yu rui* (Cold waves threaten jadelike flowers), discussed in my text, as a text that he has been unable to locate.

25. On women's employment options in Beijing and other nontreaty port cities that did not develop an industrial manufacture sector during the Republican period, see Luo Suwen, *Nüxing yu jindai Zhongguo shehui* (Women and modern Chinese society) (Shanghai: Renmin chubanshe, 1996), 247–69. Luo points out that prostitution was perhaps the most important profession available to women in early Republican Beijing (256–68).

26. On women's participation in cottage industries, see Luo, *Nüxing yu jindai Zhongguo shehui*, 253–56.

27. Employment opportunities for middle-class women seem to have been rare in the 1910s. For one, Lu Xun pessimistically remarked that, if a middle-class woman (like Ibsen's Nora) left her bourgeois husband and home, most likely she would fail to find suitable work to support herself and would eventually have to either return home or become "a fallen woman" for a living. However, the situation may have changed

somewhat for well-educated middle-class women after the mid-1920s. Luo Suwen points out that starting in the mid-1920s a considerable number of educated women entered the teaching profession in Beijing. By 1928, every elementary school in Beijing had at least one female teacher (Luo, *Nüxing yu jindai Zhongguo shehui*, 250).

28. Beijing was renamed Beiping when the Nationalists made Nanjing the national capital. The name Beiping was used until 1949.

29. The novel, unlike most other works by Wang, had never been serialized before appearing in book form. It consists of two volumes that bear individual titles. My analysis of the second volume, *Han bo yu rui*, will be based on the 1948 Shanghai Lili edition. I have not been able to find a copy of the same edition of *Qi shi fang pa*. Therefore, my citations of *Qi shi fang pa* will be keyed to the 1951 Hong Kong Kwong Yick reprint, which seems identical to the 1948 edition.

30. Wang Dulu, *Qi shi fang pa* (Fragrant buds on a splendid market) (Hong Kong: Kwong Yick, 1951), 69.

31. For details see Shi Mingzheng, "From Imperial Gardens to Public Parks: The Transformation of Urban Space in Early Twentieth-Century Beijing," *Modern China* 24, no. 3 (1998): 219–54.

32. Robert E. Park, "The City: Suggestions for the Investigation of Human Behavior in the Urban Environment," in *The City*, ed. Robert E. Park, Ernest W. Burgess, and Roderick D. McKenzie (Chicago: University of Chicago Press, 1925), 40–41.

33. Henri Lefebvre, *The Production of Space*, trans. Donald Nicholson-Smith (Oxford: Blackwell, 1991), 404.

34. Eryu voices this question (Wang, *Qi shi fang pa*, 43).

35. For a revisionist treatment of Chinese popular fiction of the 1910s, see Denise Gimpel, *Lost Voices of Modernity* (Honolulu: University of Hawaii Press, 2001). For efforts to reassess the "progressive" qualities of the work of Zhang Henshui, the best-known popular novelist of the Republican era, see, for instance, Yuan Jin, *Zhang Henshui pinghzuan* (A critical appraisal and biographical study of Zhang Henshui) (Changshang: Hunan wenyi chubanshe, 1988). For a monumental survey of the developments of all major popular genres from the late Qing to 1949, see *Zhongguo jinxiandai tongsu wenxueshi* (A history of the popular literature of modern China), ed. Fan Boqun et al. (Nanjing: Jiangsu jiaoyu chubanshe, 2000).

13

Virtue at Work

Rural Shaanxi Women Remember the 1950s

Gail Hershatter

In 1996, working with Chinese researcher Gao Xiaoxian,[1] I set out to explore a curious historical wasteland—the first decade of rural socialist construction in the 1950s. Whether one looks at gender or at a host of other issues, China scholars have a radically impoverished notion of that era. In our teaching, we usually reduce the 1950s to a series of campaigns and their aftermath. Yet we know virtually nothing about the 1950s outside the center of political power, much less history at the margins.[2] Material for a cultural or social history, even of the political campaigns about which we know so much, is fragmented, scattered, or nonexistent.[3] We can say little about the relationship between state pronouncements and what people inside and outside state organizations understood to be happening then, or what they remember now, when they recall the early years of socialism almost half a century later. And one of the main sources with the potential to complicate, contradict, embellish, or contextualize state documents—the individual and collective memories of China's farmers—is growing less accessible every year, as people age and die.

Among these rapidly disappearing rural memories, those of women have concerned us most. If farmers were about 80 percent of the total Chinese population in the 1950s, then women farmers were probably close to 40 percent. In spite of their numerical significance, they were doubly marginalized, by virtue of both location and gender. Marginalized does not mean neglected, however: the 1950s state intervened actively in agriculture (collectivization) and gender relations (the Marriage Law). Yet the responses of these women to state initiatives, the degree to which their daily lives were affected by 1950s policies, the levels—economic, social, psychological—at which change occurred are not represented with any depth in the written records of that time. A focus on rural women requires that we move beyond policy pronouncements to ask how official actions and local practices were mutually implicated in changing the social landscape. What happens to our sinological truisms about turning points in twentieth-century Chinese social and economic life when gender is placed at the center? As Joan Kelly might have said if she had been writing about China instead of Europe, did women have a Chinese revolution? And if so, when?[4]

Exploring these questions, Gao Xiaoxian and I have interviewed mainly in four research sites in central and south Shaanxi province (Guanzhong and Shaannan), with a scattering of supplementary interviews elsewhere.[5] We have collected life histories of approximately seventy women over the age of sixty and interviewed a smaller number of men who held local leadership positions during the collective period.

Asking how the collective period is remembered and understood by rural women can enable us to assess its multiple legacies and to view "gender in motion" over the latter half of the twentieth century. These legacies include rapid fundamental rearrangements in work life, slower but significant shifts in the organization of families, and the subtle reworking of notions of female virtue. Reworking, not rupture, for in their accounts of a remembered self, these women draw on conceptions of the virtuous woman from a variety of prerevolutionary as well as revolutionary genres.

In this essay, I first assess the limitations of the dominant revolutionary genre in which rural women have been heard, "speaking bitterness" stories. I then comment briefly on questions of method and memory when collecting oral narratives at a significant remove from the events of the 1950s. The remainder of the essay is devoted to three self-characterizations that appeared repeatedly in our interviews with rural women: pitiful, capable, and harmonious. Although the specific content of these terms has shifted over time, each has provided rural women with continuity in lives repeatedly disrupted by upheaval of many sorts. Each has allowed them to devise a remembered self that stakes important claims to female virtue.

Speaking Bitterness and Its Discontents

Although the scarcity of written sources by rural women can reduce a historian to despair, we do have a small but significant set of first-person accounts for the period of initial regime change and land reform: speaking bitterness stories. These were most often elicited from poor peasants and women in a public forum to break the power of local elites. Speaking bitterness, as a public practice, was intended to mobilize the listeners and alter their sense of what was permissible and possible.[6] It was meant at the same time to transform the speaker, through the act of narrating, from one who accepted a bitter fate to one who moved beyond it into a happier future. All speak bitterness narratives, by definition, were denunciatory—of particular oppressors and more generally of "the old society," the socius inhabited and controlled by those oppressors.[7]

Speaking bitterness in public meetings organized by party/state cadres was a novel practice in the early years of Chinese Communist Party (CCP)–led social transformation. It has been revived periodically since then, and its narrative conventions have not disappeared from Chinese social life; they continue to exert a pull on the memories and self-conceptions of those who once spoke bitterness or heard it spoken. Yet attention to speaking bitterness as *the* model of revolutionary self-narration has diverted our attention from a host of important questions about how the revolutionary process was understood at its inception and how it has been remembered and reworked over the past half century.

Women certainly told us stories of profound transformation in many aspects of village life. Encouraged by the Marriage Law campaigns of the early 1950s, some of them broke off parentally arranged engagements or ended marriages; others asserted their own preferences in choosing a husband. Many learned to read in winter literacy classes, were trained as new-style midwives, or took on responsibility as women's cadres. All of them participated in the process of collectivization, the enthusiasms and hardships of the Great Leap Forward, and years of field labor with other women, in some cases becoming labor models. Their lives as young adults, in short, were marked in measurable daily ways by party/state initiatives. They felt themselves to be different from and more fortunate than their mothers, and many of them contrasted their ability to move through public space in the 1950s with childhoods that were more spatially and materially constrained.[8]

Nevertheless, the dramatic rupture at the heart of speak bitterness stories is absent from the accounts of these women. Instead, they spoke in perduring self-characterizations, statements of stable identity that spanned the 1949 divide and the recent reform era as well: I was never feudal; I was always capable; I worked for family harmony; I was a person of principles; I have always been kindhearted. Or, in a less optimistic register: My life was bitter and pitiful in the collective period and the present as well as the pre-Liberation past. These are each declarations by an individual, yet they are also statements about subjectivity in the sense that Alessandro Portelli describes it, "the cultural forms and processes by which individuals express their sense of themselves in history."[9]

Express themselves, but not exactly as they please. The recurring themes in these stories draw on prerevolutionary notions of female virtue, reworked and intertwined with more recent categories of self provided by the revolution. Their accounts of their own virtue are not centered on chastity (though they sometimes mention it). In this they depart from accounts of virtuous chaste women in the Late Imperial and Republican periods, ubiquitous in local gazetteers and biographies. But several of the qualities the women emphasize—industriousness, competence, the ability to manage human relationships deftly—draw on culturally durable notions of the "good woman," even though the physical and social locations of these virtues are no longer confined to the household and may indeed be performed in the service of the collective. The quality of being "pitiful," while not virtuous in itself, is a recognized characteristic of the oppressed classes, and thus it can be said to ally one with revolutionary virtue. In these women's stories, however, being pitiful indicates something else as well—an oblique criticism of both the party/state and the family for the ways in which both have failed to recognize the virtuous sacrifices of the storytellers.

The women we interviewed must assimilate a complex political history. The Nationalist regime under which they spent their childhood has been thoroughly repudiated in the People's Republic of China (PRC). The PRC regime, however, has not been repudiated, even as its promises of development and equality through collectivization began to ring hollow, even as collectivization itself has lost popular support and been reversed in the name of "market socialism." Furthermore, in the 1950s when many of these women rejected the marriage practices and gendered work arrangements of "the old society," they did so not as rebels but as activists supported by the state. Although they seldom express direct dissatisfaction with state policy, women describe themselves as virtuous and capable in meeting the demands of both state and family, while coping with lack of support and attention from both quarters. The construction of a remembered self in commonly understood terms of virtue—and the assertion that the speaker was constant in her virtue no matter what the circumstances—create a contrast with broader political change, which is variously implied to have been too quick, too thorough, not quick enough, or insufficiently thorough. At the same time, the virtuous remembered self indicts members of the younger generation for displaying insufficient virtue of their own and failing to recognize it in their elders.

Methods and Memory

Work with oral narratives raises (at least) two issues: how do we adjust for the circumstances under which they are collected, and how do we assess the significance of memory?[10] Like speak bitterness tales, these oral narratives were not proffered spontaneously; they were elicited through prompting by us, when we asked about events now more than half a century old. Under such circumstances, what is "the remembered self"? The self these women remember (alone, in company with friends, in conversation with children)? The one we elicited through questioning? Or the one they chose to present to us? The answer is clearly "some combination of the above," with the caveat that these are not discrete categories: women may remember a particular aspect of self only in the process of answering our questions or of choosing what and what not to say to us. They may see themselves as being in conversation not only with us but also simultaneously with their families and their neighbors (living and dead)—and may use the opportunity to exhume old grievances, rehearse new ones, or salve injuries past and present. What people remember is the product of a continual process of reworking, recitation, invention, and sometimes carefully guarded silences that help shape what is said.[11]

This essay is devoted to the things we learned *without* asking: the self-characterizations that people offered us as a by-product of describing their childhoods, their marriages and families, or their work in the collective. This is information that we wanted but did not solicit directly; women chose to present it to us. Statements about their own characters served as a core around which numerous tales were spun. These statements deserve special attention.

Events are constantly reinterpreted, and even rearranged outright, in the light of subsequent events and present circumstances. This process of reworking is particularly intricate when women remember the 1950s. For the women we interviewed, collectivization required both dramatic efforts and demanding daily work. Now those feats are being recalled two decades after collectivization was dismantled, by women who are well aware that it never delivered on its promise of economic abundance. They often recall those years as times of unremitting fieldwork, domestic work, and childbearing.[12] To complicate matters further, older rural women understand themselves to have benefited from the subsequent economic reforms, yet simultaneously to have been disadvantaged by them. The stories of virtue, fortitude, and suffering they tell provide explicit comparisons with their current circumstances. They lament the difficult circumstances of the collective years in contrast to the more abundant present. This is an ironic twist on the state description of speaking bitterness: "recalling the bitter [of the prerevolutionary past] while savoring the sweet [of the collective period]." When these women refer to "the old society," they are as likely to be talking about the 1950s and 1960s as about the prerevolutionary past. At the same time, in telling these stories they celebrate their own resourcefulness, reproaching grown sons and daughters-in-law (but, interestingly enough, not daughters) who know less than they do about hardship and do not appear to appreciate virtue. What this material requires is attention to all its messages, all the ways in which female virtue, performed in the service of the revolution, also provides a critique of that revolution and its progeny.

What difference does it make that the speakers are women? Is this womanly virtue we are hearing about, or generic virtue, or even male virtue as practiced by women who have been authorized by the state to transgress and reconfigure gender boundaries? Their memories are certainly gendered, centered on women's collective work, the burden of domestic tasks and children, and the centrality of relations with a husband and his family in the context of virilocal marriage practices. But we talked to far fewer men than women. Our initial project was primarily concerned with women and collective work, and, to complicate matters further, few of the men of that generation were still alive or cognizant in any of the villages where we interviewed. I can report that the men with whom we spoke hewed much more closely to official terminology and periodization and said very little about themselves, but I cannot say much about the question of virtue among men. Similarly, I cannot know whether interviews conducted in 1955 (or 1975 or 1930) would have turned up the same vocabulary of virtue among women. I cannot track what they might have said about themselves at other times and compare it to the vocabulary of newspapers or policy directives or the varying intensities of campaign language. Since rural women generally left no written records, and time travel is not in the historian's toolbox, I know much less than I would like about the temporality of the vocabulary in question, across the putative boundary of 1949 or even across the course of the People's Republic. Whether virtue has recently made a comeback under the trying circumstances of the reforms or has been there all along, and, if so, with what variations of nuance, are all troubling and undecidable matters. What I *can* say is that *pitiful*, *capable*, and *harmonious* were ubiquitous in interviews with women in every village, showing up across variations in local political economy, education, current material comfort, and involvement with local leadership or activist roles.

Pitiful

The starting point of the speak bitterness narratives discussed earlier, the initial description around which a tale of liberation cohered, was the state of being pitiful (*kelian* or, in Shaanxi parlance, *xihuang*). Naming the sources of one's prerevolutionary suffering was a necessary prerequisite to recognizing oneself as oppressed and moving toward revolutionary action. In some of our interviews, particularly when they offered an initial recitation rather than responding to questions, women referred to their childhood selves or their mothers in this familiar chronological frame. Ke Ruiyin[13] praised her widowed mother's determination, while denouncing the demands for chastity that kept her family poor:

> As for my family, in the old society, it was really pitiful. My father died early. I was not yet a year old when my father died. Women in the old society were very pitiful. My mother brought up two of us, my elder brother and me. . . . The family was very pitiful. You can't imagine how pitiful it was. If we compare things now with the old society, it is really the difference between heaven and hell (*tian rang zhi bie*). . . . In the old society, chastity was highly praised and could not be sold. It was not good to sell one's chastity. No matter how hard life was, no matter how pitiful, she brought us two children up. Finally it was Liberation in 1949. It was Liberation and she should have had a better life then. But my mother passed away in 1949. . . . Aiya, my pitiful mother. She never enjoyed even a bit of good fortune. At home, we never had anything good to eat. Even at New Year's, she never had the happiness of eating rice or anything like that. Even a pasty gruel was considered quite special. Even under these circumstances, she did not want to marry again. Others tried to persuade her to remarry, but she refused. In 1949, it was Liberation. But she passed away.

For Ke, the state of being pitiful ended in 1949, when demands for widow chastity and the oppression of women were supposed to have disappeared.[14] In other interviews, however, "pitiful" seeps beyond the confines of prerevolutionary time. Fang Shufeng describes the early years of collectivization in terms usually reserved for the dark days before 1949:

> I always taught my two grandsons and granddaughter, "Your grandma was the most pitiful one." . . . At that time, I even hated to throw away that small amount of leftover and burned rice. I would soak it in hot water or boil it with some vegetables and then eat them. Now you kids, even for the food left from breakfast, such white rice, would say, "Grandma, throw it away. I can't eat it." If it is left over from last night or one day before, maybe you can't eat it. But this is only from breakfast. "How can people eat this? Grandma, you will be sick after you eat this." They have a point. But we people from the 1950s lived such an awful life. My husband always criticizes me: "You son of a turtle, you must have died from hunger in a former life. You hate to waste even a kernel of grain."

The content of "pitiful" has shifted in these accounts of the collective period. It no longer describes a state of reactive suffering from remote, abstract societal forces. Instead, women use it to accentuate statements of their own capacity for hard work and virtue. They are pitiful/skilled at needlework or pitiful/thrifty. Or, as Deng Fangcun comments elsewhere in her narrative, they are pitiful because they worked so hard at political activism, as when she went door to door in 1957 mobilizing her neighbors for nighttime work: "When the moon came out, I was so pitiful that I brought my winnowing fan to every door to ask people to winnow wheat."

If "pitiful" is sometimes transmuted so that it becomes an oblique statement of virtue, in other tales of the collective era it becomes an equally oblique criticism of the state. Wang Falan uses the language of bitterness and pitifulness to denounce the state's belated attention to birth control (which came to her village, as to much of rural China, only in 1971):

> WFL: When we were working in the collective, the state was in charge of everything. They took charge of telling us to grow the grain properly, harvest more, and eat more. But they didn't take charge of births (*zhua wa*). They did not control childbirth. To have more children means to suffer more, to be worn out. I have eight children, and you might think it's too funny, two sons and six daughters. I had lots of children, I starved, I endured extreme bitterness (*zhuasile, esile, kusile*). . . . After Liberation, I had so many children that I got angry. Why didn't they control it and tell people not to have more children? It was pitiful. . . .
>
> GXX: You had many children at that time. Did you ever think of having fewer children or planning births at that time?
>
> WFL: What family planning? Finally when I had the tenth, family planning started. Who ever talked to us about family planning?
>
> GXX: Were there any folkways of having fewer children among the people?
>
> WFL: People said to take a certain kind of medicine and to go to the doctors. But the doctor said why did you come to me—it was immoral (*sangde*) and sinful (*zaonie*). So people were really pitiful.

In the past twenty years of economic reform, the improved supply of consumer goods and generally rising incomes have obviated the need for needlework or grain winnowing at night. The state's struggle to impose birth control in the countryside has also rendered Wang Falan's complaint of historical interest only, although it provides an important reminder that women's desires and state policies are both shifting phenomena. Yet even as rural economic life has once again shifted dramatically, and as the Wang Falan generation has moved beyond childbearing age and the years of nighttime farm tasks and needlework, the term *pitiful* has remained in circulation. Now women use it to describe the troubles of their old age in an environment where the rules of filiality have changed.

Deng Fangcun's contemporary pitiful condition began when her husband died in 1982. Soon thereafter, as the reforms made it possible for farmers to leave their home villages, her grown son, already married with two children, decided to go to Xinjiang as a contract laborer. Although Deng didn't want him to go, her daughter-in-law blamed her for the departure, and life at home became very tense. With the family's main labor power gone, Deng found herself scrambling for money to start a microbusiness, borrowing at her son's behest from relatives in Henan. She was deeply hurt when she found that her son had been mailing remittances home to his wife to augment their savings, rather than to clear the family debt. Speaking with us in 1999, many years after the event, she was still in one-sided dialogue with an unfilial son:

> He told his wife to count the money and save the spare money. I heard his words. Listen to his words. You knew I had no money even when you were at home. You asked me to go to Henan to borrow two hundred *kuai*. But you mailed money to your wife. . . . When I think about that time, I say, you, my son, are blind in your heart. You asked me to borrow money. But you mailed money to your wife. Why don't you let your mother do business? You asked me to borrow money. You mailed money to your wife and she couldn't spend all the money, so she saved the rest.

Feeling herself in an untenable situation, Deng accepted a marriage proposal from a widower, only to find out after she moved in with him (and *his* grown children) that his sons were violently opposed to the match.

> They were not willing and so it was very awkward. At every meal he explained to them. It was pitiful. At every meal he explained to his children. He would talk. That was how we came back [to live in her new husband's home], explaining and explaining. Later, my teeth ached. It was so strange. My teeth ached very badly. My teeth felt as though they were on fire. All night I didn't sleep. I couldn't sleep. I didn't want to eat during the day. At some meals, I only had half a bowl of rice. At some meals I only had one bowl of food. Sometimes I didn't eat at all. Thus I couldn't do anything. I was not in good health.

Deng, feeling that she could not return to the home of her daughter-in-law (although legally it was her home) moved out to stay with a friend. But her new husband was unable to cope with the abuse from his own children:

> I was living here, in this house on the market street. My old man (*renjia lao hanr*) came and said, "At home there is always too much talk" (*wuli zongshi zuicui lali*). The old man was shaking when he was here. . . . The old man never stopped shaking. He took off his shoes and lay there on the *kang*. The old man said the following, "The old ox ploughed the field and died at knifepoint" (*lao niu li di dao jian si*). . . . We all said, what does this mean, and why was [he] talking this way. . . . "The old ox" meant that he, the old man, brought up his children for all his life. Now the ox was old. So the point of the knife butchered you, because they no longer needed you. The old ox plowed the field and died at knifepoint. The bones . . . the meat could be eaten. The bones could be sold for money. The beef

> could be eaten, the beef and the bones could all be sold for money. . . . The group of us couldn't understand, didn't understand what he was saying. . . . He left and didn't come back. [He went to] the cooperative clinic. They had built a shack where sick people could come and be treated. They also cooked there. He got into the room and hanged himself.
>
> Why? It was because his sons weren't willing. They were always quarreling and arguing at home. I had been sleeping over here at this house on the market street and I didn't know. . . . From the time I [married] there until my husband died, until the day he was buried, it was only one hundred days.

Deng Fangcun eventually returned home to live with her son, who had returned from Xinjiang. She felt entitled to do so because this was her natal village; her first husband had been called in as a son-in-law, and she had built the house herself. Nevertheless, it took a court order to persuade her son and daughter-in-law to take her back:

> I went to the commune first. The commune mediated and asked me to wait for a while and they called my son there. He saw me sitting there and he scrambled off and ran away. . . . It's difficult to move an inch if you are unreasonable. He was unreasonable, so he couldn't move forward. He couldn't move. Later we went to court and sat at the table. The judge put on his robes and put on his hat. He said, "Cunshan, you go and sit beside your mother." The judge blamed him. He said that if Cunshan didn't accept me, didn't acknowledge me, didn't acknowledge that I was his flesh and blood, he said he would punish him to set an example for other sons, for other young men, for not supporting the older generation financially. The judge would punish him as an example for others to see. . . . He said, "If you take your mother back this afternoon, I will say nothing. If you don't support your mother financially, you will see what happens (*zai shuo*)." Then he got up and left. That's what the judge said. I followed in back of him and came back. My daughter-in-law was secretly listening outside the door. She stood there with her daughter in her arms. I went back. My daughter-in-law lay in bed for six days. She lay there for six days. I cooked for six days. I cooked for six days. I cooked but she didn't eat. I went to the store to buy dried fruit for her to eat. This showed that I was not angry. From then on things got better. It blew over and she got better.

Beyond the painful particulars of this case is a wider story of aging women, particularly in mountainous areas where reform-era prosperity has been slow to arrive. Deng and her neighbors have children who are themselves already at middle age; few have been able to head for the coast or even the inland cities to spend years as contract laborers. Under economic pressure, grown sons grow surly toward their (mostly) widowed mothers, while daughters-in-law try to preserve resources for their own nuclear families. Families usually separate households when the children marry—a trend that grew increasingly common during the collective period—and most of the old people in the village eat alone. Deng Fangcun, because the house is her natal family property, is unusual in her willingness to claim the right to live there. But she speaks for many older village women in her terse assessment of the present and future, in which "pitiful" is once again predominant:

DFC: When people get old, they are pitiful.
GXX: When people get old, they are pitiful?
DFC: Yes. In villages when people get old, they are pitiful. You can't make money. You just hang on this way. I also smoke. I have to buy cigarettes. I have to . . . .
GXX: This is all with money you have earned yourself?
DFC: Yes, all with money I have earned myself.
GXX: You are so capable. You work in the field and do the housework.
DFC: Yes. I am capable. If I didn't do it, what would my whole family do?
GXX: What about when you can't get around anymore?
DFC: I'll be in trouble when I can't get around anymore.

Sadly, *pitiful* remains a durable term with which older rural women assess their lives. The causes they cite have changed, from a society of raw privation and danger (in which most spent their youth), to one that extracted endless work and effort from them, to one that has failed to provide them with a secure and happy old age. Only in speaking of their pre-1949 youth do they name the state and local norms for women as sources of active oppression. For their middle years and old age, the targets of their discontent (remembered and current) are more diffuse and less explicit: state demands (for fieldwork), state neglect (of birth control), changing attitudes about family and household (again, with state-initiated change in the unstated background). "Pitiful" is no longer an all-consuming state of existence, nor is it the departure point for a shared speak bitterness narrative about suffering and redemption. It appears repeatedly in the narratives of village women as a claim to virtue and a declaration of resilience, demanding acknowledgment from an uncaring world.

Capable

Unfavorable circumstances often become the backdrop for a woman's recitation of her virtues, notably her status as a capable farmer, needleworker, house manager, mother, and (sometimes but not always) local cadre. "Capable," unlike "pitiful," has traversed the collective and reform eras with its content virtually unchanged. Cao Zhuxiang, who became a regional labor model in the 1950s, first learned to do farmwork as a young wife and widow in the 1930s and 1940s. In those years, although women from poor families commonly worked in the fields at sowing and harvest, year-round fieldwork was not a respectable or safe occupation for a woman.[15] Yet Cao escaped opprobrium and garnered praise, she remembers, because she was considered capable: "No matter what I was doing, I threw myself into it. My neighbors said that my family had never before had such a capable person. In the fields I quietly threw myself into the work (*maitou kugan*). I would work until the time was up and then go home. I didn't gossip or waste time. So they had no basis for idle talk."

For the younger generation of women cadres who came of age during the 1950s, proving one's capability often meant a conscious struggle for women's equality. Qi Zhufeng describes a struggle for equal work points that lasted for several years:

> **QZF**: In the fields, at that time [during the early years of the collective], men's work points were somewhat higher and women's were somewhat lower. So every time we had to fight on behalf of women for equality between men and women, equal pay for equal work. We had done the same work as you, so we should get the same compensation. That's why those people called me "cockfighting old eight" (*zheng jizi lao ba*). I said, I am not fighting for myself; furthermore what I am fighting for is, all of our women should be like this. That's to say I am not fighting for my own benefit. You see, some are doing the same job, but are compensated differently. Men get ten points, and women are given eight. This is not something we cannot change. At last in 1958, in the people's commune, that was totally "distribution according to your labor" (*anlao fenpei*). When we labored, we proposed equal pay for equal work. When transplanting seedlings, you transplant one row, [and] I transplant one row. At the end of the day, I should get paid as much as you do. If you get ten points, I want ten points, too.
>
> **GXX**: Did you achieve that?
>
> **QZF**: Yes. We did.
>
> **GXX**: Did you achieve it during the LPC (lower producers' cooperative) or the APC (advanced 'producers' cooperative)?
>
> **QZF**: APC. Equal pay for equal work. When carrying urine, you got a strip of paper for each trip telling how much work you had done. At the end of the day, your trips would be counted. For example, if one trip carrying urine was half a point, ten trips would be five points. Twenty trips would ten points. If a man carried it, that's how much it was. If I, a woman, carried it, that's also how much it was. . . . If you kept up with the number of rows when digging seedlings, at the end of the day, you got paid the same.
>
> **GXX**: How long did it stay like this?
>
> **QZF**: Aiya, let me see—it lasted straight through until the land was distributed to households in the '80s, 1982.

Capability, then, fit nicely with the new requirements that women participate in collective labor and provided grounds on which they could argue for equal pay for that labor. Its efficacy as a claim about self, however, was not confined to the new, state-sanctioned collective sphere. Women cited as well their ability to work hard and thus support their families through difficult times in the collective era. Su Xiaming's husband left the village in 1955 to work on the railroad in various provinces. For years, she heard nothing from him and received no remittances, while responsibility for supporting her in-laws and children depended on her alone:

> When Old Yi [Su's husband] left, there were only my father-in-law, my mother-in-law, and my son, altogether four people. My father-in-law enjoyed eating but never worked. My mother-in-law was a small-foot, and therefore could only work at home and take care of the child. My son could not walk yet. My mother-in-law could be helpful. She had a nickname, "*erbobo*," meaning sometimes clever while sometimes stupid. I never requested too much. Only to take good care of my child and the family was enough. Then I would have no complaint no matter how exhausted I was from working. . . .
>
> Well, he never sent me one cent or one letter for three years. . . . Every letter he sent was kept by my father-in-law, and he did not mention it to me sometimes. I was too honest. I only cared about housework and wanted to make the family better. . . . I also made some sideline products such as palm fiber (*zong*) boxes and palm fiber rope. One *jin* of palm fiber rope was worth four *jiao*. I usually made palm fiber rope at night because I had no time during the daytime. It was cold, so I just sat in the room and made the rope without light. I could make one *jin* of rope in about three or four nights. That was just pocket money, or in case my child was ill. People were all very thrifty, and four *jiao* at that time was worth one or two yuan now. Cloth was only three *jiao* for one *chi*. . . . My husband never sent a letter or one cent to me till my eldest son was five.

Su's in-laws concealed remittances from her, kept all the best food for themselves, and generally acted in a selfish and irresponsible manner. She describes her own reaction as filiality, punctuated by an occasional quarrel. Eventually she went to track down her husband, and after that, he sent small amounts of money so that she could buy grain from the collective to make up the shortfall in her work-point earnings. Still, life remained very difficult:

> I suffered a lot—went to search for green firewood and yellow firewood in the rocky valley no matter whether it was summer or winter. I went out together with the men before dawn. They usually carried the firewood on their shoulders. I only took a cold rice ball because I had no flour to make steamed bread. I did not know how to tie the firewood up and had to ask others for help. I just followed them carrying the firewood on my back. My mother-in-law wasted a lot of firewood—one bunch of firewood could only last two or three days. Then I had to go out again for firewood. I searched for the thin leaves in winter and one day cut firewood and the next day searched for grass. Then my second son was born. It was

only I who could earn work points in the collective (*dajiti*). The grain ration was not enough. . . .[Luckily] school fees were cheap at that time and all clothes and shoes were made by me. I never bought any. I worked during the daytime and sewed and made ropes at night. It was so hard for me to raise the children.[16]

Because she was the only responsible adult at home, Su passed up a chance to get a wage-paying job far from the village but near her husband:

SXM: Just imagine, the two old ones in my family never worked—they all depended on me. . . . If I had left at that time, they could not survive. . . . They could not get enough food from the team. They wrote to me saying that. That was why I hurried back. The collective (*dajiti*) controlled (*ka*) you in this way. . . . [After my father-in-law's death], I had an old person (mother-in-law), four children, and me. There was nothing left of my husband's thirty or so yuan after his eating and drinking. He never even left me five yuan whenever he came back. There were three children in school. You could not see the children and the old starve to death. My third child once said, "Mom, the porridge we eat is so thin that we can see the reflection of bamboo leaves." I was sad whenever I recalled this [she cries]. I would just grind a bowl of rice into paste, then add some water. The five of us just drank this. I cried at home and put on a smiling face when I went out for meetings, and then would be worried again when I came back home. It was in the 1970s. Life was really hard at that time. . . . All of this would make a good novel [laughter].

GXX: OK. Just say and I will write the novel for you [laughter].

Su's tale contains many other subplots: her struggle to build a house, her determined and ultimately successful campaign to clear her husband's name when he was accused of misdeeds in his factory during the Cultural Revolution, and her reform-era career as a peddler in Baoji city, from which she had returned to the village shortly before we met her. The intertwining of *capable* with *pitiful* in this account is obvious, although Su herself does not dwell on either term. What is most interesting is how she draws on her behavior during the collective period to bolster her sense of worth. Her capable hard work, she says, has brought her the respect of her children and the wider community as well:

GXX: Who, do you think, made the greater contribution to the family, you or Old Yi?

SXM: My contribution was greater. My children always speak gently in my presence. They are always smiling. My daughters-in-law are also nice. Just like the old saying, if you are filial to the old, your children will be filial to you. I have that very experience. . . .

GXX: Why do you think you made a greater contribution to the family than Old Yi?

> **SXM:** I just wanted to show them. Just think of the two old ones and the children. . . .
>
> **GXX:** It seems that it was mainly you who supported the family.
>
> **SXM:** Yes. If I had not supported the family, his family would already have collapsed long ago. People in Old Yi's factory [where he worked after his stint on the railroad] all know that my prestige is high. People in Village T, in B commune, all trusted me.

Su is able to look back with satisfaction from a comfortable old age (for which she accumulated most of the resources herself), surrounded by grown sons who treat her well and daughters-in-law who mostly seem to stay out of conflicts with her. She has not forgotten old injuries, but her manner of talking about them indicates that they, like their perpetrators, belong to the past. When she mentions her capable performance, it does not have the force of a contemporary accusation. Nevertheless, she invokes a past spent in virtuous hard work in order to support a claim on the present, a claim for attention, economic support, and above all recognition.

Harmonious

As this last story suggests, a woman's sense of her own capabilities could come not only from fieldwork or cadre responsibilities but also from skill at supporting a family. Closely linked to the virtue of being capable was the ability to maintain harmony, primarily in the family but also in a network of village relationships often riddled with tensions. Labor models, celebrated for their fieldwork, were also chosen based on the stability and (putative) harmony of their domestic lives. They then used their prestige as labor models to advocate family harmony in the homes of their younger neighbors. Zhang Qiule, in the 1950s a newly married woman in the village of labor model Cao Zhuxiang, asserts:

> Under the leadership of Secretary Cao, women of my generation all had harmony in the family. Because Secretary Cao said to us, "Although you are working outside all day long, coming out early and going back late, when you come back everything has been done by the older generation (*tuoren*), so you have to repay the kindness of the older generation. The older generation raised you from the time you were small. Now you have gone out, and they are doing the work at home. You have to do everything well. When you go back home, you should respect the older generation. If you respect the older generation, then they will treasure you. You should respect your mothers-in-law and love your mothers." She talked to daughters-in-law who had married here and to people in their families. So the families were harmonious. Daughters-in-law from other

places had no one to talk to at home (*waitou na xifu, wuli mei ren jiang*), so that wasn't too good.

That is to say, young people are at a crossroads. It depends on where you lead them. If you lead them well, they will take the high road (*tianming lu*). If you don't lead them well, they will go down that other road.

For Zhang herself, putting this teaching into practice came at high personal cost. Her grandfather had arranged for her to marry a close cousin, in violation of the Marriage Law.

GXX: The Marriage Law talked about freedom of marriage. You never sought out a cadre to say that you wanted to make your own decision?

ZQL: I didn't want to do that. I didn't dare to go, for fear that it would make my grandfather die of anger. As it was, my grandfather died three months after I got married. Why? My mother and my grandfather had a terrible quarrel. I was already gone, and my mother said to my grandfather, "Sending her to their *kang* is your doing" (*ba ta xian kangli jiu dao ni xinshang*). She made my grandfather so angry that he lowered his head and didn't talk. Three months later he died. I have always felt that it was me and my mother who caused my grandfather to die of anger.

Later Zhang considered divorcing her bad-tempered husband, but Cao the labor model dissuaded her, apparently deeming family harmony more important than the state's message about the right to divorce. Zhang's mother-in-law admonished her son to improve his behavior, "and that's how we got to where we are today," says Zhang, consigning her negative feelings about the marriage to the past. Moments later, she erupts into a tirade about young women in the 1990s, staking a claim to superior virtue on her ability to maintain harmony in the family:

ZQL: They can't match me. They have not suffered bitterness. All they know is having money to spend, but they don't know where the money came from. They throw away their clothing before it is worn out. If the food doesn't taste good, they dump it. They know nothing about frugality. In a difficult struggle, they would be no match for me.

GXX: What is the status of women now compared to you at that time?

ZQL: They can't compare with me. Younger people nowadays, most don't have harmonious households. They also cannot match me in respecting the old.

Here a question about status is converted by Zhang into one about ethics, allowing her to occupy the moral high ground and derive emotional satisfaction from her management of a difficult marital history. For Zhang, harmony, like capability, is an attribute of the virtuous. These descriptions of how village women maintained family harmony function are a sideways indictment of those who were, or are, less virtuous than they. What is interesting here is the standard by which proper womanly behavior is measured. Capability and the state of being "advanced," it turns out, are fully compatible with—perhaps even require—filiality and family harmony, and here the younger generation (as well as many of the elders of the speaking women) fall short. These stories offer a combination of past and present claims: "I hewed to virtue in a world where the people who espoused it failed to practice it," and "I value virtue in an age in which it is no longer valued by the young."

Gender in Motion

Gender, as it figures in these narratives, is not inert. These women have lived in times in which the work considered appropriate for women, as well as important elements of daughterly and wifely and motherly behavior, have shifted not just once but continually. But if gender is in motion, what sort of motion is it? Linear? Cyclical? Brownian?

Linear motion usually implies either a progressive or a devolutionary story, and neither is adequate here. Speaking bitterness remains a familiar mode for village women, and every account we heard bore some traces of it. But the speak bitterness trajectory from oppression to liberation does not begin to exhaust the varieties of problems, or the compelling elusiveness of revolutionary promises, presented in these narratives. At the same time, the devolutionary story of "we practiced virtue but our successors do not," while prominent in many stories, usually coexists with an assessment that women today have material goods and possibilities our older speakers could not have imagined for themselves. Even a combination of the two stories ("the world is much better for women, but individual women are less worthy than we were") implies a kind of instability in gender arrangements that is not about linear change.

The motion of gender in these narratives is not cyclical, either. The reform era, in spite of the early fears of many feminist scholars, has not brought a return of the patriarchal household and the skilled but subservient wife. We cannot say that gender subordination ever disappeared or that it has returned in a recognizably antiquated form. As for Brownian motion, even if the orderly heart of a historian could abide the thought of so much random activity, it fails to account for the degree of artfulness and deliberation in the living of these lives, especially in the telling of them.

We are left, then, with a more modest sense of gender's motion, where the meanings of gender are sometimes stripped away and more often accrete slowly. Many of the elements in these tales would be recognizable to the grandmothers of these storytellers. Certainly the pride in one's own industriousness, the deft handling of a household and a family, even the well-developed sense of grievance animating the statement "I was pitiful," echo venerable elements of female virtue. But the world in which those stories are played out has added new venues for the performance of gendered virtue, while discrediting and eliminating some of the practices that once formed its core. Maintaining one's chastity is no longer the central feature of these stories, although loyalty to marital family still looms large. But the ability to perform well as a cadre, or to lead heroic efforts in collective labor, has been added to a repertoire of virtuous practices. These stories describe changes in the conditions that enable and require female virtue, as well as changes in the ways it can be diminished or highlighted.

The deep generational markers in the tales of all these women, the mixed unease and approbation with which they regard their successors, remind us that gender is not the only useful category of analysis and that its intersection with other categories necessarily undermines it as a unifying description. It would probably be more accurate to think of multiple (female) genders, marked deeply by age and locale, each with its own array of subordinations, norms, and transgressions, circulating simultaneously in contemporary China. Perhaps most sobering for the historian, these gendered accounts are themselves in motion, even in the contemporary moment in which they are uttered. When they assert the stability of their virtuous remembered selves across time, these women create continuity in the face of inconstant attention from state authorities and neglect by many of their families. They also redeem the present: in crafting a remembered self, they scour the past for usable stories, for meanings of gender that speak powerfully to present dilemmas and injuries.

Notes

Various stages of this research have been funded by the Pacific Rim Research Program of the University of California (UC), the Committee on Research at UC Santa Cruz, and the Luce Foundation's U.S.–China Cooperative Research Program. A sabbatical year of research and writing in 2000–2001 was supported by the UC President's Fellowship in the Humanities, the Chiang Ching-kuo Foundation, and the National Endowment for the Humanities. I am grateful for the capable research assistance of Jin Jiang, Lyn Jeffery, Wenqing Kang, and Xiaoping Sun. This essay benefited from thoughtful readings by Wendy Brown, Bryna Goodman, Emily Honig, Wendy Larson, Susan Mann, Elizabeth Perry, and all the participants in the conference "Gender in Motion: Divisions of Labor and Cultural Change in Later Imperial and Modern China," held October 5–7, 2001, at the University of Oregon. Any remaining problems are my sole responsibility.

1. Gao Xiaoxian is the research office director of the Shaanxi Provincial Women's Federation and head of the Women's Research Association. Our research has been fully collaborative, and I have benefited enormously from discussions of this material with her, but we plan divergent writing projects for different audiences as a result of this research. Gao Xiaoxian plans to use the material from our joint research trips in preparing two books for publication in Chinese: a collection of oral histories and a history of rural women's labor in Shaanxi over the past half century. I take full responsibility for the ideas expressed in this essay, which is part of my ongoing project entitled *The Gender of Memory.*

2. Portions of this paragraph also appear in Gail Hershatter, "The Gender of Memory: Rural Chinese Women and the 1950s," *Signs: Journal of Women in Culture and Society* 28, no. 1 (Fall 2002): 43–70.

3. An important recent exception is Neil J. Diamant, *Revolutionizing the Family: Politics, Love, and Divorce in Urban and Rural China, 1949–1968* (Berkeley: University of California Press, 2000), which uses legal and other records to examine the effects of the Marriage Law in both urban and rural locations.

4. Variations on the preceding four sentences also appear in Hershatter, "Gender of Memory."

5. Our research has centered on four villages in central and southern Shaanxi, far from the more famous north end of the province where the communists had their main wartime base area. Although none of these villages had a substantive communist presence before 1949, in other respects their local histories diverge. Village B, in the cotton-growing belt of Guanzhong in central Shaanxi, is the home of a prominent woman labor model. Village T is in the southwest part of the province, close to Sichuan, with a local economy organized around tea and rice. It has no regionally famous labor models, but it consistently has been honored as an "advanced village" with many active women's cadres. Village Z, in Shaanxi's southeastern mountains near Henan and Hubei provinces, has women's traditions of spinning, weaving, and embroidery, but none of these activities has ever won the village any official accolades. Village G, in the northern part of central Shaanxi (Weibei), sits on the edge of a dramatic gorge and suffers persistent problems with water supply. Even today most middle-aged women weave on handlooms for ceremonial occasions, and local amateur opera performances in which women are active are a major feature of local life.

6. Ann Anagnost, *National Past-times: Narrative, Representation, and Power in Modern China* (Durham, N.C.: Duke University Press, 1997), 28–44; Anne E. McLaren, "The Grievance Rhetoric of Chinese Women: From Lamentation to Revolution," *Intersections* 4 (September 2000), available at http://wwwsshe.murdoch.edu.au/intersections/issue4/mclaren.html.

7. Speaking bitterness stories have important links to a number of prerevolutionary genres, which I cannot explore here. McLaren, "The Grievance Rhetoric," compares them to bridal laments; one might also trace their derivation from practices of public complaint and expressions of anger, particularly by women. My thanks to Susan Mann for suggesting these similarities.

8. Some of these themes, along with the reconfiguration of village social space brought by state policies in the 1950s, are discussed at more length in Gail Hershatter,

"Local Meanings of Gender and Work in Rural Shaanxi in the 1950s," in *Re-Drawing Boundaries: Work, Household, and Gender in China*, ed. Gail Henderson and Barbara Entwisle (Berkeley: University of California Press, 2000), 79–96.

9. Alessandro Portelli, *The Death of Luigi Trastulli and Other Stories* (Albany: State University of New York Press, 1991), ix.

10. On both of these issues in another venue, see Emily Honig, "Striking Lives: Oral History and the Politics of Memory," *Journal of Women's History* 9, no. 1 (Spring 1997): 139–57.

11. The vast literature on memory generated by psychologists, historians, sociologists, literary scholars, and others cannot be summarized here; particularly useful sources include James W. Pennebaker and Becky L. Banasik, "On the Creation and Maintenance of Collective Memories: History as Social Psychology," in *Collective Memory of Political Events: Social Psychological Perspectives*, ed. James W. Pennebaker, Dario Paez, and Bernard Rimé (Mahwah, N.J.: Erlbaum, 1997), 3–19; and Portelli, *The Death of Luigi Trastulli.*

12. Hershatter, "Local Meanings of Gender."

13. To preserve the anonymity of those recounting often painful memories, I use pseudonyms for all of the women in this article, with the exception of the publicly known labor model Cao Zhuxiang, and Wang Falan, who is identified in Hershatter, "Gender of Memory."

14. Widow chastity as an indicator of virtue has had a remarkably tenacious afterlife in China. Cao Zhuxiang, a regional labor model, was a widow aged thirty-two in 1949. She described at length for us her decision to protect her children by not remarrying, making it one of the major themes in her narrative self-fashioning as a virtuous person. I discuss this at length in "Local Meanings of Gender" and "Gender of Memory."

15. Hershatter, "Local Meanings of Gender."

16. Like others described in this essay, Su shuttles back and forth in her account from past hardships to present conflicts. Here she adds, "When I mentioned it later, my eldest daughter-in-law would say unreasonably, 'Only you raised children while others never have.' I seldom criticized my daughter-in-law and always tried to be close to her. That couple often quarrels." On shuttle work, see Portelli, *The Death of Luigi Trastulli*, 65–66.

Index

About the Contributors

Madeleine Yue Dong is associate professor in the Department of History and the Jackson School of International Studies of University of Washington. Her recent publications include *Republican Beijing: The City and Its Histories* (2004). Her current research involves popular concepts and narratives of history at the turn of the twentieth century.

Bryna Goodman is associate professor in the history department at the University of Oregon. She is author of *Native Place, City and Nation: Regional Networks and Identities in Shanghai, 1853–1937* (1995). Her current work focuses on public culture in 1920s Shanghai, particularly newspapers and public associations, and new understandings of gender, economics, and morality.

Gail Hershatter is professor of history and the director of the Institute for Humanities Research at University of California, Santa Cruz. Her books include *The Workers of Tianjin, 1900–1949* (1986) and *Dangerous Pleasures: Prostitution and Modernity in Twentieth-Century Shanghai* (1997). Her coedited works include *Engendering China: Women, Culture, and the State* (1994) and *A Guide to Women's Studies in China* (1999). Her current project is on rural Chinese women in the 1950s.

Ellen R. Judd is professor of anthropology at the University of Manitoba. Her publications include *Gender and Power in Rural North China* (1994) and *The Chinese Women's Movement between State and Market* (2002). Her current research is on women and migration in rural west China.

Joan Judge is associate professor in the history department at the University of California, Santa Barbara. Her most recent publications include "Blended Wish Images: Chinese and Western Exemplary Women at the Turn of the Twentieth Century," in the journal *Nan nü*. Her current research project is on China's "women's question" and the uses of history at the turn of the twentieth century.

Wendy Larson is professor of Chinese in the East Asian languages and literatures department at the University of Oregon. Her publications include *Literary Authority and the Modern Chinese Writer: Autobiography and Ambivalence* (1991) and *Women and Writing in Modern China* (1998). She is working on a study of the Cultural Revolution and sexuality in post-Mao culture.

Luo Suwen is a researcher at the History Institute of the Shanghai Academy of Social Sciences. She is author of *Nüxing yu jindai Zhongguo shehui* (Women and modern Chinese society) (1996) and numerous works on Shanghai and urban history.

Susan Mann is professor of history at the University of California, Davis. She is the author of *Precious Records: Women in China's Long Eighteenth Century* (1997) and coeditor of *Under Confucian Eyes: Writings on Gender in Chinese History* (2001). She is currently writing a history of the family of Zhang Wanying.

Kenneth Pomeranz is professor of history at the University of California, Irvine. His publications include *The Making of a Hinterland: State, Society and Economy in Inland North China, 1853–1937* (1993) and *The Great Divergence: China, Europe, and the Making of a Modern World Economy* (2000). His current projects include a follow-up volume to *The Great Divergence* and a study of the goddess of Taishan in the social and cultural history of North China.

Tze-lan Deborah Sang is associate professor of Chinese in the East Asian languages and literatures department at the University of Oregon. Her recent publications include *The Emerging Lesbian: Female Same-Sex Desire in Modern China* (2003). Her current research involves popular fiction, gender, and urbanism in early twentieth-century China.

Matthew H. Sommer is associate professor of history at Stanford University. His publications include *Sex, Law, and Society in Late Imperial China* (2000). His current research focuses on wife selling, polyandry, and sex work as survival strategies in Qing and Republican China.

Wang Zheng is associate professor of women's studies at the University of Michigan. She is the author of *Women in the Chinese Enlightenment: Oral and Textual Histories* (1999) and coeditor of *Some of Us: Chinese Women Growing Up in the Mao Era* (2001). Her current research examines gender and socialist transformation in Shanghai in the 1950s.

Catherine Vance Yeh is research associate at the Institute for Chinese Studies, University of Heidelberg. She is the author of *City, Courtesan, and Intellectual: The Rise of Entertainment Culture in Shanghai 1850–1910* (2005). Her current research involves the rise of the star culture in early Republican China, in particular the female impersonator in Peking opera on his way to becoming a national icon and, as represented by Mei Lanfang, the symbol of Chinese culture internationally.

Printed in Great Britain
by Amazon